COMMAND PERFORMANCE

Y0-BVQ-850

APPLEWORKS™

COMMAND PERFORMANCE

APPLEWORKS™

CHARLES RUBIN

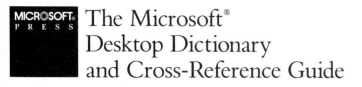

The Microsoft®
Desktop Dictionary
and Cross-Reference Guide

PUBLISHED BY

Microsoft Press
A Division of Microsoft Corporation
16011 N.E. 36th, Box 97017, Redmond, Washington 98073-9717

Library of Congress Cataloging in Publication Data
Rubin, Charles, 1953–
  Command performance.
  (Command performance)
  Includes index.
  1. AppleWorks (Computer program)
  2. Business—Data processing
I. Title.   II. Series.
HF5548.4.A68R84   1986   650'.028'55369   85-31954

ISBN 0-914845-72-1

Printed and bound in the United States of America.

1 2 3 4 5 6 7 8 9 RRDRRD 8 9 0 9 8 7 6

Distributed to the book trade in the
United States by Harper and Row.

Distributed to the book trade in
Canada by General Publishing Company, Ltd.

Distributed to the book trade outside the
United States and Canada by Penguin Books Ltd.

Penguin Books Ltd., Harmondsworth, Middlesex, England
Penguin Books Australia Ltd., Ringwood, Victoria, Australia
Penguin Books N.Z. Ltd., 182-190 Wairau Road, Auckland 10, New Zealand

British Cataloging in Publication Data available

For Doris and Daniel.

Acknowledgments

Much of the pleasure I derived from writing this book, and most of the insight I was able to bring to the task, is due to my having worked with a very fine bunch of people.

The book owes its existence to the enthusiastic collaboration of several people. The original concept of the Command Performance series came from Eddie Adamis. The idea of applying this concept to AppleWorks was first suggested to me by Claudette Moore, and it was further refined during a series of meetings between Claudette, Salley Oberlin, and myself. My manuscript was ruthlessly scrutinized by David Laraway, Dave Rygmyr, and JoAnne Woodcock, whose collective composure in the face of my occasional tantrums during the editing process leaves me in awe. Ken Sanchez, Bonnie Dunham, Carol Luke, Becky Geisler, and Greg Hickman saw the book through production, and the combined talents of Larry Levitsky, Theresa Mannix, and Karen Meredith saw it into your bookstore. As usual, everyone at Microsoft made being an author as pleasant as possible.

I would also like to thank Kelly Stiern at Apple Computer, who knows the technical side of AppleWorks better than anyone except Bob Lissner, and who never balked at sharing his encyclopedic knowledge with me. I'm grateful to Bob Lissner himself for taking time out of a brutal schedule for occasional words of encouragement.

Lastly, I want to thank Steve High, who is without a doubt the world's most enthusiastic booster of AppleWorks, and who gave me many valuable ideas for the book, along with a seemingly endless supply of support and good cheer.

Introduction

This book is a ready-reference guide to the AppleWorks program. It is organized with individual, alphabetized entries covering every command and major program feature of AppleWorks. Most of the entries include illustrations and examples to help you understand how to use each program feature or command.

If you're already familiar with AppleWorks, you can use this book to quickly learn more about specific program features or operations. If you're new to AppleWorks, you can use the book to acquaint yourself with the program, and then learn as you go.

For beginning AppleWorks users, the book includes a number of general tutorial entries that describe the basic operating features of the program—its user interface, printer-configuration options, its use under the ProDOS operating system, and its word-processor, spreadsheet, and database applications. If you haven't worked with AppleWorks before, you may want to read the entry called Interacting with AppleWorks, as this will show you how to enter commands and select options in the program.

The tutorial entries called Printer Configuration and Printer Interface Configuration will help you understand how to make Appleworks work with your printer. If you want to use a hard-disk drive with AppleWorks, the entry called Using a Hard Disk will show you what to do.

The other tutorial entries in the book offer general information about the operation of each of the three AppleWorks applications. These entries are: Database Overview, Database Printing, Database Report Formats, Spreadsheet Overview, Spreadsheet Planning, Spreadsheet Printing, Word Processor Overview, and Word Processor Printing. Like the other entries in the book, these are located alphabetically.

The tutorial entries will give you the basic working knowledge you need to set up AppleWorks for your printer or hard disk and begin using the three applications. When you need more specific information about a particular program feature or command, you can probably find it in a specific alphabetical entry. All the alphabetical entries, including the tutorial entries, are listed in the Appendix.

In some cases, program concepts or features are common to more than one alphabetical entry. When one entry refers to other program concepts or commands, superscripted page numbers refer you to the appropriate entry.

Along with the alphabetical organization of entries, the cross-referencing scheme, and the index, the book uses icons to help you find specific information more quickly:

indicates the word processor

indicates the spreadsheet

indicates the database

Some entries, such as those for the Copy, Move, and Insert commands, contain different sections of information relating to each of the AppleWorks applications. In these entries, each AppleWorks application is represented by a unique icon, and the section covering the use of a command or program feature for each application is headed with an icon indicating the application being explained. If you want to find out about using the Copy command in the database, for example, you can look under the Copy entry for the database icon and begin reading at that point.

■ **Beyond this book**

Command Performance: AppleWorks is a complete reference guide to using the AppleWorks program, and you should be able to find the answer to any question regarding the operation of the AppleWorks program. What this book does not do, however, is explain how to apply your knowledge of AppleWorks to solve personal and business problems. The companion book to this volume, *AppleWorks* (Microsoft Press, 1985), contains dozens of suggested applications and user tips that will help you make the most of your AppleWorks expertise.

@ABS

- **Structure**

  @ABS(argument)

- **Definition**

  @ABS is a spreadsheet function that calculates the *absolute value* of an argument, and places the value in the cell where the function is entered. The absolute value of a number is its value without a prefixed plus or minus sign.

The argument can be:	*Such as:*
A numeric value	@ABS(−402)
A cell reference	@ABS(B4)
A mathematical expression	@ABS((−402+B7)−B9)

- **Usage**

  Use @ABS when an expression may produce a negative number, and you want the result displayed as an unsigned, or positive number.

- **Example**

  Suppose you are calculating back orders and want to show the total number of out-of-stock items as a positive number. You might set up a spreadsheet like this one:

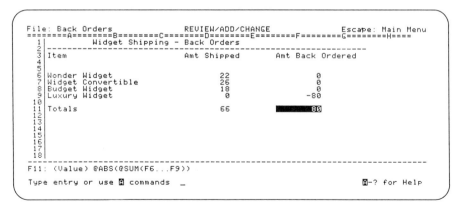

@ABS returns the absolute (unsigned) value of a value or expression.

In this example, items shipped are shown as positive numbers, and items back-ordered as negative numbers. The @ABS function in cell F11, however, is used to represent the negative number produced by the @SUM function as a positive number in the *Totals* row. The procedure is this:

1. Place the cursor on cell F11.
2. Type *@ABS(@SUM(F6.F9))* and press **RETURN**.
3. AppleWorks calculates the expression and enters its absolute value in cell F11.

■ **Comments**

The @ABS formula can be used with arguments which themselves contain other functions, as in the above example.

Add Files menu

■ **Definition**

The *Add Files menu* contains the options for loading existing files onto the AppleWorks Desktop,[97] and for creating new files.

■ **Usage**

When you choose option 1, *Add files to the Desktop*, from the Main Menu,[158] AppleWorks presents the Add Files menu, which lists five options:

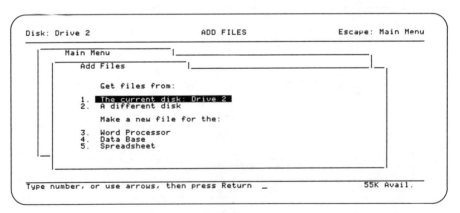

The Add Files menu.

■ **The Add Files menu options**

To use the Add Files menu, you:

1. Choose the desired option.
2. Depending on the option you choose, either select the file to add, specify the different disk location from which to add files, or choose the source of the new word-processor, database, or spreadsheet file, as described in the following entries.

Option 1—The current disk: This option produces a listing of the Apple-Works files available on the disk currently designated as the data-disk location. You can then choose the file or files to add with the → key and load them by pressing **RETURN**.

If you are adding only one file to the Desktop, that file will be loaded and displayed.

If you are adding more than one file to the Desktop, the files will be loaded one at a time. When they are all loaded, you will be prompted to use ⌂-Q to display the Desktop Index[98] and select the particular file you want to work with. Once you select that file and press **RETURN**, the file will be displayed.

Option 2—A different disk: If the files you want are located on a disk that is not the currently designated data-disk location, you can use this option to change the location of the current disk. Choosing this option accesses the Change Current Disk[25] menu, from which you can select either Drive 1, Drive 2, or a ProFile or other ProDOS[246] directory.

If you choose a ProFile or other ProDOS directory, you will then be prompted to enter the pathname[188] of the directory.

Option 3—Make a new file for the Word Processor: Choosing this option produces the Word Processor menu,[362] which allows you to either create a new word-processor file from scratch, or to use an existing ASCII file[13] as the source for the new file.

If you choose *From scratch*, you will be prompted to enter the name of the new file. When you do and then press **RETURN**, a new, blank word-processor document will then be displayed.

3

If you choose *From a text (ASCII) file*, you will be prompted to enter the pathname of the file. When you do and then press **RETURN**, the file is loaded to the Desktop as an AppleWorks word-processor document. Before it is displayed, however, you will first be prompted to enter a name for the Apple-Works word-processor document you are creating from the ASCII file. When you enter the file name and press **RETURN**, the file is displayed.

Option 4—Make a new file for the Data Base: Choosing this option produces the Data Base menu,[55] which allows you either to create a new database file from scratch, or to use an existing text (ASCII) file, Quick File,[254] or DIF[100] file as the source for the new file.

If you choose *From scratch*, you will be prompted to enter the name of the new database file. When you do and then press **RETURN**, you can then create the database file.

If you choose *From a text (ASCII) file*, you will be prompted to enter the number of categories you wish the new file to contain and then you will be prompted to enter the pathname of the text file. After the file is converted to a new database file, but before it is actually displayed, you will be prompted to name the new file. Once you enter the file name and press **RETURN**, the new database file is displayed.

If you choose *From a Quick File (TM) file*, you will be told that Quick File files will be read from the current disk drive or subdirectory. If the Quick File file you want is located in the current disk drive or subdirectory, press **RETURN**, and a list of the available Quick File files will be displayed. Select the file you want from the list.

If the file you want is not on the current disk or subdirectory, insert the correct disk in the current disk drive, or change the current pathname. After the new disk is inserted or the pathname is changed, press **SPACE** and select the file you want from the list displayed. The file will be loaded to the Desktop as a database file, but before it is displayed, you will be prompted to type a name for the new file. Once you type a name for the new file and press **RETURN**, the new file will be displayed.

If you choose *From a DIF (TM) file*, you will be prompted for the pathname of the DIF file. Once you enter the pathname and press **RETURN**, the file will be converted to an AppleWorks database file. Before it is displayed, you will be prompted to type a name for the new AppleWorks file. Once you enter the name and press **RETURN**, the file will be displayed.

Option 5—Make a new file for the Spreadsheet: Choosing this option produces the Spreadsheet menu,[296] which lets you create a new spreadsheet file from scratch, from an existing DIF file, or from an existing VisiCalc file.

If you choose *From scratch*, you will be prompted to type a name for the file. Once you type the file name and press **RETURN**, the new, blank worksheet will be displayed.

If you choose *From a DIF (TM) file*, you will be prompted to enter the pathname of the DIF file you want to use. After you type the pathname and press **RETURN**, the DIF file will be converted to an AppleWorks spreadsheet file. Before the spreadsheet is displayed, you will be prompted to type a name for the new AppleWorks spreadsheet file. When you do and then press **RETURN**, the file will be displayed.

If you choose *From a VisiCalc (R) file*, you will be prompted to type the pathname of the VisiCalc file you wish to use. After you type the pathname and press **RETURN**, the VisiCalc file will be converted to an Apple-Works spreadsheet file; but before the new file is displayed, you will be prompted to type a name for the new file. Once you type a name for the new file and press **RETURN**, the new file will be displayed.

■ **Comments**

When adding files from the current disk or a different disk, AppleWorks assumes you want to add only AppleWorks files. If the disk contains other types of files, they will not appear in the directory. To list other types of files on a disk, you must use the option, *List all files on the current disk drive*, from the Other Activities menu.[178]

Regardless of how small the files are, individually or as a group, you can never add more than 12 files to the Desktop at a time. But the actual number of files you can add at one time really depends on the amount of Desktop space (memory available for files) you have. If you have 55K of Desktop space, for example, you can't add two 30K files to the Desktop, but you can add twelve 4K files to the Desktop.

When selecting a group of files to add to the Desktop, you must be sure to mark all the files you wish to add by using the → key. If you don't mark the last one of the files you want to select, it won't be added to the Desktop, even though it is highlighted at the time. If you are only adding one file, however, the highlighted file will be loaded when you press **RETURN**.

AppleWorks lets you add two copies of the same file to the Desktop. But when you ask it to add a file that has the same name as a file already on the Desktop, AppleWorks will prompt, *You are about to have more than one copy of this file on the Desktop.* At the bottom of the screen, a question will appear: *Do you really want to do this?* If you press **Y**, a second copy of the file will be added.

Add a Printer menu

- **Definition**

  The *Add a Printer menu* is a list of printer names from which you select a printer, name it, tell AppleWorks how to access it, then optionally configure it so it can be installed in AppleWorks.

- **Usage**

  Use the Add a Printer menu when you want to add a new printer configuration to those currently available to you in AppleWorks. AppleWorks can store up to three printer configurations at a time. To use the Add a Printer menu:

  1. Choose option 5, *Other Activities*, from the AppleWorks Main Menu.[158]

  2. Choose option 7, *Specify information about your printer(s)*, from the Other Activities menu.[178]

  3. Choose option 2, *Add a printer*, from the Printer Information menu.[212] The Add a Printer menu will appear.

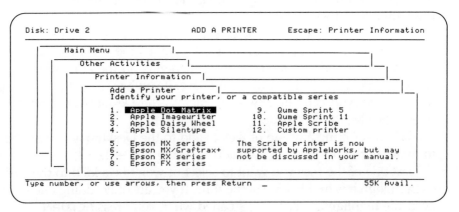

The Add a Printer menu lets you choose among several printer configurations to be stored in AppleWorks.

4. From the menu, choose the printer whose configuration you want to install in AppleWorks. After you choose the printer, you will be asked to type a name up to 15 characters long. You then tell AppleWorks how to access the printer, then optionally change the default configuration settings. The printer will then be installed, and when you choose ⌥-**P** to print from an application, that printer will be identified on the Print Menu by the name you typed in.

■ **Comments**

The AppleWorks Program disk contains default configuration settings for all of the brand-name printers listed in the Add a Printer menu. If you choose the custom printer configuration because your printer is not listed or is not compatible with one of the printers in the Add a Printer menu, you must enter the configuration settings yourself, using your printer's manual as a guide. Custom printers are discussed in detail in Printer Configuration.[200] AppleWorks can store up to three printer configurations at once, but only one of them can be a custom printer configuration.

Argument

■ **Structure**

An *argument* is always enclosed in parentheses, but can have several structures, depending on the function it is used with.

■ **Definition**

An argument is a value, range, list, or mathematical expression that is acted upon by a spreadsheet function.

■ **Usage**

The type of argument you specify for a given function depends on the function. Different functions require arguments with different structures, and these differences are explained in the entry for each function. There are four basic structures for arguments:

☐ A *value*, which is a single number or cell reference: *356, B4*, and *−402* are all values.

☐ A *range*, which is a continuous group of cells in a row, column, or block. To specify a range, you enter only the locations of the first and last cells in the group, separated by a period (.). If you wanted to specify the range of cells from B5 through B15, for example, the range in the argument would be entered as *(B5.B15)*. Once you enter a range (by pressing **RETURN**), AppleWorks automatically converts it to standard range format, which uses three periods instead of one to separate the first and last cell references. For example, AppleWorks would convert the range *(B5.B15)* to *(B5...B15)*. If you wish, you can enter ranges with all three periods to separate the end points, but it isn't necessary.

☐ A *list*, which is a collection of values, cell locations, ranges, or expressions in which each item is separated from the others by a comma. Here are some sample lists:

(B5,B8,B19)

(B5,B14−B13,350)

(B5.B9,B14−B13,B12,350)

(123,345,67,−23)

☐ An *expression*, which is a mathematical equation that produces a value. Expressions can contain functions themselves, so that functions may be nested inside arguments for more complex calculations. Here are some examples of expressions:

(B5+B7+B9)

((B5+B7)−B9)

(@SUM(B5.B12)/3)

Arithmetic functions

- **Definition**

Arithmetic functions are the spreadsheet tools that perform arithmetic calculations, as opposed to logical calculations. The arithmetic functions in the AppleWorks spreadsheet are listed in the following table.

@ABS	Displays the absolute value of an argument.[1]
@AV	Displays the average value of an argument.[15]
@CHOOSE	Displays one value from a list specified in the argument, based on the contents of the cell specified first in the list.[32]
@COUNT	Computes the number of cells containing values in a list or range.[47]

@ERROR	Causes the message ERROR to appear in the cell where it is entered, and in all arguments that refer to it.[105]
@INT	Produces the integer value of the number or expression in the argument.[130]
@LOOKUP	Sequentially searches a row or column you've set up as a table, and when it finds a value less than or equal to the one specified in the argument, it displays the value from the corresponding cell in an adjacent row or column that you've set up as a second table.[155]
@MAX	Displays the largest value in a list or range.[160]
@MIN	Displays the smallest value in a list or range.[161]
@NA	Places the message NA (not available) in the cell where it is entered, and in any cell whose argument refers to it.[170]
@SQRT	Calculates the square root of an argument.[327]
@SUM	Calculates the sum of a list or range of values.[341]

- **Usage**

You can use arithmetic functions only in the AppleWorks spreadsheet. The rules and limitations of each function's use are described in the entry for each function. Except for @ERROR and @NA, all of these functions must be entered with arguments that specify the values, cells, or expressions upon which their calculations are to be performed. (See: Argument;[7] Spreadsheet Overview.[298])

Arithmetic operators

- **Definition**

An *arithmetic operator* is a symbol that denotes the action of a mathematical process (such as addition or subtraction) on a value or values. The arithmetic operators in AppleWorks are:

+ adds two values.

− subtracts two values, or indicates a negative value.

* multiplies two values.

/ divides two values.

^ denotes that the number following it is an exponent.

■ **Usage**

You can use arithmetic operators to calculate values in both the spreadsheet and the database. In the spreadsheet, the operators are entered with values in individual cells as mathematical formulas. In the database, the operators are used in the Report Format screen when you define Calculated Categories.[18] When entering spreadsheet formulas, keep in mind that AppleWorks always evaluates mathematical expressions from left to right, except when you are using parentheses. (See: Spreadsheet Overview;[298] Database Report Formats.[79])

Arrange (⌂-A)

■ **Definition**

The *Arrange* command (⌂-**A**) lets you sort the rows in a spreadsheet or the records in a database file in alphabetic, numeric, or chronological order, based on the contents of a specified spreadsheet column or database category.

■ **Usage**

To use the Arrange command, in general:

1. Place the cursor on the spreadsheet column or database category you wish to arrange.

2. Press the Arrange command (⌂-**A**).

3. Highlight the range of spreadsheet rows you want to arrange.

4. Choose the order by which you would like the selected portion of the file sorted.

   The sorting options you have depend on whether you are sorting a spreadsheet or database file.

■ **Example: Arranging data in the spreadsheet**

Suppose you were using a spreadsheet to compile a simple list of office supplies for an inventory and ordering system. In the left column you might list the names of supply items, and in the other columns you might have categories for the quantity on hand, the price of each item, and total value when you make your order, as shown in the following example.

```
File: Supplies                    REVIEW/ADD/CHANGE              Escape: Main Menu
=======A========B========C=======D=======E========F=========G========H====
  1|                          Office Supplies
  2|
  3|Item                         Count    Price    Total
  4|
  5|Envelopes, Manila
  6|Tape, Scotch
  7|Envelopes, Window
  8|Folders, Legal
  9|Blotters, Large
 10|Folders, Regular
 11|Pens, Green
 12|Tape, Masking
 13|Blotters, Small
 14|Tape, Cassette
 15|Pens, Red
 16|Tape, Microcassette
 17|Pens, Black
 18|Tape, Packing
-----------------------------------------------------------------------------
A5: <Label> Envelopes

Type entry or use ⌂ commands  _                            ⌂-? for Help
```

You can arrange the items on this spreadsheet in alphabetic order with the Arrange command.

You enter the names of supply items at random, as you think of them, but then it occurs to you that it would be better to have the items alphabetized. Use the Arrange command:

1. Place the cursor on the column containing the names of supplies, and on the row that begins the group of entries you want to arrange (cell A5). You don't want to arrange rows 1 through 4, because you will then be moving the column headings from their current positions.

2. Press the Arrange command (Ć-**A**). The highlight bar will appear across the row where your cursor is located. Move the cursor down to row 18, to highlight all the office-supplies rows, and then press **RETURN**.

3. This menu of arranging options will appear:

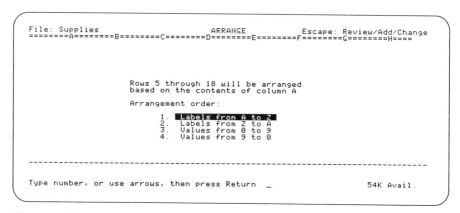

```
File: Supplies                        ARRANGE            Escape: Review/Add/Change
=======A========B========C========D========E========F=========G========H====



              Rows 5 through 18 will be arranged
              based on the contents of column A

              Arrangement order:

                    1.  Labels from A to Z
                    2.  Labels from Z to A
                    3.  Values from 0 to 9
                    4.  Values from 9 to 0


-----------------------------------------------------------------------------

Type number, or use arrows, then press Return  _            54K Avail.
```

The menu of spreadsheet Arrange options.

Choose option 1, *Labels from A to Z*. The rows you highlighted in the spread-sheet will then be arranged by the contents of column A, from A to Z.

■ Comments

When you use the Arrange command, be sure not to include rows that contain column titles, since they will also be arranged and moved from their proper places atop each column.

You can only arrange a spreadsheet file based on the contents of one column at a time.

If your spreadsheet contains functions that use cells in their arguments, such as @SUM, arranging rows may change the results of those formulas. If an @SUM formula's argument includes cells in rows 6 through 10, for example, and you use Arrange so that row 6 becomes row 11, the @SUM formula will no longer total all the rows you want.

 ### Example: Arranging data in the database

Suppose you have compiled an alphabetic list of companies that are customers of yours, and now your boss wants you to put them into a sales report, organized by salespersons' names. Your list is organized like this:

```
File: Customers              REVIEW/ADD/CHANGE              Escape: Main Menu

Selection: All records


Name              Company              Phone         Salesperson    YTD Sales
============================================================================
Olive Ogilvy      Ace Jackhammer       555-6666      Brohammer      10,635.25
Mort Drucker      Drucker Drayage      555-2345      Smith           1,025.00
Aldo Pastarelli   Pesto's Pasta        555-1111      Drohammer         355.90
Boris Boronzhova  Jetson Steel         555-8787      Jones          12,875.95
Fortuna Maldonado Furniture City       555-2222      Brohammer       2,500.85
Edwina Gumm       Fritzi Fashions      555-7890      Smith              87.50
Ed Frobish        Frobish Linen Service 555-1234     Smith          15,325.00
Walter Canary     Flippo Dog Food      555-8606      Jones             125.60
Fred Fong         Fong Machine Tools   555-8765      Jones           4,675.20
James Pennington  Linda's Typewriter Rep 555-4443    Brohammer         100.25
Arnold Ormsby     Flecko Paints        555-4567      Jones             787.35
Alex Abidikian    Imperial Dry Cleaning 555-0505     Smith           1,024.00
Barney Flint      Howard's U-Rent 'Em  555-7608      Brohammer       3,257.60
Wilson Peck       Apex Canning         555-3232      Smith           5,350.00
Wilson K. Jeeves  Butlerware, Inc.     555-3334      Smith             575.30
----------------------------------------------------------------------------
Type entry or use ⌂ commands                                  ⌂-? for Help
```

Here's how to use the Arrange command to sort the list:

1. Place the cursor on the category you want to sort (*Salesperson*).

2. Press the Arrange command (⌘-**A**). A menu of sorting options similar to the one shown above will appear.

3. Choose option 1, *From A to Z*, and then press **RETURN**. The records will be arranged by the category containing salespersons' names in alphabetic order, so all the records with the same salesperson's name will be together.

■ **Comments**

The database can have categories containing dates and times, and when you select a category with the words *date* or *time* in the category name to be arranged, you are given two additional options to arrange the data: in either ascending or descending chronological order, in addition to the standard options of alphabetically or numerically. If you're working in the Multiple Record layout[168] and the category you want to sort isn't visible, you can use ⌘-**Z** to zoom to the Single Record layout,[293] move the cursor to the category you want sorted, then use the Arrange command.

As with the spreadsheet, you can only arrange the records based on the contents of one category of data at a time in the database.

ASCII file

■ **Definition**

An *ASCII file* contains text and numbers stored in ASCII format—a common method of representing computer data used by many personal computer programs. ASCII is the acronym for American Standard Code for Information Interchange.

■ **Usage**

ASCII files are typically unformatted; they are a continuous stream of words or numbers without any line spacing, justification, or margins, as shown in the following example:

```
December 13, 1985Mr. Ed FrobishFrobish Linen Service335
Ramona Ave.San Jose, CA 95551Dear Ed:We think you're a super
customer, and I wanted to tell you how much all of us at
Acme Widgets appreciate your business.  That's why we wanted
you to be the first to know about our new Widget
Convertible--the sturdiest, most flexible, most cost-
effective widget around.I'd like to schedule a time to drop
by your office and demonstrate the advantages of the new
Widget Convertible, so I'll be giving you a call during the
next week to make an appointment.In the meantime, think what
the world's first all-purpose widget will mean to your
profits!Sincerely Yours,Fred Smith
```

A typical ASCII file is unformatted.

When you create new files with AppleWorks, the files have a unique format and they can't be shared by other programs. If you want to share Apple-Works files with other programs, you can save your files to disk as ASCII files. Since many other programs can use ASCII files, you can use this format as a way of sharing data. All three AppleWorks applications can save their files to disk in ASCII format. To store an AppleWorks file in ASCII format:

1. Display the Review/Add/Change screen of the file you want to print, and then press the Print[193] command (⚚-P).

2. Select the portion of the file you want to print, and press **RETURN**.

3. Choose *A text (ASCII) file on disk* as the print destination, and press **RETURN**.

4. Type the complete ProDOS pathname[188] under which you want to store the ASCII file, and press **RETURN**. The file will then be saved on the current disk as an ASCII file.

You can also use ASCII files as sources for new AppleWorks database and word-processor files. This allows you to make use of ASCII data created by other programs. To use an ASCII file in AppleWorks, choose *From a text (ASCII) file* as the source of your new file, and then type the pathname where the ASCII file is located. (See: Add Files menu.[2])

If you are using an ASCII file to create a word-processor document, you will probably have to add some formatting (line spacing, margins, carriage returns, indents, and so on) to make it look the way you want. (See: Word Processor Overview.[363])

If you're using an ASCII file to create a new database file, you will be asked how many categories you want the new file to contain. When the data is transferred, AppleWorks will take the data between carriage returns and place it into each category. (See: Add Files menu.)

Since ASCII is such a common format, it is also the easiest way to send computer data via modem. Most modems, commercial electronic mail services, and communications programs for personal computers are set up to send and receive ASCII files. If you want to send an AppleWorks file via modem, you will have to save it to disk as an ASCII file first.

■ **Comments**
You can send ordinary AppleWorks files to another Apple user if you are both using Apple's ACCESS II communications software. Other communications programs may be made available that will be able to send AppleWorks

files directly, as well. If you're not sure about the software or capabilities of the system you are communicating with, however, the safest course is always to send an ASCII file.

@AVG

- **Structure**

  @AVG(argument)

- **Definition**

  @AVG is a spreadsheet function that computes the average of several values, and displays the result in the cell where the function is entered.

The argument can be:	Such as:
Numeric values	@AVG(102,134,520,440)
Cell ranges	@AVG(B4.B23)
Lists	@AVG(B4,D4,F4)
Mathematical expressions	@AVG((119/6),(33*14))

- **Usage**

  The @AVG function is commonly used to find the average of a continuous *range* of cells, or a *list*[154] of separate cells in a spreadsheet.

- **Example: Averaging a range**

  Suppose you want to use this spreadsheet to compute the average number of widgets made per day:

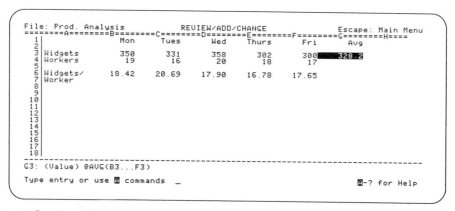

The @AVG function saves you the trouble of building mathematical expressions that compute averages.

15

To use @AVG to calculate the average in this example:

1. Move the cursor to cell G3.
2. Type *@AVG(B3.F3)* and press **RETURN** to enter the formula.
3. The average will appear in cell G3.

■ **Example: Averaging a list**

If the numbers you want to average aren't in a continuous range of cells in a row or column, you must specify them individually in a list separated by commas. Suppose you wanted to average the number of employees for only Monday, Wednesday, and Friday in the preceding spreadsheet, and place the average in cell G4. You would take these steps:

1. Place the cursor in cell G4.
2. Type *@AVG(B4,D4,F4)* and press **RETURN**.
3. The average would appear in cell G4.

Blank (⌂-B)

■ **Definition**

The *Blank* command (⌂-**B**) is used to erase the data in a spreadsheet cell, row, column, or block of cells.

■ **Usage**

When you use Blank, you erase not only the labels or data in the area where you apply the command, you also erase any custom formats you have applied to that area.

To use the Blank command:

1. Place the cursor on the cell, row, or column you wish to erase, or the cell that begins the block of cells you wish to erase.
2. Press ⌂-**B**.
3. Choose *Entry, Rows, Columns,* or *Block* as the area to be blanked.
4. If you are blanking an entry in a single cell, simply press **RETURN**. But if you are blanking rows, columns, or a block, choose the appropriate command, then use the Arrow keys to highlight the area you want to blank and press **RETURN**.

■ **Example**

Suppose you are working with this budget worksheet:

```
File: Budget.Proj              REVIEW/ADD/CHANGE              Escape: Main Menu
========A=========B=========C=========D=========E=========F=========G=========H====
   3
   4
   5                 Jan       Feb       Mar       Apr       May       June
   6 Rent           2000      2000      2000      2000      2000      2000
   7 Utilities       502       489       480       455       419       391
   8 Material       2500      2495      2350      2410      2300      2280
   9 Salaries       2000      2000      2000      2000      2000      2000
  10 Promotion       500       475       300       300       425       375
  11
  12 Total Expenses 7502      7459      7130      7165      7144      7046
  13
  14
  15
  16
  17
  18
  19
  20
-------------------------------------------------------------------------------
F4: (Label, Layout-R) Apr

Type entry or use ⬛ commands  _                              ⬛-? for Help
```

The Blank command can erase entire sections of a spreadsheet at once.

You decide that instead of doing a six-month projection, you only want to do a three-month projection from January through March. You want to blank the columns containing the data for April, May, and June. Here's how:

1. You want to erase the block of data that includes the labels *Apr, May,* and *June,* as well as the numbers below them, so place the cursor over the label *Apr.*

2. Press ⌂-**B**. The prompt line will ask you to select an area to be blanked. Choose *Block,* either by moving the highlight bar to *Block* and pressing **RETURN,** or by pressing **B.**

3. Extend the cursor across to the column labeled *June* with the → key, and then down to the row containing total expenses with ↓ , so that a block of data is highlighted.

4. Press **RETURN,** and the block of data will disappear.

■ **Comments**

Be sure you want to completely eliminate the data you select when you use the Blank command. Once you blank the data, it is gone forever, along with any cell formatting you have applied. If you want to replace entries instead of removing them, typing over the existing entries to edit them is safer than blanking the cells they occupy.

Calculate (⌂-K)

■ Definition

The *Calculate* command (⌂-K) has a completely different effect in each of the three applications. It creates page breaks in word-processor files, recalculates values in spreadsheets, and creates Calculated Categories in database reports.

Calculating page breaks in the word processor

Before you print a file on paper, you often want to know just where each printed page will end. You can find out with the Calculate command. When you use the command, a dashed line containing the page number appears at the end of each page showing where page breaks will occur.

To use the Calculate command in the word processor:

1. Make sure the file whose page breaks you want to determine is displayed on the Review/Add/Change screen.

2. Press ⌂-K—the screen will change to a menu showing you which print destinations are available to you at the time.

3. Select where the file will ultimately be printed.

4. The file will be displayed again, and the page breaks will appear as dashed lines, as in this example:

```
File: Sales Letters              REVIEW/ADD/CHANGE            Escape: Main Menu
=====|====|====|====|====|====|====|====|====|====|====|====|====|====|===

I'd like to schedule a time to drop by your office and demonstrate the
advantages of the new Widget Convertible, so I'll be giving you a call
during the next week to make an appointment.

In the meantime, think what the world's first all-purpose widget will mean
to your profits!

Sincerely Yours,


Fred Smith
- - - - - - - - - - - - - - End of Page 1 - - - - - - - - - - - - - - - - -
December 13, 1985

Mr. Ed Frobish
Frobish Linen Service
335 Ramona Ave.
------------------------------------------------------------------------
Type entry or use ⌂ commands          Line 36  Column  1        ⌂-? for Help
```

The Calculate command displays page breaks in word-processor files.

It's also useful to display page breaks when you only want to print certain pages of a file. With the page breaks displayed, you can move the cursor to the first page you want, and then use the Print[193] command (⌘-P) to print from the current page. (See: Word Processor Printing.[371])

Page breaks are displayed only until you modify the text on the screen. Once you enter, delete, or rearrange text, the page-break lines disappear.

Calculating values in the spreadsheet

Suppose you are entering a lot of figures in the spreadsheet. Normally, the spreadsheet is set to automatic recalculation, which means the entire spreadsheet recalculates every time you enter or change a number. Since it has to pause to recalculate, this activity slows down your data entry, especially if you have a large spreadsheet.

You decide to change the spreadsheet's Standard Values[330] so it recalculates manually; that is, it only recalculates when you tell it to by using the Calculate command. This way your data entry will be faster. When you have entered all the values you need and you want to recalculate the spreadsheet, all you have to do is:

1. Make sure the spreadsheet file is displayed on the Review/Add/Change screen.

2. Press ⌘-K—the values in the spreadsheet will recalculate.

You can use the Calculate command if the spreadsheet is set to automatic recalculation, which can be useful if you have a spreadsheet containing iterative calculations. (See: Iterative Calculations.[138])

Making Calculated Categories in database reports

In the database, the Calculate command is used to create Calculated Categories on the Report Format screen. A Calculated Category is a separate category you create that will contain the result of a calculation made on one or more exisiting categories in that report. You can use the standard arithmetic operators (+, −, *, /) to perform the calculation. The formula can contain only category-column labels (such as B*C), or category-column labels and values you enter yourself (such as C/1.25). Calculated Categories thus allow you to perform some calculations in database reports that you would otherwise have to do in the spreadsheet.

Suppose you are creating a database report to use as an order form for office supplies, like this:

```
File: Supplies            REPORT FORMAT          Escape: Report Menu
Report: Order Form
Selection: All records

=================================================================
--> or <--   Move cursor              -J  Right justify this category
  >  A  <    Switch category positions  -K  Define a calculated category
-->  A  <--  Change column width        -N  Change report name and/or title
 -A  Arrange (sort) on this category    -O  Printer options
 -D  Delete this category               -P  Print the report
 -G  Add/remove group totals            -R  Change record selection rules
 -I  Insert a prev. deleted category    -T  Add/remove category totals
-----------------------------------------------------------------

Item                        Qty.   Price        L
-A------------------------  -B----  -C---------  e
Blotters, Large              10     1.95         n
Blotters, Small              5      1.50         5
Envelopes, Regular, Box 250  2      11.50        2

-----------------------------------------------------------------
Use options shown above to change report format        44K Avail.
```

You have already entered the quantity and price of each item, and you want to create a Calculated Category on the right side of the report that contains the total cost of each item. Here's how:

1. With the Report Format screen displayed, place the cursor on the category of the file where you want the Total category to appear. (In our example, you would place the cursor on the *Len 52*, since we want the Calculated Category to be on the right.)

2. Press ⌘-K—a new category, named *Calculated*, will appear at the cursor position.

3. The prompt line at the bottom of the screen will show the default category name *Calculated* and will ask you to enter a different category name. Delete the name *Calculated* by using ⌘-Y, and enter a new name (in our example *Totals*). Press RETURN, and the new name will appear at the top of the category.

4. The prompt line will ask you to enter the calculation rules. In this case, you want to multiply category B (*Qty.*) by category C (*Price*), so you type: $B * C$, as shown in the following example, and press RETURN.

```
File: Supplies                 DEFINE CALCULATED              Escape: Erase entry
Report: Order Form
Selection: All records


===============================================================================
--> or <--    Move cursor                      @-J  Right justify this category
   >  @   <    Switch category positions        @-K  Define a calculated category
-->  @   <--   Change column width               @-N  Change report name and/or title
@-A  Arrange (sort) on this category            @-O  Printer options
@-D  Delete this category                        @-P  Print the report
@-G  Add/remove group totals                     @-R  Change record selection rules
@-I  Insert a prev. deleted category             @-T  Add/remove category totals
-------------------------------------------------------------------------------
Item                              Qty.  Price         Totals           L
-A------------------------------- -B--- -C----------  -D---------      e
Blotters, Large                   10    1.95               9999999999  n
Blotters, Small                   5     1.50               9999999999  6
Envelopes, Regular, Box 250       2     11.50              9999999999  5
-------------------------------------------------------------------------------
Type calculation rules (Example: A+B+C/5.75):  B*C_
```

In the database, the Calculate command creates a new category based on calculations of two or more existing categories.

5. The prompt line will ask how many decimal places you want the calculated results to show (the default is zero). This category will show dollars and cents, so type *2* and press **RETURN**.

6. The prompt line will ask how many blank spaces to leave after the category. This is the rightmost category in the report, so it really doesn't matter. Press **RETURN** to enter the default, *3*.

7. The Calculated Category will now be set up and ready to go.

On the Report Format display, a Calculated Category is indicated by a row of 9s across each record. A decimal point will appear in each row of 9s to show how many decimal places you chose. The actual, calculated results only appear when you print the report. To see the results without printing the report on paper, print the report to the screen.

You can also specify Group Totals[118] and a Category Total on a Calculated Category. With our sample order form, using the Category Total command on the calculated category will produce a total for the entire order when the report is printed.

Caret

■ Definition

The *caret* symbol (^) in word-processor documents shows the locations of printer-option settings you've chosen for that file. In the spreadsheet, the caret symbol denotes an exponent. The caret is also the character you must type in order to exit from the Printer Codes and Special Codes screens. (See: Printer Options.[217])

Use in the word processor

In the word processor, the caret symbol appears on the Review/Add/Change screen at the locations in a document where you have entered printer options. The caret symbol indicates only printer options that can be specified within text lines, such as boldfacing, super- or subscripting, underlining, or printing of page numbers. You can tell which printer option is being represented by a given caret symbol by placing the cursor on that caret and then looking at the line-indicator window at the bottom of the screen: The option being represented by the caret is displayed there.

Use in the spreadsheet

In the spreadsheet, the caret symbol is used in a formula or value to denote an exponent. The value 2^3, for example, is stored in the spreadsheet as 2 raised to the power of 3, or 8. The value 10^6 equals 10 raised to the power of 6, or 1,000,000.

■ Use with printers

When you are entering printer-control codes on either the Special Codes screen from the Printer Options menu, or the Printer codes screen (available from the Add a Printer menu[6] for custom printers), you must type the codes exactly as they appear in your printer's manual. Some of these codes use the **ESC** key as one of their keystrokes, so you cannot press **ESC** to exit a code-entry screen. Instead, AppleWorks tells you to type the caret (Shift-6) symbol to indicate when you are finished entering codes.

It is possible that the caret may itself be part of a printer-control code. If so, you won't be able to enter that code into AppleWorks: The program will think you have finished entering the code as soon as you type the caret, and the caret keystroke won't be stored as part of the code itself. (See: Printer Options;[217] Printer Configuration.[200])

Case sensitive text

■ **Definition**

Case sensitive text is a selection option that is available whenever you use the Find (⌘-**F**) or Replace (⌘-**R**) commands in the word processor.

■ **Usage**

Use the *Case sensitive text* option whenever you want to search for or replace words with distinctive spelling, capitalization, or punctuation.

■ **Example**

Suppose you are working on a report about sales of standard-sized widgets. The name of the product is *Widget Standard*, but there are several references to *standard*, or *standard-sized* products from other companies. Suppose you want to change the product name to *Widget Superior*. You can do this with the word processor's Replace[270] command, but if you choose the *Text* option instead of the *Case sensitive text* option, the program will find and replace every occurrence of the word *standard*, whether it is capitalized or not. You wouldn't want this to happen, so you would specify the *Case sensitive text* option, and then enter the word *Standard* as the text to be searched for. Since the first letter of the text you enter is capitalized, only the capitalized occurrences of *Standard* will be replaced.

■ **Comments**

Often a word you want to replace in a document will be found in locations where you *don't* want it replaced. To minimize this, use the *Case sensitive text* option as much as possible. (See: Find[109] (⌘-**F**); Replace Text[270] (⌘-**R**).)

Category

■ **Definition**

A *category* contains individual entries that usually have one specific type of information in a database file. Each category is assigned a *category name* (discussed below).

■ **Usage**

Use categories to separate the data in each record you want to store in a database file into logical groups or classifications.

In database files, information is arranged in two ways. *Categories* usually contain specific kinds of information, such as names, addresses, ages, salaries, birth dates, or employee numbers. *Records* are groups of categories. Each record contains the same categories—name, address, salary, and other data, for example—but the specific entries in each category can be different in each record.

You can see these two arrangements of data in this sample database (the categories are columns, and the records are rows):

```
File: Customers              REVIEW/ADD/CHANGE              Escape: Main Menu
Selection: All records

Name             Phone        Street          City         ST/Zip
=============================================================================
Aldo Pastarelli  555-1111     1439 Commerce   Milpitas     CA 94002
Alex Abidikian   555-0505     687 Bullis Lane Fremont      CA 95003
Arnold Ormsby    555-4567     6690 Livingston San Jose     CA 95555
Barney Flint     555-7608     878 14th St.    San Jose     CA 95550
Boris Boronzhov  555-8787     1450 Carson Ave Milpitas     CA 95558
Ed Frobish       555-1234     335 Ramona Ave. San Jose     CA 95551
Edwina Gumm      555-7890     3325 State St.  Sunnyvale    CA 94008
Fortuna Maldona  555-2222     1839 Water St.  San Jose     CA 95555
Fred Fong        555-8765     3867 Fortney St Sunnyvale    CA 95004
James Penningto  555-4443     3897 107th Ave. San Jose     CA 95553
Mort Drucker     555-2345     123 State St.   Sunnyvale    CA 94000
Olive Ogilvy     555-6666     112 Sumter St.  Santa Clara  CA 95550
Walter Canary    555-8606     3359 W. Hudson  Milpitas     CA 95554
Wilson K. Jeeve  555-3334     907 Broad St.   Santa Clara  CA 95554
Wilson Peck      555-3232     8904 Fremont St San Jose     CA 95554
-----------------------------------------------------------------------------
Type entry or use ⌘ commands                                 ⌘-? for Help
```

Categories of data in each record contain the same type of information.

Before you can begin entering data into a database file, you must create categories for the information. Once you have finished creating categories, you can begin entering the data into those categories for each record. (See: Record;[258] Database Overview.[58])

■ Category names

Category names are most useful if they are short and descriptive. If a category will be used to store a person's name, for example, you might use *Name* as the category name, as in the preceding example. If more than one file category will contain people's names, then you will have to use category names that are more specific, such as *Contact* or *Employee*.

You enter category names when you create a new database file, and you can change those category names at any time, even after the file has been created. In addition, you can delete entire categories of information, or add new categories to an existing data file. (See: Database Overview;[58] Change Name/Category.[27])

■ **Category Totals**

A *Category Total* is an option in database reports that sums the values in a category. Category Totals are useful when you have one or more categories containing values in a database report, and you want the total of those values to appear at the bottom of those categories at the end of the report.

You specify a Category Total by using the Set Totals[286] command (⌂-T) on the Report Format screen in a database file.

Cell

■ **Definition**

A spreadsheet is a grid of 999 rows numbered from 1 through 999 and 127 columns labeled A through DW. (See: Column;[37] Row.[280]) Each intersection of a row and a column is a *cell* where one item of information (a value, a label, or a formula) is entered and displayed.

■ **Usage**

Each cell has a unique location, because every row/column intersection in a spreadsheet is unique. When you refer to a cell in a formula, you always refer to it by its *coordinates*—the letter of the column followed by the number of the row that intersect at its location. The intersection of column A and row 1 is cell A1, for example. Since cells have unique locations, it's easy to remember where you have put each item of information in the spreadsheet.

The cell indicator at the bottom-left corner of the screen shows the coordinates of the cell where the cursor is located at any given time.

You can't enter a value, label, or formula into a cell unless the cursor is located in that cell. When you create spreadsheet formulas, you often refer to cell contents by the cell location. (See: Spreadsheet Overview.[298])

Change Current Disk menu

■ **Definition**

The *Change Current Disk menu* lets you select a different disk drive where AppleWorks will load, store, delete, or catalog files.

■ **Usage**

The Change Current Disk menu can be used in a variety of operations in AppleWorks. Generally, anytime you are working with files from the Main Menu[158] (such as saving them, removing Desktop[97] files, or adding files to the

Desktop), you have the option of changing to a different disk or directory. If you choose that option, the Change Current Disk menu is displayed in order to give you options about which disk AppleWorks will work with. At other times, the only way you can move directly to the Change Current Disk menu is to choose option 1 from the Other Activities menu: *Change current disk drive or ProDOS prefix*. To do this:

1. Choose option 5, *Other Activities*, from the Main Menu.

2. Choose option 1, *Change current disk drive or ProDOS prefix*, from the Other Activities menu.

3. The Change Current Disk menu will appear, and you can choose the disk drive or subdirectory you want to work with from the list of options shown.

You can use the Change Current Disk menu when working with these AppleWorks functions:

☐   If you choose *Add files to the Desktop* (option 1) from the Main Menu, then choose the option to get the files from a different disk, the Change Current Disk menu will appear next, to let you choose where you will add the files from.

☐   If you choose *Save Desktop files to disk* (option 3) from the Main Menu, and you select the option to save the files on a different disk, the Change Current Disk menu will appear after you have selected the files to be saved, to let you choose where each file will be saved. (See: Save Files screen.[282])

☐   If you choose *Remove files from the Desktop* (option 4) from the Main Menu, and the files have changed, you may choose to save them on a different disk. If you do, the Change Current Disk menu appears after you have selected the files to be removed, to let you choose where new or changed Desktop files will be saved. (See: Remove Files screen.[266])

☐   If you choose *Quit* (option 6) from the Main Menu, and there are files on the Desktop that are new or changed, and you choose to save the files to a different disk, the Change Current Disk menu will appear so you can choose where they will be saved before the program quits. (See: Quit screen.[255])

Change Name/Category screen (⌘-N)

■ **Definition**

The *Change Name/Category screen* (⌘-N) displays the file names and category names in a new or existing database file and allows you to change them.

■ **Usage**

Once a database file contains information, you can use the Change Name/Category screen to change the file name, add new categories, delete existing categories, or change category names. This screen also appears when you create a database file from scratch, because you must define data categories for a new file by naming them before you can enter information into it.

To use the Change Name/Category screen with a new database file:

1. On the Data Base menu,[55] which gives you four options for creating a new file, choose option 1, *From scratch*, and then press **RETURN**.

2. You will be prompted to type a name for the new file. Once you type a name and press **RETURN**, the Change Name/Category screen appears, as shown in the following example, and you can type names for the data categories in your new file.

```
 File: Customers           CHANGE NAME/CATEGORY     Escape: Review/Add/Change


 Category names
 ================================================================
 Category 1
                                  Options:

                                  Change category name
                                  Up arrow    Go to filename
                                  Down arrow Go to next category
                                  @-I         Insert new category




 ----------------------------------------------------------------
 Type entry or use @ commands                          43K Avail.
```

The Change Name/Category screen is used to enter new category names, to change existing category names, or to add or delete data categories.

3. To change the first category name, position the cursor on the beginning of the default category name (*Category 1*), and press ⌘-Y. This will erase that name, and you can then type a new one.

4. Once you have finished typing the first category name, press **RETURN**. The cursor will automatically move down to the next line, so you can type the second category name.

You can type up to 30 category names in a database file. When you have typed the first 15 category names, you will have used all the available spaces on the left side of the *Category names* area, and the cursor will jump to the right of your first category name on the top line.

To use the Change Name/Category screen with an existing database file, choose the Name Change[171] command (⌂-**N**) while you are working with an existing database file to display the Change Name/Category screen.

At this point several actions are available to you: Changing the file name, or adding, inserting, deleting, or changing the category names.

To change the file name: When the screen first appears, the cursor will be located at the beginning of the file name, at the bottom of the screen. To change the file name, press the Clear[34] command (⌂-**Y**). The existing file name will disappear. Type the new file name, and then press **RETURN**. The file name at the top of the screen will be changed, and the cursor will move to the beginning of the first category name in the *Category names* area. If you don't wish to change the file name but want to work instead with the category names, simply press **RETURN** when the Change Name/ Category screen first appears, and the cursor will move from the file name to the first name in the *Category names* area.

To add a new category at the end of the list: Move the cursor to the beginning of the blank space below the last category name in the *Category names* area, and type the new category name.

To insert a category between two existing categories: Move the cursor to the first character of the category where you want the new category to appear, and press the Insert[127] command (⌂-**I**)—the category you have the cursor on will be moved down a line, and a blank line will then appear at the cursor position, ready to receive your new category name.

To delete a category: Place the cursor on the first character of the category you want to delete, and press the Delete[92] command (⌂-**D**). The categories below the one you deleted will move up to fill the gap created. If you delete a category in a file that already contains information, AppleWorks will warn you first, and ask if you really want to delete the category. You then have to answer *Yes* (by pressing **Y**) to this question to actually delete the category. Once a category is deleted, the information stored in it is deleted, too. Any report formats or formatting you have created will be removed from that file if you delete a category containing information.

To change a category name: Place the cursor on the first character in the name you wish to change, and choose the Clear command (⌂-**Y**)—the category name will be erased, and you can type a new one and press **RETURN**.

■ **Comments**

You can move the cursor anywhere in the *Category names* area to add, delete, or rename categories.

A category or file name won't be changed unless you press **RETURN** after you type it. If you don't press **RETURN**, or if you press **ESC** to cancel the operation instead, the old category or file name will reappear.

Change A Printer menu

■ **Definition**

The *Change A Printer menu* is a list of pre-stored printer settings, which can be changed to suit your specific needs.

■ **Usage**

Use the Change A Printer menu when you want to change the configuration settings on a printer you have already stored in AppleWorks via the Add a Printer menu.[6] To use the Change A Printer menu:

1. Choose option 5, *Other Activities,* from the AppleWorks Main Menu.[158]

2. Choose option 7, *Specify information about your printer(s),* from the Other Activities menu.[178]

3. Choose *Change printer specifications* (option 4, 5, or 6, depending on the number of printer configurations you have stored) from the Printer Information menu.[212] The Change A Printer menu will appear, as shown in this example:

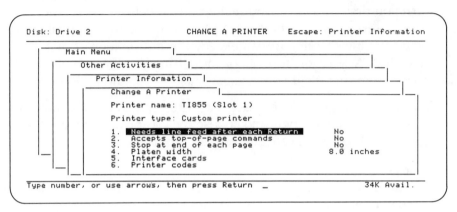

```
Disk: Drive 2              CHANGE A PRINTER     Escape: Printer Information
     _____
    |  Main Menu           |_____
    |     Other Activities      |_____|__
    |        Printer Information   |_____|__
    |           Change A Printer     |_____|__
    |           Printer name: TI855 <Slot 1 >
    |           Printer type: Custom printer
    |                 1.  Needs line feed after each Return       No
    |                 2.  Accepts top-of-page commands            No
    |__               3.  Stop at end of each page                No
        |__           4.  Platen width                            8.0 inches
            |__       5.  Interface cards
                      6.  Printer codes
     _____
    Type number, or use arrows, then press Return  _              34K Avail.
```

The Change A Printer menu lets you redefine printer-configuration settings on a printer.

4. Select the specific printer-configuration setting you wish to change by highlighting the item with the Arrow keys, or by typing the number of the item, then pressing **RETURN**.

5. The prompt line will change to read: *Change the value? No Yes.* Respond to the prompt by pressing **N** (for *No*) or **Y** (for *Yes*).

■ **Comments**

If you haven't configured any printers, or if you've removed all printer configurations from AppleWorks with the *Remove a printer* option on the Printer Information menu, the *Change printer specification* portion of the Printer Information menu won't appear on the screen.

If you are changing the codes for the printer-interface cards (option 5), this change won't take effect while the computer is running. You must quit AppleWorks and then turn the computer off and turn it on again to put this change into action. The other settings will change as soon as you indicate them on the screen.

Further information about printer configuration will be found under the entry, Printer Configuration.[200]

Characters-per-Line indicator

■ **Definition**

The *Characters-per-Line indicator* shows the number of characters that will be printed on each line by your printer.

■ **Usage**

AppleWorks displays the estimated number of characters that can be printed on a line with the current printer-options settings in the spreadsheet and the database Printer Options menus.[217] The estimate is calculated as the platen width in inches multiplied by the number of characters being printed per inch minus any left or right margin settings. If the platen width is 8 inches, for example, and the Characters-per-Inch (CI) setting is 10, and both margins are zero, then the number of estimated characters on each line will be 80, as shown in this example:

```
File: Supplies                 PRINTER OPTIONS            Escape: Report Format
Report: Order Form
=============================================================================
-------Left and right margins--------      ------Top and bottom margins-------
PW: Platen Width           8.0 inches       PL: Paper Length          11.0 inches
LM: Left Margin            0.0 inches       TM: Top Margin             0.0 inches
RM: Right Margin           0.0 inches       BM: Bottom Margin          2.0 inches
CI: Chars per Inch        10                LI: Lines per Inch         6

    Line width             8.0 inches           Printing length       9.0 inches
    Char per line (est)   80                     Lines per page       54

    --------------------Formatting options--------------------
    SC:  Send Special Codes to printer                      No
    PD:  Print a Dash when an entry is blank                No
    PH:  Print report Header at top of each page            Yes
         Single, Double or Triple Spacing (SS/DS/TS)        SS

       "Specify information about your printer" (on menu of Other
        Activities) gives you additional control over printers.
-----------------------------------------------------------------------------
Type a two letter option code  _                                   48K Avail.
```

The number of characters that can be printed on each line is displayed on the spreadsheet and database Printer Options menus.

Use the Characters-per-Line estimate to determine if the current printer-options settings will accommodate the data you have selected for printing. In the database, for example, the width of a report (in characters) is shown by the *Len* indicator[154] that appears at the far right of every Tables Report Format screen. If the number of characters per line shown on the Printer Options menu is at least as large as the report width shown in the *Len* indicator, then the printed lines will be wide enough to hold all the report's data, but if the number is less, then data that exceeds the width limit that the printer options will allow, and the characters on the right side of the report that are past the line-width limit, will not be printed. There is no *Len* indicator in Labels reports, since these reports are laid out vertically and usually don't exceed the default 80-character limit. If you think a Labels report may be wider than the printer options allow for, print the report to the screen. If some of the information on the right side of the report is cut off, either adjust the settings on the Printer Options menu to allow more characters per line, or reposition the categories so that all categories fit within the screen width when the report is printed to the screen. (See: Database Printing;[67] Spreadsheet Printing.[319])

@CHOOSE

- **Structure**

  @CHOOSE(argument)

- **Definition**

  @CHOOSE is a spreadsheet function that examines the numeric value entered in a cell specified at the beginning of the argument and then displays a value from a list within the argument whose position in the list matches the corresponding value in the cell.

- **Usage**

  @CHOOSE arguments have a specific format: a cell coordinate, followed by a list of values, such as *@CHOOSE(B21,500,550,600)*. The argument must be enclosed in parentheses. For @CHOOSE to work properly, the value in the cell specified in the cell coordinate must correspond to the position of one of the entries on the list.

  The @CHOOSE function first looks at the cell specified in the first position of the argument, and then displays the value from those listed in the remainder of the argument whose position is equal to the value in the cell. In the example presented in the last paragraph, if cell B21 contained the value *2*, then the value *550* would be displayed in the cell containing the @CHOOSE function because *550* is second in the list. However, if the value in the cell referenced in an @CHOOSE argument is greater than the number of values in the argument list, or if the value in the referenced cell is less than or equal to zero, a label, or blank, @CHOOSE will return the message *NA*. In our example, if cell B21 contained the value *6*, *NA* would appear in the cell containing the formula because there are only three numbers in the argument list.

■ Example

The following sample spreadsheet uses @CHOOSE to set up a payroll-coding system. The spreadsheet contains a list of standard amounts for FICA and FIT withholdings, each of which corresponds to a certain income level. So instead of having to enter these amounts for each employee's payroll calculation, the user can simply enter a one-digit code in cell B14 (FICA) and cell E14 (FIT) to tell the worksheet which value it should enter. In the example, cell B17 is selected and the @CHOOSE formula is displayed in the formula bar.

```
File: Payroll Calc.                  REVIEW/ADD/CHANGE                 Escape: Main Menu
=========A=========B=========C=========D=========E=========F=========G=========H====
  1|              Widget Manufacturing Payroll Calculator
  2|-----------------------------------------------------------------------------
  3|    FICA              Code                 FIT              Code
  4|  ---------        ---------            ---------        ---------
  5|    38.95              1                  89.5               1
  6|    43.25              2                  93.25              2
  7|    43.79              3                  97.43              3
  8|    47.5               4                  99.5               4
  9|    49.02              5                 100.05              5
 10|
 11|-----------------------------------------------------------------------------
 12|Employee Payroll Worksheet:      Employee Name: Jones, S.
 13|-----------------------------------------------------------------------------
 14|FICA CODE          1             FIT CODE          2
 15|
 16|Salary         435.85
 17|FICA            38.95
 18|FIT             93.25
   |-----------------------------------------------------------------------------
B17: (Value) @CHOOSE(B14,38.95,43.25,43.79,47.5,49.02)

Type entry or use ⬛ commands  _                              ⬛-? for Help
```

The @CHOOSE function can be used to automatically enter one of a list of values, based on the value's position in the list.

If there is no code value in cell B14, cell B17 will display *NA*, which means one of the values needed by the formula isn't available. However, once you type a number in cell B14, the value whose position in the list matches the number will be entered in cell B17.

We have shown the actual list of values and code numbers to make things clearer. In reality, the list of code numbers and corresponding values could be on paper and not actually included on the spreadsheet itself. The @CHOOSE function is self-contained—it works with the list of values you type inside the argument. To demonstrate this to yourself, type five completely different values in the @CHOOSE argument in cell B17, in which case one value (not the values shown in the FICA list above) would appear in cell B17.

■ Comments

AppleWorks spreadsheet formulas are limited in length to 75 characters. The word *@CHOOSE* and the opening and closing parentheses occupy 9 characters themselves, so your list of values for an @CHOOSE formula is limited to 66 characters, including commas to separate them.

Clear (⌂-Y)

■ **Definition**

The *Clear* command (⌂-Y) erases data from the cursor position to the end of a word-processor line, spreadsheet entry line, database entry, or other Apple-Works data-entry line.

Using Clear in the word processor

In the word processor, the Clear command deletes text from the cursor position to the end of the current line. If you use the Clear command in the middle of a line, make sure you want to delete everything on that line from the cursor position and everything to the right of the cursor; if you only want to delete a few words in the middle of the line, use the Delete[92] command or **DELETE** key.

If you clear a line that's within a paragraph, the remainder of the paragraph will be "pulled up" to the cursor position and readjusted. You can keep clearing lines until you reach a carriage return, which the Clear command does not affect. Use the Delete command or the **DELETE** key to clear carriage returns and close up spacing between paragraphs.

Once you delete text with the Clear command, you can't directly recover it. If the file had been previously saved on a disk, however, you can go to the Main Menu,[158] choose option 4, *Remove files from the Desktop*, choose the file from the Remove Files screen,[266] then choose option 3, *Throw out the changes to the file*. After this, you can reload the file as it was when it was last saved. You will of course lose any edits that you *did* want to make, but if what you inadvertently cleared is more important, this is the only way to get it back.

Using Clear in the spreadsheet

In the spreadsheet, the Clear command only works in conjunction with the Undo[351] command (⌂-U). When you use the Undo command, the contents of the current cell appear on the entry line, just below the cell indicator, and the blinking cursor is placed at the beginning of the cell's contents. You can use Clear to delete all or part of the entry by moving the cursor to the first character you want to delete. The Clear command will delete everything from the cursor position to the end of the entry line.

If you use the Clear command and then want to restore the contents of the entry line, press **ESC** directly after you use the Clear command.

Using Clear in the database

In the database, you can use the Clear command to delete from the cursor position to the end of a category entry in both the Tables[80] and Labels[87] report formats. To restore the data you have deleted from a category with the Clear command, press **ESC** before pressing **RETURN**. You can also use Clear to erase the file name, the current category name, or report name in the database, after you use the Name Change[171] command.

■ Comments

You can also use the Clear command anywhere AppleWorks requires you to enter a name, whether it is an application file name, the name of an ASCII[13] or DIF[100] file, the pathname[188] of a subdirectory to which you are saving a file, or the name of a printer you have configured. If you type a file name, for example, and you haven't pressed **RETURN** to enter it yet, you can erase the name simply by moving the cursor to the first letter in the name and pressing the Clear command.

Clipboard

■ Definition

The *Clipboard* is a section of computer memory used by AppleWorks to temporarily store data that is being moved or copied between applications or within the same application.

■ Usage

All files you work with on the AppleWorks Desktop[97] are stored in the computer's RAM,[256] or temporary memory. The Clipboard is an area of RAM that is used to store data being moved or copied between files on the Desktop. When you move or copy data from one file to another, it is always moved via the Clipboard like this:

1. You move, copy, or print the data to the Clipboard.
2. You switch from the original file to the file where you want to move or copy the data.
3. You move or copy the data from the Clipboard to the second file.

If you are copying data within the same file, you can use the Clipboard also, but it isn't necessary because the Move[163] and Copy[40] commands have specific options that let you move data within a file.

When you *move* data to the Clipboard, you remove it from the file where you got it. When you *copy* data to the Clipboard, you take a copy of the data from the file, and the original data remains where it was. Once your data is on the Clipboard, you can paste it into a different file, or into a different location in the same file.

When you put data on the Clipboard, a copy of that data remains there—even after you paste from the Clipboard—until you either place a different set of data on the Clipboard or you quit AppleWorks. This means that you can use the Copy command to copy the same data from the Clipboard into more than one place. If you wanted to copy a certain paragraph into three different files, for example, you could copy the paragraph to the Clipboard, then use the Copy command to paste it into File 1, paste it into File 2, and paste it into File 3. You wouldn't have to re-copy the paragraph to the Clipboard each time, because the copy would remain on the Clipboard.

If you use the Move command to paste Clipboard data into an application, the Clipboard information is removed (cut) from the Clipboard after the paste operation, and the Clipboard will be empty until you copy or move something in it again.

The Clipboard permits several different kinds of data interchange within and among AppleWorks applications. If you are moving data between the same types of file (for example, from spreadsheet to spreadsheet or from one word-processor document to another), you can use the Move (⌘-M) or Copy (⌘-C) command to get the data to the Clipboard.

In addition, you can move data from the spreadsheet or database to a word-processor document. To do this, however, you must *print* the spreadsheet or database data to the Clipboard using the Print[193] command (⌘-P), and then copy or move it into the word-processor document. Data from a spreadsheet or database file cannot be moved or copied directly into a word-processor document.

■ **Comments**

The Clipboard is part of the available RAM space in your computer. Because of this, the Clipboard's actual size can vary, depending on the amount of RAM available at the time in your system. The amount of available RAM will be affected by the number of files you have on the Desktop. If you have 11 files on the Desktop and they are using nearly all of the available RAM, you won't be able to move or copy as much data via the Clipboard as you would if the Desktop were nearly empty.

The Clipboard can never hold more than 250 word-processor lines, 250 spreadsheet rows, 125 spreadsheet columns, or 250 database records at a time, even if the Desktop is nearly empty.

Column

- **Definition**

A *column* is a continuous vertical group of spreadsheet cells or a continuous vertical group of single characters in a word-processor document.

 Columns in the spreadsheet

Spreadsheets are matrices of *rows* and *columns*, as shown in this example:

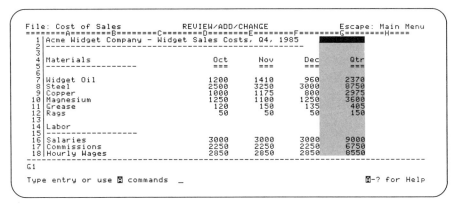

```
File: Cost of Sales            REVIEW/ADD/CHANGE              Escape: Main Menu
======A========B========C========D========E========F========G========H====
    1|Acme Widget Company - Widget Sales Costs, Q4, 1985
    2|
    3|------------------------------------------------------
    4|Materials                     Oct      Nov      Dec      Qtr
    5|------------------            ===      ===      ===      ===
    6|
    7|Widget Oil                   1200     1410      960     2370
    8|Steel                        2500     3250     3000     8750
    9|Copper                       1000     1175      800     2975
   10|Magnesium                    1250     1100     1250     3600
   11|Grease                        120      150      135      405
   12|Rags                           50       50       50      150
   13|
   14|Labor
   15|------------------
   16|Salaries                     3000     3000     3000     9000
   17|Commissions                  2250     2250     2250     6750
   18|Hourly Wages                 2850     2850     2850     8550
   --------------------------------------------------------------------
  G1

  Type entry or use Ⓐ commands   _                        Ⓐ-? for Help
```

A column is one of the two major levels of organization in spreadsheets.

Each intersection of a row and column is called a *cell*. Each row and column is labeled: Columns are labeled with letters, such as A, B, and C, and rows are labeled with numbers from 1 through 999. An AppleWorks spreadsheet can contain a maximum of 127 columns of data. They are labeled as follows, beginning at the left side of the spreadsheet:

A through Z

AA through AZ

BA through BZ

CA through CZ

DA through DW

Thus, the cell located at the intersection of the top row and the farthest left column in a spreadsheet is cell A1, and the cell on the bottom row and farthest right column is DW999.

Because a column is one of two major units of organization in a spreadsheet, it is possible to format or move data in increments of one or more columns. Within a spreadsheet, you can make individual columns or groups of columns wider or narrower, you can copy data from one column to another, and you can change the format of data in one or more columns. (See: Spreadsheet Overview;[298] Move;[163] Copy.[40])

Columns in the word processor

In the word processor, the cursor is always located at the intersection of a horizontal line and a vertical column. Lines are numbered from the top of the document beginning with 1, and columns from the left of the document beginning with 1. Thus, if the cursor is at the top-left corner of a document, it is located on line 1, in column 1. A word-processor document can be up to 80 columns wide and 2250 lines long. This example shows the cursor in column 17 in the word processor:

```
File: Sales Letter              REVIEW/ADD/CHANGE              Escape: Main Menu
====|====|====|====|====|====|====|====|====|====|====|====|====|====|====|===
December 13, 1985

Mr. Ed Frobish
Frobish Linen Service
335 Ramona Ave.
San Jose, CA 95551

Dear Ed:

I just wanted to tell you how much all of us at Acme Widgets appreciate your
business.  We think you're a ^super^ customer! That's why we wanted you to
be the first to know about our new Widget Convertible--the sturdiest, most
flexible, most cost-effective widget around.

I'd like to schedule a time to drop by your office and demonstrate the
advantages of the new Widget Convertible, so I'll be giving you a call
during the next week to make an appointment.

In the meantime, think what the world's first all-purpose widget will mean
to your profits!■
--------------------------------------------------------------------------
Type entry or use ⌂ commands          Line 22  Column 17        ⌂-? for Help
```

Columns in word-processor documents help you keep track of the cursor's location.

The numbered columns in a word-processor document are there exclusively so you can keep track of the cursor's location. You can't specify formatting or text manipulation options in the word processor by column, but only by line or character.

Column indicator: The *column indicator* is an area in the bottom-center of the Review/Add/Change screen of the word processor that shows the cursor's current horizontal location in a document.

As you move the cursor across a line in the word processor, the column indicator changes to show which column the cursor is in at any given time. In the previous example, the column indicator showed that the cursor is located in column 17.

The column indicator is most useful when you are indenting text or setting up columns of information in the word processor. By checking the column indicator, you can make sure every indent is the same size, and every line of data in a column begins in the same place.

Column width

■ **Definition**

Column width is one of the options presented when you use the Layout[146] command (⌂-L) to change the formatting of a spreadsheet file, and then choose *Columns* as the type of area whose format you want to change.

■ **Usage**

To alter the width of one or more columns in a spreadsheet:

1. On the Review/Add/Change screen of a spreadsheet, move the cursor to the column (or the first of a continuous group of columns) whose width you want to change.

2. Press the Layout command (⌂-L).

3. Choose the *Columns* option.

4. Use the → or ← key to highlight the columns whose widths you want to change, and then press **RETURN**.

5. Choose the *Column width* option.

6. Use ⌂ and → or ← keys to change the width of the column(s) you have selected. The → key will make a column wider, and the ← key will make a column narrower.

7. Press **RETURN** when the column(s) are the width you want.

■ **Comments**

Individual columns can be from 1 to 75 characters wide. Column widths can be varied individually.

If you want to change the width of every column in a spreadsheet, you can use the Standard Values[330] command (⌂-V).

Copy (⌑-C)

■ **Definition**

The *Copy* command (⌑-C) lets you copy word-processor text, database records, or spreadsheet labels, values, or formulas either directly within files, or between files using the Clipboard.[35]

■ **Usage**

Use the Copy command when you want to use existing word-processor, spreadsheet, or database data in another part of the same file, or in another file of the same type. The general procedure for copying data goes like this:

1. Move the cursor to the place in the file where you want to begin copying.
2. Press the Copy command (⌑-C).
3. Select the *copy-to* or *copy-from* destination from the prompt line (see below).
4. Highlight the word-processor text, database records, or spreadsheet cells you want to copy by using the Arrow keys.
5. After the area you want to copy is highlighted, press **RETURN**.
6. Move the cursor to the area where you want the copied material to appear.
7. Press **RETURN** to insert the copied material starting at the cursor's location.

When copying to the AppleWorks Clipboard, you are limited to 250 lines (in a word-processor document), rows (in a spreadsheet), or records (in a database file). If you try to copy more than this, you will get an error message telling you about the limit.

The Clipboard shares your Apple's RAM[256] memory with the files on the AppleWorks Desktop,[97] so while 250 lines/rows/records is the maximum allowed, the actual limit of data copied could be smaller. If the Desktop space is almost completely filled with files (52K out of 55K, for example), the amount of copying space available in the Clipboard will be smaller than it would be if the files on the Desktop occupied only 25K.

When you copy information to the Clipboard, a copy remains on the Clipboard even after you copy from the Clipboard to a file. This allows you to place the same copy in several different places by simply copying from the

Clipboard several times. When you copy a different section of information to the Clipboard, the new information replaces any that was previously being held on the Clipboard.

The copying procedure is slightly different in each of the three Apple-Works applications, as explained in the following sections.

Copying in the word processor

When copying text in the word processor, you can copy it within a document, to the Clipboard, or from the Clipboard. Highlighting the text to copy is the same, whether you're copying within the document or to the Clipboard. When you copy *from* the Clipboard, you must place the cursor at the exact location where you want the information on the Clipboard to appear. The copied text will be inserted at the cursor position, but in front of any text that follows the cursor.

Copying in the spreadsheet

When copying cells in the spreadsheet, you can copy within the spreadsheet, or to or from the Clipboard. Your ability to highlight spreadsheet areas for copying, and your ability to place the copied data, depends on the copy-to destination. Use the following sample spreadsheet to follow along as these differences are explained by example.

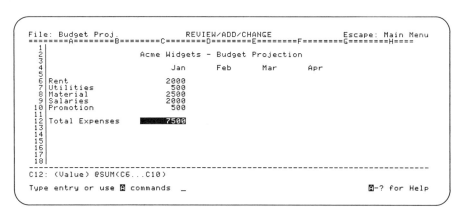

Sample spreadsheet, before copying cells.

Copying within the spreadsheet: If you are copying data within the spreadsheet, you can move the cursor to highlight cells in the current row or column only—once you highlight more than one cell in a particular row, for example, you can't move out of that row.

After you highlight the cells in the desired row or column and press **RETURN**, you can copy the data to one group of cells, or to more than one group of cells.

To copy the data to one group of cells, simply move the cursor to the new location and press **RETURN**. To copy the data to more than one group of cells, move the cursor to the first new location, press the period (.) key, and then continue moving the cursor until all the adjacent copy-to areas are highlighted. Once they are all highlighted, press **RETURN**, and the copies will be made. If you are copying data to more than one area, make sure that all the copy-to areas are adjacent—AppleWorks will not copy data to multiple locations if they are not adjacent.

Example: Copying values to one location. Suppose you want to copy the *Rent* and *Utilities* figures from the *Jan* column (cells C6 and C7) to the *Feb* column (cells D6 and D7).

1. Move the cursor to cell C6.
2. Press the Copy command (⌘-**C**).
3. Choose the option *Within worksheet* (which will automatically be highlighted at the bottom of the screen) by pressing **RETURN**.
4. Use the ↓ key to move the cursor from cell C6 to cell C7 to include this second cell in the copy selection, and then press **RETURN** to end the selection.
5. Move the cursor to the cell where you want the insertion of the copied data to begin (cell D6), and press **RETURN**. The contents of cells C6 and C7 will be copied into cells D6 and D7.

Example: Copying values to multiple locations. Suppose the *Rent* and *Utilities* figures in this projection are the same for *Mar* and *Apr,* and you want to copy them to both of these columns at once to save data-entry time. In this case, you want to place a copy of the two cells' contents in more than one location.

1. Follow steps 1 through 4 from the example above.
2. Move the cursor to the cell in the first column where you want the insertion to begin (cell E6).

3. Instead of pressing **RETURN** to end the copy-to selection, press the period (.) key. You'll see that cells E6 and E7 are highlighted. This tells AppleWorks you wish to copy to more than one destination. If you pressed **RETURN** now, instead of extending the selection, the copied information would appear in these cells only.

4. Extend the selection by moving the cursor to the second copy-to location (cell F6), which will highlight F6 and F7. End the copy-to specification by pressing **RETURN**. The contents of cells C6 and C7 will be copied to cells E6 and E7 as well as to cells F6 and F7.

The sample spreadsheet now looks like this:

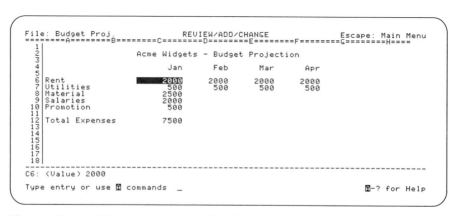

The sample spreadsheet, after copying cells C6 and C7 (see text).

Example: Copying formulas. The copy procedure is the same for both values and labels, but it is slightly different for cells containing formulas. If you are copying data cells that include formulas, you will be asked whether you want the copy to be made with *No Change* to the formulas, or with the formulas changed *Relative* to their new location.

When a copy of a formula is made with the *No Change* option, it is called an *absolute* copy, because it is an exact copy of the formula and contains the same cell references as the original. An absolute copy of the formula *A1*3* is *A1*3*. But a *relative* copy is one whose cell references have changed according to the new position of the formula. If you had the formula *A1*3* in cell A3 and copied it to cell B3 using the *Relative* option, cell B3 would contain the formula *B1*3*, since B1 is relative to B3 in relation to A1's position to A3.

The *Total Expenses* cell for January (C12) in the sample spreadsheet contains the value *7500*, but this value is actually the result of a formula that adds the values entered in the cells above (C6 through C10). The formula is *@SUM(C6...C10)*, as shown in the entry line below the cell indicator in the first sample spreadsheet. Let's copy the formula from cell C12 to cells D12, E12, and F12. This is much faster than re-entering the formula in each of the three cells. Because we want the formulas to sum the values in columns D, E, and F, however, we'll want the copied formulas to be *Relative* to their new location. Here's how:

1. Move the cursor to cell C12.

2. Press the Copy command (⌘-**C**).

3. Choose *Within worksheet* by pressing **RETURN**.

4. Press **RETURN** to end the copy-from selection, since you only want to copy that cell.

5. Move the cursor to cell D12, and then press the period (.) key to indicate multiple copy-to locations.

6. Move the cursor to the right to highlight cells E12 and F12, and then end the copy-to selection by pressing **RETURN**.

7. At this point, the entry line will show us the original formula, *@SUM(C6...C10)*, with the first cell reference (C6) highlighted. The prompt line asks if the reference to C6 in the formula should be copied with *No Change*, or copied *Relative* to its new location. This prompt always appears with the *No Change* selection highlighted. We choose *Relative* by pressing **R**.

8. The second cell reference (*C10*) in the formula is highlighted, and again we must specify whether the copies should include references to it with *No Change* or *Relative* to the new formula location. Again, we press **R** to choose *Relative*,and the copies are made.

You can check the new formula copies by moving the cursor to one of the copy-to cells (D12,E12,F12). The copied formula will show in the entry line, and you will notice that the cell references now reflect the formula's new location (for example, D12 contains the formula *@SUM(D6...D10)*. If the copies had been made with *No Change*, the references would be identical to the formula in cell C12 (C6...C10).

As this example shows, there are many instances in which you may want to copy a formula that has the same structure (such as the one in our sample that sums four cells in a column). Thanks to the *Relative* copying feature in

AppleWorks, you can copy the formula's structure and have the spreadsheet automatically change the specific cell references used so the appropriate cells are calculated in each formula copy.

You can also use combinations of *Relative* and *No change* references when copying formulas, in case you want the formula to use a cell you may have set up as a reference cell.

Copying from the spreadsheet to the Clipboard: If you are copying data from a spreadsheet file to the Clipboard to paste into another section of the current spreadsheet or a different spreadsheet, you can only highlight the data in rows. Just like copying cells within a spreadsheet, you must locate the cursor at the beginning of the copy selection *before* pressing the Copy command.

Example: Suppose we want to copy the entire sample spreadsheet to the Clipboard, so we can include this data in a different spreadsheet file.

1. Move the cursor to the top of the spreadsheet (cell A1).
2. Press the Copy command (Ú-**C**).
3. Specify *To clipboard* as the copy-to destination by using the Arrow keys to move the highlight bar at the bottom of the screen and then pressing **RETURN** or by just pressing the **T** key.
4. After **RETURN** is pressed, notice that the entire row where the cursor is currently located (row 1) is highlighted. Highlight additional rows to copy by using ↓.
5. Once you have highlighted all the rows you want to copy in the spreadsheet, press **RETURN**. The data will be copied to the Clipboard (without being removed from this spreadsheet), where it can then be copied into another section of the current spreadsheet, or into another spreadsheet.
6. Move the cursor to a new location in the current spreadsheet where you want the copied data to appear, or open another spreadsheet file and move the cursor to the location where you want the copied data to appear.
7. Press the Copy command (Ú-**C**).
8. Choose *From clipboard (paste)* by pressing **F** (or highlight the option with the → key and press **RETURN**). The data on the Clipboard will be entered in the spreadsheet, starting at the current cursor location.

Formulas versus data: One final consideration when using the Copy command in the spreadsheet is making copies of formulas versus making copies of data. If you copy a cell whose value was produced by a formula, the Copy command will copy the formula, not the value. Thus, if you tried to copy the totals in a *Totals* row, but the numbers were actually the results of @SUM formulas, the formulas—not their results—would be copied.

Copying in the database

In the database, you can copy either one record (one row in the Multiple Record[168] layout, or one screen in Single Record[293] layout) within the file, or you can copy up to 250 records from the Multiple Record layout to the Clipboard. The procedure is different in each case.

Copying within the database: When copying a single record within a database file, you can't choose the destination of the copy: Copies of a single record are automatically placed directly after the original (you can make up to 99 copies of a single record at once).

1. Place the cursor on the record you wish to copy.

2. Press the Copy command (⌘-**C**).

3. Choose *Current record* as the copy option. This option is automatically highlighted when you use the Copy command, so you can choose it simply by pressing **RETURN**.

4. You are then prompted to specify the number of copies you want to make of that record. You must enter a number (up to 99), then press **RETURN**. If you just press **RETURN** without entering a number, no copy will be made.

5. Once you press **RETURN**, the number of records you specified are placed in the row(s) directly beneath the cursor location (in Multiple Record layout) or directly after the current record (in Single Record layout).

Copying from the database to the Clipboard: In order to copy records from the Multiple Record layout to the Clipboard, the cursor must first be placed at the top or bottom of the records you want to select before you use the Copy command.

1. Repeat steps 1 and 2 from above.

2. Choose *To clipboard (cut)* as the copy-to option by moving the highlight bar to this option and pressing **RETURN**, or by just pressing **T**.

3. Highlight the remaining records you wish to copy by extending the selection with the ↑ or ↓ key.

4. End the selection by pressing **RETURN**. A copy of the selection will be placed on the Clipboard. Again, the original remains in the file you copied from.

5. Open another existing database file, or create a new one.

6. Move the cursor to the first category where you want the copied records to appear.

7. Press the Copy command.

8. Choose *From clipboard (paste)* by pressing the **F** key or by highlighting the selection with the Arrow keys and pressing **RETURN**. The records on the Clipboard will be copied into the current file.

You can also copy the records on the Clipboard into the current file by moving the cursor to the record where you want the Clipboard information to appear, pressing the Copy command, and then choosing *From clipboard (paste)*. This is an easy method of making multiple copies of multiple records within a data file.

@COUNT

■ **Structure**
@COUNT(argument)

■ **Definition**
@COUNT is a spreadsheet function that counts the number of numeric entries in a specified range or list, and displays the number in the cell where the @COUNT function is entered.

■ **Usage**
@COUNT arguments must contain either a range[308] of cells or a list[155] of cells separated by commas, within parentheses. @COUNT only counts numeric entries; text entries and empty cells are ignored.

■ **Example**

The following spreadsheet models a parts-inventory list. The @COUNT formula entered in cell C17 and displayed in the entry line returns the total number of part numbers in the list.

```
File: Inventory              REVIEW/ADD/CHANGE              Escape: Main Menu
========A========B========C========D========E========F========G========H====
   1|           Widget Inventory
   2|--------------------------------------------------------------------
   3|Name                Number              Quantity
   4|--------            --------            --------
   5|Sprockets:
   6|-----------------
   7|Small Sprockets       1001                358
   8|Med. Sprockets        1002                 21
   9|Large Sprockets       1003                188
  10|
  11|Gears:
  12|-----------------
  13|Small Gears           1004               1290
  14|Med. Gears            1005                125
  15|Large Gears           1006                190
  16|
  17|Total # of Parts: ███████████6
  18|
------------------------------------------------------------------------------
C17: (Value) @COUNT(C3...C15)

Type entry or use ⓐ commands  _                            ⓐ-? for Help
```

The @COUNT function is helpful when you want to quickly determine the number of numeric entries in a list.

Admittedly, the list isn't very long in this example, but if the list were several screens long it would be much easier to use the @COUNT function than to count the entries one by one. Notice also that @COUNT only counts the numeric entries in the list, which is all we want, and not the empty spacer cells or the text in cells C3 and C4.

■ **Comments**

You could indicate the entries you want counted by specifying them individually as a list in the argument of the @COUNT function (instead of using a range of cells) but, if you are going to bother to list each entry to be counted separately, then you might as well count the entries while you're doing so— your need for @COUNT will be gone by the time you have finished making the list you need. In other words, our @COUNT formula in cell C17 could have been written as *@COUNT(C7,C8,C9,C13,C14,C15)*, but making such a laborious list defeats the purpose of the @COUNT function.

@COUNT is affected by the @NA[170] and ERROR functions. If a cell containing @NA or @ERROR is contained in the range you specify, @COUNT will return the message *NA* or *ERROR* instead of a number.

Current disk location

■ **Definition**

The *current disk location* is the disk-drive number or ProDOS pathname[188] where AppleWorks automatically looks when you save, load, list, or delete files on disk.

■ **Usage**

The current disk location is always displayed in the upper-left corner of the AppleWorks screen when you are in the Main Menu[158] or using one of its sub-menus, such as the Add Files menu in this example:

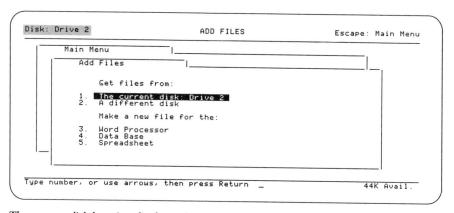

The current disk location displays which disk or ProDOS pathname is being accessed when you load, save, delete, or list files.

AppleWorks always stores the current disk location. It remembers which disk drive or pathname you last loaded files from, and assumes you want to continue working with that disk drive or pathname. You can tell which disk drive AppleWorks is remembering by looking at the current disk location in the upper-left corner of the Main Menu screen.

It's a good idea to check the current disk location when you save files, to make sure you are saving files to the proper disk or pathname. If you are listing, adding, or deleting files and you can't find the file you are looking for, check the current disk location to be sure AppleWorks is showing the right disk or ProDOS pathname. (See: Pathname; ProDOS.[246])

The current disk location is also referred to in AppleWorks as the *current disk drive,* or the *current ProDOS prefix.*

49

Cursor

- **Definition**

  The *cursor* is the place marker that shows where information you type into AppleWorks will appear on the computer screen.

- **Usage**

  When you first load an existing word-processor file or database file to the Desktop,[97] the cursor is located in the upper-left corner of the screen, which is the top-left corner of the first page of a word-processor document, or the first category of the first record in a database file. If you type information, it will appear on the screen at the cursor position. However, when you load an existing spreadsheet file, the cursor will be located in the cell it was positioned in when you last saved the file.

  The cursor's location is always shown on the screen, but:

  ☐ In the word processor, you can also tell the cursor's location from the line-and-column indicator at the bottom-center of the Review/Add/Change screen.

  ☐ In the spreadsheet, the cell indicator in the lower-left corner of the Review/Add/Change screen always shows the coordinates of the cell where the cursor is located.

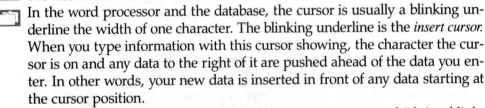 **The insert and overstrike cursors**

In the word processor and the database, the cursor is usually a blinking underline the width of one character. The blinking underline is the *insert cursor.* When you type information with this cursor showing, the character the cursor is on and any data to the right of it are pushed ahead of the data you enter. In other words, your new data is inserted in front of any data starting at the cursor position.

The other cursor you can display is the *overstrike cursor,* which is a blinking vertical rectangle the size of one character. When you type information with the overstrike cursor showing, the new data replaces any existing data in its path as you type.

In the spreadsheet, there are actually two cursors. One cursor is a highlighted rectangle that fills one cell, showing which cell you are currently working with. The second cursor appears at the bottom of the screen, following the *Type entry or use ⌂ commands* prompt. Whenever you actually enter or edit data in a spreadsheet cell, this second cursor appears in the entry line as either a blinking underline or a solid rectangle, depending on which cursor (insert or overstrike) you have selected.

Changing cursors: In all three applications, the default cursor is the insert cursor. You can change from the insert cursor to the overstrike cursor, or vice versa, with the Edit Cursor[105] command (⌂-E).

■ Moving the cursor

When you don't want your text or numbers to be placed at the upper-left corner of the screen (where the cursor is always located when you begin working with a word-processor or database file), you must move the cursor to the place where you want your data to appear before typing it. One method available in all of the applications is the *Ruler*, which lets you move the cursor quickly around a file. By pressing the ⌂ key and a number key (from 1 through 9), you can move the cursor proportionally through a file. If you press ⌂-9, for example, the cursor will move to the end of a file. If you press ⌂-5, the cursor will move to the middle of a file. If you press ⌂-1, the cursor will move to the beginning of a file. (See: Ruler[280] for more information.)

The following sections explain the key combinations for moving the cursor in each application.

Moving the cursor in the word processor

You can use the Arrow keys to move the cursor in the word processor one character left or right, or one line up or down. You can also use the ⌂ key along with the Arrow keys, the **TAB** key, or the Ruler, as follows:

⌂-↑	Moves the cursor to top of current screen, and up one screen each time after that. (When you move the cursor so new data is revealed, this is called *scrolling*.)
⌂-↓	Moves the cursor to bottom of current screen, and down one screen each time after that.
⌂-←	Moves the cursor left one word at a time.
⌂-→	Moves the cursor right one word at a time.
TAB	Moves the cursor one tab stop to the right.
⌂-**TAB**	Moves the cursor one tab stop to the left.

Moving the cursor in the spreadsheet

To move the cursor in the spreadsheet, you can use the Arrow keys, the Arrow keys in combination with the ⌘ key, the **TAB** key alone or together with the ⌘ key, or the Ruler. Here's how the individual keys and key combinations move the cursor:

↑	Moves the cursor up one cell.
↓	Moves the cursor down one cell.
←	Moves the cursor left one cell.
→	Moves the cursor right one cell.
⌘-←	Moves the cursor to left edge of current screen, and left one screen each time after that.
⌘-→	Moves the cursor to right edge of current screen, and right one screen each time after that.
⌘-↓	Moves the cursor to bottom of current screen, and down one screen each time after that.
⌘-↑	Moves the cursor to top of current screen, and up one screen each time after that.
TAB	Moves the cursor right one cell.
⌘-**TAB**	Moves the cursor left one cell.

Moving the cursor in the database

Cursor moves are different in the database, depending on which of the four possible screen formats is showing.

The Multiple Record layout screen:

←	Moves the cursor left one character.
→	Moves the cursor right one character.
↓	Moves the cursor down one record.
↑	Moves the cursor up one record.
⌘-←	Moves the cursor to the leftmost character of the current category.
⌘-→	Also moves the cursor to the leftmost character of the current category.
⌘-↓	Moves the cursor to the bottom of screen, then down one screen each time after that.

⌘-↑	Moves the cursor to top of screen, then up one screen each time after that.
TAB	Moves the cursor right one category.
⌘-TAB	Moves the cursor left one category.

The Single Record layout screen:

←	Moves the cursor left one character.
→	Moves the cursor right one character.
↓	Moves the cursor down one category. If the cursor is already on the last category in the record, it moves the cursor to the first category in the next record.
↑	Moves the cursor up one category. If the cursor is already on the first category in a record, it moves the cursor to the last category in the previous record.
⌘-←	Moves the cursor to the leftmost character of the current category.
⌘-→	Also moves the cursor to the leftmost character of the current category.
⌘-↓	Moves the cursor to the same category of the next record.
⌘-↑	Moves the cursor to the same category of the previous record.
TAB	Moves the cursor down one category.
⌘-TAB	Moves the cursor up one category.

The Tables Report Format screen:

←	Moves the cursor left one category.
→	Moves the cursor right one category.
⌘-←	Narrows the category one character.
⌘-→	Widens the category one character.
TAB	Moves the cursor right one category.
⌘-TAB	Moves the cursor left one category.

(The ↑ and ↓ keys are not active on a Tables Report Format screen.)

The Labels Report Format screen:

←	Moves the cursor left one character.
→	Moves the cursor right one character.
↓	Moves the cursor down one category.
↑	Moves the cursor up one category.
⌘-Arrow combinations	Allow you to reposition categories when the cursor is on the first character of a category name.

The **TAB** key is not active on a Labels Report Format screen.

Custom printer

■ **Definition**

A *custom printer* is a printer that is not specifically listed as an option on the Add a Printer menu,[6] and whose configuration settings must be entered into AppleWorks by you. (However, some non-listed printers are compatible with those that are listed and will work—check with your dealer to find out if your printer is compatible.)

■ **Usage**

To set up AppleWorks to work with a particular printer, you must use the Add a Printer menu. The Add a Printer menu lists some built-in configuration settings for several common printers, and if you have one of those (or one compatible with one listed), you can choose that printer from the menu.

If your printer is not listed or is not compatible with one listed on the Add a Printer menu, then it is a custom printer. You set up AppleWorks so it can use a custom printer by entering specific information via the Add a Printer menu about line feeds, top of page commands, platen width, the method used to underline text, and other settings specific to your printer.

Although you can set AppleWorks to work with three different printers at a time (so that you will have up to three printers to choose from when you print a file), only one of those stored printers can be a custom printer.

For complete information about configuring AppleWorks for different printers, see Printer Configuration.[200]

Data Base menu

- **Definition**

  The *Data Base menu* is a list of options that let you create a new database file in various ways.

- **Usage**

  When you choose option 4 from the Add Files menu,[2] *Make a new file for the Data Base*, the Data Base menu is displayed with these four options for creating a new database file:

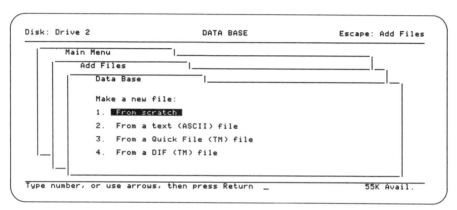

The Data Base menu

Option 1—From scratch: When you choose the *From scratch* option, the prompt line asks you to type a name for the new file. When you type a file name of up to 15 characters and then press the **RETURN** key, the Change Name/Category screen[27] is displayed. This screen allows you to enter new database category names. The first category name, which is initially displayed as *Category 1*, is displayed as an example, which you can then optionally change.

Option 2—From a text (ASCII) file: This option lets you use data in an existing ASCII file[13] as the source for a new database file. When you choose this option, the prompt line asks you how many categories the new database file will have for each record (you can specify from 1 to 30 categories).

After you enter the number of categories for the new file and press **RETURN**, the prompt line asks you to type the complete ProDOS[246] pathname[188] of the ASCII file. Once you type this pathname and press **RETURN**, the ASCII file will be loaded and converted to a new AppleWorks database file, which will contain the number of categories you have specified. You will then be prompted to type a name for the new file. When you do, press **RETURN**, and the file will be displayed.

You have to specify the number of categories in a database file made from an ASCII file because of the way AppleWorks converts ASCII files. As far as AppleWorks is concerned, every item of information between carriage returns in a file is a category entry. AppleWorks takes the items in an ASCII file sequentially, placing each item between carriage returns into a different category for as many categories as you have specified. The cycle is then repeated. With a three-category ASCII file, for example, AppleWorks would assign items between carriage returns to category 1, category 2, and category 3 for the first record, then category 1, category 2, and category 3 for the second record, and so on, until all the items had been assigned. Because of this, you have to be sure to specify the exact number of categories you need for each file, and you need to make sure the ASCII file has each item of information separated by carriage returns. If you've specified three categories for a file and you have four different types of information, the data will be mis-assigned: Item 1 will go into category 1, item 2 will go into category 2, and item 3 will go into category 3, but item 4 will go into category 1 of the next record because there's no fourth category for it to go into.

If AppleWorks is unable to locate the ASCII file at the pathname you specified, it will display the message *Cannot find the file.*

Option 3—From a Quick File (TM) file: When you choose this option, the screen displays the message, *Quick File files will be read from the current disk drive or subdirectory,* and the prompt line instructs you to press the space-bar to continue.

If the Quick File file[254] you want is stored on the current disk, press the spacebar. A list of the Quick File files on the current disk will be displayed, and you can select the file you want to use as the source for a new database file by typing its number, or by highlighting it, and then pressing **RETURN**.

Once you select the proper Quick File file and press **RETURN**, the file will be automatically loaded as a new AppleWorks database file. The new file will contain the same number of categories as the original Quick File file. You'll have to type a name for the new file and press **RETURN** before the file is displayed.

If there are no Quick File files on the current disk, you will get a message that says *Getting errors trying to read Quick File catalog on [current disk]* (the name of the current disk will be shown). To change the current disk, you must either change the floppy disk in the current drive, or change the current disk location. To change the current disk location:

1. Press **ESC** twice to return to the Main Menu.

2. Choose option 5, *Other Activities*, from the Main Menu.

3. Choose option 1, *Change current disk drive or ProDOS prefix*, from the Other Activities menu.

4. Choose the new current drive (Drive 1 or Drive 2), or type the new ProDOS prefix.

Option 4—From a DIF (TM) file: When you choose this option, the prompt line tells you to type the complete ProDOS pathname of the DIF file[100] you wish to use. When you type the pathname and press **RETURN**, Apple-Works gets the file from the current disk. The prompt line then asks you to type a name for the new file. After you type the name and press the **RETURN** key, the new AppleWorks database file will be displayed.

If AppleWorks cannot locate the DIF file under the pathname you specify, it displays the message *Cannot find the file.*

DIF files have a specific format when stored on a disk. They normally contain text and numbers arranged in rows and columns, as in a database file or spreadsheet. Data stored on disk from another program in the DIF format can be arranged in either row or column order, but the Apple-Works database expects DIF files to have been stored only in column order. If the data you load from another program's DIF file was stored in row order, your new AppleWorks database file will be misordered (that is, data that should be arranged across rows will be arranged down columns). In that case, the DIF file cannot be used, and you will either have to enter the data manually or, if possible, have the original file saved again in column order.

■ **Comments**

When you use an existing ASCII, DIF, or Quick File file as the source for a new database file, a copy of the original file also remains on the disk in its original format.

When an AppleWorks database file created from an ASCII or DIF file is first displayed, the categories will be named *Category 1*, *Category 2*, and so on. You can change these category names with the Name Change[171] command.

Database overview

Perhaps the best way to conceptualize the structure of the AppleWorks database is to imagine owning a small business, and imagine that in the office you have an overflowing, four-drawer filing cabinet in which you cram bills and receipts and orders and countless other bits of paper relating to your business. In that cabinet, for example, you probably have a manila *file* folder labeled *Customers*. And in this folder you have a sheet of paper for each of your customers that contains information about them, such as names, addresses, phone numbers, lists of purchases, and so on. You probably think of these sheets as your customer *records*, and each piece of information on them as *categories*. We can think of these three elements as being arranged in a hierarchy, like this:

I. Files
   A. Records
      1. Categories

So, when you want to add, delete, change, or simply consult information about a particular customer, you pull out the *Customers* file, sort through the records, pull out the record with the customer's name on it, and scan the record for the particular category you're interested in.

The AppleWorks database is structured very much like this hypothetical filing cabinet. In it, you create *files* in which you store *records* containing *categories* of useful information. In an AppleWorks file, you also keep entries (like names and addresses) and numbers (like phone numbers). But that's about as far as the analogy goes. Because unlike records in a file folder, you can search database records far faster and in considerably more detail and with greater accuracy than you can riffling through sheets of paper in a manila folder, and you can also generate reports based on the information contained in the records. For example, suppose you had a manila folder stuffed with 50 customer sheets, and you wanted to find out the total amount of goods all of them had bought from you during the past month. Sounds like a long session with a calculator, doesn't it (and a lot of numbers to key in accurately). If these were records in an AppleWorks database file, you could discover the sum almost instantly, with just a few keystrokes. And suppose you wanted to find out which particular pieces of merchandise sold the most and least for the month: If your records contained merchandise categories, you could discover these critical bits of information almost instantly. What's more, in an AppleWorks database file you can also have date and time categories, and sort records chronologically on this information as well.

In short, the AppleWorks database is a sophisticated, electronic filing cabinet that lets you organize and analyze your information efficiently and accurately.

■ Working with the database

In the AppleWorks database, you can either work with an existing file or create a new one, just as you would either pull out a file folder from a file cabinet if you wanted to work with an existing file, or else take out a new file folder and label it before setting up records to put in it. Your first step in either case begins with option 1 on the Main Menu,[158] *Add files to the Desktop.* This produces the Add Files menu.[2] To work with an existing AppleWorks database file, choose either option 1 (if your data disk is in the current drive), or option 2 (if your data disk is in a different drive). Whichever you choose as appropriate, the AppleWorks Files menu appears, and you can choose the database file you want to work with.

If you want to create a new file, you choose option 4 from the Add Files menu, *Make a new file for the Data Base.* This produces the Data Base menu.[55] You choose option 1 on this menu, *From scratch.* Next, you must name the file before you can begin working with it. The name must begin with a letter, and can be up to 15 characters long. (From the Data Base menu, you can also load an existing ASCII,[13] DIF,[100] or Quick File[254] file into the database; these options are covered in detail in their individual entries.)

If you load an existing AppleWorks file, you can simply begin working with it: The categories are already created. If you create a file from scratch, you must decide how many categories of information you want and then name them before you can enter any data. Because you can only create category names on the Change Name/Category screen,[27] AppleWorks starts you out there, as in this example:

```
  ┌─────────────────────────────────────────────────────────────────────┐
  │  File: Customers          CHANGE NAME/CATEGORY     Escape: Review/Add/Change
  │
  │
  │  Category names
  │  ═══════════════════════════════════════════════════════════════════════
  │  Category 1
  │                                      │ Options:
  │                                      │
  │                                      │ Change category name
  │                                      │ Up arrow    Go to filename
  │                                      │ Down arrow  Go to next category
  │                                      │ ⌂-I         Insert new category
  │                                      │
  │                                      │
  │                                      │
  │  ──────────────────────────────────────────────────────────────────
  │  Type entry or use ⌂ commands                          53K Avail.
  └─────────────────────────────────────────────────────────────────────┘
```

New database files must first have their data categories defined on the Change Name/Category screen.

This is the screen where you add, change, or delete category names. You can return to the Name Change/Category screen simply by pressing the Name Change command (⌂-N) from the Review/Add/Change screen.

As you can see from the preceding screen display, when you create a new database file from scratch, the screen is first presented with the name *Category 1* entered in the first category. This name is for reference only: You can change *Category 1* to the first of your category names. To change it, press ⌂-Y to delete the current name, and then type the name you want (category names can be up to 20 characters long). When you press **RETURN**, the cursor moves down to the next line, ready for you to type your next category name. You can have up to 30 category names in a database file.

After you finish entering your category names, you press **ESC** to actually begin entering data. A message appears telling you there are no records in the file yet, and that you will be automatically placed into the Insert New Records feature. Pressing **SPACE** brings up the Insert New Records screen, where you begin entering data, as shown in the following example.

```
 File: Customers              INSERT NEW RECORDS      Escape: Review/Add/Change


 Record 1 of 1
 ================================================================================
 Name: -
 Phone: -
 Street: -
 City: -
 ST/Zip: -
 Salesperson: -
 Start Date: -
 Last Date: -




 -----------------------------------------------------------------------------
 Type entry or use ⌧ commands                                        53K Avail.
```

After you've defined data categories in the Change Name/Category screen, press **ESC**
and then **SPACE** *to display the Insert New Records screen to begin entering data.*

The cursor appears in the first category, and to enter data, you simply begin typing. When you press **RETURN** at the end of each entry, the cursor automatically moves down to the next category. You can move the cursor
within a category by using the — or → keys, or from one category to the
next by using the | or | keys, or by pressing **TAB** or ⌕-**TAB**. Entries can be no
longer than 76 characters; however, the category name itself takes up its
share of the allotted space (up to 20 characters). In the last screen display, for
example, an entry in the category *Salesperson* can't be as long as an entry in
the category *Name*, because *Salesperson* is seven characters longer than *Name*.

When you enter the last category of the current record and then press
RETURN, you'll be in the first category of the next record. The records are
numbered consecutively from 1 as you create them. After you create more
than one record, you can scroll through them using ⌕ with the | and | keys,
or with the Ruler.[280]

When you finish entering information into the records, press the **ESC**
key. The screen then changes to the Review/Add/Change screen, which displays the records using one of the two AppleWorks viewing options: Single
Record layout[293] (if you only entered one record) or Multiple Record layout[168]
(if you entered more than one).

The Single Record layout lets you view and enter data into one record at a
time. However, there will often be times when you will want to view and

work with several records at once. To do this, you use the Zoom[376] command
(⌘-Z) to display the other viewing option, which is the Multiple Record
layout[168]screen, as in this example:

```
File: Customers              REVIEW/ADD/CHANGE           Escape: Main Menu
Selection: All records

Name           Phone       Street         City         ST/Zip
================================================================================
Aldo Pastarelli 555-1111    1439 Commerce  Milpitas     CA 94002
Alex Abidikian  555-0505    687 Bullis Lane Fremont     CA 95003
Arnold Ormsby   555-4567    6690 Livingston San Jose    CA 95555
Barney Flint    555-7608    878 14th St.   San Jose     CA 95550
Boris Boronzhov 555-8787    1450 Carson Ave Milpitas    CA 95558
Ed Frobish      555-1234    335 Ramona Ave. San Jose    CA 95551
Edwina Gumm     555-7890    3325 State St.  Sunnyvale   CA 94008
Fortuna Maldona 555-2222    1839 Water St.  San Jose    CA 95555
Fred Fong       555-8765    3867 Fortney St Sunnyvale   CA 95004
James Penningto 555-4443    3897 107th Ave. San Jose    CA 95553
Mort Drucker    555-2345    123 State St.   Sunnyvale   CA 94000
Olive Ogilvy    555-6666    112 Sumter St.  Santa Clara CA 95550
Walter Canary   555-8606    3359 W. Hudson  Milpitas    CA 95554
Wilson K. Jeeve 555-3334    907 Broad St.   Santa Clara CA 95556
Wilson Peck     555-3232    8904 Fremont St San Jose    CA 95554
--------------------------------------------------------------------------------
Type entry or use ⌘ commands                              ⌘-? for Help
```

The Multiple Record layout arranges categories horizontally, and each record is in one row.

As you can see, the categories in the Multiple Record layout are placed horizontally. If your file contains more records than you can see on one Multiple
Record layout screen, you can scroll through the records using the Arrow
keys or the Ruler. If each record contains more *categories* than you can see at
once on the screen, you'll have to move the cursor to the record you want to
view, then use the Zoom command to view that record in the Single Record
layout, where you can see all the categories for that record.

You can edit existing data in the records, or add data to blank categories
in existing records. When you add or change data in a category using the
Multiple Record layout and press **RETURN**, the cursor normally moves down
to the same category in the next record.

You can, however, change the direction the cursor moves to horizontal in
the Multiple Record layout screen. You do this by first displaying the Layout
screen[146] with ⌘-L, and then pressing **ESC**: You're given the option to accept
the default *Down* cursor movement, or change cursor movement to *Right*,
which means that in the Multiple Record layout, the cursor will move to the
next category to the right on the same record, instead of moving to the same
category of the next record.

If you want to add new records to a file displayed in Multiple Record
layout, you must use the Insert[127] command (⌘-I). The first step is to move
the cursor to the location where you want the new record and press ⌘-I.

When you do, you're presented with the Insert New Records screen, which is much like the Single Record layout, with the categories arranged vertically. You simply enter your data, pressing **RETURN** after entering each category. When you complete the last category and press **RETURN**, you remain on the Insert New Records screen and can continue inserting records. When you finish the last record, press **ESC** to return to the Review/Add/Change screen: The new record will be inserted at the cursor position and the following records will be moved down and renumbered. (Actual record numbers are only visible in the Single Record layout.)

One consideration with the Multiple Record layout is that you can only see and enter data into the categories that are visible on the screen. Since the Apple display only shows 80 characters across the screen, it's quite possible that your data file will have more categories than can be displayed horizontally at one time. You have two alternatives. If you have only one or two off-screen data categories to enter, you can use the Layout[146] command (Ò-L) to temporarily rearrange the order of the categories and move the categories you couldn't see to the left; when you've filled them in, you can return to the Layout screen and move them back to their original positions. However, it's probably more efficient in most cases to simply use the Single Record layout screen, which lets you view all the categories for a record. You can switch between Single and Multiple Record layout with the Zoom command (Ò-Z). When you press Ò-Z from the Multiple Record layout screen, the record the cursor is on will be displayed in Single Record layout.

Another consideration of the Multiple Record layout is that you may not be able to see all the data in each category. In the last screen display, for example, some of the customer names in the *Name* category aren't completely visible. You can widen or narrow individual category columns with the Ò-→ or Ò-← key in the Layout (Ò-L) screen.

Changing and deleting data: Once data is entered in categories, it can be changed or deleted. You can use the Clear[34] command (Ò-Y) in both Single and Multiple Record layouts to erase data in a category from the cursor position to the end of the category, or you can use **DELETE** to erase characters to the left of the cursor. If you want to delete entire records, however, you must use the Delete[92] command (Ò-D) on either the Single Record or the Multiple Record layout. When you press Ò-D on the Multiple Record layout, the entire record the cursor is on becomes highlighted, and you have the option of highlighting more than one record to delete. Then, when you press **RETURN**, the selected records are deleted and those following them are moved up and renumbered. When you press ⌃-**D** and then press **RETURN** on the Single Record layout, you are asked if you want to delete the current record, and must answer *Yes* to delete it.

■ **Database format defaults**

Text and numbers appear in the database just as you type them. Unlike the spreadsheet, you cannot set the database so values are automatically formatted with dollar signs, for example. There are no options for changing the formatting of database entries on the Review/Add/Change screens, but you have some flexibility when you create or print a report. The Report Format[79] screen and Printer Options[217] menus contain options for calculating categories, line spacing, justification of entries, margins, and other format settings.

■ **Moving data via the Clipboard**

Database records can be copied and moved within a file, or between database files, using the Clipboard.[35] Only entire records can be copied to the Clipboard, although individual category entries can be copied between adjacent records in the Multiple Record layout. When several records contain much of the same information, the Standard Values[330] command (⌃-**V**) can be used to fill the same information into new records automatically.

Records from the database can also be transferred to word-processor documents. To do this, you must first create a database report using the Report Format screen, and then issue the Print[193] command (⌃-**P**) to print the report to the Clipboard, where it can then be copied into a word-processor document. Database reports can also be printed on paper, onto a disk in DIF or ASCII format, or to the screen. Printing a report to the screen lets you preview the appearance of a report before you print it on paper. (See: Database Printing.[67])

■ **Database file-size limits**

AppleWorks database files can contain up to 30 categories, each of which can contain a maximum of 76 characters. The database maintains all of its records in RAM[256] to make sorting much faster, but this means that a database file can only be as large as the amount of available space on the Desktop[97] will allow. The following table shows the maximum size of an AppleWorks database file, along with the typical sizes of a file on Apple systems with different

RAM configurations and Desktop sizes. The actual number of records you can store in a file will vary, depending on the number of categories in a file, and the length of entries in each category.

Maximum Size	1350 Records
Typical size with a 10K Desktop (64K system)	140 Records
Typical size with a 55K Desktop (128K system)	750 Records

■ Arranging and sorting records

No doubt you will want to impose some sort of order on the records you enter into the database. In a *Customers* file, for example, you would probably want the individual customer records arranged in alphabetic order. However, when you're entering records in the AppleWorks database, you don't have to worry about their order as you enter them, because the Arrange[10] command (⌂-A) allows you to change their order whenever you want. The Arrange command lets you sort the records based on any one of the categories *alphabetically* from A to Z, or in reverse order, from Z to A, or *numerically* from lowest number to highest, or in reverse, from highest to lowest. If you have created categories containing the words *Date* or *Time* in the category name, you can also sort records based on them (see: Date[90]; Time[343]). Categories that include these words in their titles give you two more sorting options—chronological and reverse chronological.

If you define your categories and later decide that you want them in a different order, you can swap their positions using the Layout (⌂-L) screen.

Sometimes you will want to view a subset of records in a file according to specific criteria in certain categories. For example, you might decide to send a special letter to those customers who purchased more than $2000 worth of goods from your company. The Record Selection Rules[259] command (⌂-R) lets you specify criteria such as this using logical operators.

■ Performing calculations in the database

Although you can't do sophisticated mathematics in the database like you can in the spreadsheet, you can use the basic arithmetic operators to perform useful calculations to the values in a database report. These operators are + (add), − (subtract), * (multiply), and / (divide).

These arithmetic operators must be used in conjunction with the Calculated Category[23] command (⌂-K) on the Report Format screen. This command lets you perform arithmetic operations on one or more categories, and place the result in the new category, which is automatically created when you use the command.

Probably the most common arithmetic operation on number categories is adding up an entire category. Because this is such a common operation, AppleWorks provides the Set Totals[286] command (⌂-T). When you enter the Set Totals command, the values in a category are summed, and the total is placed, with an asterisk beside it, at the bottom of the category at the end of a *printed* report.

The only way to view the result of a totaled category or a calculated category without printing a hard copy is to print the report to the screen from the Print the Report menu. (See: Database Printing.)

■ **Database command summary**

Although we've only been able to cover the highlights of working with the database in this entry, complete information about each option and command is contained in their individual entries. The following is a list of the commands and a brief description of their functions:

⌂-A	Arrange or sort a category.[10]
⌂-C	Copy records.[40]
⌂-D	Delete records or a category in a report.[92]
⌂-E	Toggle between overstrike and insert cursor.[105]
⌂-F	Find records by matching their contents with a search string.[109]
⌂-G	Create or remove group totals in a report.[118]
⌂-H	Print the current display on a printer.[122]
⌂-I	Insert a record or a previously deleted report category, or a category "hidden" using the Layout options.[127]
⌂-J	Justify a report category.[142]
⌂-K	Define a calculated category in a report.[18]
⌂-L	Modify the category layout.[146]
⌂-M	Move (cut) records to or from the Clipboard.[163]
⌂-N	Change file, category, or report name.[171]
⌂-O	Show printer options.[217]
⌂-P	Display report menu, or print a report from the Report Format screen.[193]

⌘-Q	Show Desktop Index.[252]
⌘-R	Set record selection rules.[259]
⌘-S	Save current file to disk.[281]
⌘-T	Create or remove report category totals.[286]
⌘-V	Modify standard values.[330]
⌘-Y	Delete from cursor to end of entry.[34]
⌘-Z	Toggle between Multiple and Single Record layouts.[376]
⌘-1 to ⌘-9	Move through a file proportionally.[280]
⌘-?	Display list of commands (help).
⌘-↑ or ⌘-↓	Scroll one screen up or down in direction of arrow.
⌘-← or ⌘-→	Change category widths in the Layout or Report Format screen.

■ **Where to find more database information**

☐ Database Printing[67]

☐ Reusing Data[276]

Database printing

As explained in the Database Report Format[79] entry, you must create a report format for a database file before you can print it. After you create the format, there are up to six different destinations where you can send the report for printing:

☐ To a printer for a paper copy;

☐ To a disk printer;

☐ To the screen for previewing a report's appearance;

☐ To an ASCII file[13] on disk as unformatted data;

☐ To a DIF file[100] on disk as formatted ASCII data;

☐ To the Clipboard,[35] for moving into a word-processssor document.

We will investigate each of these options in the following sections. But first, let's look at the general procedures for printing all database files.

■ General printing procedures

When you print a database file, you must always follow the same basic sequence of steps:

1. Make sure the document you want to print is displayed on the Review/Add/Change screen.

2. Press the Print[193] command (⌂-P) to display the Report Menu,[273] as in the following example, and then choose an option to either make a new report format or work with an existing format.

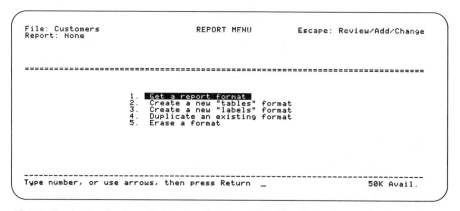

```
File: Customers                    REPORT MENU            Escape: Review/Add/Change
Report: None


================================================================================

                      1.  Get a report format
                      2.  Create a new "tables" format
                      3.  Create a new "labels" format
                      4.  Duplicate an existing format
                      5.  Erase a format




----------------------------------------------------------------------------------
Type number, or use arrows, then press Return  _                    50K Avail.
```

All printing in the database begins by choosing an existing report format or creating a new one with the Report Menu.

3. When the Report Format screen is displayed, format the report the way you want it by inserting or deleting categories, widening or narrowing report columns, reorganizing the order in which categories appear, or creating Calculated Categories.[18] (See: Database Report Formats.[79])

4. Press the Options[217] command (⌂-O) to display the Printer Options menu, and then optionally change any printer options you want for that file. Return to the Report Format screen when you are finished by pressing **ESC**. Changing any printer options affects only that report.

5. Press the Print command (⌂-P) again, and select the print destination from the Print the Report menu. Although this menu can vary, depending on the printer configurations you've set, it will probably look similar to the one that follows.

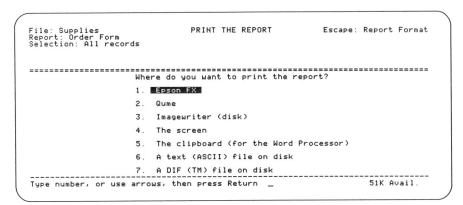

```
File: Supplies              PRINT THE REPORT        Escape: Report Format
Report: Order Form
Selection: All records


=========================================================================
                    Where do you want to print the report?
                    1.  Epson FX
                    2.  Qume
                    3.  Imagewriter (disk)
                    4.  The screen
                    5.  The clipboard (for the Word Processor)
                    6.  A text (ASCII) file on disk
                    7.  A DIF (TM) file on disk
-------------------------------------------------------------------------
Type number, or use arrows, then press Return  _            51K Avail.
```

The Print the Report menu allows you to choose the destination for your database print file.

The preceding steps are always the same, no matter which print destination you choose for the file. The steps you take from here on will vary according to the print destination you select.

■ **Printing on printers**

When you print to a printer, you must be sure that AppleWorks has been configured for that printer, that the printer is properly connected and turned on, and that the printer can handle any printer options you may have specified for the report. Once you complete steps 1 through 5 above, the basic procedure goes like this:

1. Choose one of the printers listed on the Print the Report menu as the destination for your file. The selection of printers available will depend on the printers for which you previously configured AppleWorks. You can store up to three printer configurations at a time. (See: Printer Configuration.[200])

2. After you choose the printer on which you want the file printed, you can optionally enter a date to be printed at the top of the database report. If you don't want a date printed, press **RETURN**. In either case, the date won't be printed if you have the PH (print report header at top of page) printer option set to *No*. (See: Printer Options.[217])

3. When you press **RETURN**, the prompt line asks how many copies you want printed. You either press **RETURN** to print one copy, or type the number you want (up to 9) and press **RETURN**. After this, the report will be printed.

If your printer doesn't begin printing the file, check to make sure it is turned on, and that the printer cable isn't loose. Most printers also have an "on line," or "ready," or "selected" indicator that shows whether the printer is ready to print. Make sure this indicator shows the printer is ready (there may be a "select" or "on line" button you push to light the indicator), and that there is paper in the printer. If your problem persists after this, call your Apple dealer and ask for further advice.

Checking the report line length: Beyond actual printer problems, there are characteristics of database reports that must be checked before they can be printed the way you want them. The first of these characteristics to check is the line length of a report.

The default printer options in the database allow for 80 characters on a printed line. When you print a database report, the amount of data that is actually printed on a printer is limited by the current printer options. The right and left margins, the platen width, and the Characters-per-Inch (CI) setting all combine to determine the number of characters that can be printed on each line of a report. The Characters-per-Line indicator found on the Printer Options menu shows how wide each printed report line can be, as shown in this example:

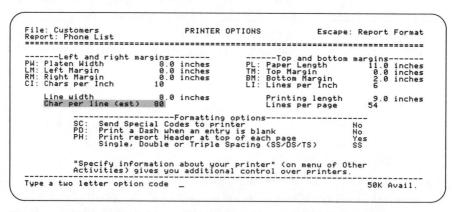

Database reports can only be as wide as the printer options allow, as shown by the Characters-per-Line indicator on the Printer Options menu.

If your report is wider than the Characters-per-Line setting allows, some of the data in the report won't be printed. With a Labels report,[79] you probably won't have a problem with the width of the data because the report is arranged vertically, and each category can be on its own line. The only way to make sure the printer options are set so that all the data in a Labels report will be printed is by printing the report on paper—changing the printer options has no effect on the appearance of a labels report printed to the screen. In a Tables report, you can tell how wide your database reports are by scrolling to the right edge of the Report Format screen. The *Len* indicator there shows how wide the report currently is, in characters (see: Database Report Format[379]). Before printing a report, check the *Len* indicator to make sure the width of the report is less than or equal to the Characters-per-Line reading on the Printer Options menu.

If the *Len* indicator shows that a Tables report is 88 characters wide, for example, and the Characters-per-Line indicator on the Printer Options menu shows 80 characters per line, some of your report will not be printed. To remedy this, you can either delete or narrow one or more of the categories in the report, or change the PW (Platen Width), CI (Characters-per-Inch), or LM or RM (Left and Right Margins) on the Printer Options menu to allow for more characters on a line.

Checking the category width: Along with the overall report width, you must also make sure individual categories in a report are wide enough to accommodate all the data entries in them. In a Labels report, for example, you might place two categories on the same line, such as *City* and *ST/Zip*. Unless you justify the right category so its starting position adjusts to the length of the entries in the category at the left, some entries may be too long to fit in the space you have allowed, as shown in this sample report:

```
File:    Customers
Report: Labels


Olive Ogilvy
Ace Jackhammer Service
112 Sumter St.
Santa CCA 95550


Wilson Peck
Apex Canning
8904 Fremont St.
San JosCA 95554


Wilson K. Jeeves
Butlerware, Inc.
907 Broad St.
Santa C95556
```

You can overcome this problem by left justifying the categories that are to the *right* of the first category when there is more than one category on a line in a Labels report (see: Justify[142]). If you want to preview the appearance of the data in categories in a Labels report, you can print the report to the screen (discussed below), but you should remember that screen-printed Labels reports are not affected by changes to the number of characters per line in the printer options.

In a Tables report, you must make sure every category is wide enough to accommodate all the data entries in it. Since the Tables Report Format screen only shows the first three records in a file, you must print the report to the screen to see if there are any entries not visible on the Report Format screen that may be too wide for the width of their categories.

Once you have determined that your categories are wide enough for all the data that will appear in them, and that your printer options are set to accommodate the overall width of your reports, you should have no problem printing from the database.

Troubleshooting printer problems: If your printer is printing your database report but it isn't printing it the way you expected, there are two likely causes: the *printer options* and the *printer configuration settings.*

The first thing to do is check the printer options. If a file is printing with single spacing and you want double spacing, for example, check the Printer Options menu to make sure the double-space option is specified. (The default for a Labels report is single spacing, so if you haven't specified the double-space option, you won't get double-spaced printing.)

If you are sure you have set all the printer options correctly, then you should check your printer-configuration settings. These settings are covered in detail in Printer Configuration,[200] but it's important to remember that many of the printer options you specify won't take effect if your printer configuration isn't properly set. For example, if you change the size of a file's printed characters from 10 CI (Characters-per-Inch) to 12 CI by using the Printer Options menu, this change won't actually be printed if you haven't configured your printer using the Change A Printer[29] menu to print at 12 CI on your custom printer. If you're using a printer specifically listed on the Add a Printer menu, most of the settings are made for you, but if you're using a custom printer, you'll have to enter the settings yourself (see: Printer Configuration[200]). So if you aren't getting the right printing effects on paper and you're sure your printer options are set correctly, check the printer configuration for that printer to see if you have configured Apple-Works to make your printer perform those options. You can check a configuration setting by choosing *Specify information about your printer(s)* from the Other Activities menu, and then choosing *Change A Printer* by selecting the printer whose settings you want to check.

Another configuration-related problem might be that you haven't configured AppleWorks properly for your printer interface. Check the interface code you have entered (or check to see whether you entered one at all). See the Printer Interface Configuration[214] entry for more about configuring interface cards.

One final thing to check when sorting out printer problems is the printer itself. You can specify certain printer options, and AppleWorks can be configured properly to handle them, but they still won't take effect if your printer can't handle them. It won't do you any good to enter a configuration for 24 CI printing, for example, if your printer physically can't print smaller than 16 CI. Check your printer manual before configuring AppleWorks to work with the printer, and make sure the configurations you enter are supported by your printer.

■ **Printing to a disk printer**
When you want to store a database file on disk with all the formatting it would have if printed on paper, you must print it to a printer configured as a *disk printer.* It's useful to print a file to a disk printer when you want to send it to someone via modem, because the file is printed to the disk as a formatted ASCII file. It's also useful if you plan to give the file on disk to someone else who will print it out later, because the file is printed with the specific formatting enhancements you specified. Someone using a word-processing program can then load it into their program and print it out exactly the way you intended—with margins and justified categories already in place.

A disk printer is set up just like an ordinary printer—by configuring it from the Printer Information menu.[212] The only difference is the way this "printer" is connected to your Apple. To configure a disk printer:

1. Choose option 2, *Add a printer*, from the Printer Information menu.

2. Choose a printer that matches the printer on which the file will ultimately be printed.

3. Give the printer a descriptive name.

4. After you name the printer, you are prompted to choose how the printer is accessed. Instead of choosing a slot number, choose the option *Print onto disk or on another Apple*. When you do this, any file printed to this printer will be printed as a formatted ASCII file on the disk in the current disk drive.

Once you have set up the printer this way, it appears on the Print Menu along with any other printers you may have configured (you can have a total of three printers). To help you remember that this is a disk printer, Apple-Works puts the word *disk* in parentheses after the disk-printer name when you are choosing which printer to print a file on.

To print your file to the disk, choose the disk-printer destination and the file is printed there. All the margins, line spacing, and other options you specified will be retained in the format of the file on disk. Also, as with printing to any other printer, reports wider than the printer options allow for will be truncated.

■ **Printing to the screen**

You can print a database report to the screen to preview the appearance of the report before you print it on paper, as explained before. This is a good way to make sure that your report format is set so your data prints properly.

With a Labels report, it usually isn't necessary to print the report to the screen, because you can see how the report will print by looking at the Report Format screen. You normally don't have more than two or three data categories on the same line in a Labels report, and the entries in each category are usually short enough so that all of them can fit on an 80-character line (the line-width default) with no problem.

If your data entries on a line in a Labels report are unusually long, however, you can print the report to the screen to see if they fit within the 80-character limit. You can also screen-print the report to make sure there's room for every data entry when you have multiple categories on one line of the report.

To print a Labels report to the screen, display the Report Format screen, press the Print command (⌕-P), and choose *The screen* as the print destination. The prompt line will ask if you want a date to appear in the report header. When you enter a date and press **RETURN**, or just press **RETURN** to bypass it, the report appears on the screen. (When you print a report to the screen, you only see a few records at a time; you must press **SPACE** to display additional portions of the report.)

The screen will show up to 80 characters on a line. Thus, if some data in your report is cut off at the right side when it is printed to the screen, you know that your printer options must be set up to accommodate more than 80 characters. Unfortunately, the screen won't show more than 80 characters on a line and will cut off entries even if the printer options are set for lines wider than 80 characters, so you'll have to guess at the correct line length necessary when you print a Labels report.

You can also print a Tables report to the screen. Normally, you do this because you can only see three of the file's records on the Report Format screen, but if you print to the screen you can preview all the records and categories (except the categories that don't begin within the first 80 columns of the report). You have to move the categories that begin after the 80th character to the left so they begin before the 80th character in order to view the contents of those categories when printed to the screen.

Suppose you have a report with the categories in this example:

```
File: Customers              REPORT FORMAT              Escape: Report Menu
Report: Phone List
Selection: All records


===========================================================================
--> or <--    Move cursor                 ⌕-J  Right justify this category
  >    <      Switch category positions   ⌕-K  Define a calculated category
--> or <--    Change column width         ⌕-N  Change report name and/or title
⌕-A  Arrange (sort) on this category      ⌕-O  Printer options
⌕-D  Delete this category                 ⌕-P  Print the report
⌕-G  Add/remove group totals              ⌕-R  Change record selection rules
⌕-I  Insert a prev. deleted category      ⌕-T  Add/remove category totals
---------------------------------------------------------------------------

Name            Company              Phone         Salesperson  YTD Sales   L
-A------------- -B------------------- -C----------- -D---------- -E--------- e
Aldo Pastarelli Pesto's Pasta        555-1111      Brohammer    526.30      n
Alex Abidikian  Imperial Dry Cleaning 555-0505     Smith        16,098.00   7
Arnold Ormsby   Flecko Paints        555-4567      Jones        4129.57     6
---------------------------------------------------------------------------
Use options shown above to change report format               50K Avail.
```

On the Report Format screen of a Tables report, you can preview the category contents for only the first three records.

You want to preview the category contents for all the records, to make sure the categories are wide enough to accommodate every data entry. To do this, you press the Print command (⌂-**P**), choose *The screen* as the print destination, and then print the report.

```
File:    Customers                                              Page  1
Report: Phone List
Name             Company              Phone        Salesperson  YTD Sales
-------------    --------------------  ------------  -----------  ----------
Aldo Pastarelli  Pesto's Pasta        555-1111     Brohammer    526.30
Alex Abidikian   Imperial Dry Cleaning 555-0505    Smith        16,098.00
Arnold Ormsby    Flecko Paints        555-4567     Jones        4129.57
Barney Flint     Howard's U-Rent 'Em  555-7608     Brohammer    1426.45
Boris Boronzhov  Jetson Steel         555-8787     Jones        21,247.50
Ed Frobish       Frobish Linen Service 555-1234    Smith        3540.00
Edwina Gumm      Fritzi Fashions      555-7890     Smith        125.00
Fortuna Maldona  Furniture City       555-2222     Brohammer    518.99
Fred Fong        Fong Machine Tools   555-8765     Jones        1859.90
James Penningto  Linda's Typewriter Re 555-4443    Brohammer    85.95
Mort Drucker     Drucker Drayage      555-2345     Smith        3318.00
Olive Ogilvy     Ace Jackhammer Servic 555-6666    Brohammer    1024.50
Walter Canary    Flippo Dog Food      555-8606     Jones        323.06
Wilson K. Jeeve  Butlerware, Inc.     555-3334     Smith        1500.67
Wilson Peck      Apex Canning         555-3232     Smith        10,567.00



Press Space Bar to continue  _                                50K Avail.
```

Printing Tables reports to the screen shows you whether all the categories are wide enough to accommodate their data.

Notice that the screen-printed report shows us that some of the data entries in certain categories have been cut off because the categories aren't wide enough. Knowing this, you can then return to the Report Format screen and widen these categories so all their data will print completely when you print the report on paper. When you print a report to the screen, you can also see actual numbers displayed in Calculated Categories and a total at the bottom of a category containing numbers formatted with the Category Totals option.

■ Printing to an ASCII file

The third possible print destination for a database file is to disk as an ASCII file. Unlike printing to a disk printer, the ASCII file created in this case is unformatted. An ASCII file normally contains ordinary characters without any formatting (see: ASCII[13]), and when you print the file to disk (rather than to a disk printer), you lose all the formatting the file had in the database report format from which it was printed. This distinction can be confusing, but it helps to think of the disk printer discussed previously as a kind of filter that arranges the ASCII data in the format dictated by the report format from which the file came. If you print to disk without a disk printer, you lose the formatting from the report format.

While it's sometimes useful to print to a disk printer (so someone using a different word-processing program could load one of your formatted database reports from a disk file, for example), it's easier to print straight to an unformatted ASCII file on disk when you don't require that the report's original formatting be maintained. When you're sending a file via modem, for example, you may not need to retain the file's original format, so you would save the file to disk as an unformatted ASCII file. Standard AppleWorks files have a unique format that can't be read properly by other programs, so the ability to produce files in ASCII format makes it easy to share files with many other programs.

You will have to decide when it's appropriate to use unformatted ASCII files as opposed to formatted files made by printing to a disk printer. Remember that unformatted files lose all their row-and-column formatting.

If you wanted to share your report with another database program, for example, you would probably save the file to disk as a DIF file,[100] since this is the format easiest to read by database files (DIF is discussed in the next section). If you wanted to share your report with another word-processing program, printing to a disk printer would be the best method, because the file would retain all its original formatting when you load it into the new word-processor document. If your main goal is to have the data in ASCII format, and you don't care about formatting, then save the file to disk as ASCII.

To save a database file to disk as an ASCII file:

1. Display the report you want to print and press the Print command (⌂-P), just as you do when printing to a printer.

2. Choose *A text (ASCII) file on disk* as the print destination.

3. Type the complete ProDOS pathname[188] under which you want the file stored on the disk, and then press **RETURN**. The file will now be stored on disk.

You don't have to worry about whether the printer options can accommodate the width of your data selection when printing to an ASCII file. In this case, AppleWorks ignores the printer-options limits and it prints the whole file in one continuous stream.

- **Printing to a DIF file**

A DIF file is much more suitable than an ASCII file for storing database data you want to share with another spreadsheet or database program, because it maintains the original orientation of the data in a format that can be read by other programs (see: DIF[100]). It won't maintain formatting options (such as margins and justification) like a disk printer, however. To print to a DIF file, you follow most of the same steps you do when printing to an ASCII file.

When printing to a DIF file, you press the Print command (Ó-**P**). Then:

1. Choose *A DIF (TM) file on disk* as the print destination.

2. Type the complete ProDOS pathname[188] under which you want the file stored, and then press **RETURN**. The file will be printed to disk.

- **Printing to the Clipboard**

The final print destination to which you can send database files is the Clipboard. Printing files to the Clipboard is different from copying data to the Clipboard: When you copy or move database data to the Clipboard, you can only use that data in database files, but when you *print* data to the Clipboard, the data is converted into a format that can be used in word-processor files. Thus, you must print database data to the Clipboard when you want to move the data into an AppleWorks word-processor document.

Printing to the Clipboard is much like printing to a printer. You choose Ó-**P** from the Report Format screen, then choose *The clipboard* as the destination. Just as with printing to a printer, you must be sure that the data you select is narrow enough to fit within the width limits set by the printer options. If your data is too wide, then only the part of the data that fits within the printer-options limits will be printed to the Clipboard. Also, you must make sure the categories in your report are wide enough to accommodate all the entries in the file; if they aren't, some of the data will be cut off.

Just as with printing to a printer, you have the option to print a report date in the header at the top of the file when you print to the Clipboard. Once you print your data to the Clipboard, AppleWorks displays the following notice telling you that the data is on the Clipboard.

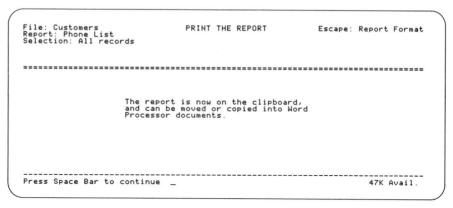

```
File: Customers                   PRINT THE REPORT              Escape: Report Format
Report: Phone List
Selection: All records


================================================================================



                         The report is now on the clipboard,
                         and can be moved or copied into Word
                         Processor documents.




------------------------------------------------------------------------------------
Press Space Bar to continue  _                                        47K Avail.
```

When you print database data to the Clipboard, AppleWorks tells you when the operation is complete.

Once your data is printed to the Clipboard, you must press **SPACE** or **ESC** to return to the database's Report Format screen.

■ **For more information**

For more information about printing database reports, see Database Report Formats.[79]

Database report formats

AppleWorks allows you to print database files in one of two *report formats*: as *Tables* or as *Labels*. Before you can actually print a new database file—either to the screen, to a printer, or to disk as an ASCII[13] or DIF[100] file—you must create one of these formats for the file from which you are printing. You do this via the Report Menu.[273] Each database file has its own report formats—you can't create a report format and use it with more than one file.

Each of the report formats has its own Report Format screen, as we'll see in the following sections. When you configure the report's format with the Report Format screen, you can choose to include only specific data *categories* or specific *records* in a report, and also adjust the report's final printed appearance. In Tables reports, you can also perform basic arithmetic calculations on categories containing numbers.

■ Tables report format

Database reports with the *Tables* format present data categories in columns, and individual data records in rows, just like the Multiple Record layout. These reports are most useful when you want to view a lot of records on one printed page, and you don't need to see every data category in a report.

To use the Tables Report Format screen to create a new report:

1. Press the Print[193] command (⌘-P) while a database file is displayed on the Review/Add/Change screen. The Report Menu[273] will appear.

2. Choose option 2, *Create a new "tables" format*, from the Report Menu.

3. Type a name for the new report, which can be up to 19 characters and can be the same as the file's name, and press **RETURN**. The Report Format screen for a Tables report format will appear, as in this example:

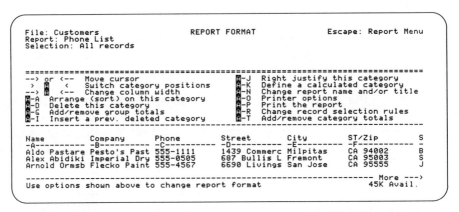

The Tables Report Format screen is used to create, view, and modify Tables-style database reports.

Once you have named a new report the report is attached to that datafile, and you can use it anytime thereafter. To do this, you choose option 1, *Get a report format*, from the Report Menu. You're then presented with a list of named report formats you've created, and you can choose the one you want.

All reports have a default format when you create them: They include all categories and records in the file. As you can see in the example, all the options available for modifying a report format are displayed at the top of the screen. In the screen's lower half, the first three records are displayed with as many categories as will fit across the screen.

The report will print on paper exactly as it is shown on the screen, except that all the categories in the report will print, not just those shown on the screen (see Database Printing[67] for more information). In the preceding example, the arrow at the lower-right corner of the screen indicates that there are more categories in the report off screen to the right. To see off-screen categories, use → to scroll sideways. The off-screen categories will begin to appear when you scroll past the last category on the screen.

The right edge of the report is indicated by the *Len* indicator,[154] which is displayed vertically along the right side of the last category in the file, as in the following example. The *Len* indicator also shows you how many characters wide the report will be when printed on paper.

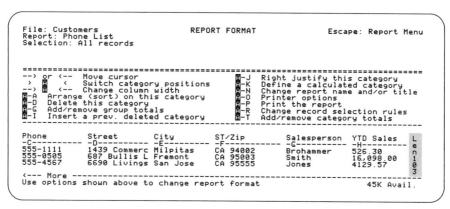

The Len indicator at the right of the report shows you how many characters wide the printed report will be.

Adjusting the width of categories: You can adjust the overall width of a Tables report by making individual categories wider or narrower, or by deleting or inserting previously deleted categories from the report.

1. Move the cursor to the category you want to widen or narrow.

2. Press ⌂-← to narrow the category width, or ⌂-→ to widen it.

Deleting and inserting categories: As mentioned, you can also delete categories from a report if they're not relevant to the specific purpose of that report. You can use the Delete[92] command to delete as many categories as you want, as long as the report retains at least one category. When you delete a category, you simply delete it from the report—the category still exists in the file, and will still be visible on the Review/Add/Change display. If you change your mind and want to replace a category you have deleted, you can use the Insert[127] command.

To delete a category:

1. Move the cursor to the category you want to delete.

2. Press the Delete command (⌘-D).

To insert a category:

1. Move the cursor to the category that you want to appear to the right of the inserted category.

2. Press the Insert command (⌘-I).

3. The Insert A Category screen appears, listing previously deleted categories. Select the category you want to insert by moving the highlight bar with the Arrow keys, or typing the number of the category, and pressing **RETURN**.

4. You will be returned to the Report Format screen, the category will be inserted at the cursor position, and the category the cursor was on and all categories to the right of it will be moved over.

Changing the order of categories: Sometimes you will want to alter the position of categories in a report. To change the order of categories:

1. Move the cursor to the category whose position you want to change.

2. Press ⌘-< to move the category to the left, or ⌘-> to move it right. (You don't have to press the Shift key when pressing < or >.)

Arranging data in categories: You can arrange the records in a file so they appear in a certain order. To do this, you use the Arrange[10] command (⌘-A). You can only arrange data in a file based on the contents of one category at a time. If a file contains names, addresses, and phone numbers, for example, you could use the Arrange command on the *Name* category to place the records in alphabetic order by name. By arranging a zip-code category, you can place the records in ascending order by zip code.

To arrange records in a file:

1. Place the cursor on the category on which you want the arrangement of records to be based.

2. Press the Arrange command (⌂-**A**).

3. The following Arrange screen will appear, and you can then choose the method by which you want the records arranged, after which you will automatically be returned to the Report Format screen.

```
File: Club Members              ARRANGE (SORT)           Escape: Report Format
Report: Birthdays
Selection: All records


=============================================================================
                      This file will be arranged on
                      this category: Birthdate

                      Arrangement order:
                           1.   From A to Z
                           2.   From Z to A
                           3.   From 0 to 9
                           4.   From 9 to 0
                           5.   Chronological
                           6.   Reversed chronological


-----------------------------------------------------------------------------
Type number, or use arrows, then press Return  _              43K Avail.
```

The Arrange (Sort) screen lists options for arranging the records in a file based on one category.

The options for arranging records chronologically that are shown in the preceding screen are only presented when you are arranging records with the cursor placed on a category whose name contains the word *date* or *time*. AppleWorks automatically knows that these categories will contain dates or times, and gives you extra sorting options for them (options 5 and 6).

You can only sort a file on one category of data at a time, but sometimes you want to sort a file on more than one category. In a customer list, for example, you might want to sort the records by zip code, and then alphabetically within each zip code. To do this with AppleWorks, you can simply arrange the file twice: Arrange the records by the secondary criterion first (in this case, alphabetically), and then arrange the file by the primary criterion (zip code, in this case).

Selecting records: Sometimes you don't want a database report to contain all the records in a file. To print only some of the records from a file, you can use the database's Record Selection Rules[259] command (⌘-**R**). The record-selection rules allow you to include certain records in a report based on the contents of those records' categories.

If you had a customer list with a *Date* category, for example, you might want to print only records where the date is after August 1, 1985. The record-selection rules in the database let you select records based on up to three different criteria. A selection might include records where the date is after August 1, 1985, the date is before December 1, 1985, and the customer name begins with A, for example.

To use the record-selection rules in the Report Format screen:

1. Make sure the report format you want to work with is displayed.

2. Press the Record Selection Rules command (⌘-**R**). If you have already selected certain records using the record-selection rules, the prompt line will ask you *Select all records? No Yes.* If you choose *Yes*, any rules will be removed, and you must press the Record Selection Rules command again. If you choose *No*, previous record-selection rules will be erased, and the following will occur:

3. A list of the categories included in the current report will appear. Choose the first category on which you want the record selection to be based.

4. A list of record-selection options will appear. Choose the option you want, and then type the comparison information.

5. Choose a second category to narrow your record selection, if you like, and then choose a second selection option and enter comparison information. (If you want to end the selection rules, press **ESC**.)

6. Choose a third category and selection option, and enter comparison information, if you like, or press **ESC** to end the selection.

7. Once you press **ESC** to end the record-selection process, only the records matching the criteria you have specified will be included in the report.

For further information about the record-selection rules, see Record Selection Rules.

Calculating data in Tables reports: The Tables report format allows you to perform some limited calculations on data. You can total numeric entries in a category with the Set Totals[286] command, which causes the total to appear at the bottom of the column *when the report is printed*. You can also create Calculated Categories, in which one or more categories are calculated, and the result is placed in a new category which is created when you use the Calculate[18] command (⌘-K). None of these calculated results appears on screen, however, unless the report is printed to the screen or on paper.

Creating Category Totals: To total the numbers in one category:

1. Place the cursor on the category you want to total.
2. Press the Category Totals command (⌘-T).
3. The prompt line will ask you to specify the number of decimal places to be used in the total. You can specify up to four decimal places.
4. The prompt line will then ask how many blank spaces you want after (to the right of) the category. The number of blank spaces you can specify depends on the original width of the category itself (see: Set Totals[286]).

Category Totals can be removed from a report by issuing the Category Totals command again when the cursor is placed on the totaled category.

Calculating Group Totals: When you create Category Totals, you can tell the database to sum all of the values contained in the category and place the total at the bottom of the column in the printed report. Sometimes, however, you want subtotals of values in a column.

Suppose, for example, that you have an inventory valuation report for a stock that contains *Widgets*, *Valves*, and *Pipes*. Your Category Totals command can total all the items in your inventory, but it won't produce subtotals of widgets, valves, and pipes. You can use the Group Totals[118] command (⌘-G) to make these subtotals.

The Group Totals command creates subtotals in a column of numbers, but the groups themselves are controlled by another column of data in the report. In our example of *Widgets, Valves,* and *Pipes,* you'd use the category *Item Name* to sort records into the proper groups for totaling. Here's how:

1. Place the cursor on the category where the types of items (*Widgets, Valves,* and *Pipes*) are located (in our example, *Item Name*).

2. Use the Arrange command (⌘-**A**) to arrange the file's records alphabetically on the Item Name category. This will group all the like items together in the report (records will be sorted so that all *Pipes* records will be placed above all *Valves* records, and all *Valves* records will be placed above all *Widgets* records).

3. With the cursor still on the item category, press the Group Totals command (⌘-**G**). You will be prompted to choose whether you want only group totals printed, or whether you want group totals as well as the rest of the information in the report. In this case, you want only the group totals of items and not the bulk of the report, so you choose *Yes* in answer to the prompt, *Group Totals Only?* (If you had chosen *No* to the prompt, you would have been asked whether you wanted each set of group totals to be placed on a different page—the printer would start a new page for each group—since the bulk of the report would have been included with the group totals.)

4. After you make this selection, the report will produce group totals of the numbers of items by item type, and will then produce a grand total of the number of items at the bottom of the column containing the number of items.

    For complete information about group totals, see Group Totals.[118]

Creating Calculated Categories: The detailed procedures for creating Calculated Categories are explained in the Calculate entry. But the general steps you take are:

1. Place the cursor where you want the new category to appear.

2. Press the Calculate command (⌘-**K**).

    A new category called *Calculated* will appear at the cursor position, moving all categories to the right of the cursor, including the one the cursor was on, to the right. Type a new name for the category, or press **RETURN** to accept the default name *Calculated.*

3. Type the calculation rules (formula) that will produce the numbers you want in the new category.

4. Type the number of decimal places you want to be used in the calculated numbers when they are printed.

5. Type the number of blank spaces you want inserted to the right of the category.

Calculated Categories can be removed from a report with the Delete command (⌃-**D**).

■ Labels report format

Database reports with the *Labels* format present data categories vertically, stacked on top of each other, just like the Single Record layout. This type of report is most useful when it is more important to see all the data in an individual record than it is to see data grouped in categories, or when you want the data laid out in a particular format for things such as mailing labels.

To use the Labels Report Format screen to create a new report:

1. Press the Print command (⌃-**P**) while a database file is displayed on the Review/Add/Change screen. The Report Menu will appear.

2. Choose option 3, *Create a new "labels" format*, from the Report Menu.

3. Type a name for the new report (up to 19 characters), and press **RETURN**. The Report Format screen for a Labels report format will appear, as in this example:

```
File: Customers                REPORT FORMAT              Escape: Report Menu
Report: Labels
Selection: All records


======================================================================
Name
Company
Phone
Street
City
ST/Zip
Salesperson
YTD Sales
-----------------------Each record will print  8 lines----------------------




--------------------------------------------------------------------
Use options shown on Help Screen                         ⌂-? for Help
```

The Labels Report Format screen is used to create, view, and modify Labels-style database reports.

Once you have named a new report, you can use it anytime thereafter for that file. To do this, you choose option 1, *Get a report format*, from the Report Menu. You're then presented with a list of named report formats you've created, and you can choose the one you want by highlighting it with the Arrow keys, or typing its number, then pressing **RETURN**.

As you can see in the example, Labels database reports show each record with its categories stacked vertically. This layout doesn't lend itself to either Calculated Categories or Category Totals, so these options aren't available in this report format. Also, unlike Tables reports, you don't have to worry about not being able to see all the categories in the report on the screen at once, because Labels reports begin with all of their categories showing.

Repositioning, deleting, and inserting categories: You can change the position of categories on the screen, delete categories, or insert them, as in a Tables report, and you can also justify categories that are on the same line and to the right of another category so that there isn't any blank space left between two categories when both are printed. These options are very useful when you are creating a report to print mailing labels.

Repositioning categories: To change the position of a category:

1. Place the cursor on the first character of the name of the category you want to move.
2. Use ⌂ with the Arrow keys to move the category name up, down, or to the right or left on the screen.

Deleting categories: To delete a category:

1. Place the cursor on the first character of the name of the category you want to delete.
2. Press the Delete command (⌂-**D**).

Inserting deleted categories: Just like a Tables-style report, deleted categories aren't really deleted, they are just hidden from view. You can reinsert previously deleted categories if you change your mind. To do this:

1. Place the cursor where you want the inserted category name to appear.
2. Press the Insert command (⌂-**I**).
3. The Insert A Category screen appears, listing previously deleted categories. Select the category you want to insert by moving the highlight bar with the Arrow keys and pressing **RETURN**.

4. You will be returned to the Report Format screen, and the category you have inserted will be placed at the cursor position.

Inserted categories in Labels reports are often placed over other category names, as in the following example, where *Phone* was placed over *Company*:

```
File: Customers                    REPORT FORMAT              Escape: Report Menu
Report: Labels
Selection: All records


================================================================================
Name
C Phone

Street
City
ST/Zip
Salesperson
YTD Sales
-----------------------Each record will print  8 lines-----------------------




--------------------------------------------------------------------------------
Use options shown on Help Screen                              ❖-? for Help
```

When you insert previously deleted categories on a Labels report, the inserted category is often placed over the name of another category.

To move an inserted category to its own line, or to move it to the right of the category name underneath it:

1. Place the cursor on the first letter in the inserted category's name.
2. Press ♂ with an Arrow key to move the category name.

Inserting blank lines between categories: If you want to insert a blank line between two categories, you can choose *A spacing line above cursor position* or *A spacing line below cursor position* from the Insert A Category screen, instead of choosing a category name. There don't have to be category names listed (previously deleted) for you to use this option.

Justifying categories: In Labels reports, you can place more than one category of information on each line. A common example of this might be the *City*, *State*, and *Zip* categories in a mailing label.

AppleWorks doesn't automatically adjust the amount of space allowed for each category of data in a Labels report—it normally gives each category as much space as it needs when each category prints. When there is more than one category on a line, however, the data in one category can overlap the data in the category to the right. To prevent this from happening, you can use the Justify[142] command so that categories to the right of another category will automatically be placed starting one space after the data in the first category ends.

If a city name is San Francisco, for example, the *State* information will automatically be placed one space after the end of Francisco. If the city in the next record is Davis, the *State* category will begin one space after the Davis entry ends. To justify a category:

1. Place the cursor on the first character of the category name to the right of the first category on the line.

2. Press the Justify command (⌘-J).

3. A less-than sign will appear in front of the justified category to show that it has been justified, and this category will automatically adjust itself to the length of the category to the left of it when the report is printed.

All the formatting and category-manipulating options for Labels reports are listed when you type the Help[123] command (⌘-?) while a Labels report is displayed.

■ **Where to find more information**
You can find further information about the commands used with database reports in the entries for the individual commands and screens: Delete,[92] Insert,[127] Help,[123] Justify,[142] Print,[193] Report Menu,[273] Printer Options,[217] and Change Name/Category screen.[27]

Date

■ **Definition**
A special type of data entered in a database file.

■ **Usage**
Use the word *Date* (or *date*) in a database category name when you want the database to automatically format all your date entries the same way, and you want to be able to sort date entries chronologically.

A database file will store any type of numeric or text information. Normally, the data you enter is formatted just the way you enter it, and the data in any category can be arranged in either alphabetic or numeric order using the Arrange[10] command (⌂-A). If you use the word *Date* in a category name, however, AppleWorks automatically applies a consistent format to date information entered, and lets you then use the Arrange command to sort that information chronologically in addition to alphabetically or numerically.

In the following file, for example, we have used the word *Date* in the category name *Hire Date*. Because of this, the dates we enter are always formatted MMM DD YY, no matter what format we type the date in. We could well have entered Brohammer's hire date as *7-16-84*, or *July 16 84*, and AppleWorks would automatically translate it to the *Jul 16 84* format shown.

```
File: Employees              REVIEW/ADD/CHANGE           Escape: Main Menu
Selection: All records

Name          Phone          Title         Hire Date      Start Time
=========================================================================
Susan Best    555-0707       Salesperson   Oct  9 85       9:00 AM
Audie Brohammer 555-6543     Salesperson   Jul 16 84       9:00 AM
Fred Smith    555-2342       Salesperson   Nov  3 84      10:00 AM
Martin Grunion 555-8099      Clerk         Apr 13 85       8:30 AM




-------------------------------------------------------------------------
Type entry or use ⌂ commands                              ⌂-? for Help
```

If you use the word Date *in a category name, dates you enter are automatically formatted consistently, no matter what format you enter the date in.*

Another advantage to using the word *Date* in a category name is that it makes it possible to arrange that category chronologically. If we press the Arrange command with our cursor located on the *Hire Date* category in the example, the options *Chronological* and *Reversed chronological* will appear on the Arrange (Sort) screen.

■ Comments

You must use the word *Date* in a category name to tell AppleWorks that you are working with date information. If you enter dates in a category whose name doesn't contain the word *Date*, the database will treat the data as ordinary text—it won't be formatted consistently, and you won't be able to sort it chronologically.

Default

- **Definition**

  A *default* is an option setting that is preset in AppleWorks, and one that you may or may not be able to change.

- **Usage**

  There are dozens of AppleWorks program options whose settings you can alter as you use the program, from printer options in the word processor to layout settings in the database to the standard location of a data disk. For every option that lets you change its setting, AppleWorks has a default setting that it automatically uses unless you specify another.

  In many cases, defaults are built into the program, and the default can't be changed. Printer options are a good example: Even though you can set new printer options for an existing file as often as you want, you can't change the default settings that AppleWorks automatically uses for every new file.

  In some cases (such as the standard location of a data disk), you can change the default so that, for example, the standard data-disk location displayed when you start AppleWorks each day is one you have chosen yourself.

  You'll find instructions for changing default options in specific entries dealing with each of the options themselves.

Delete (⌂-D)

- **Definition**

  The *Delete* command removes data from word-processor, spreadsheet, and database files.

- **Usage**

  The Delete command works differently for each application, but in general is used like this:

  1. Move the cursor to the beginning of the data you want to delete.

  2. Press the Delete command (⌂-D).

  3. Use the Arrow keys to highlight the data you want to delete, and then press **RETURN**. The data will be deleted from the file.

     You can also use the **DELETE** key to delete text or data.

Deleting data in the word processor

Suppose you are composing the sales letter shown in the following document. Frobish has been a customer of yours for years, and you decide upon re-reading the letter that you really don't have to urge him on with that final paragraph.

```
File: Sales Letter                REVIEW/ADD/CHANGE                Escape: Main Menu
=====|====|====|====|====|====|====|====|====|====|====|====|====|====|====|===
December 13, 1985

Mr. Ed Frobish
Frobish Linen Service
335 Ramona Ave.
San Jose, CA 95551

Dear Ed:

We think you're a ^super^ customer, and I wanted to tell you how much all
of us at Acme Widgets appreciate your business.  That's why we wanted you
to be the first to know about our new Widget Convertible--the sturdiest,
most flexible, most cost-effective widget around.

I'd like to schedule a time to drop by your office and demonstrate the
advantages of the new Widget Convertible, so I'll be giving you a call
during the next week to make an appointment.

In the meantime, think what the world's first all-purpose widget will mean
to your profits!
-----------------------------------------------------------------------------
Type entry or use ⌂ commands              Line 3  Column  1         ⌂-? for Help
```

With the Delete command, you can delete anywhere from one character to an entire file's worth of text in the word processor.

Here's how to delete the final paragraph in this letter:

1. Place the cursor at the beginning of the paragraph (on the letter *I* in the word *In*).
2. Press the Delete command (⌂-**D**).
3. Use the Arrow keys to extend the selection to the paragraph marker at the end of the paragraph (to the space past the exclamation point), and press **RETURN**.
4. The paragraph will disappear.

Comments: If you are deleting only one line, it may be faster to place the cursor at the beginning of the line and use the Clear[34] command (⌂-**Y**). The Clear command deletes from the cursor position to the end of the current line.

When you use the Delete command, all the carriage returns in the file appear on the screen. When highlighting an area of text to delete, be sure to include those carriage returns you need to eliminate so there won't be too many blank spaces above and below the deleted text.

Deleting data from the spreadsheet

Suppose you are working with this spreadsheet:

```
File: Cost of Sales          REVIEW/ADD/CHANGE          Escape: Main Menu
=======A========B========C========D========E========F========G========H====
   1│Acme Widget Company - Widget Sales Costs, Q4, 1985
   2│-----------------------------------------------------------------------
   3│
   4│Materials                Oct      Nov      Dec      Qtr
   5│------------------       ===      ===      ===      ===
   6│
   7│Widget Oil              1200     1410      960     2370
   8│Steel                   2500     3250     3000     8750
   9│Copper                  1000     1175      800     2975
  10│Magnesium               1250     1100     1250     3600
  11│Grease                   120      150      135      405
  12│Rags                      50       50       50      150
  13│
  14│Labor
  15│------------------
  16│Salaries                3000     3000     3000     9000
  17│Commissions             2250     2250     2250     6750
  18│Hourly Wages            2850     2850     2850     8550
-------------------------------------------------------------------------
A12: ⟨Label⟩ Rags

Type entry or use ⬛ commands  _                        ⬛-? for Help
```

In the spreadsheet, the Delete command eliminates entire rows or columns of data.

You have decided to combine the expenses for grease and rags in one row in the *Materials* section, so you want to delete the *Rags* row. Here's how you would delete the *Rags* row (row 12) from the spreadsheet:

1. Place your cursor in row 12 (it doesn't matter which column the cursor is in).

2. Press the Delete command (⌂-D).

3. The prompt line will ask if you want to delete *Rows* or *Columns*. Choose *Rows*, either by pressing **RETURN**, or by typing the letter *R*.

4. The row where your cursor is located will be highlighted. Since this is the only row you want to delete, press **RETURN**, and the row will be deleted.

Comments: Once an entire row or column is highlighted, you can use the Arrow keys to highlight additional rows or columns. If you want to delete large portions of a file, use the Ruler[280] or ⌂ and ↓ or ↑ for rows, or the → and ← for columns to move the cursor through the file and highlight one screen or several screens of data at a time.

There is a difference between deleting rows or columns and blanking them with the Blank[16] command. When you delete a row, it is removed from the spreadsheet, and all the rows under it move up and are renumbered. When you blank a row, on the other hand, you simply erase the entries and any formatting applied to the cells in the row, and the empty row itself remains in the spreadsheet. The same goes for columns; when you delete a column, all columns to the right of the deleted column move to the left and are re-lettered. If you blank a column, the entries in that column are erased and the empty column remains in place.

Deleting data from the database

In the database, the Delete command performs more than one function. It can be used to delete entire records, or to delete individual category names, which in turn deletes all the information in that category from all the records. It can also be used to "hide" categories, either from a layout you use to view data, or from a report format you will be printing. Your data-handling goal determines how you use the Delete command in the database.

Deleting records: Deleting groups of records allows you to eliminate one or more records from the database without changing the structure or formatting of the file in any way. The steps for deleting groups of records are:

1. Display the Review/Add/Change screen in either Single Record[293] or Multiple Record layout.[168]

2. Position the cursor on the first record you want to delete.

3. Press the Delete command ($\circleddash$-**D**). In the Multiple Record layout, the record your cursor is on will be highlighted, and you will be prompted to use the Arrow keys to highlight additional records to be deleted. Once you select all the records you want to delete, press **RETURN**. In the Single Record layout, the prompt line will ask whether you want to delete the current record. If you choose *Yes* (or simply press **Y**), the record will be deleted and the next record in the file will appear on the screen. You will again be asked if you want to delete the record. You can delete several records this way by simply continuing to answer *Yes* to the prompt as each additional record appears.

Deleting categories from a layout: You can use the Delete command in the Change Record Layout screen only to have the Multiple Record layout "hide" certain categories from view. This method doesn't remove categories of data from the file itself, but just removes them from the display. You can't delete categories to hide them in the Single Record layout.

To delete categories:

1. Make sure your database file is displayed in the Multiple Record layout.
2. Press the Layout[146] command (⌂-L) to produce the Change Record Layout screen.
3. Place the cursor on the category you want to delete from the layout, and press the Delete command (⌂-D). The category will be hidden from the layout.

Comment: You can insert a deleted category by using the Insert[127] command on the Change Record Layout screen.

Deleting categories from a report: No matter what layout is shown on the Review/Add/Change screen, all reports begin with all categories included in them. You can delete (hide) categories from a report on the Report Format screen. To do this:

1. Press the Print command (⌂-P) while either the Single Record or Multiple Record layout of a database file is displayed.
2. Either get an existing report format or create a new report format by choosing the appropriate option from the Report Menu.[273]
3. Once the Report Format screen is displayed, move the cursor to the category you want to remove from the report and press the Delete command (⌂-D). The category will be removed from the report.

Comments: Deleting categories from a report this way doesn't actually remove them from the file, or from either layout in the Review/Add/Change screen. You can replace a previously deleted category in a report by using the Insert command (⌂-I).

Deleting categories from a file: If there are categories of data that you no longer need in a file, you can delete them—and the data they contain—from the file. To do this:

1. Press the Name Change[171] command (⌂-N) from the Review/Add/Change screen of a database file. This will produce the Change Name/Category screen[27].
2. Use ↓ or ↑ to move the cursor to the category you wish to delete, and press the Delete command (⌂-D).

3. The screen will display a message warning you of the consequences of deleting a data category (see Comments below). Press *Y* to answer *Yes* to the question *Do you really want to do this?*

4. The category name and the data in the category will be deleted from the file.

Comments: When a file contains information, permanently deleting a data category affects the structure of the file. When you try to delete a category, AppleWorks warns you that all report formats will be deleted, and all custom options you have specified for Review/Add/Change layouts will be set back to the default options. If you have a lot of custom reports already defined, you may not want to delete a category, since you will then have to re-create the reports. It would be easier to simply delete (hide) the category temporarily from the Review/Add/Change layout and any report formats if you no longer need it.

Desktop

■ **Definition**

The *Desktop* is the portion of your computer's RAM[256] that is used to store files you are working with.

■ **Usage**

The AppleWorks Desktop is simply your computer's memory—the place into which you load files you work with during a session. The Desktop can store various sizes of files, depending on the amount of RAM in your computer, but it can't store more than 12 files total no matter how large or small they may be. Nevertheless, the ability to have more than one file in memory at once is one of AppleWorks' great benefits.

In a 64K Apple system, there is 10K of Desktop space available for files. In a 128K system, there is 55K of Desktop space. Some third-party manufacturers make RAM expansion cards that can increase the AppleWorks Desktop to more than 2000K. No matter how much RAM you have, though, you are limited to 12 files. It's possible, especially in systems with a 10K Desktop, that you will run out of Desktop space once you have more than four or five files in memory. If you run out of Desktop space, a warning message will alert you, and you can then remove one or more files from the Desktop to make more space.

You can always see how many files are on the Desktop at a given time by displaying Desktop Index[98] with the Quick Change[252] command (⌂-Q).

Desktop Index (⌂-Q)

■ **Definition**

The *Desktop Index* is a listing of files currently on the AppleWorks Desktop.[123]

■ **Usage**

The Desktop Index is used to select a Desktop file to work with, or simply to remind you which files are currently on the AppleWorks Desktop.

The Desktop Index is not a complete AppleWorks screen by itself; rather, it is a window that opens in the middle of the screen you are currently working on. The Index can be displayed in either of two ways: By selecting *Work with one of the files on the Desktop* (option 2) from the Main Menu,[158] or by using the Quick Change[252] command (⌂-Q) from any screen in AppleWorks, including the Main Menu.

When you produce the Desktop Index, the files currently on the Desktop will appear in a window in the middle of the screen, as in this example:

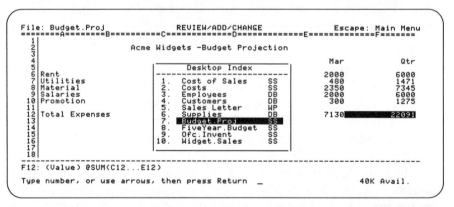

The Desktop Index is a fast way to see which files you currently have on the Desktop, and to change which file you are working with.

When you display the Desktop Index, the highlight bar is always on the file you are currently working with. If there are no files on the Desktop when you display the Desktop Index, the Desktop Index window will still open, but instead of a list of files it will display the message *There are no files on the Desktop.*

Switching files with the Desktop Index: Because you can display the Desktop Index from anywhere in AppleWorks and then select a file to work with from it, the Desktop Index is the fastest way to switch from one file to another. To select one of the Desktop Index files, either move the highlight bar with the ↓ or ↑ key to the filename you want to work with and press **RETURN**, or type the number of the file you want and press **RETURN**.

The file you choose will be displayed on the screen, and the Desktop Index will disappear.

Returning to the current file: If you display the Desktop Index and then decide not to change files, there are two ways to return to the file you were working with. Because that file will be the one that is automatically highlighted when you display the Desktop Index, you can then simply press **RETURN** and the Desktop Index will disappear and you will be back in the file. Your other option is to press **ESC**: You will be returned to the Main Menu, and you can then press **ESC** again to return to the file you were working with before you displayed the Desktop Index.

■ **Example**

Suppose you are working with the *Budget.Proj* worksheet shown in the last example, and you want to switch to working with the *Sales Letter* file:

1. Press ⌂-Q: The Desktop Index will appear.

2. Move the highlight bar until *Sales Letter* is highlighted, and press **RETURN**; or, type the number of the *Sales Letter* file (5), and then press **RETURN**.

3. The Desktop Index will vanish, and the *Sales Letter* file will appear on the screen.

■ **Comment**

The Desktop Index can contain a maximum of 12 files, because this is the maximum number of files you can have on the Desktop at once.

DIF file

■ **Definition**

A *DIF (Data Interchange Format)* file is a special type of ASCII file[13] in which the data is organized in a specific order of rows and columns.

■ **Usage**

DIF files were originally created by VisiCalc.[357] VisiCalc was the first spreadsheet program, and the DIF format became popular with many other programs as well, including database programs, graphics programs, and other spreadsheets because they enabled users to exchange data files. The AppleWorks database and spreadsheet can both use DIF files as sources for new files, and they can print their own data in the DIF format so other programs can use it as well.

Unlike standard ASCII files, which store data as a continuous stream, DIF files preserve the row and column orientation of the data in spreadsheets and database files. If you print a database file to disk as a DIF file, all the data in categories (columns) will be stored on disk in those columns, and all the data in rows (records) will be stored in rows. This means that if you print a database file to disk as a DIF file, then use that DIF file as the source for a new spreadsheet with AppleWorks or other DIF-compatible programs, the data will transfer automatically into neat rows and columns, just as it was arranged in the database.

In some cases, you have to tell AppleWorks (or other programs that create or use DIF files) how to store or load their data. The DIF format keeps track of groups of data in rows and columns, but sometimes you have to tell a program which data is stored in row form, and which data is stored in column form.

When you print a DIF file to disk from the AppleWorks spreadsheet, for example, you are asked whether the data is to be ordered in rows or columns. How you answer depends on how the program that will be using the DIF file expects the data to be ordered. The AppleWorks database, for example, expects DIF data to be stored in column order. If you specify the wrong storage order, data that should have been stored in columns (as in the first spreadsheet on the next page) will end up in the new file in rows (as in the second spreadsheet on the next page). As you can see in the second spreadsheet, the data that should be in rows has been placed into columns, and the result is unintelligible.

```
File: Cost of Sales          REVIEW/ADD/CHANGE           Escape: Main Menu
=======A========B========C========D========E========F========G========H====
   1|Acme Widget Company - Widget Sales Costs, Q4, 1985
   2
   3
   4|Materials                    Oct      Nov      Dec      Qtr
   5|------------------           ===      ===      ===      ===
   6
   7|Widget Oil                  1200     1410      960     2370
   8|Steel                       2500     3250     3000     8750
   9|Copper                      1000     1175      800     2975
  10|Magnesium                   1250     1100     1250     3600
  11|Grease                       120      150      135      405
  12|Rags                          50       50       50      150
  13
  14|Labor
  15|------------------
  16|Salaries                    3000     3000     3000     9000
  17|Commissions                 2250     2250     2250     6750
  18|Hourly Wages                2850     2850     2850     8550
-----------------------------------------------------------------------------
A1: (Label) Acme Widg

Type entry or use ⌂ commands  _                         ⌂-? for Help
```

DIF files store data in rows and columns just as in this spreadsheet.

```
File: Costs                  REVIEW/ADD/CHANGE           Escape: Main Menu
=======A========B========C========D========E========F========G========H====
   1|Acme Widg-              Materials-               Widget OiSteel
   2|et Compan-                        -              1
   3|y - Widge-
   4|t Sales C-              Oct      ===                  1200     2500
   5|osts, Q4,-             Nov      ===                  1410     3250
   6| 1985     ------       Dec      ===                   960     3000
   7                        Qtr      ===                  2370     8750
   8
   9                        Jan      ===                 850.5      567
  10                        Feb      ===               893.025   595.35
  11                        Mar      ===             937.67625 625.1175
  12                        6Mos     ====             6251.201 10537.46
  13
  14
  15
  16
  17
  18
-----------------------------------------------------------------------------
A1: (Label) Acme Widg

Type entry or use ⌂ commands  _                         ⌂-? for Help
```

You have to specify the storage order of an AppleWorks spreadsheet file you want to save as a DIF file so it matches the order expected by the program using it. (The AppleWorks database automatically stores DIF files in column order only.) Here, a DIF file stored in row order has been loaded into the AppleWorks spreadsheet, which expects DIF data in column order.

To understand which storage order a program expects DIF files to be in, you will have to consult the program's manual. In AppleWorks, both the spreadsheet and the database expect DIF files to be stored in column order.

▪ Comments

Because they store data according to the ASCII standard, DIF files can be sent to other computers via modem.

For further information about printing DIF files from the spreadsheet or the database, see Spreadsheet Printing[319] and Database Printing.[67]

Displaying a database report

In the AppleWorks spreadsheet and word processor applications, the Review/Add/Change screen shows you almost exactly what a file will look like when printed. In the database, you choose formatting options on the Report Format screen, but you can't see how they will look on paper. If you make a category narrower, for example, you only see the effect of that change on the first three records in the file—the other records don't appear on the Report Format screen. Likewise, when you total a category or create a Calculated Category,[18] you can't see the results of these calculations on the Report Format screen.

You can, however, print a database report to the screen to preview its appearance on paper. To do this:

1. Press the Print[193] command (⌘-P) from the Report Format screen.

2. Choose *The screen* as the print destination.

3. Type in a report date, or just press **RETURN** if you don't want one.

4. The report will be displayed on the screen as it will appear on paper. Every record in the report will be shown (you may have to scroll through several screens by pressing **SPACE** to see the entire report), and the formatting you have chosen will appear as it will on paper.

Displaying database reports on the screen is a good way to make sure you haven't truncated some entries in a category by making the category too narrow. It's also a good way to see a category total or to see values in a Calculated Category without printing the report on paper, since neither of these features is displayed on the Report Format screen. There is, however, one basic limitation to displaying database reports on the screen: Reports wider than 80 characters won't be displayed completely—only the categories that begin within the first 80 characters from the left of the report will be displayed. Thus, if you want to preview categories in a report that begin to the right of the 80th character, you have to redesign the report so those categories fall within the 80-character limit, either by narrowing or temporarily deleting some categories from the report format, or by changing the positions of the categories.

For further information about database reports, see Database Report Formats.[79]

Ditto (⌘-')

- **Definition**

  The *Ditto* command (⌘-') simply copies the entry in the category above the cursor in a database record into the entry the cursor is on in the record below. The Ditto command works only in the Multiple Record layout.[168]

- **Usage**

  Use the Ditto command when one or more existing records in a database file should contain the same information. To use the Ditto command:

  1. Place the cursor on the database entry you wish to replace with the entry from the category directly above.

  2. Press the Ditto command (⌘-'). The entry your cursor is on will be replaced with the entry in the record directly above.

- **Example**

  Suppose you are working with the *Customers* file shown in the following example. You have reassigned salesperson *Smith* to the *Drucker Drayage* account, and you want to change the *Jones* entry to *Smith*.

```
File: Customers            REVIEW/ADD/CHANGE            Escape: Main Menu
Selection: All records

Name            YTD Sales      Company        Salesperson  Phone          S
===========================================================================
Wilson Peck     5,350.00       Apex Canning    Smith        555-3232       8
Wilson K. Jeeve 575.30         Butlerware, Inc Smith        555-3334       9
Mort Drucker    1,025.00       Drucker Drayage Jones        555-2345       1
Arnold Ormsby   787.35         Flecko Paints   Jones        555-4567       6
Walter Canary   125.60         Flippo Dog Food Jones        555-8606       3
Fred Fong       4,675.20       Fong Machine To Jones        555-8765       3
Edwina Gumm     87.50          Fritzi Fashions Smith        555-7890       3
Ed Frobish      15,325.00      Frobish Linen S Smith        555-1234       3
Fortuna Maldona 2,500.85       Furniture City  Brohammer    555-2222       1
Barney Flint    3,257.60       Howard's U-Rent Brohammer    555-7608       8
Alex Abidikian  1,024.00       Imperial Dry Cl Smith        555-0505       6
Boris Boronzhov 12,875.95      Jetson Steel    Jones        555-8787       1
James Penningto 100.25         Linda's Typewri Brohammer    555-4443       3
Aldo Pastarelli 355.90         Pesto's Pasta   Brohammer    555-1111       1

---------------------------------------------------------------------------
Type entry or use ⌘ commands                                ⌘-? for Help
```

The Ditto command copies the entry from a category directly above the cursor.

Here's how to use Ditto to replace *Jones* with *Smith* in record number three in the *Customers* file:

1. Place the cursor on the *Jones* entry, in record number 3 (the cursor can be on any character in the entry).

2. Press the Ditto command (⌘-'). The entry above (*Smith*) will replace the current entry (*Jones*).

103

■ **Comments**

The Ditto command is most useful when you want to change several entries in one data category, and the information you want to substitute is located in a category above the entry to be changed.

When pressing the command, make sure you press the unshifted *apostrophe* (') key together with ⌂; if you try to use *quote* (")—the shifted apostrophe key—the command won't work.

DOS-ProDOS Conversion Program

■ **Definition**

The DOS-ProDOS Conversion Program is a program on the ProDOS User's Disk that converts ProDOS files[246] to DOS 3.3 files, or vice versa.

■ **Usage**

AppleWorks runs under the ProDOS operating system, and the files it creates are unique types of ProDOS files. When you save AppleWorks files to disk as DIF[100] or ASCII[13] files, you can then use those files with other ProDOS-based programs.

If you want to use your DIF or ASCII files with programs that run under the older DOS 3.3 operating system, you must convert them to DOS 3.3 format. If you want to use DOS 3.3 DIF or ASCII files in AppleWorks, you must convert them to ProDOS files first. These conversions can only be done with the DOS-ProDOS Conversion Program.

The DOS-ProDOS Conversion Program is one of several utility programs on the ProDOS User's Disk. If you don't have a copy of the ProDOS User's Disk, you can buy one, along with a ProDOS User's Manual, for about $40 at your Apple dealer. The ProDOS User's Manual explains how to use the DOS-ProDOS Conversion Program.

Edit Cursor (⌂-E)

- **Definition**

  The *Edit Cursor* command (⌂-E) toggles the cursor between the *insert* mode and the *overstrike* mode.

- **Usage**

  Use the Edit Cursor command when you want to change the way the cursor enters data into AppleWorks. The default setting for the cursor in all three applications is *insert* mode. In insert mode, everything you type at the cursor position is inserted in front of any data to the right of it. The insert mode is indicated by the shape of the cursor: a blinking underline. By pressing the Edit Cursor command (⌂-E), you change the cursor to *overstrike* mode, in which each character you type replaces the character at the cursor position. In overstrike mode, the cursor is a blinking rectangle. The Edit Cursor command toggles back and forth between these two modes, so that when you use it, you change the cursor from its current mode to the other mode.

- **Comments**

  If you use the Desktop Index[98] to change to another file, even one for a different application, the cursor will remain in the mode you had in the previous application.

@ERROR

- **Structure**

  @ERROR

- **Definition**

  @ERROR is a spreadsheet function that causes the message ERROR to be displayed in the cell where it is entered, and in all cells that refer to that cell.

- **Usage**

  You enter the @ERROR function by itself in a cell without an argument.

- **Example**

Let's use the @ERROR function in the column of numbers in this worksheet:

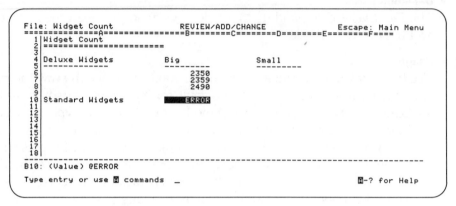

```
File: Widget Count              REVIEW/ADD/CHANGE              Escape: Main Menu
=================A===============B=========C=========D=========E========F====
   1|Widget Count
   2|========================
   3|
   4|Deluxe Widgets          Big                 Small
   5|---------------         ---------           ---------
   6|                            2350
   7|                            2359
   8|                            2490
   9|
  10|Standard Widgets        ▓▓▓▓▓ERROR
  11|
  12|
  13|
  14|
  15|
  16|
  17|
  18|
----------------------------------------------------------------------------
B10: (Value) @ERROR

Type entry or use ▣ commands  _                            ▣-? for Help
```

You can use the @ERROR function as a reminder, so a cell isn't accidentally included in a formula's calculation.

Suppose we want to sum the figures in column B, and we want to be certain that cell B10 is not used in the calculation.

1. Place the cursor in cell B10.

2. Type *@ERROR*, and press **RETURN**.

3. The ERROR message will appear in B10, and it will also appear in any formula that uses cell B10 as a reference.

ERROR

- **Definition**

ERROR is a spreadsheet message reporting that one of the values necessary for a formula to calculate is incorrect or missing.

- **Usage**

The ERROR message is displayed in the cell where the formula is located, so that instead of presenting the result of a calculation, the cell shows an error condition. ERROR occurs when cells or cell contents used in the argument of a formula render the formula incapable of producing a correct result— for example, if the formula attempts to divide by zero, which AppleWorks does not allow.

- **Example**

  You are a widget manufacturer, and you want to know how many widgets each worker is producing per day. To track this, you set up this worksheet:

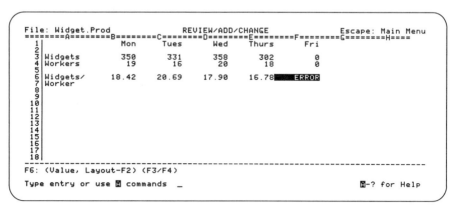

```
File: Widget.Prod              REVIEW/ADD/CHANGE              Escape: Main Menu
=========A=========B=========C=========D=========E=========F=========G=========H====
  1              Mon      Tues      Wed     Thurs      Fri
  2
  3│Widgets      350       331      358       302        0
  4│Workers       19        16       20        18        0
  5
  6│Widgets/    18.42     20.69    17.90     16.78�████ ERROR
  7│Worker
  8
  9
 10
 11
 12
 13
 14
 15
 16
 17
 18
-----------------------------------------------------------------------------
F6: (Value, Layout-F2) (F3/F4)

Type entry or use ⬚ commands  _                              ⬚-? for Help
```

  The ERROR message appears when a formula can't calculate properly because of missing or inappropriate values.

  An ERROR message is produced because the formula in cell F6 divides the number of widgets by the number of workers. In this case, Friday was a holiday and nobody was working, so the formula in F6 therefore divides by zero, which is an illegal value.

- **Comments**

  The ERROR message often appears when you delete rows or columns that contain cells referenced by a formula. If a formula sums values in rows 1 and 2, for example, and then row 2 is later deleted, the formula may produce the ERROR message. Also, if a formula refers to a cell with the @ERROR[105] function in it, an ERROR message will be displayed in that cell.

File

- **Definition**

  A *file* is a collection of information that is stored under one name on a disk or on the Desktop.[97]

- **Usage**

  Each of the three applications in AppleWorks creates a different type of file; the files created by each application are not directly compatible with the others, or with other programs. You can't load a spreadsheet file into the word processor, for example. You can, however, transfer parts of spreadsheet and database files into word-processor documents by using the Clipboard,[35] and transfer data between the spreadsheet and the database by creating DIF[100] or ASCII[13] files. You can also create DIF or ASCII files from the three applications so their data can be used by other programs (see: Reusing Data[276]).

As soon as you choose the option to create a file from scratch from the Add Files menu[2] and then name the file, that file exists in your Apple's memory. If you turn off the computer at this point, that file will disappear. You must save new files to disk before quitting AppleWorks if you want to use them again later.

Files on the Desktop: It's possible to work with up to 12 files at a time on the Desktop, but the actual number depends on both the size of the files and the amount of RAM your system has (see: Desktop).

Files on the disk: You can store up to 51 AppleWorks files on a 5¼" floppy disk, and up to 130 files in a hard-disk subdirectory, depending on the size of the files being stored. Since you can store a maximum of 143K of data on a 5¼" floppy disk, for example, you couldn't store 51 files if each file was 10K. (See: Pathname;[188] Using a Hard Disk.[353])

Naming files: Whenever you create a file in AppleWorks, you must give it a name. There are some restrictions on the names you can give files:

☐ File names can't contain more than 15 characters (letters, numbers, spaces, or periods).

☐ File names must begin with a letter.

☐ File names can't contain other punctuation marks or symbols, such as *, /, +, or −.

If you try to type an improper symbol as part of a file name, AppleWorks will beep and you won't be able to enter that character.

Every file you name in AppleWorks must have a unique name, because the program only knows that files have different contents by their names. Suppose you have two completely different reports in word-processor files, for example. The first file is named *Report*, and is stored on disk. You have just created the second file and named it *Report*. If you save the second file on the same disk where the first file is stored, the first will be replaced with the second: Since the names are the same, AppleWorks assumes that the files are the same. You could maintain files with the same names on different disks, but that could get confusing, so it isn't a good idea.

Find (⌘-F)

- **Definition**

The *Find* command (⌘-F) locates text, numbers, or database records, depending on the type of file in which it is used.

- **Usage**

The specific operation of the Find command differs, depending on the application in which you use it. In general, though, to find something:

1. Press the Find command (⌘-F).

2. The prompt line will ask you which Find option you want to use. These differ among the three applications. Depending on what you want to do, select the appropriate Find option.

3. Enter the reference information or comparison data for the Find command to match against the file, and press **RETURN**. The cursor will move to the data matching your comparison entry, and, depending on the application, the matching data will be highlighted.

In the word processor and spreadsheet, the Find command only searches from the cursor position in a file toward the bottom. If you want to search through an entire file, therefore, you must move the cursor to the beginning of the file.

If the Find function doesn't find the data you specify, the computer beeps, and the prompt line tells you the data wasn't found.

▣ Using Find in the word processor

When you press ⌘-F while in the Review/Add/Change screen of the word processor, the prompt line changes to read:

Find? Text Page Marker Case sensitive text Options for printer

Text: Whenever you press **RETURN** (or **T**) to choose the *Text* option, the prompt line changes to read *Find what text?* When you type the text you want found and press **RETURN**, Find jumps to the next occurrence of the characters following the cursor position, highlights them, and the prompt line changes to read *Find next occurrence? No Yes.* If you press **RETURN** (or **N**), you are returned to the Review/Add/Change screen. If you press **Y** to choose the *Yes* option, Find jumps to the next occurrence of the characters, highlights them and again prompts you to choose whether or not to find the next occurrence. You can keep finding the specified text by pressing **Y**. When AppleWorks reaches the last occurrence of the text in the document, your next attempt will result in an audible beep, and the message *Not found, press Spacebar to continue* displayed on the screen.

If you choose to find *Text*, the function will stop at every occurrence of the text you specify, including occurrences of the characters within longer words. Also, the Find command with the *Text* option is not case sensitive: It will find any occurrence of the characters, even those not capitalized exactly the way you entered it. If you specify the word *do*, for example, Find will locate the word *Do* as well as *don't, dose,* and *Dossier.*

Page: If you press **P** to choose the *Page* option when the Find prompt line is displayed, the prompt line changes to read *Page number?* When you type a page number and press **RETURN**, Find jumps to the page-break indicator at the *end* of the specified page. The prompt line then changes to *Find next occurrence?* at which point you can press **RETURN** or **N** to end the search, or **Y** to continue looking for pages with the same page number.

You can find a page only if you have used the Calculate[18] command (⌂-**K**) to paginate the document first.

Marker: *Markers* are simply numbers you can place in a word processor file from the Printer Options menu.[217] If you press **M** to choose the *Marker* option when the Find prompt line is displayed, the prompt line changes to read *Marker number?* When you type a marker number and press **RETURN**, Find jumps to the marker you specified and highlights it. The prompt line then changes to read *Find next occurrence?*, at which point you can press **RETURN** or **N** to end the search, or **Y** to continue searching for markers with the same number.

Case sensitive text: If you press the **C** key to choose the *Case sensitive text* option when the Find prompt line is displayed, the prompt line changes to read *Find what text?*, just as with the *Text* option. With the *Case sensitive text* option, however, you can specify exact matches according to lower- and uppercase characters. For example, if you type *Do* in response to the prompt, Find will jump over occurrences of *do* or *don't* or *dossier* but will stop at occurrences of *Do* or *Don't* or *Dossier.*

Options for printer: If you press **O** to choose the *Options for printer* option when the Find prompt line is displayed, a version of the Printer Options menu called Find Printer Options appears in the lower half of the screen. When you type the two-character code for the printer option you want and press **RETURN**, the menu disappears, the first occurrence of the option is highlighted in the document, and the prompt line gives you the option to *Find next occurrence*. If the option is not found, the computer beeps and you are prompted to press **SPACE**, which will return you to the Review/Add/Change screen.

It's useful to find printer options when you want to change them in a file. If part of a file is single-spaced, for example, and you want to change it to double-spacing, you can choose the *Options for printer* option to display the Printer Options menu and type *SS* to quickly locate the single-spaced section.

Example: In the following example document, *Convertible* was specified as the text to find:

```
File: Sales Letter                 FIND          Escape: Review/Add/Change
=====|====|====|====|====|====|====|====|====|====|====|====|====|====|===
Mr. Ed Frobish
Frobish Linen Service
335 Ramona Ave.
San Jose, CA 95551

Dear Ed:

We think you're a ^super^ customer, and I wanted to tell you how much all
of us at Acme Widgets appreciate your business.  That's why we wanted you
to be the first to know about our new Widget Convertible--the sturdiest,
most flexible, most cost-effective widget around.

I'd like to schedule a time to drop by your office and demonstrate the
advantages of the new Widget Convertible, so I'll be giving you a call
during the next week to make an appointment.

In the meantime, think what the world's first all-purpose widget will mean
to your profits!

----------------------------------------------------------------------
Find next occurrence? No  Yes
```

Using Find in the spreadsheet

When you press ⌂-**F** in the spreadsheet, the prompt line offers you these four options:

Find? **Repeat last** **Coordinates** **Text**

Repeat last: When you press **R** (or **RETURN**) to choose *Repeat last*, AppleWorks repeats the last Find option you specified. If you specified *do* as the text to find, for example, the first occurrence of that particular word following the cursor would be highlighted. But if you pressed ⌂-**F** again and then **R**, the next occurrence of the string would be highlighted. If there are no more, the prompt line will tell you. If you haven't specified any Find options in the spreadsheet before, AppleWorks will beep and present the Find options again. This option will also locate coordinates specified as the last find criteria.

Coordinates: When you press **C** to choose *Coordinates*, the prompt line will change to read *Coordinates?* All you need do is type the coordinates of the cell you want to find and press **RETURN**: The cursor will jump directly to the cell and highlight it. (This is a good way to jump quickly to a distant cell in the spreadsheet.)

Text: When you press **T** to choose *Text*, the prompt line will change to read *Comparison?* When you type the text you want to find and press **RETURN**, the cursor jumps to the cell containing the text string and highlights it; if there are no occurrences of the text string, you'll hear a beep and the prompt line will tell you. The Find command searches the spreadsheet from top to bottom, left to right from the cursor position.

As in the word processor, if the text you specify is part of other words on the spreadsheet, those words will also be found. For example, if you specified *do* as the word to find, AppleWorks would find *dossier* as well. Also, the Text option in the spreadsheet is not case sensitive, so Find highlights all text entries containing the specified letters regardless of case.

When searching for text in the spreadsheet, the Find command will only locate text contained within one cell—if you typed in a label that spilled over into another cell, you could only search for as much text as would fit into one cell. For example, if you typed *Net Profit* into cell A5, the *t* in *Profit* would actually be entered into cell B5, and to locate this label you would have to specify *Net Profi* as the search text, since that is all that fits into cell A5. You can, however, widen the cell so that all the text fits in it, in which case the Find command would locate the entire entry.

Example: In the spreadsheet on the following page, *Pencils* was specified as the text to find.

```
File: Ofc.Invent                        FIND           Escape: Review/Add/Change
==================A================B=======C========D=======E========F====
   1|                                 Office Supplies
   2|
   3|Item                             Count    Price    Total
   4|
   5|Blotters, Large
   6|Blotters, Small
   7|Envelopes, Regular
   8|Envelopes, Window
   9|Envelopes, Manila
  10|Folders, Regular
  11|Folders, Legal
  12|Pencils
  13|Pencils, Red
  14|Pens, Black
  15|Pens, Blue
  16|Pens, Green
  17|Pens, Red
  18|Rulers
-----------------------------------------------------------------------
A12: (Label) Pencils

Find? Repeat last  Coordinates  Text
```

Using Find in the database

You can use the Find command in the database to list only those records with categories containing information you specify. The information can be text, a number, a date, or a time.

When you press ⌂-F while the Review/Add/Change screen of a database file is displayed, the records disappear from the screen and the prompt line reads *Type comparison information.* When you type the information and press **RETURN**, only those records with categories containing the comparison information appear on the screen. But if no records are found, the message *No records match your request* will be displayed. Then, to return to the normal Review/Add/Change screen, press **ESC**.

When you search for text or data in the database, the Find command will display all records containing matching information, even if the information occurs in different categories within different records. For example, suppose you have a file with a record containing *Millicent Fremont* in a name category and another record with *Fremont* in a city category. If you specify *Fremont* as the comparison information, the Find command will list both records.

Because the Find command only works from the Review/Add/Change screen, you won't be able to use the Find command to selectively locate records to print in a report. If you sort records with the Find command and then choose ⌂-P to print the records, you'll notice that all records—even the ones that did not match the Find criteria—will be included in the report. To select only certain records to use in a report, you must use the Record Selection Rules[259] command.

113

Example: In the following database, *Brohammer* was specified as the text to be found:

```
File: Customers                 FIND RECORDS        Escape: Review/Add/Change
Find all records that contain BROHAMMER
Press ⌘-F to change Find.

Name              Company              Phone      Salesperson   YTD Sales
========================================================================
Olive Ogilvy      Ace Jackhammer       555-6666   Brohammer     10,635.25
Aldo Pastarelli   Pesto's Pasta        555-1111   Brohammer        355.90
Fortuna Maldonado Furniture City       555-2222   Brohammer      2,500.85
James Pennington  Linda's Typewriter Rep 555-4443 Brohammer        100.25
Barney Flint      Howard's U-Rent 'Em  555-7608   Brohammer      3,257.60




-------------------------------------------------------------------------
Type entry or use ⌘ commands                              ⌘-? for Help
```

Fixed Titles (⌂-T)

- **Definition**

  Fixed Titles are spreadsheet row or column titles that remain on the screen when you scroll through the spreadsheet.

- **Usage**

  When you scroll around a spreadsheet, the rows or columns move off the screen as you reveal new parts of the file. If you scroll to the right, columns move off the screen to the left as you do so. If you scroll down, rows move off the screen at the top as you do so.

  Sometimes, however, you don't want row or column titles to move off the screen when you scroll. In those situations you can use the Fixed Titles command to "lock" a set of row and/or column titles on the screen so that when you scroll through your spreadsheet, the titles will remain displayed even when other columns or rows scroll out of view.

- **Example**

  Suppose you are preparing a five-year budget projection, part of which is shown in the following example.

114

```
┌──────────────────────────────────────────────────────────────────────────┐
│ File: FiveYear.Budget          REVIEW/ADD/CHANGE           Escape: Main Menu │
│ ========A========B========C========D========E========F========G========H==== │
│  1                                                                          │
│  2              Acme Widgets - Budget Projection                            │
│  3                                                                          │
│  4                    Q185      Q285      Q385      Q485      Q186      Q286 │
│  5                                                                          │
│  6 Rent               2000      2000      2000                              │
│  7 Utilities           502       489       480                              │
│  8 Material           2500      2495      2350                              │
│  9 Salaries           2000      2000      2000                              │
│ 10 Promotion           500       475       300                              │
│ 11                                                                          │
│ 12 Total Expenses     7502      7459██████7130                              │
│ 13                                                                          │
│ 14                                                                          │
│ 15                                                                          │
│ 16                                                                          │
│ 17                                                                          │
│ 18                                                                          │
│ ----------------------------------------------------------------------      │
│ E12: (Value, Layout-F0) @SUM(E6...E10)                                      │
│                                                                             │
│ Type entry or use ▣ commands  _                          ▣-? for Help       │
└──────────────────────────────────────────────────────────────────────────┘
```

When a spreadsheet is very wide, the row labels will disappear when you scroll to the right to view off-screen cells.

Because there are so many columns in the spreadsheet, many of them are located off the screen to the right. If you scroll over to the fifth year to enter figures, the row labels you have put in columns A and B will scroll off the screen, and you will have trouble remembering which expense figure goes in which row. You can set a Fixed Titles area so the row labels are always on the screen, and only the columns with data in them scroll. To do this:

1. Place the cursor in the column to the right of the area in which you want to fix titles (in our example, column C).

2. Press the Fixed Titles command (♵-T). The prompt line will ask if you want to fix the titles at the top of the spreadsheet, at the left side of the spreadsheet, or in both places. In this example, you would choose the left side.

3. The titles to the left of the cursor (in columns A and B) will now be fixed on the screen, and when you scroll to the right, they will remain visible.

■ **Removing fixed titles**

To remove titles, simply press ♵-T from anywhere in the spreadsheet. The prompt line will say *Titles? None* and the word *None* will be highlighted. Pressing **RETURN** or **N** will remove any titles you have fixed.

■ **Comments**

Set the Fixed Titles area at the left of the screen if you want the row labels to remain visible when you scroll the spreadsheet horizontally. Set a Fixed Titles area at the top of the screen when you want the column labels to remain visible when you scroll vertically. The entries you fix on the screen can be either numbers or labels—the Fixed Titles command fixes a portion of the spreadsheet on the screen, not a specific type of data.

To set a Fixed Titles area at the top of the screen, place the cursor in the row directly below the titles you want to fix.

To set a Fixed Titles area for both the top and the left side, place the cursor in the cell at the intersection of the first row below the top titles, and the first column to the right of the left titles. In this case, think about the titles area as an inverted L-shaped bar—you want to place the cursor in the cell directly inside the corner of the inverted *L*.

Setting a Fixed Titles area for both the top and left titles doesn't mean that both sets of titles will always appear on the screen, however. If you fix both groups, the left titles will stay on the screen when you scroll from left to right, and the top titles will stay when you scroll from top to bottom.

Also, you'll notice that if you have fixed a portion of the spreadsheet, like columns A and B in our example, and you scroll all the way to the left, you'll see that the columns you fixed are actually duplicated, and by scrolling all the way to the left you'll have two copies of the columns on your screen, although you'll only be able to enter data or change information in the unfixed portion of the spreadsheet.

Formula

■ **Definition**

A *formula* is a mathematical expression that calculates values and places the result in the cell where the formula is entered.

■ **Usage**

Formulas can be combinations of values, functions,[117] and logical[125] or arithmetic[9] operators that calculate them. (Values can be represented by individual numbers, cell coordinates, ranges of cell coordinates, lists of numbers and/or cell coordinates, or the results of mathematical expressions.) A formula might perform a simple calculation, such as *2+2* or *A1+A2*, or it might perform a complex calculation, such as *@SUM((A1/10^6)*(B23+(B39/12)))*.

For more complete information about using formulas, see Spreadsheet Overview.[298]

Functions

- **Definition**

A *function* is a special type of built-in spreadsheet formula that performs a specific kind of calculation or data-handling operation.

- **Usage**

Functions are used in spreadsheet formulas as easy ways to produce certain calculations. The @SUM[341] function, for example, adds the list or range of values specified in its argument. To add the contents of cells A1, A2, and A3, for example, you could specify the function *@SUM(A1.A3)*. This is much simpler than adding the three cells with the formula *A1+A2+A3*.

These are the functions available in the AppleWorks spreadsheet:

Function:	Description:
@ABS	Absolute value of the argument.[1]
@AVG	Average value of the argument.[15]
@CHOOSE (list)	Finds a value according to its position in a list, based on the contents of an indexed cell.[32]
@COUNT	Counts the number of numeric entries in a list.[47]
@ERROR	Displays the message *ERROR* in a cell.[105]
@IF	Applies a logical condition to an expression, and presents one of two different results specified in the argument, depending on whether the condition is true or false.[125]
@INT	Converts a decimal number to its integer value.[130]

Function:	Description:
@LOOKUP	Finds a value in a table according to the corresponding position of the comparison value named in the argument from a lookup table.[155]
@MAX	Returns the largest value in a list.[160]
@MIN	Returns the smallest value in a list.[161]
@NA	Displays the message *NA* in a cell.[170]
@NPV	Finds the current value of a predicted future cash flow at a specified discount rate.[175]
@SQRT	Displays the square root of the argument.[327]
@SUM	Sums values in a range or list.[341]

■ **Comments**

You can find specific information about each of these functions under their individual entries. General information about functions is located in the entry, Spreadsheet Overview.[298]

Group Totals (⌘-G)

■ **Definition**

The *Group Totals* command (⌘-G) calculates subtotals for groups of related entries in a database report.

■ **Usage**

Use the Group Totals command on the Report Format screen in the database whenever you want to total one or more numeric categories (with the Set Totals[286] command), but you also want the records subtotaled in groups based on the entries in another category. Although a Group Total can be specified for any category in a report, the Group Totals command will only produce a useful result under these conditions:

☐ The numeric category or categories whose values you want to subtotal must first be totaled with the Category Totals command.

☐ The category you want to base the groups on should contain non-numeric information and must have the Group Totals command applied to it.

118

☐ The category with the Group Totals command must be sorted with the Arrange[10] command, so all the records in each group in that category are grouped together in the report.

Group totals are actually subtotals of values in a numeric category that have been totaled with the Category Totals option. The Category Totals option only produces a grand total at the bottom of the totaled category. To produce subtotals, you must tell AppleWorks how to create groups of values that will be added to make up the subtotals. To do this, you should use a non-numeric category to control or determine the makeup of each subtotaled group. You do this by arranging the category you want the subtotals based on (so all the records in the report with the same entry in that category are grouped together), and then you specify a group total on that category, so AppleWorks knows it must subtotal the values in the totaled numeric category based on those groups.

■ **Example**

Suppose you have a *Customers* file that contains customer names, their year-to-date purchases, and the name of the salesperson assigned to each customer. You want to produce a report that shows not only total sales, but also the subtotals of the sales by salesperson. Here's how to do it with the Group Totals command:

1. With the Review/Add/Change screen of the *Customers* file showing, press the Print[193] command (⌘-P) to produce the Report Menu.[273]

2. Select the option to create a new Tables report, and name the new report *Sales/Salesperson*. Once you do this, the Report Format screen will be displayed.

3. Use the Delete[92] command (⌘-D) to eliminate all categories from the report, except for *Company, Salesperson,* and *YTD Sales.*

4. Move the cursor to the YTD Sales category and press the Category Totals command (⌘-T). The prompt line will change to read *Decimal places for this category?* Since the category is money amounts, type *2* so cents amounts are included, and press **RETURN**. The prompt line will read *Blank spaces after this category?* Press **RETURN** to accept the default of 3 spaces. A row of 9s will be displayed to indicate that the entire *YTD Sales* category will be totaled, as shown in the example on the next page.

```
File: Customers              REPORT FORMAT           Escape: Report Menu
Report: Sales/Salesperson
Selection: All records


=================================================================
--> or <--   Move cursor                  ⌂-J   Right justify this category
 >   ⌂   <    Switch category positions    ⌂-K   Define a calculated category
--> ⌂ <--    Change column width           ⌂-N   Change report name and/or title
⌂-A  Arrange (sort) on this category       ⌂-O   Printer options
⌂-D  Delete this category                  ⌂-P   Print the report
⌂-G  Add/remove group totals               ⌂-R   Change record selection rules
⌂-I  Insert a prev. deleted category       ⌂-T   Add/remove category totals

Company                      Salesperson  YTD Sales        L
-A-------------------------- -B---------- -C-----------     e
Ace Jackhammer Service       Brohammer    9999999999.99     n
Drucker Drayage              Smith        9999999999.99     5
Pesto's Pasta                Brohammer    9999999999.99     7
                                          =============
-----------------------------------------------------------------
Use options shown above to change report format.            36K Avail.
```

When you create a category total on the Report Format screen of the database, a row of 9s is displayed to indicate this.

5. Move the cursor to the *Salesperson* category, and press the Arrange command (⌂-**A**). When the Arrange Options screen appears, press **RETURN** to accept the default option to sort the category alphabetically from A to Z. The names in the *Salesperson* category will now be arranged in alphabetical order.

6. While the cursor is still on the *Salesperson* category, press the Group Totals command (⌂-**G**). The Group Totals indicator will appear in the upper-left part of the screen, below the selection indicator, and the prompt line will ask if you want to print only the group totals, like this:

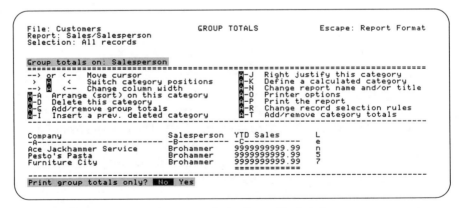

```
File: Customers              GROUP TOTALS           Escape: Report Format
Report: Sales/Salesperson
Selection: All records

Group totals on: Salesperson
=================================================================
--> or <--   Move cursor                  ⌂-J   Right justify this category
 >   ⌂   <    Switch category positions    ⌂-K   Define a calculated category
--> ⌂ <--    Change column width           ⌂-N   Change report name and/or title
⌂-A  Arrange (sort) on this category       ⌂-O   Printer options
⌂-D  Delete this category                  ⌂-P   Print the report
⌂-G  Add/remove group totals               ⌂-R   Change record selection rules
⌂-I  Insert a prev. deleted category       ⌂-T   Add/remove category totals

Company                      Salesperson  YTD Sales        L
-A-------------------------- -B---------- -C-----------     e
Ace Jackhammer Service       Brohammer    9999999999.99     n
Pesto's Pasta                Brohammer    9999999999.99     5
Furniture City               Brohammer    9999999999.99     7
                                          =============
-----------------------------------------------------------------
Print group totals only? No  Yes
```

When you use the Group Totals command, the Group Totals indicator appears to show it is in effect for the selected category.

7. Press **N** (or **RETURN**) to answer *No* to the prompt. (If you print only the totals, only the subtotals and Category Total, along with one element of each group of the category you used for Group Totals to identify the subtotal, will appear in the report. In this case, we want the company and salesperson's name to appear in the report as well.)

8. A second prompt will ask if you want each new group to be printed on a new page. Press *N* to answer *No*. (This is a short report, so that would be a waste of paper.)

9. The report is now ready: The records are arranged by the names of the salespeople, and the Group Totals command assures that each salesperson's name will be used to form a separate group of records. The Category Totals command in the *YTD Sales* category will produce a grand total of the amounts in that category, and because we have used the Group Totals command in the *Salesperson* category as well, the group defined by each salesperson's name will be subtotaled in the *YTD Sales* category.

10. Print the report, and the group totals will be shown in it, as you can see here:

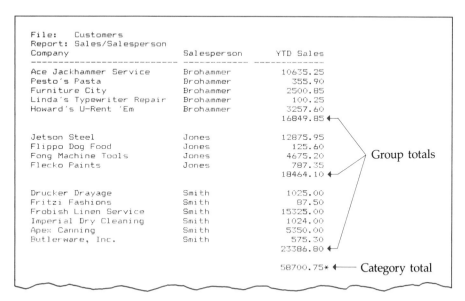

The Group Totals command lets us subtotal values in a report by groups based on the contents of another category. In this case, we have subtotaled YTD Sales *by* Salesperson.

■ **Comments**

You can't see the subtotals produced by the Group Totals command unless you print the report, either to the screen or to a printer.

You can't specify a group total in the *Labels* report format. You can only specify one Group Total in a report, but you can have more than one Category Total based on the category with the Group Totals, so you could subtotal several categories of numeric information on the same report.

The Group Totals command is useful when you have a report containing numeric values that must be subtotaled. Examples of such reports include sales reports (where subtotals could be based on different products, salespeople, or types of customers), invoices (where subtotals could be based on whether the item is food, dry goods, or tax, for example), or inventory valuation reports (where subtotals could be based on product classes).

Hard Copy (⌂-H)

■ **Definition**

The *Hard Copy* command (⌂-H) sends the contents of an AppleWorks screen to your printer for a hard-copy printout (also called a *screendump*).

■ **Usage**

Use the Hard Copy command (⌂-H) to print the current screen you're working with in AppleWorks. The command will print any screen, anywhere in the program.

When you print the screen, all the AppleWorks interface elements such as the file name, the screen name, the Escape path, and the prompt line are printed along with the data in your file.

To use the Hard Copy command:

1. Make sure your printer is on and is connected properly to your computer.

2. Press the Hard Copy command (⌂-H).

3. The currently displayed screen will be printed on paper exactly as it appears on your display.

■ **Comments**

The only screen elements that don't print when you use the Hard Copy command are the cursor and highlighting. Because the cursor blinks, it is not "captured" by the Hard Copy command, and consequently is not reproduced on paper. Highlighting is produced by the video display, and can't be reproduced on a printer.

To check which printer will be used when you use the Ć-H command, choose *Other Activities* from the Main Menu,[158] then choose *Specify information about your printer(s)* from the Other Activities menu. Option 1 on the Printer Information menu will show you the printer currently selected as the Open-Apple-H printer. To change it, simply press **RETURN** (the option's already highlighted), and choose the printer you want from the list that appears. Note that AppleWorks will not print Ć-H information to a printer configured as a Disk printer (see: Printer Configuration[200]).

Further information will be found in the Printing the Display[245] entry.

Help (Ć-?)

■ **Definition**

The *Help* command (Ć-?) produces information screens that list and explain the commands available in the word processor, the spreadsheet, the database, and AppleWorks in general. The screen produced at any given time is appropriate to the application you're currently working with.

■ **Usage**

Use the Help command when you're not sure which command to use, or when you can't remember the keystrokes for a certain command. The list of commands that appears when you press Ć-? depends on which application you are using at the time—AppleWorks displays the list of commands and brief command explanations for the specific application you are working with. (Note that you don't have to hold down the **SHIFT** key when pressing **?** together with Ć.)

When you press the Help command from the Main Menu,[158] the Help screen lists and explains the commands that work the same throughout AppleWorks. The first three entries are:

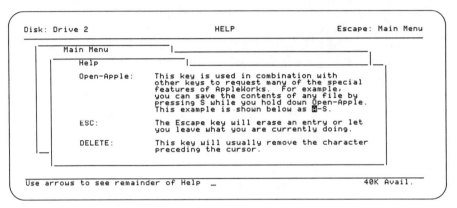

```
Disk: Drive 2                    HELP                 Escape: Main Menu

       Main Menu            |_____
         Help             |_____|_
         Open-Apple:      This key is used in combination with
                          other keys to request many of the special
                          features of AppleWorks.  For example,
                          you can save the contents of any file by
                          pressing S while you hold down Open-Apple.
                          This example is shown below as ⌂-S.

         ESC:             The Escape key will erase an entry or let
                          you leave what you are currently doing.

         DELETE:          This key will usually remove the character
                          preceding the cursor.


Use arrows to see remainder of Help  _                    40K Avail.
```

Pressing the Help command (⌂-?) from the AppleWorks Main Menu displays a general list of commands.

■ Comments

Most of the Help screens AppleWorks displays are too long to fit on one screen, but you can use the ↓ and ↑ keys to scroll through the list. The Help command isn't available when the spreadsheet's or word processor's Printer Options menu[217] is displayed, or when the database's Tables Report Format screen is displayed.

When you press the Help command keys from the Review/Add/Change screen in the spreadsheet, the Help screen lists and explains all the spreadsheet's ⌂ and cursor-movement commands, as well as the beginning characters you must type to tell AppleWorks that you are entering a value or a label. The Help screen in the spreadsheet also gives a list of the current Standard Values[330] settings.

When you press the Help command keys from the Review/Add/Change screen in the database, the Help screen lists all the database's ⌂ and cursor-movement commands. There is another Help screen available in the database, however. The Tables Report Format screen lists the available report commands at the top, but there isn't room to list these commands on a Labels Report Format screen. If you want to see the list of commands available for use with Labels report formats, you can press the Help command from the Labels Report Format screen, and a list of commands will appear.

@IF

- **Structure**

  @IF(logical condition, value (if true), value (if false))

- **Definition**

  @IF is a spreadsheet function that examines a logical condition contained within its argument, and then displays one value specified within its argument if the logical condition proves true, or a second value specified within its argument if the condition proves false.

- **Usage**

  The @IF function is used when the contents of a cell will depend on whether a logical condition is true or false. The argument for @IF is always specified inside parentheses. To use an @IF formula, you must list three elements in its argument in this order: (1) a logical condition, (2) a value to be returned if the condition is true, and (3) a value to be returned if the condition is false.

- **Example**

  In the commission schedule shown in the following spreadsheet, the figure placed in the commission rate applied to a sale depends on the amount of the sale: If the amount is $1000 or more, the rate is 3 percent; if it's less than $1000, the rate is 5 percent.

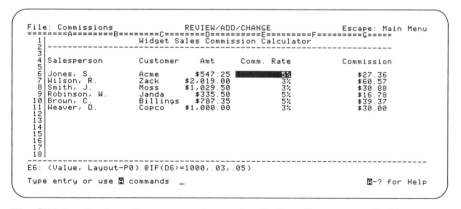

The @IF function is used to put one of two values in the cell containing the @IF function, depending on whether the contents of another cell pass or fail a logical test specified within the function's argument.

Once the commission rate is calculated, then the sale amount is multiplied by the commission rate, and the commission payment is calculated. To use the @IF function in the entry for salesperson Jones:

1. Place the cursor in cell E6.

2. Type *@IF*, followed by a left parenthesis.

3. Type the logical condition to be satisfied. In this case, we want different results depending on whether the amount of the Jones sale is $1000 or more, so we specify:

   D6>=1000.

Be sure you don't include a dollar sign—the function expects numbers only.

4. Type a comma to separate the logical condition from the values.

5. Type the value to be returned if the condition is true. Here, we want to apply a 3 percent commission rate if the sale amount is $1000 or more, so we type *.03*.

6. Type a comma to separate the true value from the false value.

7. Type the value to be returned if the condition is false. In this case, we want to apply a 5 percent commission rate if the sale amount is less than $1000, so we type *.05*.

8. Type a right parenthesis to complete the argument, and then press **RETURN** to enter the formula. The rate of *5%* will appear in cell E6, as shown in the example.

You can't specify a number with a percent sign in a formula, so you have to enter the percent amounts as decimals. In the example, the number appears with a percent sign after it because column E has been formatted for percent using the Layout[146] command (⌘-L).

The @IF function is a *logical function* that allows you to select a value according to the outcome of a logical condition, using logical principles that consist of math-like formulas and operators. When you enter @IF formulas, you can use the logical operators in the following table to create the conditions you want to satisfy.

Operator:	Description:
<	Less than
>	Greater than
<=	Less than or equal to
>=	Greater than or equal to
=	Equal to
<>	Not equal to

If one of the values needed to test the logical condition, or one of the values returned if the logical condition is met, is a cell containing the @NA function, the cell where the @IF formula is placed will show the message *NA*. Likewise, if one of the values in the logical condition, or one returned by the logical condition, references a cell containing the @ERROR function, the message *ERROR* will be displayed in the cell containing the @IF function.

Insert (⌘-I)

- **Definition**
  The *Insert* command (⌘-I) inserts blank rows or columns in a spreadsheet, or blank records in a database file.

- **Usage**
  The Insert command works slightly differently, depending on whether you are working with a spreadsheet or database file, but the general procedure is the same:

  1. Move the cursor to the spreadsheet row or column, or the database record where you want the blank row, column, or record inserted.

  2. Press the Insert command (⌘-I).

  3. Select whether you want to insert rows or columns (in the spreadsheet), then type the number of blank rows or columns you wish to insert, or enter the new data in the blank record (in the database).

Example: Inserting rows in the spreadsheet

Suppose you are working with this budget-projection spreadsheet:

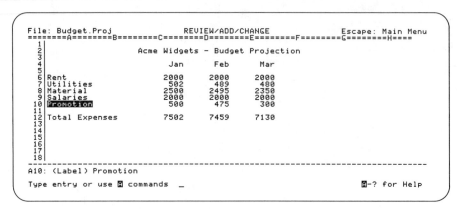

```
File: Budget.Proj              REVIEW/ADD/CHANGE              Escape: Main Menu
========A========B========C========D========E========F========G========H====
  1
  2                      Acme Widgets - Budget Projection
  3
  4                         Jan      Feb      Mar
  5
  6 Rent                    2000     2000     2000
  7 Utilities                502      489      480
  8 Material                2500     2495     2350
  9 Salaries                2000     2000     2000
 10 Promotion                500      475      300
 11
 12 Total Expenses          7502     7459     7130
 13
 14
 15
 16
 17
 18
----------------------------------------------------------------------------
A10: (Label) Promotion

Type entry or use ⌂ commands  _                          ⌂-? for Help
```

You can insert rows or columns anywhere in a spreadsheet with the Insert command.

You realize that you forgot to include rows for *Insurance* and *Benefits*. You will have to insert two rows in this spreadsheet to add the new expense categories. You want them to appear between the rows that are labeled *Salaries* and *Promotion.* Here's how:

1. Place the cursor on the row labeled *Promotion* (row 10). It doesn't matter which column the cursor is in.

2. Press the Insert command (⌂-I). The prompt line will ask if you want to insert *Rows* or *Columns:* Choose *Rows* by pressing **RETURN** or **R.**

3. The prompt line will ask how many rows you want to insert: Type *2,* and then press **RETURN.**

4. The row labeled *Promotion* will move down two rows to row 12, and two blank rows will appear as rows 10 and 11. You can then enter your new expense categories.

You can insert blank columns by choosing the *Columns* option from the Insert prompt line. The first new column appears in the column where your cursor is located when you use the Insert command, and if you specify multiple columns, the rest will follow to the right of the first.

Comments: You can insert up to nine rows or columns into a spreadsheet at a time. If you want to insert more than nine, you must use the Insert command twice.

Example: Inserting records in the database

Suppose you are working with this *Customers* database file:

```
File: Customers              REVIEW/ADD/CHANGE           Escape: Main Menu

Selection: All records


Name            Company         Phone         Salesperson   Street          Y
=============================================================================
Aldo Pastarelli Pesto's Pasta   555-1111      Brohammer     1439 Commerce    3
Alex Abidikian  Imperial Dry Cl 555-0505      Smith         687 Bullis Lane  1
Arnold Ormsby   Flecko Paints   555-4567      Jones         6690 Livingston  7
Barney Flint    Howard's U-Rent 555-7608      Brohammer     878 14th St.     3
Boris Boronzhov Jetson Steel    555-8787      Jones         1450 Carson Ave  1
Ed Frobish      Frobish Linen S 555-1234      Smith         335 Ramona Ave.  1
Edwina Gumm     Fritzi Fashions 555-7890      Smith         3325 State St.   8
Fortuna Maldona Furniture City  555-2222      Brohammer     1839 Water St.   2
Fred Fong       Fong Machine To 555-8765      Jones         3867 Fortney St  4
James Penningto Linda's Typewri 555-4443      Brohammer     3897 107th Ave.  1
Mort Drucker    Drucker Drayage 555-2345      Smith         123 State St.    1
Olive Ogilvy    Ace Jackhammer  555-6666      Brohammer     112 Sumter St.   1
Walter Canary   Flippo Dog Food 555-8606      Jones         3359 W. Hudson   1
Wilson K. Jeeve Butlerware, Inc 555-3334      Smith         907 Broad St.    5
Wilson Peck     Apex Canning    555-3232      Smith         8904 Fremont St  5
-----------------------------------------------------------------------------
Type entry or use ⌂ commands                                ⌂-? for Help
```

You can use the Insert command to insert a new database record in either the Multiple Record layout (shown) or the Single Record layout.

You want to insert a new record at the top of the file. To do so:

1. Move the cursor to the first record (in our example, *Aldo Pastarelli*).

2. Press the Insert command (⌂-I). A new, blank record will appear in Single Record layout.[293] You can then enter data in the record. The new record will be given record number 1, and all the records below it will be renumbered.

3. You can keep entering records, until you press **ESC** to return to the Multiple Record layout screen.

When you want to insert records in the Single Record layout,[293] you use the Insert command the same way as in the Multiple Record layout, except that the records will be displayed in Single Record format when you press **ESC** to indicate that you are through inserting records.

Comments: Inserted records are always entered in the Single Record layout mode. Even if you choose the Insert command from the Multiple Record layout, the screen will change to Single Record layout when you enter the information. Once you're in the Insert mode, you can keep entering records until you press the **ESC** key. After pressing **ESC**, you'll be returned to the Multiple Record layout if you chose the Insert command from that screen. To enter blank records, you simply press the **RETURN** key for each category. If you want to enter a group of blank records in the Multiple Record layout, first create one blank record, press **ESC** to return to Multiple Record layout, and then copy the blank record as many times as you like (see: Copy[40]).

@INT

- **Structure**
@INT(argument)

- **Definition**
@INT is a spreadsheet function that displays the integer portion of a value or expression in the cell where it is entered.

- **Usage**
The @INT function reduces any value or expression to its integer equivalent. An *integer* is a whole number (either negative, positive, or zero) that contains no decimal point. Thus, the @INT function will reduce a value or expression with a decimal point to a whole number.

You can use @INT with an argument that contains an individual value, or an expression that results in an individual value. The argument must be specified inside parentheses.

- **Example**
The inventory-classification system in the following spreadsheet arranges parts by weight in column C. The @INT function is used in column E to reduce the decimal values to integers, and thus make classification easier.

```
 File: Weight Classes            REVIEW/ADD/CHANGE            Escape: Main Menu
 =======A========B========C========D========E========F========G========H====
    1|          Widget Part Weight Classes
    2|---------------------------------------------------------------
    3|Name              Weight            Class
    4|---------          --------          ---------
    5|Sprockets:
    6|-------------------
    7|Small Sprockets     1.32             1
    8|Med. Sprockets      2.04             2
    9|Large Sprockets     4.15             4
   10|
   11|Gears
   12|-------------------
   13|Small Gears         1.75             1
   14|Med. Gears          2.83             2
   15|Large Gears        12.25            12
   16|
   17|
   18|
 E7: (Value) @INT(C7)

 Type entry or use ▣ commands  _                        ▣-? for Help
```

The @INT function turns decimal numbers into integers.

Although this list is fairly short, you can see that @INT would be helpful in classifying a large collection of parts.

The @INT function can also be used with expressions, even those containing other functions, to reduce the result of a calculation to an integer. In the example shown, we could reduce the average weight of small gears and sprockets to an integer by typing *@INT(@AVG(C7,C13))*.

- ■ **Comments**

@INT doesn't round decimal numbers—it simply displays the integer portion of a value. Thus, you could enter either *12.35* or *12.98* as the value, and @INT would display the number *12* in both cases.

Interacting with AppleWorks

AppleWorks is fairly simple to learn and use because it relies heavily on menus, lists, questions, and simple commands to receive instructions from you, and it tells you what it expects from you via prompts and error and warning messages. Before looking at these specific program-control devices, though, let's look at the elements common to most AppleWorks screens.

- ■ **The AppleWorks interface**

Most AppleWorks screens contain certain elements that help you understand where you are in the program and what your options are at that point. The program's Main Menu[158] is a good example:

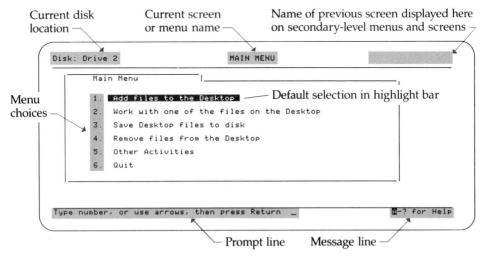

The AppleWorks Main Menu.

The menu itself appears between the horizontal lines at the top and bottom of the screen. The elements above the top line and below the bottom line are common to almost every screen in AppleWorks.

The *current disk location* is shown at the left, above the top line. This indicates the disk drive where AppleWorks will retrieve and save files if you tell it to add, save, or delete them. The current disk location appears only on menu screens; when you display a particular file on the Review/Add/Change screen, this area displays the name of the file you're working with.

In the top center of the line, you can see the *name* of the screen or menu being displayed. Every screen and menu in AppleWorks has a name.

In the upper-right corner, AppleWorks displays the *Escape* destination. As you will see, you can use the **ESC** key to exit the screen you are on and return to the screen you were working with before (a menu, for example). When you first start the AppleWorks program, of course, there is no previous screen, so the Escape destination is not shown (as in our example).

Below the bottom line you will find the AppleWorks *prompt line*. The contents of this line change depending on the screen being displayed.

■ Menus

Many of AppleWorks major functions (creating, saving, or deleting files, for example) are accomplished through menus like the Main Menu. All of these menus and their options are described individually in separate entries that are headed with the name of the menu, such as Main Menu, or Add Files menu.[2] When it comes to choosing options from the menus, though, they all work in the same way.

There are two ways to select menu options:

☐ Use the ↑ or ↓ keys to move the highlighted bar until the option you want is highlighted, and then press the **RETURN** key, *or*

☐ Type the number of the menu option and press the **RETURN** key.

Every AppleWorks menu appears with one of its options already highlighted. This *default* selection is the option you'll most likely want to choose. If it is, you can simply press **RETURN** to select it.

To cancel a menu selection and return to the previous screen (which is shown in the upper-right corner of the screen), you can press **ESC**. Even if you are far into AppleWorks (in the Report Format screen in the database, for example), pressing **ESC** three or four times will quickly return you to the program's Main Menu.

■ Lists

When you are required to choose from several files (when adding files to the Desktop,[97] saving files, or deleting files, for example), AppleWorks presents you with a list of files on the current disk drive, as in this example:

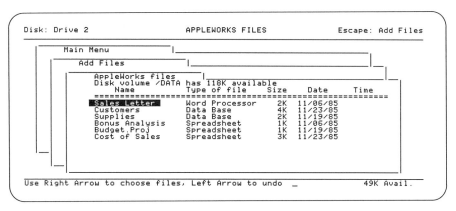

When you need to choose from several files on a disk, AppleWorks presents a list like this.

To choose one file from a list, use the ↑ and ↓ keys to move the highlight bar until the file you want is highlighted, and then press **RETURN**.

To choose more than one file from a list, move the highlight bar to the first file you want and select it by pressing →. An arrow will appear next to the file name, indicating that it has been selected. Then move the highlight bar to the next file you want and select it with →, as in this example:

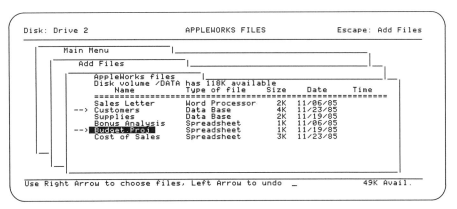

You can select more than one file from a list by selecting each file with the → key.

When all the files you want have been selected with →, press **RETURN** to add, save, remove, or delete them according to the menu you're in.

When selecting more than one file, AppleWorks will ignore files that do not have an arrow next to them, even if a file is highlighted.

■ Questions

When an AppleWorks command is complex (requiring more than one set of keystrokes from you), or when AppleWorks wants to double-check a command you have given it (it always double-checks to make sure you want to quit the program or delete a file, for example), it presents a question in the prompt line at the bottom of the screen, followed by the available choices. Sometimes, the choices are simply *Yes* or *No*, and sometimes there are multiple choices. In any case, you can respond to questions in either of two ways:

☐ Use the → or ← keys to move the highlight bar until it's over the choice you want, and then press **RETURN**, *or*

☐ Type the first letter of the choice you want (such as **Y** for *Yes*).

In most cases, answering a question will complete a command, but sometimes a further response from you is required. In these cases, a prompt will follow your response to a question.

■ Simple commands

Most AppleWorks functions are effected by pressing the ⌘ key together with another of the keyboard keys. These commands are represented in this book as ⌘-*key*, where *key* is the second key in the sequence. Note that you need to hold down the ⌘ key while pressing the second key to carry out a command.

■ Prompts

Unless it is asking you for confirmation about a command, AppleWorks always displays a prompt at the bottom of its screens, as shown in the examples. The prompt suggests the action you should take at the time. If you're not sure what to do on any screen, check the prompt line for a suggestion.

■ Error and warning messages

When AppleWorks is unable to do something you tell it to, or it thinks you are asking it to do something you might regret, it displays an error or warning message. These messages have two basic forms.

When AppleWorks wants to warn you that it can't carry out a command completely, or that a command you've given has serious consequences, it usually presents a warning message, like this:

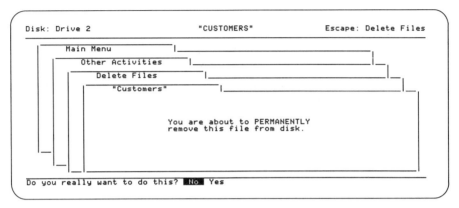

```
Disk: Drive 2                    "CUSTOMERS"            Escape: Delete Files
        _____
       | Main Menu           |_____|
       |  _____ |
       | | Other Activities    |_____| |
       | |  _____ |  |
       | | | Delete Files        |_____| | |
       | | |  _____ | |  |
       | | | | "Customers"         |_____| | | |
       | | | |                                                     | | | |
       | | | |         You are about to PERMANENTLY                 | | | |
       | | | |         remove this file from disk.                 | | | |
       | | | |                                                     | | | |
       | |_| |                                                     | | | |
       | |___|                                                     | | | |
       |_____|_____|_| |
 _____
 Do you really want to do this? No  Yes
```

This warning message alerts you that a file will be erased.

In the spreadsheet, AppleWorks warns you that a column is too narrow to display a number by filling the affected cell or cells with number (#) signs, as in this example:

```
File: Budget86                    REVIEW/ADD/CHANGE              Escape: Main Menu
=======A========B========C========D========E========F========G=====
  1|              Acme Widget Company - 1986 Budget
  2|----------------------------------------------------------------
  3|              Jan       Feb       Mar       Apr       May
  4|
  5|Expenses
  6|===================
  7|Rent        $1,750.00 $1,750.00 $1,750.00 $1,750.00 $1,750.00
  8|Utilities     $350.00   $350.00   $350.00   $350.00   $350.00
  9|Phone         $450.00   $450.00   $450.00   $450.00   $450.00
 10|Salaries    $8,000.00 $8,000.00 $8,000.00 $8,000.00 $8,000.00
 11|Advertising   $250.00 $1,000.00 $1,000.00 $1,000.00 $1,000.00
 12|Insurance   $1,200.00 $1,200.00 $1,200.00 $1,200.00 $1,200.00
 13|Materials   $9,000.00 $9,000.00 $9,000.00 $9,000.00 $9,000.00
 14|
 15|Totals      ##########################################################
 16|
 17|Income
 18|===================
----------------------------------------------------------------
C15: (Value, Layout-D2) @SUM(C7...C13)

Type entry or use ▯ commands  _                        ▯-? for Help
```

This error signal tells you the numbers in row 15 are too large to display completely within the current column width.

Sometimes, the messages simply tell you that AppleWorks couldn't carry out your request completely (it wasn't able to add to the Desktop all the files you selected, for example). In these cases, you are simply being made aware of the condition. Most of the time, however, AppleWorks tells you something isn't right and gives you a chance to cancel your request or alter it so that it can be carried out. AppleWorks contains a prepared message for virtually every problem you might encounter.

If you make a mistake entering a command (you press **M** instead of **Y** or **N** in response to a prompt, or you try to use an ⌂-*key* command that isn't available to you at the time, for example), the computer beeps to tell you that you've made a keystroke error.

The spreadsheet also displays an error message in a cell when it can't perform a calculation or function. This is discussed in the ERROR[106] entry.

Internal Rate of Return (IRR)

■ **Definition**

Internal Rate of Return (IRR) is a common measurement of the soundness of a business investment.

■ **Usage**

Internal Rate of Return is a measurement of an investment's quality based on the theory of discounted cash flows, which assumes that the money returned on an investment diminishes in value over time due to the rate of inflation.

Typically, a business has a required rate of return it expects to receive for its investments. This is normally a rate that guarantees the investment will earn money over time, over and above the rate of inflation. (If safe investments of this quality aren't available, then the required rate is simply the highest rate a company can safely earn from investing in treasury bills or other conservative securities.) Internal Rate of Return calculations are used to match the return rate of a potential investment with a company's required rate of return.

You can determine the IRR of an investment by using the @NPV function in the AppleWorks spreadsheet. The @NPV function returns the *Net Present Value* of an investment, assuming a certain annual discount (or inflation) rate. In other words, it calculates the real value of an investment's future cash flow in today's dollars.

The Internal Rate of Return of an investment is the discount rate that causes an investment's Net Present Value to be equal to the amount originally invested. You can find this by trial and error—you simply test different discount rates in a Net Present Value calculation until the NPV is equal to the amount of the original investment. Let's look at an example.

Suppose you are thinking of investing $10,000 in a piece of equipment, and the equipment will return $2500 per year for five years. At the end of the fifth year, you can sell the equipment for $1500. Your company has a required rate of return of 11 percent, and you want to know if the IRR of this investment is greater or less than 11 percent. You can analyze this investment with this spreadsheet:

```
File: Investment                REVIEW/ADD/CHANGE          Escape: Main Menu
=======A========B========C========D========E========F========G========H====
   1             Investment Analysis
   2
   3 Investment Amount: $10,000
   4 Discount Rate:          .11
   5 Net Present Value: $10,130
   6
   7
   8  Year 1    Year 2    Year 3    Year 4    Year 5
   9
  10  $2,500    $2,500    $2,500    $2,500    $4,000
  11
  12
  13
  14
  15
  16
  17
  18
------------------------------------------------------------------------------
  C5: (Value, Layout-D0) @NPV(C4,A10...E10)

  Type entry or use █ commands  _                            █-? for Help
```

The @NPV function calculates the present value of future cash flows from an investment.

We begin the analysis by entering each of the yearly cash flows in separate columns, as shown. The last year's cash flow includes the equipment's salvage value, which is the amount it will be sold for at the end of that year.

At the top of the worksheet, we create a reference area that shows the amount originally invested (cell C3), the discount rate (cell C4), and the Net Present Value (cell C5). Cell C4 is referred to in the @NPV formula in cell C5, so that if we change the rate in cell C4, the @NPV formula automatically recalculates. This is the only formula in the spreadsheet.

With this formula entered, we need to find the exact discount rate that will produce an NPV figure of $10,000 in cell C5. We can start with 11 percent, because that is our required rate of return. At 11 percent, the NPV of the investment is still greater than $10,000 (as you can see in the example), so we must try a slightly higher discount rate. We continue trying different rates in cell C4 until the NPV figure in cell C5 is exactly $10,000.

After a little trial and error, we determine that the rate that produces an NPV of exactly $10,000 is 11.48 percent. This is the investment's Internal Rate of Return. Since 11.48 percent is nearly half a percent higher than our required rate of return (11 percent), the investment is a good one from that point of view.

■ **Comments**

You must enter the discount percentage rate as a decimal number (as in our example) when you use the @NPV function. For further information about the Net Present Value function, see @NPV.[175]

Iterative calculations

■ **Definition**

Iterative calculations are successive recalculations needed to solve two or more mutually dependent formulas in the spreadsheet.

■ **Usage**

Most spreadsheet formulas are fairly straightforward—they calculate using the values stored in certain cells as AppleWorks moves through the spreadsheet from top to bottom, or from left to right, depending on how the Standard Values[330] are set to recalculate the spreadsheet. These kinds of formulas can be completely solved with one recalculation of the spreadsheet.

Some formulas, however, require repeated, or *iterative*, calculations before they can be completely solved. Iterative calculations are required with what are called *circular references*—where the result of one or more formulas at the end of a row or the bottom of a column is itself used to calculate the result of a formula in the middle of the row or column. Formulas that rely on the outcome of other formulas are known as *dependent formulas*.

In a circular reference, all dependent formulas would have to be recalculated at the same time for the results in each formula to be accurate, since each formula depends on the outcome of the other. This presents a mathematical "catch-22" situation in that one formula can't come up with the correct value until it receives a correct value from the other formula, and that formula can't come up with the correct value until the first formula produces a correct value. In the AppleWorks spreadsheet, the only way around this problem is to keep recalculating the entire spreadsheet with the Calculate[18] command (⌘-K) until the values produced by these formulas stabilize (don't change any more when you press ⌘-K).

■ **Example**

Suppose you want to pay your salespeople a bonus equal to 10 percent of the company's net profit. The net profit itself, however, is figured as the gross profit minus the bonus you are paying. The spreadsheet might look like this:

```
 File: Bonus Analysis             REVIEW/ADD/CHANGE               Escape: Main Menu
 ========A========B========C========D========E========F========G========H====
    1 Sales Bonus Analysis
    2
    3
    4
    5 Sales                  280000
    6 Cost of Sales          190000
    7 -------------------
    8 Gross Profit            90000    C5-C6
    9 Bonus Paid               9000    C11*.1
   10 -------------------
   11 Net Profit              81000    C8-C9
   12
   13
   14
   15
   16
   17
   18
 ----------------------------------------------------------------------------
 C11: (Value, Layout-F0) +C8-C9

 Type entry or use ⧉ commands  _                        ⧉-? for Help
```

Circular references, where the result of one equation depends on the result of another, require iterative calculations. (The formulas actually in cells C8, C9, and C11 have been entered as labels in column D, so you can see the formulas and their results at the same time.)

After the last formula is entered in cell C11, the spreadsheet automatically recalculates (it recalculates after each entry is made unless you specify otherwise using the Standard Values command), and presents the results shown. This is because the formula in cell C9 returned a value of zero when it was first entered, because there was nothing in cell C11 yet. Then, when the formula in C11 was entered, it initially contained a value of *90,000* (C8 minus C9). When the spreadsheet recalculated (after the formula was entered), cell C9 displayed a value of *9000*, which is 10 percent of the value in cell C11 when C9 recalculated. Then, because of the order in which the cells recalculate, C11 recalculated itself and produced a value of *81,000*—which is C8 minus C9.

Since the *9000* currently in cell C9 is not 10 percent of the *81,000* in cell C11, you can see that this spreadsheet needs to be recalculated, until the values in the two dependent cells (C9 and C11) stabilize with correct values.

If we use the Calculate command (⌂-**K**) to recalculate these formulas, the results will change. In this example, the spreadsheet has to be recalculated four times before the values in cells C9 and C11 stabilize.

An important consideration for multiple recalculation is the display formatting for the dependent cells. In the preceding example, the fourth recalculation would produce the value 8181.9 in cell C9, and 81818.1 in cell C11. This degree of accuracy may cause more iterations of recalculation than necessary for the two cells to stabilize. By using the Layout[146] command (⌘-**L**) to format these cells for Fixed display with no decimal places, which we did in the example, the spreadsheet won't require as many iterations to produce the stabilized values shown below:

```
 File: Bonus Analysis             REVIEW/ADD/CHANGE              Escape: Main Menu
 =======A========B========C========D========E========F========G========H====
   1|Sales Bonus Analysis
   2|
   3|
   4|
   5|Sales                    280000
   6|Cost of Sales            190000
   7|-------------------
   8|Gross Profit              90000   C5-C6
   9|Bonus Paid                 8182   C11*.1
  10|-------------------
  11|Net Profit                81818   C8-C9
  12|
  13|
  14|
  15|
  16|
  17|
  18|
 --------------------------------------------------------------------------
 C11: (Value, Layout-F0) +C8-C9

 Type entry or use ⌘ commands  _                          ⌘-? for Help
```

After four iterative calculations, these circular-reference formulas are finally solved to a meaningful degree of accuracy.

When working with circular references involving iterative calculations, there are two possible solutions to a situation, depending on the structure of the formulas involved: *convergent* and *divergent* results. A convergent result, which was achieved in the preceding example, means that the results produced by the formulas involved will eventually stabilize and further recalculations of the spreadsheet will not change these results significantly. In a divergent situation, as shown in the following example, the results can never stabilize because the mathematical relationship between the formulas makes convergence impossible (the formulas used in column C have been entered as labels in column E for reference).

```
File: Interest Calc.            REVIEW/ADD/CHANGE              Escape: Main Menu
========A========B========C========D========E========F========G========H====
  1|
  2|Interest Calculations
  3|
  4|
  5|Balance              $121.90              C8
  6|Interest Rate             2%              .02
  7|------------------
  8|New Balance          $124.34          C5*(1+C6)
  9|
 10|
 11|
 12|
 13|
 14|
 15|
 16|
 17|
 18|
-----------------------------------------------------------------------------
C8: (Value, Layout-D2) +C5*(1+C6)

Type entry or use ⌂ commands  _                            ⌂-? for Help
```

Recalculating a spreadsheet with divergent circular references will never produce a stable result.

These situations demonstrate the need for careful planning when entering formulas into a spreadsheet, especially when there are circular references involved. There are situations when dependent formulas can appear to converge on a stable result through iterative calculations, then begin to diverge and return meaningless results. Through careful planning, instances of circular references via dependent formulas can be avoided, thus minimizing the chance of calculation error.

A simple way to check your AppleWorks spreadsheet for divergent circular references is to manually recalculate it using the Calculate command, checking to see if any of the values start producing illogical results.

■ **Comments**

AppleWorks doesn't automatically perform iterative calculations when they are needed. You must use the Calculate command each time you want to recalculate the formulas.

You can avoid circular-reference formulas by designing your spreadsheet so that formulas will calculate in the proper order—top to bottom or left to right. For more information see Spreadsheet Planning.[314]

Jump Windows (⌘-J)

- **Definition**

  The *Jump Windows* command (⌘-J) moves the cursor from one window to another in the spreadsheet.

- **Usage**

  Sometimes when you are working with a large spreadsheet you will split the screen into two windows, so you can see two different parts of the spreadsheet at once (see: Window[360]). The cursor, however, is only located (and therefore active) in one window at a time. To move the cursor from one window to the other, simply press the Jump Windows command (⌘-J): The cursor will jump from the current window to the other window.

- **Comments**

  The Jump Windows command is a toggle: Each time you use it, the cursor moves from the current window to the other window, jumping to the first row (in horizontal windows) or column (in vertical windows) on the other side of the window dividing line.

Justify (⌘-J)

- **Definition**

  In the database, the *Justify* command (⌘-J) creates left-justified categories in Labels reports that have more than one category on a line.

- **Usage**

  In a mailing-label report, for example, you might have categories for *City* and *ST/Zip* on the same line. If the entry for a city is small, you might not want the large space that is left between the printed entries for *City* and those for *ST/Zip*. You would use the Justify command to left justify the *ST/Zip* category, so its entries are always printed close to the end of the *City* category's entries.

- **Example**

  Suppose you have a Labels report containing customer information. The report format contains the two categories, *City* and *ST/Zip*, on the same line, as in the example on the next page.

```
File: Customers                    REPORT FORMAT              Escape: Report Menu
Report: Labels
Selection: All records


================================================================================
Name
Company
Street
City    ST/Zip
------------------------Each record will print  6 lines------------------------




------------------------------------------------------------------------------
Use options shown on Help Screen                                    ■-? for Help
```

Labels report formats can contain two or more categories on the same line.

In this report format the two categories, *City* and *ST/Zip*, are not justified. When this report is printed, the entries in these categories will begin printing in the same places each time, so some long entries for *City* will be overwritten by entries for *ST/Zip*. You can see this effect in the following example, where the file has been printed to the screen:

```
File:   Customers                                              Page   1
Report: Labels

Olive Ogilvy
Ace Jackhammer Service
112 Sumter St.
Santa CCA 95550

Wilson Peck
Apex Canning
8904 Fremont St.
San JosCA 95554




Press Space Bar to continue  _                          48K Avail.
```

With categories unjustified, entries are begun in the same position in every record, and some long entries may be overwritten.

To eliminate this problem, you can use the Justify command. The category you want to justify is the *ST/Zip* category. When it is justified, its entries will automatically be printed starting one space after the end of the *City* entry in each record, no matter how long that entry is. To use the Justify command:

1. Place the cursor on the first character in the *ST/Zip* category name on the Report Format screen.

2. Press the Justify command (⌂-**J**). A less than (<) symbol will appear at the beginning of *ST/Zip* to indicate that the category is now justified.

3. When the report is printed now, the entry in the *ST/Zip* category will always begin one space after the end of the entry in the *City* category.

```
File:    Customers                                    Page  1
Report: Labels


Olive Ogilvy
Ace Jackhammer Service
112 Sumter St.
Santa Clara CA 95550

Wilson Peck
Apex Canning
8904 Fremont St.
San Jose CA 95554




Press Space Bar to continue  _              48K Avail.
```

The Justify command prevents one category's entries from overwriting the entries of another category on the same line.

■ **Comments**

You can justify as many categories on a Labels report as you like, but it only applies to categories that are on the same line and to the right of another category. If there are three categories on the same line, for example, you would probably want to justify the two categories to the right.

The Justify command isn't necessary or active in Tables reports.

K

■ **Definition**

The symbol *K* represents one thousand.

■ **Usage**

In computing terms, the symbol *K* represents roughly 1000 bytes, or one *Kilobyte*, of storage on a floppy disk or in RAM.[256] Strictly speaking, however, one *K* is equal to 1024 bytes, so when the Desktop space indicator in the lower-right corner of the screen shows 55K available, you actually have 56,320 bytes of storage space to work with.

Computer memory, space on disks, and files are almost always measured in thousands of bytes, or *K*.

Keyboard

■ **Definition**

The *keyboard* is the device on which you enter commands and type information into AppleWorks.

■ **Usage**

The keyboard on your Apple computer works much like the keyboard on a standard typewriter. The only keys with symbols on them that don't produce corresponding characters on the screen are the ⌂, , and Arrow keys.

The symbol keys: ⌂ is pressed in combination with various letter keys to issue commands in AppleWorks. Pressing ⌂ and **S** at the same time, for example, saves the current file to disk. The commands you type with ⌂ are explained in the individual entries.

The key does not currently perform any function in AppleWorks—it is reserved for future enhancements.

The Arrow keys are used to move the cursor[50] around the screen, or to view different parts of a file.

The labeled keys: ESC exits the current AppleWorks screen and returns to the previous screen, or lets you cancel certain operations (See: Interacting with AppleWorks[131]).

TAB moves the cursor.[50]

The **CONTROL** key is pressed in combination with other keys to perform AppleWorks and Apple-system functions. Pressing **CONTROL** and **Y** at the same time, for example, deletes the data on the current line from the cursor position to the right edge of the line, cell, or category.

SHIFT works exactly like the shift key on a typewriter: When you press it and a letter, number, or symbol key, you type a capital letter (if you're pressing a letter key) or the upper symbol shown on the keycap. **SHIFT** does not have any effect when pressed together with the ⌂, , or the Arrow keys.

CAPS LOCK causes every letter key to type a capital letter on the screen. When you press **CAPS LOCK**, it locks down; if you press the key again, it releases. In the down position **CAPS LOCK** produces capital letters, but unlike the shift-lock key on a typewriter it doesn't produce the upper symbols on number or symbol keys: You must press **SHIFT** to produce the upper symbols on symbol or number keys. **CAPS LOCK** doesn't have any effect when pressed together with ⌂, , or the Arrow keys.

RETURN has different effects, depending on which AppleWorks application you are using. In the word processor, it inserts a carriage return in a document and moves the cursor down one line. In the spreadsheet and database, it enters the data you have typed in a cell or category.

DELETE moves the cursor one place to the left each time you press it. If there is a character to the left of the cursor when you press **DELETE**, that character is deleted when the cursor moves into its position.

RESET is used to reset the Apple system. It is not used in AppleWorks, but it can be used to reset the computer and load another program when you're finished working with AppleWorks (see: Reset[274]).

Layout (⌂-L)

- **Definition**
  The *Layout* command (⌂-L) changes the arrangement of database data or the appearance of a spreadsheet on the screen.

- **Usage**
  Use the Layout command to alter the appearance or formatting of spreadsheet or database data on the Review/Add/Change screen. The layout options are very different in the spreadsheet and database.

Layout options in the spreadsheet
With the spreadsheet's layout options, you can alter the formatting of values or labels in one or more cells, rows, columns, or a block of cells; you can also change the width of one or more columns; and you can protect one or more cells, rows, columns, or a block against changes to their contents.

- **Selecting a layout area**
  If you are changing the layout of only one cell, you must place the cursor on that cell before pressing the Layout command. If you are changing the layout of more than one cell, you must first place the cursor at the top, bottom, left,

146

or right corner of the area whose layout you want to change, and then press the Layout command (⌂-L).

1. Place the cursor on the cell whose layout you want to change, or at the top, bottom, left, or right corner of the area you want to change, and press the Layout command (⌂-L).

2. When you press the Layout command in the spreadsheet, the prompt line shows this menu:

   Layout? Entry Rows Columns Block

Choose the option for the kind of area whose layout you want to change by pressing either the first letter of an option, or by using the Arrow keys to highlight one and pressing **RETURN**. Depending on the area you select, you have different layout options.

■ The Entry layouts

If you choose *Entry* as the area whose layout you want to change, the layout options you select will affect only the cell where your cursor is currently located. The prompt line displays this menu of options:

   Layout? Value format Label format Protection

Value format: The *Value format* option changes the format of values in a cell. When you choose this option, you see this menu:

   Value format? Fixed Dollars Commas Percent Appropriate Standard

Fixed format displays numbers with a specific number of decimal places. When you choose the *Fixed* format, you are prompted to enter the number of decimal places (from 0 to 7) you want the value in the selected cell to have.

Dollars format displays numbers as dollars and cents, with a dollar sign in front of them. When you choose the *Dollars* format, you are prompted to enter the number of decimal places you want the value in the selected cell to have.

Commas format displays numbers with commas every three digits to mark thousands, hundreds of thousands, and so on. When you choose the Commas format, you will also be prompted to enter the number of decimal places you want the value in the selected cell to have.

Percent format displays numbers with a percent sign (%) after them. When you choose the *Percent* format, you will also be prompted to enter the number of decimal places you want the value in the selected cell to have. Bear in mind, however, that this option will multiply the value contained in the cell by 100, so if you want a cell to display *2%* after being formatted for percent, the value would have to be entered as *.02*.

Appropriate format displays numbers as you type them, as closely as possible. This is the default *Value format* layout option in the spreadsheet. When you enter numbers into cells with this option, decimal places will appear as they are when you enter each number, but you can't use dollar signs, commas, or percent signs with those numbers.

Standard format lets you restore the selected cell back to the format options you have set using the Standard Values[350] command. Use this option to remove a custom format option from a cell (to change a *Dollars*-formatted cell back to *Appropriate* formatting, for example, or whatever the Standard Values for that cell have been set to). If the Standard Values haven't been changed, this command will restore a cell to Appropriate, the default cell layout.

Label format: The *Label format* option changes the format of the label in the cell you have selected. When you choose the *Label format* option, you see this menu:

> **Label Format? Left justify Right justify Center Standard**

Left justify aligns the label in the selected cell flush with the left edge of that cell. This is the default cell layout for labels.

Right justify aligns the label in the selected cell flush with the right edge of that cell.

Center centers the label between the left and right edges of the selected cell.

Standard sets the default spreadsheet label format option to the one you have set using the Standard Values command for the selected cell. If no Standard Values have been set for that cell, it is returned to the default format, which is left justified.

Protection: The *Protection* option lets you allow or exclude the entry of certain kinds of data in the cell you have selected. Note, however, that in order for *Protection* options to work, the *Protection* option under the Standard Values menu must be set to *Yes*, its default setting. (See: Standard Values.[330])

When you choose the *Protection* option, this menu is displayed:

Allow? Labels only Values only Nothing Anything

Labels only allows you to enter only text into the cell you have selected, and not values.

Values only allows you to enter only values into the cell you have selected, and not text (labels).

Nothing essentially "freezes" the contents of the cell, so that you're unable to enter anything into the cell you have selected.

Anything allows you to enter any type of label or value in the cell you have selected. This is the default *Protection* option.

■ The Rows layouts

When you choose *Rows* from the Layout menu, the row the cursor is currently on is highlighted, and you are prompted to highlight the rows whose layout you want to change. By using the ↑ or ↓ keys, you can highlight rows above or below the cursor's current position. When you want to change the layout of rows, therefore, you must first move the cursor to the top or bottom row in the group you want to change before pressing the Layout command.

After you press **RETURN** to select the highlighted rows, you are presented with the same menu that is displayed for the Entry option:

Layout? Value format Label format Protection

These options are identical to the options explained in the section on Entry layouts.

■ The Columns layouts

When you choose *Columns* from the Layout menu, the column the cursor is currently in is highlighted, and you are prompted to highlight the columns whose layout you want to change. By using the → or ← keys, you can highlight columns to the left or right of the cursor's current position.

After you press **RETURN** to select the highlighted columns, the following menu is displayed:

Layout? Value format Label format Protection Column width

The first three options on this menu are identical to the options in the Entry and Rows menus.

The *Column Width* option lets you change the width of the column or columns you have selected. After choosing this option, press ⌘-→ to make the selected column(s) wider, and ⌘-← to make the selected column(s) narrower, and press **RETURN** after the columns are the widths you want them. Spreadsheet columns can be from one character to 75 characters wide.

■ The Block layouts

When you choose *Block* from the Layout menu, the prompt line instructs you to move the cursor to highlight the block of cells you want formatted, and then press **RETURN**. After you highlight the block of cells and then press **RETURN**, the prompt line changes to the Layout menu discussed in the section on Entry layouts on page 146.

Comment: All of the spreadsheet-label and value-format options are described in the entry, Spreadsheet Overview.[298]

Layout options in the database

The layout options in the database are used to change the appearance of the Review/Add/Change screen. The Layout command lets you change the position of categories, change the width of categories in the Multiple Record layouts, delete ("hide") categories from the layout, or insert previously deleted (hidden) categories into the layout. Because it lets you delete or insert previously deleted categories or change the position of categories, the Layout command is your means of selecting the specific categories of data you see on the screen, and arranging their display.

As explained in their individual entries, there are two formats for viewing data in the database: as *Single Record layout*[293] or *Multiple Record layout.*[168] Each has its own set of unique layout options, and changing the layout of records in one format does not affect the layout in the other. The options for each format are covered in the following sections.

Layout options in Multiple Record layouts: When you press the Layout command (⌘-L) from the Multiple Record layout's Review/Add/Change screen, the Change Record Layout screen then appears, as shown on the next page.

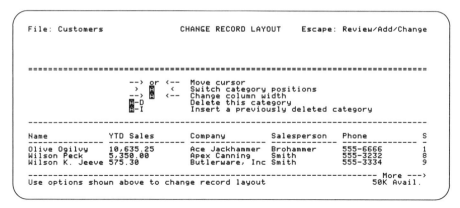

```
File: Customers          CHANGE RECORD LAYOUT    Escape: Review/Add/Change


========================================================================
                    --> or <--   Move cursor
                     >  ⌘  <     Switch category positions
                    -->  ⌘  <--   Change column width
                    ⌘-D          Delete this category
                    ⌘-I          Insert a previously deleted category
------------------------------------------------------------------------

Name            YTD Sales       Company        Salesperson  Phone        S
----------------------------------------------------------------------------
Olive Ogilvy    10,635.25       Ace Jackhammer Brohammer    555-6666     1
Wilson Peck     5,350.00        Apex Canning   Smith        555-3232     8
Wilson K. Jeeve 575.30          Butlerware, Inc Smith       555-3334     9
---------------------------------------------------------------- More --->
Use options shown above to change record layout              50K Avail.
```

This Change Record Layout screen lets you alter the appearance of a Multiple Record database layout.

The available options for changing the record layout appear at the top of the Change Record Layout screen. Here's how they work:

☐ ⌘ = < or ⌘ = > change the position of a category. To change a category position:

1. Use the → and ← keys to move the cursor until it is on the category whose position you want to change.

2. Use ⌘-> or ⌘-< to move the category to the right or left.

☐ ⌘-→ and ⌘-← change the width of a category. To do this:

1. Move the cursor to the category whose width you want to change.

2. Use ⌘-→ or ⌘-← to make the category wider or narrower.

☐ ⌘-D is used to delete a category. When you delete a category with the Layout command, you don't remove that category from the file, you just remove, or "hide," it from view on the layout. To do this:

1. Move the cursor to the category you want to delete.

2. Press ⌘-D, and the category will disappear from view.

☐ ⌘-I is used to insert a previously deleted category. This command has no effect if you haven't deleted any categories from the layout. If you have deleted categories from the layout, pressing ⌘-I displays a list of previously deleted categories, from which you can choose a category to insert at the current cursor position, as shown in the following example.

Inserted categories always appear at the cursor's current position, and the category the cursor was on and all categories to the right of it are moved to the right.

```
File: Customers              INSERT A CATEGORY   Escape: Change record layout




================================================================================
  1.  Street
  2.  City
  3.  ST/Zip







--------------------------------------------------------------    -------------
Type number, or use arrows, then press Return  _              50K Avail.
```

To insert a previously deleted category into a database layout or report format, you must choose from a list of deleted categories.

To insert a previously deleted category:

1. Place the cursor on the category where you want the inserted category to appear, and press Ꮕ-I.

2. The list of previously deleted categories will appear. Move the highlight bar to the category you want to insert, or type the number of the category, and press **RETURN**. The display will change back to the Review/Add/Change or Report Format screen you were working with, and the category you selected will have been inserted at the cursor position, and the category the cursor was on and all categories to the right of it will have been moved to the right.

Changing direction of cursor movement on the Multiple Record layout: When you are through changing the layout of the Multiple Record layout screen, press **ESC**. When you do, AppleWorks will ask you *Which direction should the cursor go when you press Return?* and present you with two choices, *Down (standard)* or *Right.* This option allows you to change the direction the cursor will move when you press **RETURN** when the Multiple Record layout screen is displayed. Instead of the cursor moving down to the same category of the next record (*Down,* which is the default), you can choose to have the cursor move to the next category of the same record (*Right*).

Layout options in Single Record layouts: In Single Record layouts of the Review/Add/Change screen, the only layout option you have is to change the position of a category. When you press the Layout command from the Single Record layout's Review/Add/Change screen, you see the Single Record's Change Record Layout screen, as shown in this example:

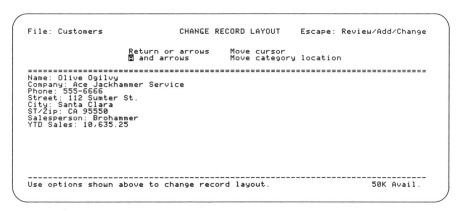

Pressing ⌂-L from a Single Record layout produces this screen, which lets you change category positions.

As you can see at the top of the screen in the example, you can't widen or narrow categories or insert or delete categories on Single Record layouts.

⌂ and an Arrow key are used to move a category up, down, left, or right on the display, depending on which Arrow key is used. You can move categories anywhere on this screen you want, even partially on top of each other. To move a category, however, the cursor must be placed on the first letter of the name of the category you want to move; otherwise, the ⌂ and Arrow keys have no effect. Also, before you can move a category up or down, you must first move it to the fourth character after the colon of the category name that is immediately above or below it. For instance, suppose in the last example that you want to move the *Salesperson* category down to the *YTD Sales* line. You would first place the cursor on the *S* of *Salesperson*, use ⌂-→ to move the category over the comma in *10,635.25*, then, finally, use ⌂-↓ to move the *Salesperson* category down.

Changing direction of cursor movement on the Single Record layout: When you press **ESC** to leave the Change Record Layout screen for the Single Record layout, and if you've reordered the categories or put two categories on the same line, AppleWorks asks you what the cursor direction will be when

Return is pressed. The two options presented to you are *Order in which you defined categories* and *Left to right, top to bottom*. If you choose the first option, the cursor will move from category to category in the order you defined the categories when you first created the datafile, regardless of their position and order on the Single Record layout screen. If you choose the second option, the cursor will then move from category to category, left to right, top to bottom, based on the arrangement of categories you created in the Change Record Layout screen for the Single Record layout.

Len indicator

■ **Definition**

The *Len indicator* shows the length of lines in a Tables[79] database report.

■ **Usage**

When you create a Tables database report, the word *Len*, short for *Length*, appears with a number below it at the right margin of the report on the Report Format screen. The number indicates the width of that report's lines in characters. In this example, the printed report will be 80 characters wide:

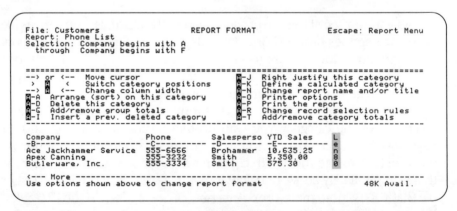

The Len indicator appears at the right margin of a Tables database report to show how wide the report will be when printed. (Since this report is too wide to be viewed completely on the screen, it has been scrolled to the right.)

■ **Comment**

When a report is too wide to be displayed completely on the Report Format screen, you may have to scroll to the right to see the *Len* indicator.

154

List

■ **Definition**

A *list* is a collection of values separated by commas specified in the argument of a spreadsheet function.

■ **Usage**

When you enter a spreadsheet function, you can either specify a list of values or cell coordinates in the argument[7] for the function to calculate, or a continuous range of cells (see: Spreadsheet Overview[298]). A list is a collection of values and/or cell coordinates separated by commas.

Unlike a range, which must be a collection of continuous cells (for example, A1 through A5), a list can contain values, expressions, or cell coordinates from anywhere in the spreadsheet. Depending on the requirements of the function you use, each item in a list can be one number, a cell coordinate, an expression, a complete formula, or a range of cells. Here are some examples of possible lists:

(A1,A3,A5,247,C302,1000)

(2,47,60,D255)

(A1,A15,(32 ∗ A47),A9)

(B35,@SUM(C1.C40),973)

@LOOKUP

■ **Structure**

@LOOKUP(value,range)

■ **Definition**

@LOOKUP is a spreadsheet function that uses a search value you supply in the argument to sequentially search a list of cells called a *lookup table*, find the largest entry in the table that is less than or equal to the search value, and then return the value located in a second table set up next to the lookup table from the cell adjacent to the entry it finds in the lookup table.

■ **Usage**

@LOOKUP is used with two adjacent sections of rows or columns set up as tables of numbers. A two-column table might look like this:

Column searched:	Column matched:
15	14
18	2
20	8
22	5

The two-row table of these numbers would look like:

| Row Searched | 15 | 18 | 20 | 22 |
| Row Matched | 14 | 2 | 8 | 5 |

The column to the left or the row on top contains values that are sequentially searched for the search value you specify in the *value* part of the argument. The column to the right or the row on the bottom contains values that are returned based on the entry found by the search value. @LOOKUP is used when you want the entries on one list to be tied to entries on a second list. The search value you specify as the first part of a @LOOKUP argument is compared with the entries in the left-hand column or top row of numbers (called the *lookup table*), and @LOOKUP finds the entry that is less than or equal to that value.

The range of cells specified as the lookup table must be continuous—there can be no blank cells or label cells in it—and the numbers must be arranged in ascending order. The values in the bottom or right group of cells don't have to be in ascending order, but they can't contain any blank cells or label cells.

■ **Example**

The two columns in the following spreadsheet contain related kinds of information: hours worked and employee numbers. In a large list, you wouldn't easily be able to locate a specific entry by scrolling through it, so you might use the @LOOKUP function to search for a value instead.

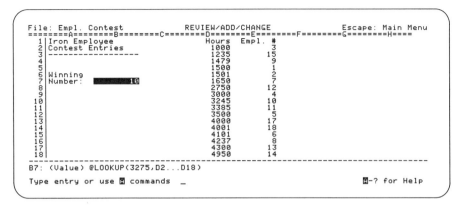

```
File: Empl. Contest          REVIEW/ADD/CHANGE             Escape: Main Menu
========A========B========C========D========E========F========G========H====
    1│Iron Employee                    Hours    Empl. #
    2│Contest Entries                  1000           3
    3│-------------------              1235          15
    4│                                 1479           9
    5│                                 1500           1
    6│Winning                          1501           2
    7│Number:        ░░░░░░10          1650           7
    8│                                 2750          12
    9│                                 3000           4
   10│                                 3245          10
   11│                                 3385          11
   12│                                 3500           5
   13│                                 4000          17
   14│                                 4001          18
   15│                                 4101           6
   16│                                 4237           8
   17│                                 4300          13
   18│                                 4950          14
  -----------------------------------------------------------------------------
  B7: (Value) @LOOKUP(3275,D2...D18)

  Type entry or use 🄰 commands  _                          🄰-? for Help
```

The @LOOKUP function locates a value in the first of two lists of related entries and returns the value in the adjacent cell.

In this example, there is an employee contest underway in which each employee is asked to guess how many hours the most durable worker put in the previous year. Each guess is listed in column D, and the number of the employee who made each guess is listed in column E. With the @LOOKUP function, you can search for a certain number of hours worked, and automatically have the spreadsheet tell you which employee came closest to the target without going over. The @LOOKUP formula entered in cell B7 and displayed in the prompt line is used to identify the employee who came closest to guessing the actual number of hours worked without going over it. The formula compares the list in D2...D18 against 3275, locates 3245 as the largest number that is less than or equal to it, matches 3245 with the number 10 in the adjacent column, and then displays the number 10 in cell B7.

■ Comments

The two columns or rows in a lookup table must be directly adjacent. Make sure there isn't a blank row or column between them.

The values in the top or left group of cells must be in ascending order, because the spreadsheet searches the list sequentially. If the values are not in order, @LOOKUP may end its search before finishing the entire list because it came upon a value greater than the search value. Also, if the @LOOKUP function comes across a blank cell, or a cell containing a label in either table, an ERROR message will be displayed in the cell containing @LOOKUP.

If the search value is smaller than the first entry or all of the entries in the list, the message *NA* will be returned. If the matching value in the lower, or right-hand group of cells is missing, or if it is a text entry instead of a number, the message *ERROR* will be returned.

Main Menu

- **Definition**

The *Main Menu* is the pathway to every other function in AppleWorks.

- **Usage**

The Main Menu lists six options:

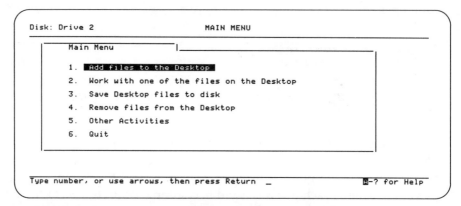

The Main Menu offers you access to all AppleWorks activities.

Option 1—Add files to the Desktop: Choosing this option accesses the Add Files menu.[2] From it you can load a file from a disk or create a new file.

Option 2—Work with one of the files on the Desktop: If there is only one file on the Desktop when this option is chosen, the Review/Add/Change screen for that file will be displayed. If there is more than one file on the Desktop at the time, the screen will show the Desktop Index,[98] and you can then select the file you want to work with from the list of files shown.

Option 3—Save Desktop files to disk: This option accesses the Save Files screen,[282] and you can choose the file(s) you want to save from the list of files presented. Saving files with this option does not remove them from the Desktop.

Option 4—Remove files from the Desktop: This option accesses the Remove Files screen.[266] Use the → key to choose files from the list that you want to remove. If you select a new file, or a file you loaded from disk and made changes to, you'll be given the option to either save the new or changed file to disk, or throw out the new/changed file.

Option 5—Other Activities: Choosing this option produces the Other Activities menu,[178] from which you can get a listing of all files on a disk, delete files on disk, create subdirectories on a disk, specify printer information, format disks, and specify different disk drives for accessing files.

Option 6—Quit: To exit the AppleWorks program, you choose *Quit*. The Quit screen[255] will appear, and you will be asked to confirm that you really want to quit. If there are files on the Desktop that have not been saved, the Quit screen will display each file name in turn, and prompt you to either save it or throw out the changes you have made to it. AppleWorks won't allow you to quit if you have unsaved files on the Desktop, unless you specifically tell it for each file that it's all right to do so.

After you have saved or thrown out all your changes to the Desktop files, the Quit command exits to ProDOS,[246] and you will be prompted to enter the ProDOS prefix, then the pathname[188] of the next application.

Margin indicator

- **Definition**

  The *Margin indicator* shows the right-hand margin of a Multiple Record database layout when you are changing the record layout.

- **Usage**

  The Margin indicator appears vertically at the right-hand edge of the Change Layout Screen for Multiple Record database layouts, as in this example:

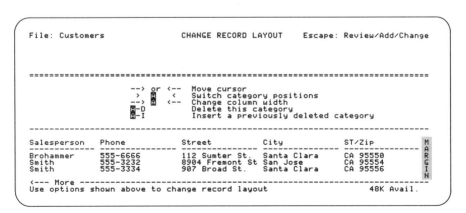

The Margin indicator shows you that there are no more categories to the right on a Multiple Record database layout.

The Margin indicator only appears when you use the Layout[146] command (⌘-L) to change the Multiple Record layout of a database file. If there are more categories in the file than can be shown on the screen at once, the word *More* will appear in the lower right corner of the screen followed by a > symbol, indicating that other categories can be seen by scrolling to the right using the → key. The Margin indicator won't appear until you scroll as far to the right in the layout as you can go.

@MAX

- **Structure**

  @MAX(argument)

- **Definition**

  @MAX is a spreadsheet function that finds the largest value in a specified range of cells or list[155] of values or cell references contained within its argument, and displays it in the cell where the function is entered.

- **Usage**

  If you use a list in the argument of a @MAX formula, the list can contain mathematical expressions or other functions. You must separate items in a list with commas, and the argument, whether it be a list or range, must be enclosed in parentheses.

The argument can include:	*Such as:*
Cell ranges	@MAX(L4...L23)
Lists	@MAX(E1...E12,F5...G5,H2,39)
Functions or mathematical expressions	@MAX(((F5+F7)−B9),@SUM(E1...G5))

■ **Example**

The following spreadsheet contains three separate lists of product totals. The @MAX formula entered in cell D17 and displayed in the prompt line reveals the highest number of small widgets:

```
File: Widget Count              REVIEW/ADD/CHANGE              Escape: Main Menu
========A========B========C========D========E========F========G========H====
  1|           Regional Widget Count
  2|-------------------------------------------------------
  3|           Big    Medium   Small
  4|
  5|East        35      89      247
  6|West       200      92      118
  7|North       90      33      230
  8|South      500     110       88
  9|Canada      31      77      412
 10|Europe     450      65      300
 11|Mexico      69     789      231
 12|Brazil     287      21      150
 13|Albania     22      24       86
 14|Gibraltar   31      32      109
 15|
 16|Lowest      22      21       86
 17|Highest    500     789      412
 18|
-----------------------------------------------------------------------------
D17: (Value) @MAX(D5...D14)

Type entry or use █ commands  _                        █-? for Help
```

The @MAX function is used to return the largest value in a list or range.

■ **Comments**

You can also nest other functions within the @MAX function's argument. If you want to determine whether the sum of values in a range (D5...D14) is larger than 35, for example, you could enter a formula that looks like this: *@MAX((@SUM(D5...D14)),35).*

@MIN is a related function that returns the smallest value in a list or range contained in its argument.

@MIN

■ **Structure**

@MIN(argument)

■ **Definition**

@MIN is a spreadsheet function that finds the smallest value in a specified range of cells or list[155] of values or cell references, and then displays it in the cell where the function is entered.

■ **Usage**

If you specify a list, the list can contain mathematical expressions or other functions. The items in a list must be separated by commas, and the argument, whether it be a list or a range, must be enclosed in parentheses.

The argument can include:	Such as:
Cell ranges	@MIN(L4...L23)
Lists	@MIN(E1...E12,F5...G5,H2,39)
Functions or mathematical expressions	@MIN(((F5+F7)−B9),@SUM(E1...G5))

■ **Example**

The following spreadsheet contains three separate lists of product totals. The @MIN formula entered in cell D16 and displayed in the prompt line reveals the lowest number of small widgets:

```
File: Widget Count                REVIEW/ADD/CHANGE              Escape: Main Menu
========A=========B=========C=========D=========E=========F=========G========H====
   1|          Regional Widget Count
   2|------------------------------------------------------------
   3|              Big    Medium    Small
   4|
   5|East           35       89      247
   6|West          200       92      118
   7|North          90       33      230
   8|South         500      110       88
   9|Canada         31       77      412
  10|Europe        450       65      300
  11|Mexico         69      789      231
  12|Brazil        287       21      150
  13|Albania        22       24       86
  14|Gibraltar      31       32      109
  15|
  16|Lowest         22       21       86
  17|Highest       500      789      412
  18|
------------------------------------------------------------------
D16: (Value) @MIN(D5...D14)

Type entry or use ▤ commands  _                          ▤-? for Help
```

The @MIN function is used to return the smallest value in a list or range.

■ **Comments**

You can also use nested functions within the function's argument. If you want to determine whether the sum of values in a given range (B14...B25) is smaller than 35, for example, you could enter a formula that looks like this: @MIN((((@SUM(B14...B25))),35).

@MAX is a related function that returns the largest value in a list or range contained in its argument.

Move (⌂-M)

■ **Definition**

The *Move* command (⌂-M) is used to move portions of data within word-processor, spreadsheet, or database files, or between any of these files and the Clipboard.[35]

■ **Usage**

The Move command works slightly differently in each application, but the general procedure is the same:

1. Place the cursor at the beginning of the data you want to move.

2. Press the Move command (⌂-M). At this point, the prompt line in the word processor and spreadsheet will give you the option of moving (1) within the document or worksheet, (2) to the Clipboard (cut), or (3) from the Clipboard (paste). If you want to move the data to another file of the same type, choose to move to the Clipboard. If you only want to move the section within the same document or spreadsheet, simply press **RETURN** to accept the default option of moving within the document. In the database, you only have the options of moving data to or from the Clipboard.

3. Use the Arrow keys to highlight the data you want to move, and then press **RETURN**.

4. If you are moving data to the Clipboard, the data will be removed from the file and placed on the Clipboard. If you are moving data within the file, move the cursor to the place where you want to relocate the data, and then press **RETURN**. The data will be moved there. If you are moving data from the Clipboard, the data will appear starting at whatever position the cursor was at before you chose the Move command.

The following sections in this entry explain the procedures for using Move in the word-processor, spreadsheet, and database applications.

Moving data in the word processor

Suppose you are working with this sales letter:

```
File: Sales Letter                 REVIEW/ADD/CHANGE              Escape: Main Menu
=====|====|====|====|====|====|====|====|====|====|====|====|====|====|====|===
December 13, 1985

Mr. Ed Frobish
Frobish Linen Service
335 Ramona Ave.
San Jose, CA 95551

Dear Ed:

I wanted to tell you how much all of us at Acme Widgets appreciate your
business.  We think you're a ^super^ customer!  That's why we wanted you to
be the first to know about our new Widget Convertible--the sturdiest, most
flexible, most cost-effective widget around.

I'd like to schedule a time to drop by your office and demonstrate the
advantages of the new Widget Convertible, so I'll be giving you a call
during the next week to make an appointment.

In the meantime, think what the world's first all-purpose widget will mean
to your profits!
----------------------------------------------------------------------------
Type entry or use ⌂ commands              Line 13  Column 12      ⌂-? for Help
```

Use the Move command to rearrange text in the word processor.

You decide to rearrange the text of the first paragraph, beginning the letter with the second sentence and combining the first sentence with it. To make these changes, you will have to use the Move command to move the second sentence. Here's how to do this:

1. Place the cursor on the first character in the second sentence (*W*).

2. Press the Move command (⌂-**M**).

3. The prompt line will show the three options for moving text: Choose *Within document* by pressing **RETURN**.

4. Use the Arrow keys to highlight the second sentence and press **RETURN**.

5. Move the cursor to the place where you want the sentence relocated (the first character in the first sentence), and press **RETURN**: The sentence will be moved, and the remainder of the document will rearrange itself to compensate for the new text order.

6. Now, you can replace the exclamation point at the end of the new first sentence with a comma, and add the word *and*.

7. Because you moved only the second sentence and not the spaces around it, you will now have to delete the two extra spaces at the end of your new opening sentence.

164

Comments: You can move up to 250 lines of word-processor text at a time with the Move command. Blank lines count as moved lines. If you move lines to the Clipboard, you can move them back into the same file, or open another word-processor file and move the data into it. Unlike the Copy[40] command, once you move data from the Clipboard, it is empty again.

Moving data in the spreadsheet

Suppose you're working with this *Cost of Sales* spreadsheet:

```
File: Cost of Sales              REVIEW/ADD/CHANGE             Escape: Main Menu
========A========B========C========D========E========F========G========H====
  1|Acme Widget Company - Widget Sales Costs, Q4, 1985
  2
  3
  4|Materials                        Oct      Nov      Dec      Qtr
  5|-----------------                ===      ===      ===      ===
  6
  7|Widget Oil                      1200     1410      960     2370
  8|Steel                           2500     3250     3000     8750
  9|Copper                          1000     1175      800     2975
 10|Magnesium                       1250     1100     1250     3600
 11|Grease                           120      150      135      405
 12|Rags                              50       50       50      150
 13
 14|Labor
 15|-----------------
 16|Salaries                        3000     3000     3000     9000
 17|Commissions                     2250     2250     2250     6750
 18|Hourly Wages                    2850     2850     2850     8550
  -----------------------------------------------------------------------
G17: (Value) @SUM(D17...F17)

Type entry or use ⌂ commands  _                              ⌂-? for Help
```

You can move entire rows or entire columns in the spreadsheet.

You decide that you would rather place the row of commission expenses (row 17) below the row of hourly wage expenses (row 18). To rearrange the spreadsheet as you want it, you can use the Move command:

1. Place the cursor anywhere in the row you want to move (row 17).

2. Press the Move command (⌂-**M**).

3. The prompt line will ask you where you want to move the data. Choose *Within worksheet* by pressing **RETURN**.

4. The prompt line will ask if you want to move rows or columns. Choose *Rows*.

5. The row in which your cursor is located will be highlighted. You can use the Arrow keys to highlight additional rows to be moved, but in this case you only want to move the one row, so just press **RETURN**.

6. Move the cursor to the row *below* where you want to relocate the data (row 19), and press **RETURN**. The *Commissions* row will be moved to where the hourly wage expenses row was, and the *Hourly Wages* row will be moved up to fill the space vacated by the *Commissions* row.

- **Comments**

You can move up to 250 spreadsheet rows or 125 columns at a time.

When moving rows or columns within a worksheet, the new position of the moved rows or columns depends on whether the rows are being moved up or down relative to their original position, and whether the columns are being moved left or right relative to their original position.

If you move rows *down* (below their original positions), the moved rows will appear starting one row *above* the row you placed the cursor on and the other rows will be adjusted accordingly. If you move rows *up* (above their original positions), the moved rows will appear beginning in the same row the cursor is on and the other rows will be adjusted accordingly.

If you move columns to the *right* of their original positions, the moved columns will appear beginning one column to the left of the column the cursor is in. And if you move columns to the *left* of their original positions, the moved columns will appear beginning in the column the cursor is in.

If you move spreadsheet data to the Clipboard, you can then move it from the Clipboard into the same file, or into another spreadsheet file.

Moving data in the database

Suppose you are working with this customer file:

```
File: Customers              REVIEW/ADD/CHANGE              Escape: Main Menu
Selection: All records


Name              YTD Sales  Company                  Salesperson    Phone
==========================================================================
Olive Ogilvy      10,635.25  Ace Jackhammer Service   Brohammer      555-6666
Fortuna Maldonado  2,500.85  Furniture City           Brohammer      555-2222
Barney Flint       3,257.60  Howard's U-Rent 'Em      Brohammer      555-7608
James Pennington     100.25  Linda's Typewriter Repair Brohammer     555-4443
Aldo Pastarelli      355.90  Pesto's Pasta            Brohammer      555-1111
Arnold Ormsby        787.35  Flecko Paints            Jones          555-4567
Walter Canary        125.60  Flippo Dog Food          Jones          555-8606
Fred Fong          4,675.20  Fong Machine Tools       Jones          555-8765
Boris Boronzhova  12,875.95  Jetson Steel             Jones          555-8787
Wilson Peck        5,350.00  Apex Canning             Smith          555-3232
Wilson K. Jeeves     575.30  Butlerware, Inc.         Smith          555-3334
Mort Drucker       1,025.00  Drucker Drayage          Smith          555-2345
Edwina Gumm           87.50  Fritzi Fashions          Smith          555-7890
Ed Frobish        15,325.00  Frobish Linen Service    Smith          555-1234
Alex Abidikian     1,024.00  Imperial Dry Cleaning    Smith          555-0505
--------------------------------------------------------------------------
Type entry or use ⌂ commands                               ⌂-? for Help
```

The Move command moves entire records in the database.

You want to move all of salesperson Brohammer's records to the bottom of the list. To make this move:

1. Place the cursor on the first record in the file.

2. Press the Move command (⌂-M).

3. The prompt line will show the database move options, *To clipboard (cut)* and *From clipboard (paste)*. Choose *To clipboard (cut)* by pressing **RETURN**.

4. Highlight Brohammer's records by pressing ↓, and press **RETURN** when you're done. The records will be placed on the Clipboard, and the other records in the file will move up to fill in the space.

When you move records from the Clipboard into a database file, the moved data appears where the cursor was located when you chose the Move command, and the record the cursor was on and all records under it are moved down. Since you want Brohammer's records to appear *below* the last record in the file, you must move data twice:

5. Place the cursor on the last record (the final Smith record), press the Move command again, and choose *From clipboard (paste)* as the option. Brohammer's records will appear above the bottom record in the file.

6. Move the cursor to the last record in the file, and press the Move command again. Choose the option, *To clipboard (cut)*, and press **RETURN**. Since the record you want to move is already highlighted, press **RETURN** again to select it. The record will be moved to the Clipboard.

7. Now, move the cursor to the first of Brohammer's records, press the Move command, choose *From clipboard (paste)*, and the record will be placed where the first Brohammer record was, and the Brohammer records will be moved down. Brohammer's records will now be the last ones on the list.

Comments: You cannot move data directly within a database file without using the Clipboard. When you paste database records into another database file, it is important to remember that categories will be pasted in by position—that is, the first category of information in the data file you are moving the records from will be pasted in the first category of information in the data file you are moving records to. It doesn't matter if the names are different, or if the type of information contained in the category is different—AppleWorks always pastes information based on category position. Also, if there aren't as many categories in the destination data file as in the original data file, AppleWorks will truncate, or cut off, any extra categories and the information in those categories will be lost. So, when moving records between two data files, make sure that each has the same number of categories, and that each corresponding category contains the same type of information.

You can move up to 250 records at once to the Clipboard, providing you have enough memory for the Clipboard. If the Desktop is nearly full, for example, AppleWorks will only allow you to move a small portion of the 250-record maximum to the Clipboard—you'll have to remove some files from the Desktop in order to move more at once.

The Move command is useful when you must split a database file because it has become too large. If the *Customers* file grew to 800 records, for example, you might be close to running out of file space. You could create a new file with the same data categories in the same order, and then move some of the records (for example, the records with customer last names beginning with M-Z) from the first file into the second file. This way, you would have two files, each of which contained part of your data.

Multiple Record layout

- **Definition**
  The *Multiple Record layout* is one of two possible views of the Review/Add/Change screen in a database file. This layout lets you see more than one record at a time.

- **Usage**
  The Multiple Record layout is the default view of the database Review/Add/Change screen.

```
File: Customers              REVIEW/ADD/CHANGE              Escape: Main Menu
Selection: All records

Name             YTD Sales   Company                  Salesperson   Phone
===========================================================================
Olive Ogilvy     10,635.25   Ace Jackhammer Service   Brohammer     555-6666
Wilson Peck       5,350.00   Apex Canning             Smith         555-3232
Wilson K. Jeeves   575.30    Butlerware, Inc.         Smith         555-3334
Mort Drucker      1,025.00   Drucker Drayage          Smith         555-2345
Arnold Ormsby      787.35    Flecko Paints            Jones         555-4567
Walter Canary      125.60    Flippo Dog Food          Jones         555-8686
Fred Fong         4,675.20   Fong Machine Tools       Jones         555-8765
Edwina Gumm         87.50    Fritzi Fashions          Smith         555-7890
Ed Frobish       15,325.00   Frobish Linen Service    Smith         555-1234
Fortuna Maldonado 2,500.85   Furniture City           Brohammer     555-2222
Barney Flint      3,257.60   Howard's U-Rent 'Em      Brohammer     555-7608
Alex Abidikian    1,024.00   Imperial Dry Cleaning    Smith         555-0505
Boris Boronzhova 12,875.95   Jetson Steel             Jones         555-8787
James Pennington   100.25    Linda's Typewriter Repair Brohammer    555-4443
Aldo Pastarelli    355.90    Pesto's Pasta            Brohammer     555-1111
---------------------------------------------------------------------------
Type entry or use Ⅲ commands                          Ⅲ-? for Help
```

The Multiple Record layout lets you view several database records at once.

This layout automatically appears when you begin working with an existing database file. If your screen shows the Single Record layout,[293] press the Zoom[376] command (⌘-Z) to change to the Multiple Record layout. When you change from Single Record layout to Multiple Record layout, the cursor will be located on the record that had been displayed in Single Record layout and it will be displayed at the top of the screen.

■ **Comments**

In the Multiple Record layout, you move from one category to another from left to right by pressing **TAB**. If you want to move right to left from category to category, press ⌘ and **TAB** at the same time.

The ↑ and ↓ keys move the cursor from one record to the next. If you press ⌘ and ↑ or ↓ at the same time, the cursor moves to the top or bottom of the screen, and then scrolls forward or backward one screen at a time each additional time you use the same keystroke combination.

The default Multiple Record layout screen displays about five categories at a time, but most database files will contain more categories than this. You can't move the cursor into categories that aren't visible in the Multiple Record layout. You must first rearrange the layout of the categories, moving the one you want to work with so it is in view on the screen. This is done with the Layout[146] command (⌘-L).

You can't add new records at the end of a file with the Multiple Record layout showing. In order to add a record at the end of a file from Multiple Record layout you must switch to Single Record layout:

1. Move the cursor to the last record in the file.

2. Press the Zoom command (⌘-Z) to change to Single Record layout.

3. Move the cursor to the last category in the record with the ↓ key, and then press ↓ once more. The screen will show a message that says you are past the last record in the file, and asking if you want to add new records. Answer *Yes* to the question, and a blank record will appear.

@NA

- **Structure**

  @NA

- **Definition**

  @NA (for *Not Available*) is a spreadsheet function that places the message *NA* in the cell where it is entered, and in cells containing formulas that refer to it.

- **Usage**

  @NA isn't used with an argument. You enter @NA in a cell by itself. Typically, you use @NA to mark cells you want to use in large spreadsheets where all the values needed in a formula or formulas aren't yet available. If a formula finds the @NA function in a cell, it displays the *NA* warning message instead of a result, so you know some needed values are still missing.

- **Example**

  Suppose you are filling in a company budget and the figures are trickling in from several departments over a period of time, making the budget incomplete, as in this example:

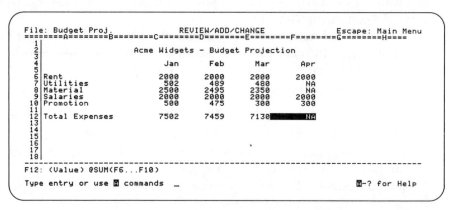

The @NA function is useful for reminding you when all the values needed by a formula haven't been entered yet.

You have entered a @SUM formula in the *Total Expenses* row for every month, but you don't want the total to show if all the expenses for a month aren't in yet. But if you simply left the cells with missing values blank, the spreadsheet would ignore them, add the rest of the values in the column, and present a total. To avoid this, you can use @NA as a placeholder for missing values.

1. Move the cursor to cell F7.

2. Type, @NA, then press **RETURN**.

3. Repeat steps 1 and 2 for cell F8.

4. With these functions entered, the @SUM formula will show the warning *NA* instead of a value, and you will be reminded that some values are missing.

- **Comments**

The @NA function is especially useful on large spreadsheets that cannot be seen on-screen all at once. With @NA, you don't have to be able to see blank cells where values are missing, because the formulas that refer to cells with missing information that you have marked using the @NA function will display a warning message.

Name Change (⌂-N)

- **Definition**

The *Name Change* command (⌂-N) is used to change the name of an Apple-Works file, a database report, or database categories.

- **Usage**

Use the Name Change command to change the name of a word-processor, spreadsheet, or database file, or database reports or categories. This command works exactly the same way on file names in the word processor and spreadsheet. It is slightly different in the database.

Changing word-processor and spreadsheet file names

Since the process is the same for changing both word-processor and spreadsheet file names, we'll step through just one example. Suppose you are working with the sales letter shown on the next page.

171

```
File: Sales Letter            REVIEW/ADD/CHANGE          Escape: Main Menu
=====|=====|=====|=====|=====|=====|=====|=====|=====|=====|=====|=====|=====|=====|=====|===
December 13, 1985

Mr. Ed Frobish
Frobish Linen Service
335 Ramona Ave.
San Jose, CA 95551

Dear Ed:

We think you're a ^super^ customer, and I wanted to tell you how much all
of us at Acme Widgets appreciate your business.  That's why we wanted you
to be the first to know about our new Widget Convertible--the sturdiest,
most flexible, most cost-effective widget around.

I'd like to schedule a time to drop by your office and demonstrate the
advantages of the new Widget Convertible, so I'll be giving you a call
during the next week to make an appointment.

In the meantime, think what the world's first all-purpose widget will mean
to your profits!
------------------------------------------------------------------------
Type entry or use ⌘ commands          Line 3  Column  1       ⌘-? for Help
```

You have finished composing it, and decide to send it to Ed Frobish, a customer. You want to rename the file so it is more descriptive. To do this:

1. Make sure the file is displayed on the Review/Add/Change screen.

2. Press the Name Change command (⌘-**N**). The file name will appear on the prompt line, and the cursor will be flashing on the first character in the name, like this:

```
File: Sales Letter             CHANGE FILENAME       Escape: Review/Add/Change
=====|=====|=====|=====|=====|=====|=====|=====|=====|=====|=====|=====|=====|=====|=====|===
December 13, 1985

Mr. Ed Frobish
Frobish Linen Service
335 Ramona Ave.
San Jose, CA 95551

Dear Ed:

We think you're a ^super^ customer, and I wanted to tell you how much all
of us at Acme Widgets appreciate your business.  That's why we wanted you
to be the first to know about our new Widget Convertible--the sturdiest,
most flexible, most cost-effective widget around.

I'd like to schedule a time to drop by your office and demonstrate the
advantages of the new Widget Convertible, so I'll be giving you a call
during the next week to make an appointment.

In the meantime, think what the world's first all-purpose widget will mean
to your profits!
------------------------------------------------------------------------
Type filename: ▮ales Letter                                45K Avail.
```

3. Delete the existing file name with the Clear[34] command (⌘-**Y**), or move the cursor to the end of the name and then erase it by backing the cursor over it with **DELETE**.

4. Type the new name (*Frobish.ltr* would be descriptive) and press **RETURN**. The file name at the top-left corner of the screen changes, and the file is renamed.

5. Press ⌘-**S** to save the file on disk under the new name.

6. Both the renamed file *Frobish.ltr* and the original file *Sales Letter* are now stored on the disk.

Comments: It is useful to change file names when you modify a file and want to keep both the modified and original versions stored separately on a disk. In the example, the *Sales Letter* file can now be a "boilerplate" file you begin with when you start a sales letter, and with each modified letter you could change the file name to reflect the modified letter's specific contents, then save it on disk so you have an exact copy.

Changing database file, category, and report names

To change the name of a database file, use the Name Change command the same way you do when changing a word-processor or spreadsheet file name. When you use the Name Change command on the Review/Add/Change screen of a database file, however, you can also change the names of categories in the file, or add or delete categories.

Let's assume you have a file of customers that contains the category *Name*, and you want to change the name of that category to *Contact*. Here's how to make the change:

1. Make sure the database file's Review/Add/Change screen is displayed (it can be in either Single[293] or Multiple Record layout[168]).

2. Press the Name Change command (⌘-**N**). The Change Name/Category screen will appear, like this:

```
File: Customers          CHANGE NAME/CATEGORY     Escape: Review/Add/Change


Category names
=====================================================================
Name
Company                              Options:
Phone
Street                               Change filename
City                                 Return    Go to first category
ST/Zip
Salesperson
YTD Sales




-------------------------------------           ---------------------
Type filename: ▊ustomers                              34K Avail.
```

You can change the file name and category names in the database with the Name Change command.

3. The cursor will be blinking on the first character of the file name. You could use the Clear command to delete the current file name and then type a new one at this point, but we'll leave the file name as it is and move into the category-name area instead.

4. Press **RETURN**. The cursor will move into the category-name area of the screen, to the first character of the first category, *Name.*

5. Press the Clear command (⌥-Y) to delete the name, *Name.*

6. Type in the new name, *Contact,* and press **RETURN**. The new category name will replace the old one.

7. Press **ESC** to return to the Review/Add/Change screen.

You can also use the Name Change command on the database Report Format screen to change the name of a report format (you can't, however, change the name of a category). When you use the Name Change command on the Report Format screen, you can also enter a report title line above the category names in the report itself. The title line you enter will appear when the report is printed. Suppose you have a report format called *Sales,* for example, and you want to change the name to *YTD Sales,* and use that same name as the title line of the report. To do this:

1. Make sure the *Sales* report format is displayed on the screen.

2. Press the Name Change command (⌥-N). The prompt line will display the report name, and the cursor will be flashing on the first character in the name.

3. Since you simply want to insert the characters *YTD* in front of the name *Sales,* you can simply type them at the cursor position, along with a space to separate *YTD* from *Sales,* and then press **RETURN** (assuming you are using the insert cursor[50]). The new name, *YTD Sales,* will replace the old name in the upper-left corner of the Report Format screen.

4. Once you type the new report name, the cursor will move to the space above the category names in the report, and the prompt line will suggest that you type a title line for the report, as shown in the following example.

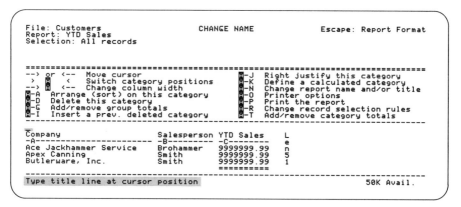

```
File: Customers                    CHANGE NAME              Escape: Report Format
Report: YTD Sales
Selection: All records

==============================================================================
--> or <--    Move cursor                      ■-J  Right justify this category
  >  ■   <    Switch category positions        ■-K  Define a calculated category
--> ■   <--   Change column width              ■-N  Change report name and/or title
■-A  Arrange (sort) on this category           ■-O  Printer options
■-D  Delete this category                      ■-P  Print the report
■-G  Add/remove group totals                   ■-R  Change record selection rules
■-I  Insert a prev. deleted category           ■-T  Add/remove category totals
------------------------------------------------------------------------------
Company                      Salesperson YTD Sales   L
-A---------------------- -B--------- -C--------      e
Ace Jackhammer Service       Brohammer   9999999.99  n
Apex Canning                 Smith       9999999.99  s
Butlerware, Inc.             Smith       9999999.99  1
                                         ==========
------------------------------------------------------------------------------
Type title line at cursor position                          50K Avail.
```

The Name Change command lets you enter a report title above the category names in a report.

5. Type the title, *YTD Sales*, and then press **RETURN**. This title will now be printed with the report.

■ **Comments**

The database's Change Name/Category screen can also be used to delete categories from a file, although doing this will erase any report formats you have created and reset the layout options to their defaults. AppleWorks warns you about these consequences when you try to delete a database category. Just as you can delete categories, you can also create new ones, but doing this has the same consequences as deleting a category.

@NPV

■ **Structure**

@NPV(interest rate,range)

■ **Definition**

@NPV (for *Net Present Value*) is a spreadsheet function that calculates the current value of future cash flow, when the value of the cash flow over time is discounted at a constant rate.

- **Usage**

@NPV is typically used to measure the actual return on an investment that produces income over a period of years. In financial analysis, money is recognized as being worth less as time goes by because of inflation. The Net Present Value (NPV) of an investment is the current value of the dollars you will receive over time, with a discount rate (the rate at which you feel the value of the money declines) figured in.

- **Example**

Suppose somebody asks you to invest $10,000 in a new business venture, and promises to pay you back with interest over five years. The first year you will receive $2500, and the amount you receive each subsequent year will increase by $250 over the previous year's payment through the fifth year, when the investment ends. You enter these cash flows in a spreadsheet, as in row 5 of this example:

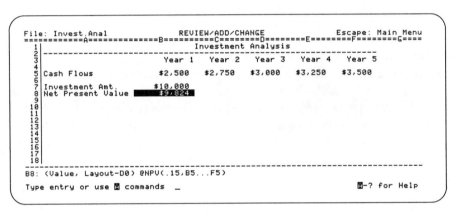

The @NPV function helps you determine whether an investment is worthwhile.

For reference, you place the amount of the original investment underneath the row of yearly cash flows. This investment seems like a good one, but you know you can invest your $10,000 in a second deed of trust and earn 15 percent interest for those five years. To find out how the business investment compares with the trust deed, you enter the @NPV formula shown in the prompt line into cell B8:

1. Place the cursor in cell B8.

2. Type *@NPV*, followed by an open parenthesis.

3. Type the rate at which you want to discount the cash flows, *.15*, followed by a comma to separate the rate from the range where the cash flows are located.

4. Type the range of cells containing the cash flows, *B5.F5*, and then type a closed parenthesis to complete the argument.

5. Press **RETURN** to enter the formula.

6. The formula calculates the Net Present Value of the cash flows in cells B5 through F5, and places the result in cell B8.

You can see in the last example spreadsheet that the proposed business-venture investment yields less than the present value of your cash on hand ($10,000), and isn't such a great deal after all. For this investment to make sense, the NPV should be greater than $10,000.

■ **Comments**

The rate specified in the argument of an @NPV formula must be entered as a decimal—AppleWorks won't accept rates expressed with a percent sign.

You must determine a required rate of return (the rate at which you will discount the cash flows) before you enter the formula. Typically, businesses and individuals arrive at a required rate of return by considering other investments in which the risk is lower—if you know you can safely invest your money at 15 percent, for example, it makes sense to require that riskier investments perform better.

The cash flows in an @NPV formula can either be uniform throughout the period, or they can vary during the period. If one or more of the cells specified in the range of the argument is blank, or contains a label, then the @NPV formula will produce the message *ERROR* in the cell where it was entered. Also, if you try to specify a list of cells or more than one range instead of a single range, you will also get an *ERROR* message in the cell.

Other Activities menu

■ Definition
The *Other Activities menu* is a list of options that lets you adjust how Apple-Works interacts with printers and disk drives, or manage files on disks.

■ Usage
Choose option 5, *Other Activities*, from the AppleWorks Main Menu.[158] The Other Activities menu will appear, listing these seven options:

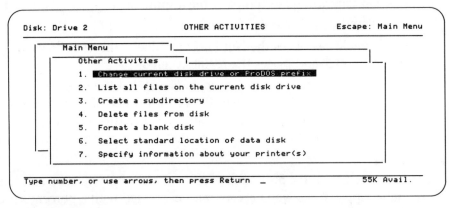

The Other Activities menu.

These options each let you perform the following activities:

Option 1. Change current disk drive or ProDOS prefix: This option produces the Change Current Disk screen:

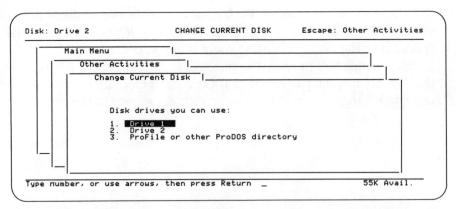

This screen lets you change the current disk drive, so you can access files from a different disk or directory.

The current disk drive is a physical device—a floppy disk drive; the current directory (called a *pathname*[188] on the AppleWorks screen) is a section or subsection of a ProFile hard disk drive, or a floppy disk you have designated as the location for certain files. When you add files to the Desktop, save files, list files, or delete files, AppleWorks automatically assumes you want to perform one of these operations with the current disk drive or directory. You use option 1 from the Other Activities menu to replace the current disk location with another one via the Change Current Disk screen.

As you can see in the Change Current Disk screen, AppleWorks presents you with three options for choosing a new current disk. When you choose this option, Drive 1 is highlighted. To change the drive number:

1. Highlight the option you want by pressing the corresponding number and **RETURN** (or use ↓ or ↑ to move to the option you want, then press **RETURN**).

2. The drive you select will become the current disk location.

   If you want to select a directory or subdirectory, choose option 3, *ProFile or other ProDOS directory*. To use this option:

1. Select *ProFile or other ProDOS directory* by highlighting the option or typing its number and pressing **RETURN**.

2. The prompt line will tell you to type the ProDOS prefix—the pathname to the directory—you want to use as the current location.
   You must type the complete prefix: If you are specifying a directory, the prefix will be */directory* (where *directory* is the name of the directory you want to access). If you are specifying a subdirectory, the prefix will be */directory/subdirectory* (where *directory* and *subdirectory* correspond to the names you want).

3. When you type the ProDOS prefix and press **RETURN**, the current disk is changed to that prefix.

When you change the current disk drive or ProDOS prefix, you are only changing it for the current AppleWorks session—when you begin working with AppleWorks next time, the prefix will be set to the standard data-disk location. If you want to change the standard data-disk location, so a certain disk drive or prefix appears each time you begin working with AppleWorks, use option 6 on the Other Activities menu, which is explained on page 183.

Option 2. List all files on the current disk drive: When you choose this option, AppleWorks displays a list of all the files on the current disk drive, as in this example:

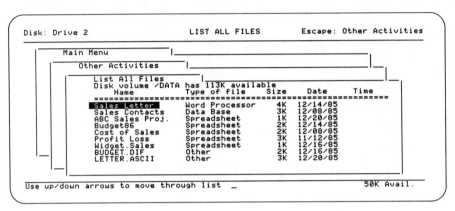

```
Disk: Drive 2                    LIST ALL FILES        Escape: Other Activities
 ┌─ Main Menu              │
 │ ┌─ Other Activities       │
 │ │ ┌─ List All Files        │
 │ │ │ Disk volume /DATA has 113K available
 │ │ │    Name           Type of file      Size   Date      Time
 │ │ │ ==============================================================
 │ │ │ Sales Letter       Word Processor    4K   12/14/85
 │ │ │ Sales Contacts     Data Base         3K   12/08/85
 │ │ │ ABC Sales Proj.    Spreadsheet       1K   12/20/85
 │ │ │ Budget86           Spreadsheet       2K   12/14/85
 │ │ │ Cost of Sales      Spreadsheet       2K   12/08/85
 │ │ │ Profit Loss        Spreadsheet       3K   11/12/85
 │ │ │ Widget.Sales       Spreadsheet       1K   12/16/85
 │ └─ BUDGET.DIF          Other             2K   12/16/85
 │ │ │ LETTER.ASCII       Other             3K   12/20/85
 └───┴─────────────────────────────────────────────────────────────
 Use up/down arrows to move through list  _                50K Avail.
```

The List All Files option displays the entire contents of a disk or directory, not just the AppleWorks files it contains.

Some of the options on the Main Menu also produce listings of files on the current disk, but these listings contain only AppleWorks files.

When you choose the List All Files option, the file listing shows Apple-Works files, subdirectories, and other files (which may be DIF files,[100] ASCII files,[13] or files created by other programs). The file listing shows the name of each file, the type, the size, the date it was last modified, and the time it was created (if you have an optional clock/calendar card in your Apple).

Option 3. Create a subdirectory: The third option listed on the Other Activities menu lets you create a subdirectory on a disk. Subdirectories are sections of a disk where you can place files for greater organization. On the disk shown in the List All Files example above, for example, we might want to create a subdirectory called *Finances*, and then store the *Profit Loss, Cost of Sales, Widget.Sales, Budget86,* and *ABC Sales Proj.* worksheets in it, so they aren't in the same list as the *Sales Letter* word-processor document and the *Sales Contacts* database file. Subdirectories are especially useful on large-capacity disks, or on floppy disks that contain dozens of individual files.

To create a subdirectory:

1. Choose option 3, *Create a subdirectory*, from the Other Activities menu.

2. A screen message will tell you to type the complete ProDOS pathname of the subdirectory. This must include the name of the directory and the name of the subdirectory, each preceded by slash marks, like this: */directory/subdirectory.*

3. Once you type the subdirectory pathname and press **RETURN**, Apple-Works will check the disk identified by the directory name you entered, and then attempt to make a subdirectory with the name you have chosen. If the attempt is successful, a message will report *Success.* If AppleWorks is unsuccessful in creating the subdirectory, it will display a message that says *Unable to create a subdirectory with the specified pathname.*

If AppleWorks can't create a subdirectory using the pathname you give it, there are three possible reasons:

☐ The directory you specified doesn't exist.

☐ The subdirectory you specified already exists.

☐ The directory you specified is full.

You can create a subdirectory on any disk currently available to Apple-Works—the subdirectory doesn't have to be on the current disk.

Suppose, for example, that your current disk drive is Drive 2, but you also have a hard disk called */Hard1* connected to your Apple. You want to create a subdirectory on the hard disk called */Finances.* To do this, you choose the option to create a subdirectory, type the pathname */Hard1/Finances*, and then press **RETURN**. AppleWorks will create the subdirectory on your hard disk, and report success. When you create a subdirectory, the current disk-drive location does not change. (See: Using a Hard Disk.[353])

Option 4. Delete files from disk: You use this option to permanently remove files from the current disk. The Delete Files option lists all files on the current disk, including non-AppleWorks files and subdirectories, and you can delete them by selecting them from the list. To delete files:

1. Choose option 4, *Delete files from disk*, from the Other Activities menu.

2. Highlight the file you want to delete, or use the → key to select more than one, then press **RETURN**. AppleWorks will present the name of

the file you have selected (or the name of the first of several files selected), and warn you that you are about to permanently remove the
file from disk. The prompt line asks if you really want to do this.

3. If you are sure you want to remove the file, choose *Yes* from the
   prompt line. If you decide you don't want to remove the file after
   all, either choose *No* or press **ESC**.

   If you select a group of files to delete, AppleWorks will warn you about
   each file before it deletes it, and will ask you to confirm each deletion.

4. Once you answer *Yes* to indicate you're certain you want the file deleted, AppleWorks will erase the file from the disk.

Option 5. Format a blank disk: This option lets you prepare a disk on which
to store your files. Every new computer disk is completely blank. You can't
store files on a blank, unformatted disk, so it must be formatted for use by
the operating system of the type of computer whose files it will store: Data
disks for an Apple and an IBM PC are formatted quite differently. Apple-
Works always formats the disk in the current disk drive.

To format a blank disk with AppleWorks:

1. Determine the current disk location by looking at the disk locator in
   the upper-left corner of the screen. It must be either Drive 1 or Drive 2.
   AppleWorks won't format portions of a hard disk or a directory, so
   if the current disk location shows a ProDOS directory, change to either
   Drive 1 or Drive 2 using the *Change current disk* option described earlier.

2. Place an unformatted disk in the current disk drive.

3. Choose option 5, *Format a blank disk.*

4. AppleWorks will display a message that tells you the formatter will
   use the drive indicated at the upper-left corner of the screen. The
   prompt line asks you to type a disk name, which can contain up to
   15 characters.

5. Type a name for the new disk, and press **RETURN** when you are
   finished.

6. AppleWorks will display a message warning that the disk to be formatted should be in the current drive. The prompt line tells you to press the spacebar to continue.

7. Press **SPACE**, and the disk in the current drive will be formatted.

You can also format disks that already contain information. Formatting erases all the previously stored data on a disk, though, so be careful not to format disks that contain data you need. If a disk contains data you no longer need, however, formatting it is a much faster way to erase the old files than deleting them one at a time with the Delete Files option described earlier.

Option 6. Select standard location of data disk: This option lets you choose the data-disk location that AppleWorks will remember from one session to the next. The current-disk location can be changed any number of times during a session with AppleWorks, but each time you start the program, it automatically uses a default, or standard-disk location. This option lets you select that location.

To select a standard data-disk location with AppleWorks:

1. Choose option 6, *Select standard location of data disk* from the Other Activities menu. AppleWorks will present a screen similar to the one for option 1, *Change current disk drive,* shown earlier.

2. Choose a disk drive, or choose the *ProFile or other ProDOS directory* option and type the pathname you want. When you're finished, press **RETURN**.

3. AppleWorks will now store your choice as its standard-disk location, and that location will be indicated whenever you start the AppleWorks program.

When you select the standard data-disk location, it also becomes the new current-disk location. If you want to work with a different current-disk location, you can use option 1 to change the current disk, as discussed earlier. That option will change the current location temporarily, but the standard location—the location shown when you begin working with AppleWorks each time—will remain the one you set.

Option 7. Specify information about your printer(s): The final option listed on the Other Activities menu provides access to AppleWorks facilities for interacting with printers of various types. Through this option, you can set AppleWorks to communicate with up to three different printers; you can modify AppleWorks to work with different brands of printer interfaces; and you can select the printer AppleWorks always uses when you print the display with the Hard Copy[122] command (Ö-**H**).

You will find specific details about printer and interface configuration in the Printer Configuration[200] and Printer Interface Configuration[214] entries. The following section contains a general description of the *Specify information about your printer(s)* option.

When you choose the option to *Specify information about your printer(s)* from the Other Activities menu, AppleWorks presents the Printer Information menu:

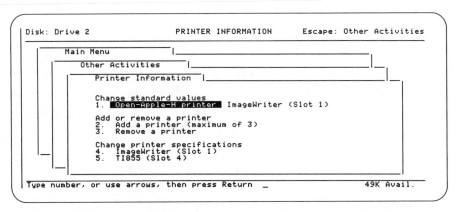

The Printer Information menu provides access to all the printer and interface configuration options in AppleWorks.

Depending on the option you choose, AppleWorks presents you with other menus or screens that let you control Appleworks' interactions with printers.

Option 1. Change standard values: This controls the printer used when you print the contents of the screen using the Hard Copy (Ö-**H**) command. AppleWorks asks you to set a printer for this function here, so you don't have to go through the steps of choosing a printer to use when you issue the Hard Copy command. When you choose this option, AppleWorks shows you a list of the printers you currently have configured, and lets you choose one of them as the (Ö-**H**) printer.

Options 2 and 3. Add or remove a printer: The *Add or Remove a printer* option lets you add printers to or remove them from the list of up to three stored configurations you can define and store at one time in AppleWorks. When you print a file from an application, you select which of the three printers (or however many you have configured) you want to use. AppleWorks will not store more than three printer configurations. If you already have three configurations stored and you want to add a new printer, you must first remove one from the list using the *Remove a printer* option.

Options 4, 5, and 6. Change printer specifications: This option lets you change the settings for a printer that has already been configured. Depending on the number of printers you have configured at the time, this option will show 1, 2, or 3 printers. You choose the printer whose specifications you want to alter by highlighting it. Once you select a printer, the specifications screen appears, and you can change the settings as you like. If you have no printers configured, this option will not appear on your screen.

Page break

- **Definition**

  A *page break* is a dashed line and page number that appear on the screen to indicate which parts of a word-processor document will be printed on separate pieces of paper.

- **Usage**

  When you create a word-processor document, it appears on the screen as one continuous block of text—there are no page breaks to separate it into what the actual printed pages will be. But when you use either the Print[193] command (⌂-P) or Calculate[18] command (⌂-K) in the word processor (discussed on the following page), page breaks are calculated and the document becomes a series of pages with visible page breaks between them.

```
File: Picnic.Outline          REVIEW/ADD/CHANGE          Escape: Main Menu
=====|====|====|====|====|====|====|====|====|====|====|====|====|====|==■
                    Acme Widget Company Picnic

                         Agenda

   I. Preparations...........................9:30 a.m.
          A. Set up tables
          B. Set up volleyball net
          C. Install direction signs

  II. Kick-off..............................11:00 a.m.
          A. Register for prize
          B. Choose volleyball teams
          C. Delegate BBQ chefs
          D. Delegate trash detail
  - - - - - - - - - - - - - - - End of Page 1 - - - - - - - - - - - - - - -

 III. Picnic Mania..........................12:00 p.m.
          A. Hamburgers & Hot Dogs
          B. Volleyball warm-ups
  -----------------------------------------------------------------------
  Type entry or use ■ commands            Line 4  Column  1      ■-? for Help
```

Page breaks show how a document will be physically divided when you print it on paper.

Displaying page breaks with the Calculate command: Press the Calculate command (⌂-**K**), and then choose the printer from a list of printers you have configured for AppleWorks that you will ultimately be printing the document on. The Review/Add/Change screen will reappear, and the page breaks will be displayed.

Displaying page breaks with the Print command: Press the Print command (⌂-**P**), and choose the portion of the document you want to print from the options presented, then choose the printer you will be printing the document on. Then, instead of printing the document, press **ESC** to return to the Review/Add/Change screen. The page breaks will be displayed.

■ **Comments**

You can insert page breaks into documents to divide printed information the way you want. You create new page breaks within a document with the NP printer option. (See: Printer Options.[217])

It's important to know which part of a document will print on certain pages so you can choose to print only the part of the document beginning on a certain page, instead of printing the entire document. The word processor gives you three choices about which part of the document you can print: (1) all of it, (2) from the current page to the end, or (3) from the cursor position to the end. Knowing which page your cursor is on will help you if you want to print only part of the document. (See: Word Processor Printing.[373]) If you want to print only the last page of a document, for example, you should calculate page breaks, move the cursor to the last page, and then choose the option to print from the current page.

If you have calculated a document's page breaks, you can also search for a particular page number with the Find[109] command (⌂-**F**) when you want to quickly move the cursor to that page.

Paste

■ **Definition**

The word *paste* is used to describe the process of copying data from the Clipboard[35] into an AppleWorks file.

■ **Usage**

When you copy or move data from the Clipboard, you are said to *paste* it into a file. Using the Copy[40] command (⌂-**C**) to paste information from the Clipboard doesn't remove that information from the Clipboard—you are simply pasting a *copy* of the data from the Clipboard. Data stored on the Clipboard remains there until you copy some other data from a file to the Clipboard, or use the Move[163] command (⌂-**M**) to cut the data from the Clipboard. New data copied or moved to the Clipboard replaces the old data stored there.

Path

■ **Definition**

Path is an indicator that appears in the current-disk-location[49] indicator of the AppleWorks screen to show that the current file location is a ProDOS pathname, rather than a disk-drive number.

■ **Usage**

The current-disk-location indicator located in the upper-left corner of the AppleWorks screen changes to reflect the location you have selected for your data. If the location you have selected is one of the floppy-disk drives (Drive 1 or Drive 2), the current disk location shows the indicator *Disk:* followed by the drive number. But if you choose *ProFile or other ProDOS directory* as the current disk location, the current-disk-location indicator changes to read *Path:* followed by the ProDOS pathname you specified, as shown on the following page. (See: Pathname;[188] Change Current Disk Menu.[25])

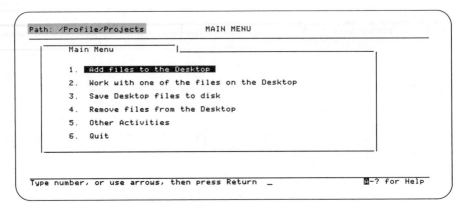

```
Path: /Profile/Projects          MAIN MENU

    Main Menu              |
    1. Add files to the Desktop
    2. Work with one of the files on the Desktop
    3. Save Desktop files to disk
    4. Remove files from the Desktop
    5. Other Activities
    6. Quit


Type number, or use arrows, then press Return  _        ⌘-? for Help
```

When your current disk location is a ProDOS pathname, the indicator shows the word Path:.

Every storage location in the ProDOS operating system has a pathname, even floppy disks in disk drives. Thus, you can identify a floppy disk in Drive 1 or Drive 2 by a pathname instead of by the drive number. If you do this, the current disk location will show the word *Path* instead of the word *Disk*.

Pathname 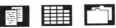   IW), IS), ID)

■ **Definition**

A *pathname* is the name by which ProDOS[246] locates an individual file.

■ **Usage**

Every pathname in ProDOS has at least two parts: the name of the volume where the file is located, and the name of the file. When you format a floppy disk, or create a hard-disk directory, you must give it a volume[359] name.

When you use ProDOS itself to work with files, you must use complete pathnames (both the volume name and the file name) to identify the volumes and files you want. When you use AppleWorks, however, you don't have to specify the complete pathname. For convenience, AppleWorks lets you refer to the location of a floppy-disk volume by the number of the disk drive where the disk is currently located (Drive 1 or Drive 2), rather than by the name of the actual disk in the drive.

Once you set the current disk location (Drive 1 or Drive 2), you can then add or save files by file name only: AppleWorks will remember the volume location. The same is true if you specify a volume name (either the name of a floppy disk or the name of a hard-disk directory) as the current disk location using option 1 or 6 of the Other Activities menu:[178] Once you specify the location, AppleWorks remembers it, and you can load or save files by the file name only.

It's important to remember that although you don't have to use a complete pathname with AppleWorks, ProDOS always uses complete pathnames. When AppleWorks lets you work with files by using only file names, that's because AppleWorks is supplying the volume name for you. Thus, you are always using pathnames, whether you know it or not. To see this, look at this example:

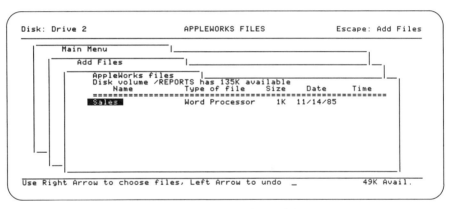

Every volume has a name in ProDOS — even a floppy disk.

As you can see, the current-file-location indicator in the upper-left corner shows that you are accessing a disk drive, but the file listing in the file menu displays the volume name of the disk, *IREPORTS*, at the top.

Although you can generally ignore pathnames when you work with AppleWorks files on floppy disks, you must use them when you create or load DIF,[100] ASCII,[13] or VisiCalc[357] files, or if you use a hard disk.[353] Hard-disk volumes and DIF, ASCII, or VisiCalc files must be identified by complete ProDOS pathnames when you want to access them.

Pathnames always have the same structure:

/volume name/file name

If you have created a subdirectory on a volume, and the file you want to work with is in that subdirectory, then you must include the name of the subdirectory[336] between the volume name and the file name. In this case, the pathname would look like this:

/volume name/subdirectory name/file name

Subdirectories are discussed in detail in the Subdirectory entry, but for now, you can think of subdirectories as sections of a volume containing a group of files.

■ **Examples**

Suppose you are formatting a new floppy disk to store a report on. When you format the disk by choosing that activity from the Other Activities menu, AppleWorks asks you to type a name for the disk. Let's say you have named the disk *Reports*. You only have to type the name itself—AppleWorks supplies the slash mark in front of the name. As far as ProDOS is concerned, this disk will be named */Reports* from now on. You save your report onto the disk under the file name, *Sales*. ProDOS now identifies this file with the pathname, */Reports/Sales*.

Now, let's suppose you want to create a DIF file called *DIF.Totals* from the spreadsheet, and you want to save the DIF file to the disk you have named *Reports*. Even though the disk is a floppy disk in Drive 2 and the current disk location is set to Drive 2, you must still use a complete pathname to save the file. In this case, the complete pathname for saving the DIF file would be */Reports/DIF.Totals*. Notice that the pathname includes the name of the floppy-disk volume, rather than the number of the disk drive where it's located, and that the pathname begins with a slash.

You always have to use a complete ProDOS pathname when you save DIF or ASCII files to a disk, when you print a file to a printer configured as a disk printer, or when you load these files from a disk. If you were loading a DIF file (called *DIF*, in this example) from a hard-disk volume, you would have to use the complete pathname as well. Suppose the hard-disk volume was named */ProFile*. The pathname for the file would be */ProFile/DIF*.

If you can't remember the volume name of the floppy disk where a DIF or ASCII file will be saved or loaded, you can find it quickly by choosing *Add files to the Desktop* from the Main Menu.[158] When AppleWorks presents the list of files stored on the floppy disk, it will show the disk's volume name at the top of the list, as shown in the example.

Pointer

■ **Definition**

A *pointer* is a set of cell coordinates that places a copy of the value in one spreadsheet cell in the cell containing the pointer.

■ **Usage**

Pointers can be used by themselves, or they can be used in spreadsheet formulas when you want the calculation to include values that already exist in other cells. When you use a pointer alone in a cell, the pointer must always have the same format: a plus sign (+) or a minus sign (−) (so AppleWorks knows you aren't typing a label), followed by the coordinates of the cell whose contents you want to use. When you use pointers in a formula, you don't need to begin them with a plus or minus sign. Let's take a look at two examples.

■ **Example: Using one pointer**

This spreadsheet analyzes a $10,000 investment.

```
File: Investment                REVIEW/ADD/CHANGE            Escape: Main Menu
=========A=========B=========C=========D=========E=========F=========G=========H====
 1              Investment Analysis
 2
 3 Investment Amount: $10,000
 4 Discount Rate:          .11
 5 Net Present Value: $10,130
 6
 7
 8   Year 1    Year 2    Year 3    Year 4    Year 5
 9
10   $2,500   ▓$2,500▓   $2,500    $2,500    $4,000
11
12
13
14
15
16
17
18
----------------------------------------------------------------------
B10: (Value, Layout-D0) +A10

Type entry or use ⌾ commands  _                          ⌾-? for Help
```

You can use cell pointers to copy the contents of one cell to other cells.

The investment will return the same cash flows for each of the first four years. We could simply enter the same value (2500) in cells A10, B10, C10, and D10 to represent these cash flows, but in this case the pointer *+A10* has been entered in cells B10, C10, and D10. The pointer "points" to cell A10, and tells the spreadsheet to use the contents of cell A10. In the example, the cursor is in cell B10, and you can see that the cell contains the pointer *+A10*.

With this pointer entered in cells B10 through D10, the values in these cells will always match whatever value is in cell A10. Thus, we can change the amount of the cash flow in cell A10, and it will change automatically in cells B10 through D10.

This is the advantage of using cell pointers: The cells containing the pointers always contain the same data as the cell being pointed to.

- **Example: Using pointers in a function**

Looking at the same spreadsheet again, we can see how to use more than one pointer to refer to the contents of many cells in a formula. In this view of the same spreadsheet, the cursor has been placed in cell C5, which contains a function that calculates the Net Present Value[175] of the cash flows in row 10:

```
 File: Investment                 REVIEW/ADD/CHANGE              Escape: Main Menu
 ========A========B========C========D========E========F========G========H====
  1|                  Investment Analysis
  2|
  3|Investment Amount: $10,000
  4|Discount Rate:         .11
  5|Net Present Value: $10,130
  6|
  7|
  8|    Year 1     Year 2     Year 3     Year 4     Year 5
  9|
 10|   $2,500     $2,500     $2,500     $2,500     $4,000
 11|
 12|
 13|
 14|
 15|
 16|
 17|
 18|
    -------------------------------------------------------------------------
 C5: (Value, Layout-D0) @NPV(C4,A10...E10)

 Type entry or use ▒ commands  _                          ▒-? for Help
```

You can use multiple pointers in a formula, as in this example.

As you can see, the function's argument uses a pointer to indicate a single cell, C4. Since the argument uses a pointer, we can change the value in cell C4 to indicate a different discount rate, and the function in cell C5 will automatically recalculate to show the effects of the change on the final amount. Some functions can only use pointers, while others can use either pointers or actual values. It's always best to use pointers whenever you can.

Print (⌂-P)

■ **Definition**

The *Print* command (⌂-P) displays the currently available print destinations where you can print word-processor, spreadsheet, or database files.

■ **Usage**

Use the Print command when you are ready to print a file, either to a printer, to a disk, or to the screen. The Print command has a different effect in each application.

Example: Using the Print command in the word processor

1. Make sure the Review/Add/Change screen for the file you want to print is displayed.

2. Press the Print command (⌂-P). This prompt line will appear:

    Print from? Beginning This page Cursor

3. Choose the option you want, and press **RETURN**. The Print Menu[196] will be displayed. It shows the possible places where you can print the data: to a printer you have configured for AppleWorks,[200] or to a text (ASCII) file[13] on disk.

4. Choose the print destination you want, and press **RETURN**.

5. If you choose one of the configured printers as the print destination, the prompt line will ask how many copies of the file you want printed. Type the number of copies you want, and press **RETURN**. The file will be printed on the specified printer.

6. If you choose a printer configured as a disk printer, or a text (ASCII) file on disk as the print destination, you will be prompted to enter a pathname[188] for the file. Type the pathname, press **RETURN**, and the file will be saved on disk under the pathname you specified.

Comments: For further information about printing from the word processor, see the entries: Print Menu[196] and Word Processor Printing.[371] Information about formatting options will be found under the entry Printer Options.[217]

▦ Example: Using the Print command in the spreadsheet

1. Make sure the file you want to print is shown on the Review/Add/Change screen.

2. Press the Print command (⌘-P). This prompt line will appear:

   Print? All Rows Columns Block

3. Choose the option you want, and press **RETURN**.

4. If you choose to print all of the file, the Print screen will be displayed. If you choose to print certain rows, columns, or a block of data, use the Arrow keys to highlight the area you want to print, then press **RETURN**.

5. Once you have selected the data you want to print, the Print screen appears. It lists the possible places where you can print the data: to a printer you have configured for AppleWorks, to a DIF file[100] on disk, to an ASCII file on disk, or to the Clipboard[35] (for transfer to a word-processor document).

6. Choose the print destination, and then press **RETURN**.

7. If you choose one of the configured printers as the print destination (including a printer configured as a disk printer), or the Clipboard, the prompt line will ask you either to type a date for the spreadsheet print-out and press **RETURN**, or simply to press **RETURN** if you don't want a date printed. Once you press **RETURN**, the data you selected will be printed at the destination you chose.

8. If you choose a printer configured as a disk printer, or choose a DIF file on disk, or an ASCII file on disk, you will be prompted to type in a pathname for the file. Type the pathname, press **RETURN**, and the file will be saved on disk under the pathname you specified.

Comments: To move spreadsheet data into a word-processor document, you must print it to the Clipboard—the data can't be transferred if you simply copy or move it to the Clipboard. You can find further information about spreadsheet printing and formatting options under the entries Spreadsheet Overview[298] and Spreadsheet Printing.[319]

Example: Using the Print command in the database

In the database, you can't print until you define a report format. Therefore, the Print command has two functions in the database. When you use it from the Review/Add/Change display, it accesses the report-generating options, so you can define a report. Once you have defined a report, you use the Print command from the Report Format display to actually print the data.

1. Make sure the file you want to print is displayed on the Review/Add/Change screen.

2. Press the Print command (⌂-P). The Report Menu[273] will appear, showing options for creating new report formats, or using an existing format.

3. When you choose the report or report-making option you want, the Report Format screen appears.

4. Use the Report Format display to arrange and calculate the data in your report the way you want. When you are finished, press the Print command again. The Print the Report menu[197] will appear, showing the available print destinations: A printer you have configured for AppleWorks, a DIF file on disk, an ASCII file on disk, or the Clipboard (for transfer to word-processor documents).

5. Choose the print destination you want, and press **RETURN**. If you choose one of the configured printers (including disk printers), the screen, or the Clipboard as the print destination, the prompt line will ask you to type a date for the report or press **RETURN**. Once you type a report date and press **RETURN** (or simply press **RETURN** if you don't want a date printed on the report), the report will be printed at the destination you chose.

6. If you choose a disk printer, or choose a DIF or ASCII file as the print destination, you will be prompted to type in a pathname for the file. Type the pathname, press **RETURN**, and the report will be saved on disk under the pathname you specified.

Comments: You must print a database report to the Clipboard if you want to transfer the data to a word-processor document. Further information about making reports and printing from the database can be found under the entries Report Menu,[273] Database Report Formats,[79] and Database Printing.[67]

Print Menu

■ **Definition**

The *Print Menu* is a list of available print destinations that appears when you issue the Print[193] command (⌂-**P**) in an AppleWorks word-processor file.

■ **Usage**

Use the Print Menu to choose a print destination for your AppleWorks word-processor file. The menu lists the printers you have currently configured for AppleWorks, as well as the option to print to a text (ASCII) file[13] on disk. To use the Print Menu:

1. Press the Print command (⌂-**P**) while you have a word-processor file displayed on the Review/Add/Change screen. This prompt line will appear:

   Print from? Beginning This page Cursor

2. Choose the option you want by pressing the first letter of its name, or by highlighting the option with → and pressing **RETURN**; the Print Menu will appear, as in this example:

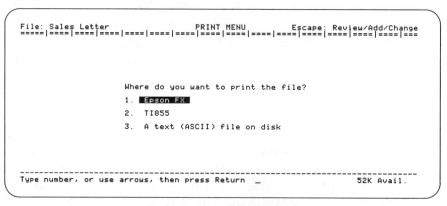

The word processor's Print Menu lets you choose a print destination for your file.

3. Choose the print destination you want by choosing one of the options from the menu and pressing **RETURN**.

4. After you choose the destination, the prompt line will ask you how many copies you want printed. Enter the number of copies and press **RETURN** (or just press **RETURN** if you only want one copy), and the file will be printed to the destination you have chosen.

If you choose *A text (ASCII) file on disk* as the print destination of your document, you will be prompted to enter a pathname[188] for the ASCII file instead of the number of copies. After entering the pathname, press **RETURN** and the file will be saved on disk with the name you specified.

■ **Comment**

Complete information on printing word-processor files will be found under the entry, Word Processor Printing.[371]

Print the Report menu

■ **Definition**

The *Print the Report menu* is a list of print destinations that are available from the AppleWorks database Report Format screen.

■ **Usage**

The Print the Report menu appears automatically as soon as you issue the Print[193] command (⌂-P) from the Report Format screen in the AppleWorks database. Use it to choose the destination where you would like the current report printed. To use the Print the Report menu:

1. Press the Print command (⌂-P) when the Report Format screen is displayed. The Print the Report menu will appear, like this example:

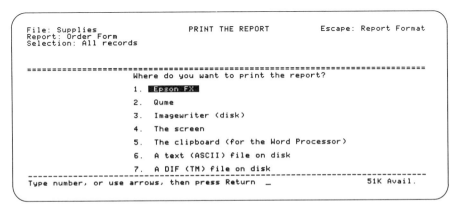

```
File: Supplies                  PRINT THE REPORT          Escape: Report Format
Report: Order Form
Selection: All records


=================================================================================
                       Where do you want to print the report?
                   1.  Epson FX
                   2.  Qume
                   3.  Imagewriter (disk)
                   4.  The screen
                   5.  The clipboard (for the Word Processor)
                   6.  A text (ASCII) file on disk
                   7.  A DIF (TM) file on disk
--------------------------------------------------------------------------------
Type number, or use arrows, then press Return  _                     51K Avail.
```

The Print the Report menu in the database lets you choose the print destination of your report.

2. Choose the print destination you want by selecting it from the list displayed.

3. If you choose one of the configured printers, the screen, or the Clipboard[35] as the print destination, the prompt line will ask you to type a report date. Either type a report date and press **RETURN**, or simply press **RETURN** if you don't want a date on the report. Once you do this, the report will be printed to the destination you have chosen.

4. If you choose either a DIF file[100] on disk or an ASCII file[13] on disk as the destination, you will be prompted to type the pathname[188] of the file you will be creating. When you type it and press **RETURN**, the file will be saved on disk under that pathname.

■ **Comment**

Complete information about printing database files can be found under the entry Database Printing.[67]

Print screen

■ **Definition**

The *Print screen* is a list of available print destinations that appears when you issue the Print[193] command (⌂-P) from the AppleWorks spreadsheet.

■ **Usage**

The Print screen automatically appears when you press the Print command (⌂-P) in the AppleWorks spreadsheet. Use it to select the printer or other print destination for the file. The screen also tells you the width, in characters, of the information you selected for printing, and compares it with the character width allowed by the currently selected spreadsheet printer options. To use the Print screen:

1. Press the Print command (⌂-P) while a spreadsheet file is displayed on the Review/Add/Change screen. This prompt line will be displayed:

    Print? All Rows Columns Block

2. Choose the data you want printed and press **RETURN**; the Print screen appears, like this:

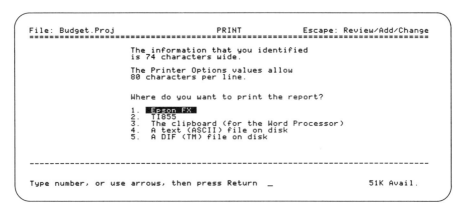

```
File: Budget.Proj                    PRINT           Escape: Review/Add/Change
================================================================================
                    The information that you identified
                    is 74 characters wide.

                    The Printer Options values allow
                    80 characters per line.

                    Where do you want to print the report?

                    1.  Epson FX
                    2.  TI855
                    3.  The clipboard (for the Word Processor)
                    4.  A text (ASCII) file on disk
                    5.  A DIF (TM) file on disk


--------------------------------------------------------------------------------

Type number, or use arrows, then press Return  _              51K Avail.
```

The spreadsheet's Print screen shows you how wide your printed selection is in characters, and lists available print destinations.

3. Compare the width of your printed selection with the width allowed by the printer options, then choose a print destination by highlighting the option you want on the menu (or typing the number of the option) and pressing **RETURN**.

4. The prompt line will ask you to type a report date or press **RETURN**. Type a report date and press **RETURN**, or simply press **RETURN** if you don't want a date to appear on the report. Once you do this, the file will be printed to the destination you have chosen.

If you choose to print the file to an ASCII[13] or DIF[100] file on disk, you will be prompted to enter a pathname[188] for the file instead of a report date. When you type the name and press **RETURN**, the file will be saved on disk under the pathname you specified.

■ **Comment**

Complete information about printing spreadsheet files will be found in the entry Spreadsheet Printing.[319]

Printer configuration

Different makes and models of printers operate differently from one another. Before you can print an AppleWorks file on a printer, you must *configure* the AppleWorks program to work with that printer. This means telling AppleWorks how the printer is connected to the computer, and how it should send data to that particular printer.

The general steps are not terribly complicated: You tell AppleWorks what name to give the printer, and you choose some configuration options for it. AppleWorks then stores the printer's name and configuration settings on the program disk. Thereafter, when you print a file, AppleWorks will present a list of configured printers (you can configure up to three at a time), and you can choose the one you want to print to at that particular time.

All activities for working with printer information in AppleWorks are done through the Printer Information menu.[212] To display the Printer Information menu:

1. Choose option 5, *Other Activities*, from the Main Menu[158] to display the Other Activities menu.[178]

2. Choose option 7, *Specify information about your printer(s)*; the Printer Information menu will be displayed, as shown in this example:

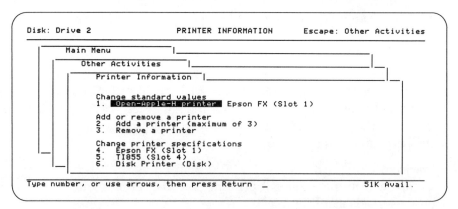

You can add, remove, or change printer settings in AppleWorks from the Printer Information menu.

As you can see, this menu lets you add or remove printers, change printer settings, and choose the *Open-Apple-H printer* where you can print paper copies of the screen (see: Printing the Display[245]). Let's look at these options:

■ **Option 1: Open-Apple-H printer**

When you print an AppleWorks file, you must choose the printer you want to use from a list of printers you currently have configured in AppleWorks. When you use the Hard Copy[122] command (⌂-**H**) to print the screen display, however, AppleWorks automatically uses one specified printer. If you only have one printer configuration stored in AppleWorks, the program will automatically print the display to that printer. If you have more than one printer configured, you can specify the one you want hard copies printed on by choosing option 1, *Open-Apple-H printer* from the Printer Information menu. When you choose this option, AppleWorks presents a list of the printers you currently have configured, and then you simply choose the printer you want Appleworks to use as the hard-copy printer whenever you press ⌂-**H**.

■ **Option 2: Add a printer**

AppleWorks makes a distinction between two basic types of printers: *standard* printers and *custom* printers. Standard printers are some of the more popular printers whose configuration settings are prestored on the AppleWorks program disk. These settings aren't ready to use, however, until you actually add a standard printer from the Add a Printer menu[6] (we'll discuss the procedures shortly).

A custom printer is one whose configuration settings are not prestored on the AppleWorks program disk, and which must be selected by you when you configure the printer. Because the AppleWorks disk is already storing several sets of standard printer-configuration settings, it only has room to store one custom printer setting at a time. Therefore, while you may have up to three printers ready to use at any given time in AppleWorks, only one of them can be a custom printer.

To configure a printer for AppleWorks:

1. Choose option 5, *Other Activities*, from the Main Menu to display the Other Activities menu.

2. Choose option 7, *Specify information about your printer(s)*, to display the Printer Information menu.

3. Choose option 2, *Add a printer (maximum of 3)*, from the Printer Information menu. The Add a Printer menu will appear.

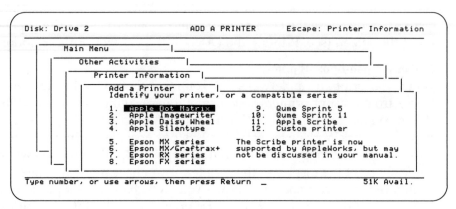

You add printer configurations to AppleWorks by choosing the printer you want from the Add a Printer menu.

4. Choose the printer you have, if that printer is listed (or is compatible with one listed). Choose option 12, *Custom printer*, if your printer is not listed, or is not compatible with one listed.

5. After you choose a printer, you will be prompted to type a name for the printer (even if it's listed). Type any name you want (up to 15 characters) and press **RETURN**.

Choosing the printer's location: Once you have chosen a printer to add and typed a name for it, you must tell AppleWorks how that printer is connected to your computer. After you enter your printer's name and press **RETURN** (step 5, above), a list of connection options appears:

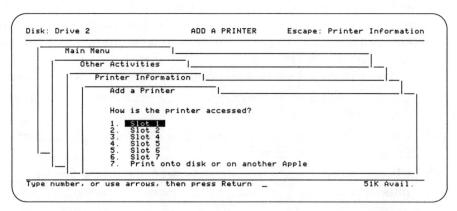

After naming a printer, you must tell AppleWorks how the printer is connected to your computer.

The slot where your printer is connected is either the number of the slot on your Apple IIe or II+ that holds your printer-interface card, or the number of the serial port on your Apple IIc. If you are using only one printer with your Apple IIc, choose *Slot 1* as the option. If you are using both serial ports on your Apple IIc and both of them contain printers, choose *Slot 2* as the second printer's slot.

Notice option 7 on the slot-location menu: *Print onto disk or on another Apple*. This option lets you set up a *disk printer,* so you can print formatted word-processor, spreadsheet, or database files to disk as ASCII files[13]complete with all their formatting options intact. Use this option when you want to send a fully formatted file to another computer via modem. (See: Word Processor Printing;[371] Spreadsheet Printing;[319] and Database Printing.[67])

Specifying printer-configuration settings: After you choose the slot for your printer, a screen of printer-configuration options will appear, like this:

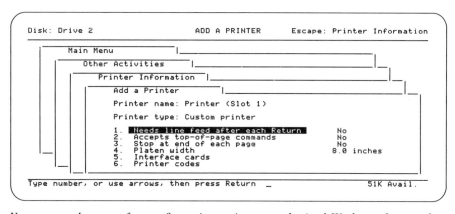

You may need to set a few configuration options to make AppleWorks work properly with your printer.

The sixth option, *Printer codes,* will only appear when you select a custom printer from the Add a Printer menu.

Let's look at each of these settings individually.

Configuration 1—Needs line feed after each Return: This setting tells Apple-Works either to send or not send a line-feed instruction after each carriage return in a file. The options are *Yes* or *No.* The default option is usually set to *No.* To change the option, select it, and then answer *Yes* to the prompt at the bottom of the screen by pressing **Y**, or by highlighting the word *Yes* with → and pressing **RETURN**. The option will change automatically.

Some printers or interface cards supply their own line feeds automatically after receiving a carriage return. The easiest way to determine whether your printer needs AppleWorks to send a line feed is to try it. If the option is set to *No* and your printer prints all your data on one line, then it needs a line feed from AppleWorks. If it prints with normal spacing when the option is set to *No*, then you have the right setting. If the option is set to *Yes* and your printer prints double-spaced text when you have set the printer options for single spacing, then you should change the option to *No*. If the line spacing is correct, then the option is set correctly.

Configuration 2—Accepts top-of-page commands: Nearly every printer made accepts top-of-page commands, and this option should usually be set to *Yes.* You change this option the same way you change the line-feed option. If your printer accepts top-of-page commands, it should automatically advance the paper to the top of the next page when it finishes printing a file. If it doesn't accept top-of-page commands, it will stop immediately when it finishes printing. You should set this option to *Yes,* and if your printer doesn't advance the paper to the top of the next page after printing a file, then it doesn't support this feature.

Configuration 3—Stop at end of each page: Use this option to have Apple-Works stop printing at the end of each page, so that if you are using single sheets of paper (letterhead, for example), you can insert a new piece of paper before AppleWorks prints the next page. If you are using continuous fanfold paper, this option should be set to *No,* unless you are printing on roll paper and you must specifically instruct your printer to stop when it's finished printing each page so you can tear off the pages individually, since roll paper isn't perforated. Most printers will stop at the end of each single-sheet page by themselves, because the printer will sense it's out of paper. If your printer won't stop when it's done printing each page, set this option to *Yes.*

Configuration 4—Platen width: This is the width of the platen, or paper roller, in your printer. It determines the physical length of lines your printer can print. Your printer's manual will tell you exactly how wide your platen is. On standard-sized printers, the platen width is usually 8 or 8½ inches. On wide-carriage printers, the platen width is about 13 inches.

To set the platen width, select the option, and then type the number of inches of your printer's platen. The option will accept both whole and decimal numbers (so you could set a platen width of 10.5, for example).

When you configure your printer, it's best to set the platen width to the printer's maximum printing width. That way, you'll be able to use the printer's full printing range when you specify printer options. You can set the platen width (or length of printed lines) individually for each file that you print with the PW (Platen Width) printer option; but the line width you specify in an application's Printer Options menu using the PW option is limited by the platen-width configuration you choose here (see: Printer Options[217]). Suppose your printer has a 13-inch platen: If you set a platen-width configuration of 8 inches on the Add a Printer screen, you will never be able to print lines longer than 8 inches from a file, even if you set that file's PW printer option to 13 inches using an application's Printer Options menu.

Configuration 5—Interface cards: Use this option to configure AppleWorks to work with your printer-interface card. You don't need to use this option if you are using an Apple IIc, an Apple Parallel Interface Card, or a serial-interface card. If you are using a non-Apple parallel-interface card in an Apple IIe or II+, you may have to specify a different initialization code for your interface than the one currently stored (which is the code for the Apple Parallel Interface Card). To do this, choose the option, answer *No* when asked if the current code is okay, and then type in the code for your printer-interface card (you will find the code in the manual for your interface card). For further information, see: Printer Interface Configuration.[214] After typing the new code, you must type a caret ($^$) symbol in order to exit this screen.

Configuration 6—Printer codes: Printer codes are codes your printer needs to produce enhancements such as boldfacing, underlining, and superscripts and subscripts. The *Printer codes* option only appears on the list of printer-configuration options if you are configuring a custom printer. If you are configuring a standard printer, these settings are already stored in AppleWorks. If you're using a custom printer, you will have to enter the settings yourself.

When you choose the *Printer codes* option, the Printer Codes menu appears, like this:

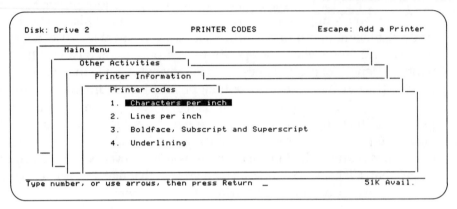

```
Disk: Drive 2                PRINTER CODES        Escape: Add a Printer
   ┌─────Main Menu────────────┐
   │     ┌───Other Activities────────┐
   │     │   ┌──Printer Information──┐
   │     │   │   ┌──Printer codes──────────────┐
   │     │   │   │   1. ████Characters per inch████
   │     │   │   │   2. Lines per inch
   │     │   │   │   3. Boldface, Subscript and Superscript
   │     │   │   │   4. Underlining
   │     │   │   │
   │     │   │
   │     │
Type number, or use arrows, then press Return  _          51K Avail.
```

You enter different print-enhancement codes for your printer on the Printer Codes menu.

You will need your printer's manual to determine the actual codes your printer needs to perform various enhancements. The codes are listed by the type of enhancement: characters per inch (pitch), lines per inch, superscript, subscript, and underlining. Here's how to enter these codes:

♦ Characters per inch: This option tells AppleWorks how to make your printer produce different-sized characters (see: Printer Options[217]). To set this option, check your printer's manual for the sizes of characters it is capable of printing. Your printer will have a different code for each size of character. Once you decide which sizes of characters your printer can print, you must configure AppleWorks for each size you want to use. If you want to configure AppleWorks to print 10, 12, and 15 characters per inch, for example, you must enter a different code for each size, and tell AppleWorks which size that code represents.

1. Choose option 1, *Characters per inch*, from the Printer Codes menu. The following Characters Per Inch menu will appear, prompting you to enter the number of characters per inch you want to configure:

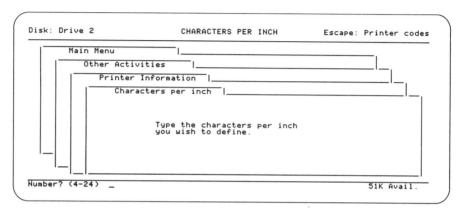

Before you can enter a code to produce a certain size of character, you must tell AppleWorks what size of character you are about to configure.

2. Type the number of characters per inch you want to configure. You can only type in whole numbers when you specify characters per inch. If your printer manual says your printer can print 16.8 characters per inch, for example, you should enter the next-lower whole number: 16. After you specify the size of print and press **RETURN**, a prompt screen appears, as shown in this example:

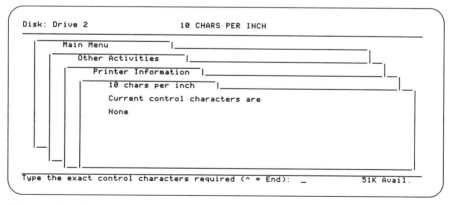

When configuring the AppleWorks characters-per-inch setting, you must type the printer codes exactly as they appear in your printer's manual.

3. Your printer's manual should specify the exact code you need for each characters-per-inch setting: Type it, and then type the caret (^) symbol when you are finished. You will then be returned to the Characters Per Inch menu, where you can enter the next size of character you want to configure, and then enter the code for that size.

For example, if the code required for 10 characters per inch was specified in your printer manual as *Esc y*, you would first press the **ESC** key, followed by **Y**, as in this example:

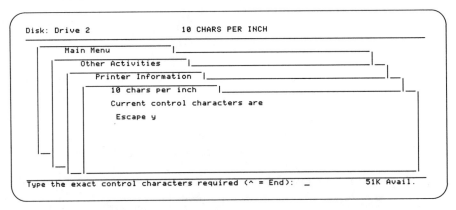

```
Disk: Drive 2                    10 CHARS PER INCH

        Main Menu           |
          Other Activities      |
            Printer Information   |
              10 chars per inch     |
              Current control characters are

                Escape y




Type the exact control characters required (^ = End):  _        51K Avail.
```

Each code sequence will appear on the screen as you type it.

Note that the word *Escape* will appear when you press the **ESC** key; trying to type the word *Escape* instead of pressing the **ESC** key will produce an incorrect code. Also, do not press **SPACE** after pressing **ESC** unless it is part of the required code.

4. Repeat these steps until you have entered a code for each size of character you want to print from AppleWorks, and then press **ESC** from the Characters Per Inch menu to return to the Printer Codes menu.

If you don't configure a specific character size, you can't produce that size of print by specifying it with the CI option on a Printer Options menu. If you didn't configure AppleWorks to print 12 CI characters on your printer, for example, then specifying an option of 12 CI with an application's Printer Options menu will have no effect when you print a file. (For more information see: Printer Options.)

♦ Lines per inch: Line spacing refers to the amount of space around each line in a document—it is not the same as single, double, or triple spacing, which refers to the number of blank lines between each printed line in a document. You can print single, double, or triple spacing and still print the lines at either 6 or 8 lines per inch.

AppleWorks lets you choose between printing 6 lines per inch and printing 8 lines per inch when you select the LI (Lines-per-Inch) printer option for each file. The Lines-per-Inch configuration option sets your printer to make the change when you use this printer option. First, check your printer's manual to see if it's capable of printing 8 lines per inch (every printer can print 6 lines per inch). If your printer can handle both types of line spacing, then choose this option. You will then be given the following Lines Per Inch menu, with options for configuring either 6 lines per inch or 8 lines per inch:

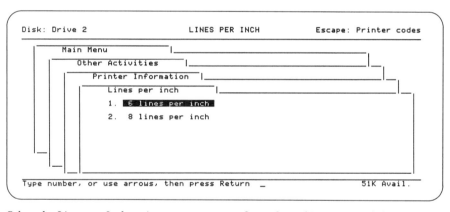

Select the Lines-per-Inch option you want to configure from this menu, and then enter the codes to make your printer print that number of lines per inch.

Choose the option for the setting you want to configure, and then enter the printer code that produces that type of line spacing. You enter the codes exactly as they appear in your printer manual, and type the caret (^) symbol when you finish entering the codes (just as you do when configuring characters per inch, as explained in the preceding section).

You can only configure either 6 or 8 lines per inch in AppleWorks. If your printer is capable of a wider variety of line spacing, you can't use those additional options with AppleWorks.

♦ Boldface, Subscript, and Superscript: These print enhancements are usually available on printers. Check your printer's manual to see whether your printer can perform them, and then look up the printer codes the printer needs for these enhancements. With these enhancements, there are usually two codes: one to begin the enhancement, and one to turn it off. You must enter the codes as explained above for the Characters-per-Inch setting: You select the option from the following menu for the code you want to enter, and then enter the code.

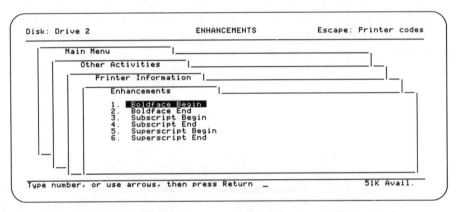

Choose the type of print enhancement you want to configure, and then enter the appropriate printer code for it.

♦ Underlining: Different printers perform underlining in different ways. This option lets you set AppleWorks to send underlining commands that your printer understands. Consult the manual to determine your printer's method of underlining, and then select the method from this menu:

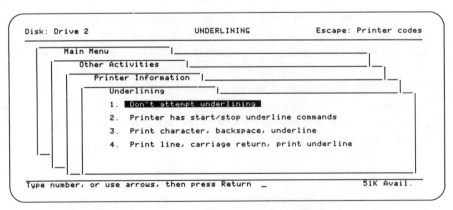

Use this menu to select the method your printer uses to underline text.

Some printers use control codes to begin and end underlining, just as for boldfacing and super- or subscripts. If your printer uses codes for this feature, choose option 2, *Printer has start/stop underline commands,* and then enter the codes to begin and end underlining as you do for Characters-per-Inch and the other enhancements.

♦ Serial interface settings: If you are using an Apple IIc, an option called *Serial interface settings* will appear at the bottom of your Printer Codes menu. Use this option to set or change the baud rate, parity, and data format settings in AppleWorks to match those expected by your serial printer. You can determine which settings are correct by looking in the manual for your printer interface.

Storing the configuration: After you set all the configuration options you want for your printer, press **ESC** until you to return to the Other Activities menu. The configuration will be stored automatically on the AppleWorks program disk.

■ Option 3: Remove a printer

You can remove a printer configuration from AppleWorks whenever you like by choosing option 3, *Remove a printer,* from the Printer Information menu. A list of stored printers will appear, and you can choose the printer you want to remove. When you select the printer and press **RETURN**, the printer configuration is removed.

■ Options 4, 5, and 6: Changing a printer's specifications

You can change your printer's configuration settings at any time. To change a setting, choose one of the options in the *Change printer specifications* section on the Printer Information menu. The list of configuration options will appear again, just as it did when you first added the printer, and you can change any option you like, except the printer's name and how the printer is accessed. If you want to change the printer's name or which slot it's connected to in your computer, you must remove the printer, add it again, and reconfigure it.

■ **If a printer doesn't work**

If you have added a printer and chosen its configuration settings correctly, but the printer still doesn't print properly, there are several things to check:

1. Make sure your printer is turned on, and that the printer cable is plugged in firmly to your printer and your interface or interface card. If you're using an Apple IIe or II+, make sure your printer-interface card is firmly seated in its slot.

2. Check all the configuration settings for the printer, to make sure you have entered them correctly.

3. Make sure the "ready" or "on-line" indicator light on your printer is on. If it isn't, press the printer's on-line or ready button.

4. If you follow steps 1, 2, and 3, and the printer still doesn't work properly, you may have a problem with your printer interface and you should double-check the configurations for it. (See: Printer Interface Configuration.[214])

Printer Information menu

■ **Definition**

The *Printer Information menu* is the main list of options for specifying which printers will be used by AppleWorks. It contains options for adding, removing, and changing printer specifications, and options for specifying which printer will be used when the Hard Copy[122] command (⌂-H) is used to print the display.

■ **Usage**

Use the Printer Information menu when you want to access one of the options for specifying which printers will be used by AppleWorks, and how they will be used. AppleWorks must be informed about a type of printer and its operating characteristics before it can use the printer properly. To use the Printer Information menu:

1. Choose *Other Activities* (option 5) from the AppleWorks Main Menu.[158]

2. Choose *Specify information about your printer(s)* (option 7) from the Other Activities menu.[178] The Printer Information menu will appear, as in this example:

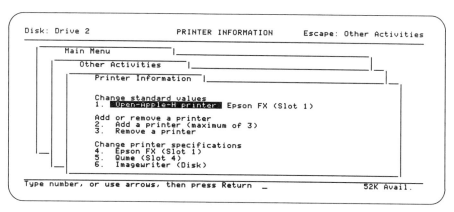

```
Disk: Drive 2              PRINTER INFORMATION      Escape: Other Activities
    _____
   | Main Menu            |_____
   |   _____
   |  | Other Activities   |_____  |
   |  |   _____                                      | |_
   |  |  | Printer Information  |_____     |  |_
   |  |  |                                                  |     |   |
   |  |  |  Change standard values                          |     |   |
   |  |  |  1.  Open-Apple-H printer  Epson FX (Slot 1)      |     |   |
   |  |  |                                                  |     |   |
   |  |  |  Add or remove a printer                         |     |   |
   |  |  |  2.  Add a printer (maximum of 3)                |     |   |
   |  |  |  3.  Remove a printer                            |     |   |
   |  |  |                                                  |     |   |
   |  |  |  Change printer specifications                   |     |   |
   |  |_ |  4.  Epson FX (Slot 1)                           |     |   |
   |  |_ |  5.  Qume (Slot 4)                               |     |   |
   |     |  6.  Imagewriter (Disk)                          |     |   |
    _____
    Type number, or use arrows, then press Return  _            52K Avail.
```

The Printer Information menu is the main pathway to all options for specifying the printers you will use with AppleWorks.

3. Choose the option you want to work with.

Change standard values (option 1) lets you select the printer that will be used when you use the Hard Copy (⌂-H) command to print the contents of an AppleWorks screen. When you choose this option, the screen shows a list of currently configured printers for AppleWorks. You can then select the printer you want AppleWorks to use when you issue the Hard Copy command.

Add a printer (option 2) produces a list of stored printer configurations, from which you can select a configuration that will be immediately available to AppleWorks when you print a file. You can add up to a maximum of three printers. (See: Add a Printer menu.[6])

Remove a printer (option 3) produces a list of currently active printer configurations which have been selected from the Add a Printer menu. You can remove a configuration by selecting it from the menu.

Change printer specifications (options 4 through 6) lets you display and alter the configuration settings for any of the up to three currently available printers you have set up for AppleWorks with the Add a Printer menu. (See: Change A Printer menu.[29])

Printer interface configuration

You need two things before you can actually print paper copies of Apple-Works files: a *printer* and a *printer interface*. There are two types of printers, *parallel* and *serial*, which require parallel and serial interfaces. But no matter what printer you use, you must *configure* AppleWorks to work with it (see: Printer Configuration[200]). Depending on the type of printer interface you have, however, you might or might not have to configure AppleWorks to work with it as well, in addition to configuring the printer itself.

Note: Versions 1.0 and 1.1 of AppleWorks don't feature the built-in interface-configuration utility described in this entry. If you have one of these versions, you will have to get a separate disk, called the AppleWorks Interface Configuration Utility, from your Apple dealer. There's no charge for the disk, and it contains complete instructions for its use.

■ **Usage**

A printer interface takes one of three forms:

☐ A *parallel-interface card* that fits into one of the slots on an Apple IIe or II+.

☐ A *serial-interface card* that fits into one of the slots on an Apple IIe or II+.

☐ The *serial ports* built into the Apple IIc.

As it's delivered from the factory, AppleWorks is set up to work with only two specific printer interfaces: the Apple Parallel Interface Card and the Apple IIc's built-in serial ports. If you have an Apple Parallel Interface Card, you only have to configure AppleWorks to work with your printer, as explained in the Printer Configuration[200] entry.

To set up a serial port on an Apple IIc, choose the Serial Interface option from the Printer Codes menu, and then set the baud rate, data format, and parity according to what your printer expects. You will find the settings you need in your printer's manual. If you are using a serial card with an Apple IIe or Apple II+, you configure it by setting the card's DIP switches. Refer to the card's user manual for the correct switch settings.

The interface situation becomes more complex when you are using a parallel interface card other than the Apple Parallel Interface Card.

There are several third-party interface cards on the market, and most of them handle data a little differently than the Apple Parallel Interface Card. You know your printer interface isn't configured properly if your printer won't print within the proper margins all the time, or if it prints a control code, such as *80N*, at the top of the page when it begins printing.

These problems occur because different parallel-interface cards expect different *initialization codes*—codes that make the card ready to receive data and pass it on to your printer. The code initializes the interface card and turns off the screen echo, so that data is not displayed on the screen as it is being printed. The default code AppleWorks sends to achieve this is *Control-I 80N*, but many other cards use a different code, such as *Control-I 99N*, or *Control-I 0N*. To compensate for this, you must configure AppleWorks for your specific interface by entering its initialization code.

When you configure a printer for the first time in AppleWorks, and you are using a non-Apple parallel-interface card, you must choose option 5, *Interface cards*, on the Add a Printer menu:[6]

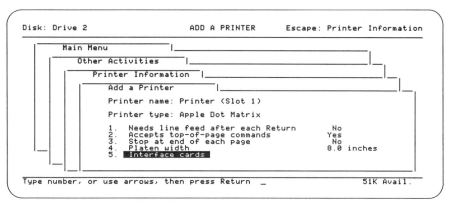

You can configure AppleWorks for different parallel-interface cards by choosing option 5 from the Add a Printer menu.

To configure your interface card:

1. Choose option 5, *Interface cards*, from the Add a Printer menu after you have chosen the type of printer you want to add. The screen will

change to an explanation about the initialization code AppleWorks sends out:

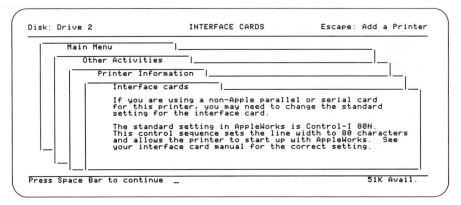

When you choose option 5, Interface cards, *from the Add a Printer menu, this screen appears.*

2. When you press **SPACE** to continue, AppleWorks displays the current interface code, and the prompt line asks if you want to change it, as in this example:

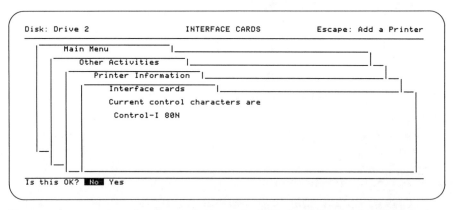

You can type new printer-interface codes to set AppleWorks up for your interface card.

3. Consult your printer-interface manual to determine the initialization code the interface uses to turn off screen echoing. If the code is the same as the one stored in AppleWorks, you can answer *Yes* to the prompt, and exit the interface configuration utility.

4. If the code for your interface card is different, answer *No* to the prompt. A blank screen appears, and you can enter the initialization code for your printer. You must type in the code with exactly the same keystrokes shown in your interface-card manual. For control sequences, such as the Control-I in the above example, hold down **CONTROL** and press I (or whatever letter is required), and that sequence will appear on the screen. When you finish entering the code, type the caret[22] symbol (^) to exit the code-entry screen. The code will then be stored, and your interface card should work properly.

■ Comments

A few parallel-printer interface cards expect to receive data in an 8-bit format. AppleWorks sends data to printers in a 7-bit format. If you have entered your interface card's proper initialization code along with the proper printer codes and your printer still won't print properly, you may have to reset a DIP switch on your interface card so it can receive data in a 7-bit format. You will find instructions for this in your interface-card manual. If your problems persist after that, you should consult the manufacturer of your interface card for further assistance.

Printer Options (Ú-O)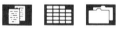

When you want to use special formatting or other printing options for AppleWorks files, you must specify them from the Printer Options menu in the application you are using. You display the Printer Options menu with the Options command, Ú-O. Each of the AppleWorks applications has its own Printer Options menu. Some of the options are unique to one menu (the word processor has many printer options not available in the spreadsheet or database), and some of the options (such as left and right margins) are common to all menus.

This section explains all the printer options available in AppleWorks. The general procedure for specifying printer options is always the same:

1. Press the Options command (Ú-O) from the word-processor Review/ Add/Change screen, spreadsheet Review/Add/Change screen, or database Report Format screen. The Printer Options menu will appear. (If you are working with the word processor, you must first move the cursor to the place where you want the printer option to begin before displaying the Printer Options menu.)

2. Type the two-letter code for the option you want to specify, then press **RETURN**. In some cases (such as margin settings), you will have to type a value after the option code. You can type as many printer options as you want, as long as the menu is displayed.

3. To return to the Review/Add/Change screen or Report Format screen, press **ESC**.

The Printer Options menus are shown in the following screen displays, and the descriptions of the options follow in alphabetical order.

```
File: Sales Letter           PRINTER OPTIONS        Escape: Review/Add/Change
=====|====|====|====|====|====|====|====|====|====|====|====|====|====|===
December 13, 1985*
*
Mr. Ed Frobish*
Frobish Linen Service*
335 Ramona Ave.*
San Jose, CA 95551*
*
Dear Ed:*
*
We think you're a super customer, and I wanted to tell you
how much all of us at Acme Widgets appreciate your business.
     PW=8.0  LM=1.0  RM=1.0  CI=10  UJ  PL=11.0  TM=0.0  BM=2.0  LI=6  SS
Option: _               UJ: Unjustified      GB: Group Begin       BE: Boldface End
                        CN: Centered         GE: Group End         +B: Superscript Beg
PW: Platen Width        PL: Paper Length     HE: Page Header       +E: Superscript End
LM: Left Margin         TM: Top Margin       FO: Page Footer       -B: Subscript Begin
RM: Right Margin        BM: Bottom Margin    SK: Skip Lines        -E: Subscript End
CI: Chars per Inch      LI: Lines per Inch   PN: Page Number       UB: Underline Begin
P1: Proportional-1      SS: Single Space     PE: Pause Each page   UE: Underline End
P2: Proportional-2      DS: Double Space     PH: Pause Here        PP: Print Page No.
IN: Indent              TS: Triple Space     SM: Set a Marker      EK: Enter Keyboard
JU: Justified           NP: New Page         BB: Boldface Begin
```

The word-processor Printer Options menu.

```
File: Bonus Analysis          PRINTER OPTIONS        Escape: Review/Add/Change
================================================================================

-------Left and right margins-------        ------Top and bottom margins------
PW: Platen Width        8.0 inches      PL: Paper Length      11.0 inches
LM: Left Margin         0.0 inches      TM: Top Margin         0.0 inches
RM: Right Margin        0.0 inches      BM: Bottom Margin      0.0 inches
CI: Chars per Inch      10              LI: Lines per Inch     6

   Line width           8.0 inches          Printing length   11.0 inches
   Char per line (est)  80                  Lines per page     66

            -------------------Formatting options-------------------
            SC:  Send Special Codes to printer                  No
            PH:  Print report Header at top of each page         Yes
                 Single, Double or Triple Spacing (SS/DS/TS)     SS



------------------------------------------------------------------------
Type a two letter option code  _                              47K Avail.
```

The spreadsheet Printer Options menu.

```
 File: Customers             PRINTER OPTIONS          Escape: Report Format
 Report: Phone List
 ==========================================================================
 -------Left and right margins--------       ------Top and bottom margins-------
 PW: Platen Width         8.0 inches      PL: Paper Length        11.0 inches
 LM: Left Margin          0.0 inches      TM: Top Margin           0.0 inches
 RM: Right Margin      •  0.0 inches      BM: Bottom Margin        2.0 inches
 CI: Chars per Inch      10               LI: Lines per Inch       6
     Line width           8.0 inches          Printing length      9.0 inches
     Char per line (est)  80                   Lines per page      54
         -------------------Formatting options-------------------
         SC:  Send Special Codes to printer                     No
         PD:  Print a Dash when an entry is blank               No
         PH:  Print report Header at top of each page           Yes
              Single, Double or Triple Spacing (SS/DS/TS)       SS



 --------------------------------------------------------------------------
 Type a two letter option code  _                            47K Avail.
```

The database Tables report format Printer Options menu.

```
 File: Customers             PRINTER OPTIONS          Escape: Report Format
 Report: Mailing Labels
 ==========================================================================
 -------Left and right margins--------       ------Top and bottom margins-------
 PW: Platen Width         8.0 inches      PL: Paper Length        11.0 inches
 LM: Left Margin          0.0 inches      TM: Top Margin           0.0 inches
 RM: Right Margin         0.0 inches      BM: Bottom Margin        0.0 inches
 CI: Chars per Inch      10               LI: Lines per Inch       6
     Line width           8.0 inches          Printing length     11.0 inches
     Char per line (est)  80                   Lines per page      66
         -------------------Formatting options-------------------
         SC:  Send Special Codes to printer                     No
         PD:  Print a Dash when an entry is blank               No
         PH:  Print report Header at top of each page           Yes
         OL:  Omit Line when all entries on line are blank      Yes
         KS:  Keep number of lines the Same within each record  Yes

 --------------------------------------------------------------------------
 Type a two letter option code  _                            46K Avail.
```

The database Labels report format Printer Options menu.

Using word-processor printer options

All of the printer options for the spreadsheet and database affect the entire file, but the word processor's printer options can affect as little as one character, word, sentence, or paragraph. Because the word processor's options can affect only part of a file, it's important for you to be able to see where printer options have been placed in a file. AppleWorks handles this in two ways.

If the option is one that can affect as little as one word or character, the option is shown as a caret[22] symbol (^) where it occurs on the screen. The same caret symbol is used to show the placement of many different printer options, including super- and subscripts, boldfacing, underlining, and page numbering, but you can tell which printer option is being indicated on the

Review/Add/Change screen by placing the cursor on the caret. When you place the cursor on any caret symbol used to indicate a printer option, the option that caret represents is shown in the line-indicator area at the bottom of the screen.

Other printer options in the word processor can't affect less than a paragraph. Such options include margins, line spacing, and pitch settings. Because these options can't fall in the middle of a paragraph, they are shown as text on the screen above the paragraph where they begin to take effect. Normally, these options are hidden from view so they don't distract you from your text editing, but you can display all these printer options by pressing the Zoom[376] command (⌂-Z). When you want to hide the options, just press Zoom again. Printer options are only displayed on the screen if you have specified settings different from the defaults, so if you don't change the default-margin or line-spacing settings, for example, these settings won't be displayed on the screen when you use the Zoom command.

Now that we've covered how printer options are inserted and displayed, let's look at the options themselves.

Boldfacing text (BB and BE, or CONTROL-B)

You can print word-processor text in boldface with two different sets of options: by specifying the Boldface Begin (BB) and Boldface End (BE) options from the Printer Options menu, or by pressing **CONTROL-B** directly from the Review/Add/Change screen. The **CONTROL-B** alternative is available because it's faster than using the Printer Options menu.

If you want to use the BB and BE options from the Printer Options menu, you must place the cursor at the beginning of text you want boldfaced before pressing ⌂-O and typing the BB option. Then press **ESC** in order to return to the Review/Add/Change screen, and then place the cursor at the end of the boldfaced text before pressing ⌂-O and typing the BE option. Because this requires displaying the Printer Options menu two different times (once each when the cursor is at the locations where you want to begin and end boldfacing), it isn't a very efficient procedure for such a common print enhancement.

The **CONTROL-B** command lets you specify boldfacing in the word processor directly from the Review/Add/Change screen, without having to display the Printer Options menu. To use **CONTROL-B**, simply move the cursor to the beginning of the boldfaced section of text, press **CONTROL-B**, and then move the cursor to the end of the boldfacing and press **CONTROL-B** again. The presence of the boldface begin and end options is shown on the Review/Add/Change screen by the caret symbol (^).

Boldfacing can only be accomplished if your printer is capable of doing it, and if AppleWorks has been configured so it can instruct your printer to print in boldface. (See: Printer Configuration.[200])

You can boldface a single character or an entire paragraph. Any Boldface Begin command will terminate at the next paragraph mark if a Boldface End command isn't applied. So if you want to boldface more than one paragraph, you will have to apply the Boldface Begin command to each paragraph.

Centering (CN), Justifying (JU), and Unjustifying (UJ) text

You can control the alignment of text in a word-processor document with three printer options: *Center* (CN), *Justify* (JU), and *Unjustify* (UJ). All three of these options are indicated on the screen as text lines, which can be revealed with the Zoom command (⌂-**Z**).

Center (CN): Use the Center (CN) option from the word processor's Printer Options menu when you want text to be centered on a line. You can use the Center option anywhere in a document, but you must use the Un-justify (UJ) option to return to the default of left-justified text.

The Center option takes effect at the first carriage return before your cursor's position. If your cursor is in the middle of a paragraph, for example, and the previous carriage return is in the space before the paragraph, the entire paragraph will be centered when you choose the Center option.

Be sure to use the UJ option to return to left-justified text, if you are only centering part of a document. Centered text is shown on the screen as it will appear when printed on paper. If you are using Characters-per-Inch (CI) settings other than the default of 10 which can't be displayed on the screen, however, each centered line may not have the same contents when printed as it does on the screen. (See the section on Pitch, below.)

Justify (JU): Use the Justify option (JU) when you want to justify both the right and left edges of the text in a word-processor document. Normally, word-processor text is left justified: The text is lined up so every line begins evenly along the left side of the document. The Justify option places extra spaces between words on each line so the text is both left and right jus-tified: Every line not only begins evenly, but ends evenly. You can see the dif-ference in this sample printout:

```
This is an example of ordinary, unjustified text, which is
text that has a justified left margin, and a typically
unjustified, or "ragged right" margin.  Notice that every
line ends at a different place.  This kind of text is
usually acceptable for most business uses, but sometimes one
wants a more formal look.

This is an example of justified text, which is text that has
both left  and right margins justified.  Notice that all the
lines begin  at the  same place,  and end at the same place.
As you can see, this look is a little more formal and crisp.
```

Text in word-processor documents is normally left justified only, but you can justify both margins with the JU option.

In this sample, you can see that the justified text contains larger spaces between words than the unjustified text. The spaces have been automatically inserted by AppleWorks to make the lines end in the same place.

You can justify as little as one paragraph of a document, if you like. If the cursor is in the middle of a paragraph when you type the Justify option, that entire paragraph and the text below it to the end of the document will auto-matically be justified.

If you only want to justify part of a document, be sure to return the docu-ment to its normal formatting by using the Unjustified (UJ) option at the end of the section you want justified.

The Justify option doesn't affect the appearance of text on the screen—the text is only justified when it is printed out.

Unjustify (UJ): Text in the word processor is normally formatted in the *Un-justify* mode. Unjustify means that text is justified only at the left margin.

All lines begin at the same place along the left margin, but lines can end in different places in relationship to the right margin, depending on the contents of each line.

Use the Unjustify option when part of your text has been either justified or centered, and you want to return the remainder of the document to the normal formatting mode. You can specify different justification options (Justify, Unjustify, or Center) as often as every paragraph in a word-processor document. The Unjustify option takes effect at the carriage return before the cursor's position. Thus, if you type the Unjustify option when the cursor is in the middle of a paragraph, that entire paragraph will be unjustified.

Enter Keyboard (EK)

The Enter Keyboard (EK) option pauses the printer to allow entry of data from the keyboard when a word-processor document is being printed. Use this option when you want to enter custom information into one or more documents that are being printed on the printer. The Enter Keyboard option lets you enter custom information into a file as the file is printed.

The Enter Keyboard option is only available in word-processor documents. When you specify it, the presence of the EK option in a document is indicated by a caret (^) symbol.

Example: Suppose you want to send the same sales letter to four different customers, and you don't want to create four separate files for printing. You can use the EK command to customize the data in each letter as you print from the same file. Here's how to customize the data in the letter's salutation:

1. Place the cursor one space after the word *Dear* in the greeting line of the letter.
2. Display the Printer Options menu with the ⌂-O command.
3. Type the EK option, and press **RETURN**.
4. Press **ESC** to continue working with your letter.

A caret symbol will appear in the greeting line, one space after the word *Dear.* When you print the letter, you will be prompted to enter the custom data when the printer reaches this point, as in this example:

```
File: Sales Letter              PRINT MENU          Escape: Review/Add/Change
=====|====|====|====|====|====|====|====|====|====|====|====|====|====|===
Dear █




                    You can type information to be placed
                    at the point marked above.

-----------------------------------------------------------------------------
Information? _                                               44K Avail.
```

When you use the EK option, AppleWorks prompts you to enter the custom information before the file is printed.

Now you can enter the name of the customer, and then press **RETURN**. (If you make a mistake typing the name, you can correct it by using **DELETE** before pressing **RETURN**.)

After you press **RETURN**, the rest of the letter will be printed, and the name you typed will be printed starting at the position of the caret symbol. Each time you print this letter, AppleWorks will prompt you to enter the custom information you want when it encounters the caret symbol.

You can use as many EK options in a document as you like. If you use EK twice, for example, you'll be prompted to enter the data for the first marker, and then part of the document will print. At the second marker, the printer will pause, and you will be prompted to enter the data for that marker.

Group Begin (GB) and Group End (GE)

The Group Begin (GB) and Group End (GE) printer options are used to keep a block of text together so it isn't split between two pages in a printed word-processor document. Neither of these options is available in the spreadsheet or database.

Use the Group Begin and Group End printer options when you have a section of text that must be printed all on one page, and you want to make sure that the word processor doesn't insert a page break in the middle of it.

You begin a group of text with the GB command, and you specify the end of the group with the GE command. In order for this feature to work properly, a group should be less than a page in length.

When you define a group, the group begins at the carriage return before the cursor position. Thus, if the cursor is in the middle of a paragraph when you type the GB option and the last carriage return is in the spacing line above the paragraph, the group will begin just before the paragraph. The GB and GE options are shown as text lines on the screen, and can be revealed with the Zoom command (Ó-Z).

When you print a document containing a group, the word processor determines whether the group will fit completely on the current page. If it will, the group is printed. If the group won't fit on the current page, AppleWorks begins a new page before it starts printing the group.

You must always end a group with the Group End command.

Headers (HE) and Footers (FO)

The Header (HE) and Footer (FO) printer options are used to insert text at the top (header) or bottom (footer) of a specified page or pages within a word-processor document.

Use the Header or Footer options when you want to specify, format, and enter text to be printed at the top or bottom of the pages in a word-processor document. The options take effect starting with the page the cursor is on when you specify them (the Page header command must be issued on the first line of the page), so it's possible to have a header or footer on some pages and not on others. It is also possible for you to change the header or footer on each page.

Example: Suppose you are creating a price list, and you want the name of the report and the date to appear at the top of each page. Here's how to use the Header option to do this:

1. Place the cursor on the first line of the page of the document where you want the Header to begin printing.
2. Display the Printer Options menu with the Ó-O command.
3. Type the HE option, and press **RETURN**.
4. Press **ESC** to return to the Review/Add/Change screen.
5. The location of the Header option will appear on the screen, and the cursor will be at the beginning of the line below it.

6. Type the text you want to appear in the Header, and then press
    RETURN to move any other text on that line down to a new line, as
    shown in this example:

```
File: Price List                 REVIEW/ADD/CHANGE           Escape: Main Menu
=====|====|====|====|====|====|====|====|====|====|====|====|====|====|===
--------Page Header
Widget Price List - January, 1986

Widgets

            Item                        Price

        Standard Widget               24.95  ea.
        Widget Deluxe                 39.95  ea.
        Widget Flexy                  59.95  ea.


Widget Supplies

        Widget Oil                     5.95  qt.
        Widget Grease                  2.95  lb.


-----------------------------------------------------------------------------
Type entry or use ⬚ commands          Line 3  Column  1        ⬚-? for Help
```

Headers can be inserted in documents by typing the HE option from the Printer Options
menu, and then typing the text of the title below the option on the screen.

7. The text you typed below the Header option will now appear on the
    first line of that page (after the top margin), and each subsequent page
    of the document.

    This process is the same with footers, except you use the FO option. The
    text of the header or footer must appear on the line directly below the HE or
    FO option on the Review/Add/Change screen. The text of the header or footer
    must be on a line by itself with a carriage return at the end.

    The HE and FO options always appear on the screen—you don't need to
    use the Zoom command to display them. The actual printed headers or foot-
    ers don't appear on each page when the document is displayed on the screen
    —they only appear when you print the document (except the one you en-
    tered when setting up the header or footer).

    You can change a header or footer within a document simply by moving
    the cursor to the top of the appropriate page (you will have to calculate page
    breaks first with the Calculate[18] command (⌘-K)), using the option again,
    and specifying different text on the line below. You can also insert page num-
    bers automatically into headers or footers. To do this, you use the PP (Print
    Page Number) option as part of the line of header or footer text. (See: Page
    Numbering on page 237.)

Indent (IN)

The Indent (IN) option indents text below the first line in a paragraph by the number of spaces you specify to create what's called a "hanging" paragraph. Use the Indent option to indent several lines of text the same distance from the left margin. The IN option is useful for indented quotations or paragraphs, or bulleted items in which each item is more than one line long. This option is only available in the word processor.

The Indent command does not indent the first line of a paragraph—it only indents the lines below the first line. Thus, you can't use the Indent option to indent a list of items in separate paragraphs that are each one line long. (You can, however, use the **TAB** or **SPACE** key to manually indent the first lines of indented paragraphs as single-line lists before you type them.)

You can think of every document as having text that is indented 0 characters. If you are indenting text in the middle of a document, you must be sure to set the indent back to 0 characters at the end of the indented portion, so the text below it will have normal margins.

When you Indent paragraphs of text, they will appear indented on the screen as they will be when printed. Normally, though, the actual settings don't appear on the screen. To check the settings, press the Zoom ($\circlearrowleft$-**Z**) command: The indent settings (as well as any other printer-option settings) will appear as separate lines on the screen, preceded by dashed lines.

Example: Suppose you want to indent a list of the features and benefits of a product in a sales brochure. The opening and closing paragraphs have normal margins, but you want the items between them indented 10 characters. Here's how:

1. Type the first paragraph of the brochure (be sure to press **RETURN** at the end).

2. With the cursor below the first paragraph, display the Printer Options menu with the $\circlearrowleft$-**O** command.

3. Type *IN* for the Indent option, and press **RETURN**.

4. A prompt line reading *Chars:* will appear below the *Option* line: Type *10* for an indent of 10 character spaces.

5. Press **RETURN**, and then press **ESC** to return to the Review/Add/ Change screen.

6. Type the indented items. (The first line of each item won't be indented, so you'll have to use the **TAB** key to move the cursor over to column 10 before you type the first line in each item.)

7. When you're finished typing the indented items, display the Printer Options menu again with Ô-**O**.

8. Type *IN* again, and then type the value *0* to return to normal indent.

9. Press **RETURN**, and then press **ESC** to return to the Review/Add/Change screen.

10. Type the last paragraph of the document, which won't be indented now that you've returned the indent value to 0.

Here's the first screen of a sample document (the indent options have been displayed with the Zoom command):

```
File: Brochure                     REVIEW/ADD/CHANGE            Escape: Main Menu
=====|==|=|====|====|====|====|====|====|====|====|====|====|====|===
Acme Widget Manufacturing Company proudly announces its
latest product, the Widget Flexy.  The Flexy is a
breakthrough in widgeting, because it combines value,
convenience, and multiple-use options in one
competitively-priced product.  Look at these features:*
*
--------Indent: 10 chars
        - Widget Flexy is equally at home in industrial,
          service-oriented, and office environments.*
*
        - Widget Flexy is available immediately in high
          volume quantities, to meet even the most demanding
          customer's needs.*
*
        - Widget Flexy is plug-compatible with every
          existing widget in the Acme line, and it outlasts
          the Standard Widget in our lineup by an average of
          150 man-years.*
--------Indent: 0 chars
*
----------------------------------------------------------------------------
Type entry or use Ô commands           Line 20  Column  1       Ô-? for Help
```

Use the Indent option to indent paragraphs that contain more than one line each.

You can indent text up to 64 characters in a word-processor document. If you are only indenting a few lines, you can do so manually by using **TAB** or **SPACE** to move the cursor to the indent point before you begin typing.

If you specify an Indent value when the cursor is in the middle of a paragraph, the option will appear above the paragraph, and that entire paragraph (except for the first line) will be indented.

Keep Same (KS)

The Keep Same (KS) printer option is used to maintain the same number of lines in all records of Labels database reports, even if all the records don't have data in every category. This option is only available in the database from the Labels report format Printer Options screen.

The KS option is an important feature when you are printing names and addresses on pre-cut mailing labels. Such mailing labels are typically an inch high, which works out to six printed lines of data. In a report of this type, you normally leave a blank line above and below the data so the data is centered on each label. The data itself is printed on four lines. Normally, this is fine with addresses that contain a name, a company, a street, and a city, state, and zip code. The data would be arranged like this:

Name

Company

Street

City, State Zip

But what happens when one of your records is missing one or more lines of data? If the name or company is missing from a record, and you have used the Omit Line (OL) option (discussed on page 234) to instruct the database to omit a line from the report when an entry is missing, then such a record will print only five lines (three data lines and two space lines). The records below will move up one line as a result, and there will no longer be a spacing line at the top of each mailing label. It would only take two five-line records to ruin the spacing of the records on the labels so that part of each record was printing on the bottom of the previous record's label. With the KS option set to *Yes*, however, AppleWorks will add the required spacing lines at the bottom of each record that is missing a data line.

The KS option works together with the Omit Line (OL) option. The OL option allows you to omit a line from a printed record if there isn't any data on the line. If the OL option is set to *No*, then records will always print the same height, because a blank line will be inserted to take up the space of the missing data. In this case, the KS option isn't visible on the Printer Options menu, because it isn't needed. If the OL option is set to *Yes*, however, then the KS option is displayed and you can set it to *Yes* or *No*. (See: Omit Line, on page 234.)

Line Spacing (SS, DS, and TS)

The default line spacing for all AppleWorks files is single spacing. However, you can change settings on the Printer Options menu and print any AppleWorks word-processor file, spreadsheet file, or database Tables report with single, double, or triple spacing between each line. You do this with the Single-Space (SS), Double-Space (DS), and Triple-Space (TS) options.

In the spreadsheet and database, you can select only one line-spacing option for the entire file. In the word processor, you can change the line spacing at every carriage return. Line-spacing options in the word processor take effect at the carriage return before the cursor. If your cursor is in the middle of a paragraph when you specify the DS option, for example, and the preceding carriage return is in the space before the beginning of the paragraph, then the entire paragraph will be double spaced. The line-spacing options are shown in the word processor as text—you can reveal them with the Zoom command (⌘-z).

If you want to double space only part of a document that is otherwise single spaced, remember that you must specify the SS (Single Space) option to return to single spacing at the end of the double-spaced section.

Lines per Inch (LI)

The Lines-per-Inch option (LI) changes the number of lines in an Apple-Works file that will be printed on each vertical inch of paper. AppleWorks permits two different LI settings: 6 lines per inch (which is the default), and 8 lines per inch. Use the settings for 8 lines per inch when you want to print as many lines on each page as possible.

In the database and the spreadsheet, one LI setting controls the entire file. In the word processor, you can change the LI setting as often as every paragraph.

In the word processor, a new LI setting takes effect at the last carriage return before the cursor's current location. Thus, if you set a new LI when the cursor is in the middle of a paragraph, the new setting will affect the entire paragraph and the rest of the document. The LI option is shown as a line of text in a word-processor document. Ordinarily, it's hidden from view, but you can display it with the Zoom command (⌘-z).

None of the AppleWorks applications show the effect of a changed LI setting on the screen—you have to print out the file to see the difference. If you change the LI in the spreadsheet or database, however, the Lines-Per-Page indicator on the Printer Options menu will change to display the new number of lines.

You can type values other than 6 and 8 after typing the LI option, but AppleWorks won't accept them. In order for the LI setting of 8 to actually affect your printed output, your printer must be capable of printing 8 lines per inch, and it must have been configured to accept this option from Apple-Works (see: Printer Configuration[200]).

For more detailed information about printing different numbers of lines per inch, see: Word Processor Printing;[371] Spreadsheet Printing;[319] and Database Printing.[67]

Margins (LM, RM, TM, BM)

The margin-setting options in all three AppleWorks applications are Left (LM), Right (RM), Top (TM), and Bottom (BM). Changing these options in a spreadsheet or database file affects the *entire* printed document, but you can't see the effects on-screen. In the word processor, however, the margin settings are not limited to the entire document. Instead, sections of text within a document can be adjusted. For example, you can set off a long quotation in an essay as a block-indented paragraph. The on-screen document will then change to show the effect of adjusted left and right margins.

The default margin settings (in inches) for the three applications are:

	Top	Bottom	Left	Right
Word Processor	0	2	1	1
Database (Tables reports)	0	2	0	0
Database (Labels reports)	0	0	0	0
Spreadsheet	0	0	0	0

The default top margin for all applications is 0 to allow for the feeding of single sheets of paper into sheet-feed printers.

A margin setting can be either a whole number, such as 2 (which yields a 2-inch margin), or a single decimal, such as 2.5 (which yields a 2½-inch margin). The maximum possible setting for any of the margins is 9 inches.

When you change a margin setting in the spreadsheet or database, the new number will appear next to the setting caption on the Printer Options screen as soon as you type it. If you forget what you set the margins at, and want to find out what they are, you must display the Printer Options menu (Ú-O). In the word processor, you can view the settings right on the document by pressing the Zoom command (Ú-Z): The settings you have changed and their values will appear on the lines where you set them (press Ú-Z to hide them again).

As mentioned, when you change a margin setting in the spreadsheet or database, the document on-screen does not change to show the effect. In both of these applications, you must either print the file on paper to find out if you've cut off part of the spreadsheet by changing the margins or check the width of the selected information against the line width allowed by the application's printer options by looking at the spreadsheet Print screen,[198] or by looking at the database Tables report *Len* indicator[154] and Characters-per-Line indicator.[31]

The location of the cursor in a spreadsheet or database file is not important when you open the Printer Options menu and change margin settings, because the entire document is affected. Cursor location is important in the word processor, however, because individual paragraphs are affected. The general steps for specifying a margin within word-processor documents are:

1. Move the cursor to the beginning of the first line of the section you want to adjust.
2. Press ⌘-O to open the Printer Options menu.
3. Press the appropriate series of keys (TM, BM, LM, or RM).
4. Press **RETURN**.
5. Type the number of inches you want the margin to be, then press **RETURN**.

If this was the only margin you intended to set, you would next press **ESC** to return to the document. If you wanted to set another margin, or choose another option from the Printer Options menu, you would simply press the appropriate sequence of keys.

In the word processor, the Top and Bottom margin options take effect above the paragraph in which the cursor is located when the option is specified. Thus, you could have different top and bottom margins for each printed page in a document.

When you change the left and right margins on a word-processor document, AppleWorks adjusts the document so that you can see the visual effect on-screen. The screen margins won't measure the settings exactly, but the content of each line will be the same as that in a printed document.

Normally, the left and right margins are the same throughout the entire document. But if you insert different left- or right-margin settings somewhere in the document, all of the text below the new settings changes to show the difference. If you want to return the remainder of the document after the section of changed text to normal settings, or a different setting, you must move the cursor to the beginning of the first paragraph of text to be affected and reset the margins.

You can see the effect of changing margin settings in the following employee productivity report, in which the Top, Left, and Right Margin settings have been adjusted at various places in the document and displayed with the Zoom command (⌂-Z):

```
File: Employee.Report              REVIEW/ADD/CHANGE              Escape: Main Menu
=====|====|====|====|====|====|====|====|====|====|====|====|====|====|===
--------Top Margin:  1.0 inches
--------Centered
                    ^Employee Report^*
*
*
--------Unjustified
This report lists employees of the Acme Widget Manufacturing
Company who distinguished themselves during the last quarter
of Fiscal Year 1985.*
*
--------Left Margin:  1.5 inches
--------Right Margin:  2.0 inches
     *
     Productivity Champs - These employees had the
     highest average number of hours worked per
     week, and the fewest unscheduled absences.*
--------Left Margin:  3.0 inches
               *
          Bruno Workaholski*
          Edith Carstairs*
----------------------------------------------------------------------
Type entry or use ⌂ commands            Line 1  Column  1      ⌂-? for Help
```

Word-processor documents show the effect onscreen of new left- and right-margin settings when you change them.

New Page (NP)

Ordinarily, when you create and print a word-processor document that's more than a page long, AppleWorks automatically determines (according to your margin settings) where to stop printing on one page and continue printing on the next. This is called *breaking pages.* You can preview on-screen where page breaks occur with the Calculate[18] command (⌂-K): A dashed line and the label *End of page [number]* appears wherever AppleWorks will stop printing one page and begin printing the next. Pressing any command or typing in text will remove the page-break labels, and you can redisplay them anytime by pressing ⌂-K again.

Sometimes when you preview a document you will discover that an automatic page break occurs where you don't want it, such as in the middle of a list or in the wrong place in an outline. In this situation, you can use the New Page (NP) printer option to override the automatic page break and force a page break where you want it.

When you use the NP option to cause a page break before an automatic page break, the automatic page breaks following the one you inserted will be recalculated to reflect the new position of text on the pages. If you force a page break in the middle of page 2 of a document, for example, the old page breaks that had been calculated for page 3 and beyond will be moved up, keeping all pages the same length.

You can specify new page breaks as often as every paragraph. Page breaks always occur at the carriage return before the position of the cursor when you type the option. If you type the option when the cursor is in the middle of a paragraph, for example, the page break will occur before that paragraph.

Omit Line (OL)

The Omit Line (OL) option removes blank lines from individual records in Labels database reports when a category doesn't contain any data. This option isn't available in the spreadsheet or the word processor, or in Tables database reports.

Use the OL option when you want to conserve space in a Labels database report. This option adjusts the height of each record in a Labels report according to the number of lines that contain data. In a typical Labels report of names and addresses, for example, you probably have the data in a format similar to this:

Spacing Line

Name

Company

Address

City, State Zip

Spacing Line

Each record will print six lines, as long as there is data on each of the data lines. If there isn't data on a data line (one of the categories in a record doesn't contain any data), however, you have a choice: You can either allow the report to be printed so that the missing data is replaced with a blank line, or you can omit the blank line using the OL option and shorten those records that are missing a line of data to five printed lines.

If you aren't printing the records on pre-cut mailing labels, you will be printing records in a Labels report vertically on a sheet of paper. In this case, you will probably want to conserve paper, and omit blank lines from records when a data line is blank.

The OL option is linked to the Keep Same (KS) option in the database Labels report Printer Options menu. If you have OL set to *No*, then missing data will be replaced with a blank line, and all records will print the same height. Since the function of the KS option is to make sure all records print the same height, this option isn't necessary when OL is set to *No*, and the KS option isn't visible on the Printer Options menu in this case. If OL is set to *Yes*, however, the KS option becomes visible on the menu, so you can choose whether or not to keep the number of lines per record the same even though blank lines (categories containing no data) are being omitted from the report.

When OL is set to *Yes* (blank data lines are omitted) and KS is set to *Yes* (to keep each record the same height), a blank line is inserted at the bottom of each record to make up for lines omitted because of missing data (if any). (See: Keep Same on the preceding page.)

Pause Each Page (PE) and Pause Here (PH)

The Pause Each Page (PE) and Pause Here (PH) printer options can be used to temporarily stop the printing of a word-processor file. These options are not available in the spreadsheet or the database. The Pause Each Page option stops the printing of a file at the end of each page in a word-processor document, while the Pause Here option stops the printing of a file at a place that you specify.

The PE and PH options are normally hidden, but you can display them with the Zoom command (⌘-Z).

Pause Each Page (PE): When you use the PE option, AppleWorks stops printing at the end of each page and prompts you to press either **SPACE** (to continue printing) or **ESC** (to cancel printing and return to the Review/Add/Change screen). The Pause Each Page option is useful when you aren't sure how a document will look when printed, and you want to examine each page as it comes out of the printer. With the PE option, you can look at each printed page, and then continue printing if you are satisfied or cancel printing if you're not satisfied. You can also use PE to pause printing when you're using single-sheet paper.

The PE option takes effect beginning with the end of the page on which the cursor is located when you type the option. You can use the PE option at the beginning of a document (to pause printing on every page) or in the middle of a document (to pause printing only on the pages after a certain point in the document). Once you specify the PE option, however, there's no way to cancel it later in the document—it will be in effect from the cursor's position to the end of the document.

Pause Here (PH): Use the Pause Here (PH) option when you want to pause printing at a specific location in a document. When you use the PH option, printing will pause at the last carriage return before the place where the cursor was located when you typed the option. Thus, if the cursor stops in the middle of a paragraph when you type the PH option, the printer will pause just before the beginning of that paragraph.

Unlike the PE option, which pauses printing on every page, the PH option only pauses printing in each place where the option is specified. When you use PH, the printer pauses at the place you choose, and you can either continue printing (by pressing **SPACE**) or cancel printing and return to the Review/Add/Change screen (by pressing **ESC**).

The PH option is useful when you want to examine a specific part of a printed document before the whole document is printed. With the PH option specified, the printer will stop, and you can see how your document looks. If you like what you see, you can continue printing; if you don't like what you see, you can cancel the printing of the rest of the document and save your printer ribbon and paper.

You can use PH as often as every paragraph in a document.

Print Dash (PD)

Quite often a database report will have records that don't contain data in every category. When you print the report, these categories will be left blank. If the report contains a lot of records with blank entries, the gaps will give the printed result a disorganized, unattractive appearance. The Print Dash (PD) option can help compensate for this, because it prints a dash in every database category that's blank, giving some substance to the printed page. Note that the Omit Line (OL) option must be set to No for the Print Dash option to work for Labels reports.

Paper Length (PL)

The Paper Length (PL) option is used to set a different page length for printed AppleWorks files. Use this option when you will be printing a word-processor, spreadsheet, or database file on paper shorter or longer than 11 inches. If you're printing on 11-inch paper, you don't have to change the PL setting (11 inches is the default), but if you will be printing on legal-sized paper (14-inch), you will have to change the PL setting so that each printed page matches the length of paper you will be using. AppleWorks will accept PL values up to 25.4 inches.

The PL option in the spreadsheet and the database can only be set once for an entire file. The PL option in the spreadsheet and database is linked to the Lines-per-Page indicator on these applications' Printer Options menus.

The number of lines per page is calculated as the paper length, minus the sum of the top and bottom margins (if any), multiplied by the number of lines per inch. Thus, a PL of 11 inches on a document with top and bottom margins set to *0* and the Lines-per-Inch (LI) option set to *6* would yield a Lines-per-Page reading of *66* ((11-0) ∗ 6). A PL of 11 inches on a document with the top and bottom margins set to *1* inch and a LI value of *6* would yield a Lines-per-Page reading of *54* ((11-2) ∗ 6).

When you set the PL option in the word processor, the setting appears as a text line in the document; you can hide or display the setting with the Zoom command (Ć-z).

Changing the PL won't affect the appearance of text on the screen. But when you calculate page breaks in a word-processor document with the Calculate command (Ć-k), the placement of page breaks will reflect the current PL setting. For example, page breaks will occur more often in a document with the PL set to *11* than they will in a document with the PL set to *14*.

Page Numbering (PP and PN)

There are two printer options that control page numbering in AppleWorks. The Print Page Number (PP) option instructs AppleWorks to print the current page number on the page where the option is used. The Page Number (PN) option lets you renumber pages beginning with any number you specify, starting on the page where the option is used. These options are only available in the word processor, not in the spreadsheet or database.

Print Page Number (PP): The Print Page Number (PP) option prints the current page number where the cursor is located when you enter the option from the Printer Options menu. You can tell where the location is by a caret symbol (^).

Used by itself, the PP option will print only the page number of the page the option was specified in. To number all the pages in a document, you include the PP option on the same line you specified header or footer text. This will include the current page number as a part of the header or footer information, and will allow you to automatically number the pages. If you don't want header or footer text on your document, you can use the PP option by itself under the line containing the Page Header or Page Footer command, so that only the current page number is printed as the header or footer information.

Page Number (PN): Use the Page Number option (PN) when you want to specify exactly which page numbers are printed on a word-processor document. The Page Number option (PN) overrides AppleWorks' automatic page numbering option, and lets you begin page numbering with a number you specify.

Like the Print Page Number (PP) option, the Page Number (PN) option takes effect on the page where the cursor is located when you enter the option. When you display the Printer Options menu and type *PN* in response to the *Option* prompt and press **RETURN**, a second prompt reading *Number* appears below it. Type in the number you want to begin renumbering pages with and press **RETURN**. AppleWorks will then number pages from that point on with whatever number you type in response.

The Page Number (PN) option will have no effect on a printed document unless the Print Page Number (PP) option is used to actually print the page number.

Unlike the Print Page Number (PP) option, which inserts a caret (^) symbol where it's entered, the PN setting is displayed as a text line that you can display or hide with the Zoom command (⌂-**Z**).

You can change the page numbering of a document on any page, but if you specify more than one PN value per page, AppleWorks will use the last specified value before the page break to begin renumbering.

The PN option is useful when you're working with a document that contains a title page, a dedication, or other pages of "front matter" before the actual text begins. With documents like this, you probably don't want to number the front-matter pages, and you want the first page of actual text to be numbered 1. If you used only the PP option on a document like this, the title page and other front-matter pages would be included in the page-number count, and the number printed on the first text page would reflect that page's position in the document. By using the PN option, however, you can specify that the page where the text actually begins in a document be given the number *1*.

Pitch and Character Spacing (CI, P1, and P2)

There are three ways to control the pitch and spacing between characters in AppleWorks. The Characters-per-Inch (CI) option controls the individual widths of characters printed, and is available in all three AppleWorks applications. The Proportional-1 (P1) and Proportional-2 (P2) options set proportional spacing between characters on a line, and are only available in the word processor.

In the word processor, CI, P1, and P2 all appear as text lines, which can be hidden and revealed with the Zoom command (⌘-**z**).

Characters-per-Inch (CI): Use the Characters-per-Inch option (CI) in the word processor, spreadsheet, or database when you want to change the density (pitch) of the printed characters in a file.

The default CI setting in every AppleWorks application is 10 CI, which means that printed characters are of such a size that 10 of them occupy one horizontal inch of printed text. Using the CI option, however, you can vary the size of printed characters from 4 characters per inch to 24 characters per inch. If you choose a CI setting that prints larger characters (4 to 9 CI), then fewer characters will fit on a line. If you choose a CI setting that prints smaller characters (11 to 24 CI), then more characters will fit on a line. The CI setting is most often used to squeeze more text on each line.

You can change the CI setting in the word processor, spreadsheet, or database. In the spreadsheet and database, you can only specify one CI setting for the entire file. In the word processor, though, you can change the CI setting at every carriage return, if you like.

There are two considerations to keep in mind when using different CI settings: your printer's configuration settings, and the amount of data that can be displayed on the screen.

Printer Configuration: In order to actually print text with a particular CI setting, your printer must be capable of printing at that density (which should be indicated in the printer's manual), and it must have been configured to print at that density when instructed to by AppleWorks. AppleWorks won't display a message or otherwise alert you that there's a printer-configuration problem—it simply prints the file with normal-sized (10 CI) characters. So if you change the CI setting and AppleWorks still prints the file with normal characters, you know either that you have not configured AppleWorks for your printer, or that your printer can't print with the specified density.

Screen Display: The AppleWorks display is only capable of showing the contents of a line if the document was printed using a print density of between 4 and 13 CI. If you specify one of these CI settings, the contents of each line on the screen will change to show the resulting number of characters that will fit on a line, but the size of the actual characters on the screen will stay the same. If you specify a CI between 14 and 24, the contents of the on-screen lines won't change because there isn't room to display more characters on the screen. If you use a CI of 18, for example, there will actually be much more text printed on a line than your screen can show.

You will find further information about printing and printer configuration under Word Processor Printing;[371] Spreadsheet Printing;[319] Database Printing;[67] and Printer Configuration.[200]

Proportional-1 (P1) and Proportional-2 (P2): Normally, all text printed from AppleWorks is printed with a fixed pitch—that is, each character of text and the space around it takes up the same amount of space as the others. Proportional printing, however, adjusts for the width of each character: An *i* will print in a narrower space than a *w*, for example. Because proportional spacing adjusts for the differences in width between different characters, there is always a constant amount of spacing between characters that are printed proportionally. Proportional printing is used in books and other professionally printed materials; the P1 and P2 options will help your documents look more professional, too.

In order to use these options, your printer must be capable of printing proportionally, and AppleWorks must be configured to print proportionally. There are two different options for proportional spacing because some printers can print proportionally in two different ways. Check your printer's manual to see if it supports two different proportional printing modes. If not, use the P1 option only.

The P1 and P2 options replace the Characters-per-Inch (CI) option in the word processor: The normal proportional printing mode prints 10 CI characters, and printers with 2 proportional printing modes usually offer 12 CI characters in the alternate mode. If you want to print in fixed-pitch mode (the default), you don't have to do anything. If you want to print in proportional mode, you must specify it with either the P1 or P2 option from the Printer Options menu.

You can change from proportional to fixed-pitch printing as often as every paragraph in a word-processor document. When you specify the P1 or P2 option, the option takes effect from the last carriage return before the cursor's current position to the end of the document. Thus, if your cursor is in the middle of a paragraph when you specify the P1 or P2 option, that entire paragraph will be printed with proportional spacing, as well as the rest of the document.

Platen Width (PW)

The rubber-covered roller in your printer is called the *platen*. Physically, the platen width is the actual width of your printer's platen, but the Platen Width (PW) setting in AppleWorks refers to the maximum width of paper across which your printer's print head will travel. Use the Platen Width option (PW) to change the maximum width of lines printed from word-processor, spreadsheet, or database files. The default Platen Width setting for all three of the AppleWorks applications is 8.0 inches (the maximum horizontal distance most printer print heads can travel), but you can specify a Platen Width setting up to 13.2 inches in one-decimal increments.

When you configure a printer for AppleWorks, you specify the width of the platen. The PW setting you specify from a Printer Options menu in AppleWorks can be less than or equal to the Platen Width setting you have configured for your printer, but it can't be greater than that setting. If your printer's print head will only travel 8 inches, for example, you can't make it travel a wider distance than that by specifying a PW of 13 inches. If you have configured AppleWorks for a wide-carriage printer, and you are using wide paper, you will have to manually change the PW setting from the default of 8.0 inches to a more useful 13 inches each time you print a file.

Although the default PW setting for all three applications is 8 inches, most of the standard-carriage printers have a maximum platen width of 8.5 inches. Consequently, you may sometimes want to alter the PW setting slightly to squeeze more data on a line. In a spreadsheet, for example, you may need all of the horizontal printing space you can get, and changing the PW setting from 8.0 to 8.5 will print a few more characters on each line.

The PW setting affects the entire file in the spreadsheet and the database, but it can be changed as often as every paragraph in the word processor. Narrow PW settings will probably force your printer to end lines earlier than they end on the screen, however, and any PW setting greater than 8.0 will result in longer lines of data being printed than can actually be displayed on the Review/Add/Change screen.

The PW setting appears as a text line in the word processor when you reveal it with the Zoom command (Ć-Z).

Set Marker (SM)

When you're preparing a long word-processor document, it's likely that you will create sections that you know you will want to go back to later, perhaps to double-check a fact or enter different data. The Set Marker (SM) option lets you insert unique numbers at those locations that you can later find easily and quickly with the Find[109] command (⌂-F), which offers a specific option to search for markers. The SM option is not available in the spreadsheet or database applications.

To set a marker, simply move the cursor to the place in your file where you want the marker to appear, display the Printer Options menu (⌂-O), type *SM*, and then type the marker number.

You can specify between 1 and 254 marker numbers in a document. Marker numbers don't have to be specified in sequential order, and you can set the same number at more than one location. Markers are placed after the last paragraph mark before the position of the cursor when you enter a marker. If your cursor is in the middle of a paragraph when you set a marker, for example, the marker will be placed at the beginning of that paragraph.

If you want to see where you have inserted markers throughout a document, display them with the Zoom command (⌂-Z).

Skip Lines (SK)

The Skip Lines (SK) option creates blank lines when a word-processor document is printed. The SK option is essentially a fast alternative to inserting a lot of carriage returns when you want to create a lot of blank lines. This option is not available in the spreadsheet or database.

If you want a title to appear in the middle of a page, for example, you could insert 15 or so carriage returns above it, but it would be more efficient to use the SK option instead. To use SK in this situation, you would move the cursor above the title on the screen, display the Printer Options menu (⌂-O), type the SK option, press **RETURN**, enter the number *15*, press **RETURN**, and then press **ESC**. Now, the printer will automatically skip 15 lines above the title when the document is printed.

In a word-processor document, you can use the SK option as often as every paragraph. The option takes effect at the last carriage return before the cursor's location whenever you enter SK. (If, for example, you type *SK* with the cursor in the middle of a paragraph, the specified lines will be skipped above the paragraph.) The SK option is hidden from view, unless you use the Zoom command (⌂-Z).

Special Codes (SC)

The Special Codes (SC) option sends special print-enhancement codes to a printer from a spreadsheet or database file. This option is not available in the word processor.

When you type the SC option from the Printer Options menu in the spreadsheet or the database, you are prompted to enter special control characters that produce a print enhancement in your printer. Since the spreadsheet and database printer options aren't as extensive as those in the word processor, the SC option here lets you add more print enhancements to your documents.

Boldface type, for example, isn't an option on the spreadsheet or database Printer Options menus, but you could send a special code to your printer that would put it into boldface printing mode. If you did that, your entire spreadsheet would be printed in boldface. Other options could include compressed, shadow, or expanded print.

The SC option only prompts you to enter one printer-control code. Since most printer features require a code to start them and another code to stop them, most features you initiate with a control code in this fashion will last until the entire file has been printed. In some cases (underlining, for example), printer-control codes only last until the end of the first printed line.

If you want to enhance the print of a spreadsheet or database file with the SC option, you will have to consult your printer's manual to determine what its control codes are, and which functions they perform, before you can enter one of them into AppleWorks.

You can change a special code, too. If you have already entered a printer code with the SC option, type *SC* anyway. You will be shown the currently stored code, and asked if it is correct. If you want to replace it, answer *No*, and then type in the new code.

When you want to do away with a stored code, just type the caret symbol (^) by itself on the code-entry screen after choosing *No*. You will be returned to the Printer Options menu, and the value for SC will have been changed back to *No*.

Superscripts (+B, +E) and Subscripts (−B, −E)

Superscript printing is placed half a line above the rest of the text on a line, while subscript printing is placed half a line below the rest of the text on a line. These printing modes are used when you are specifying footnotes, exponents, trademark symbols, and other special items that you want to set off from the rest of the text on a line. Superscript and subscript printing can only be accomplished if your printer is capable of them, and if AppleWorks has been configured so it can instruct your printer to print in these modes. (See: Printer Configuration.[200])

To specify *superscript printing*, you must begin a section of text with the +B option and end it with the +E option. Superscript printing begins where the +B option has been placed in a document, and ends where the +E option has been placed. To specify *subscript printing*, begin a section of text with the −B option and end it with the −E option. Subscript printing begins at the place where the −B option occurs, and ends where the −E option occurs. The options are indicated by the caret symbol on the screen.

Superscript and subscript printing can't be carried out over more than one line at a time, however. If you place a +B option in one line of text and put the +E option on the next line of text, for example, only the text in the first line will be printed in superscript. If you want to print more than one line in superscript or subscript, you must specify +B and +E (or −B and −E) options for each new line.

Underlining (UB, UE, and CONTROL-L)

Underlined text can be accomplished in two ways in the AppleWorks word processor: either by typing the UB (Underline Begin) and UE (Underline End) options from the Printer Options menu, or by pressing **CONTROL-L** directly on the Review/Add/Change screen. The **CONTROL-L** alternative is offered because it's faster than using the Printer Options menu.

If you use the UB and UE options from the Printer Options menu, you must place the cursor at the beginning of the text you want underlined before typing the UB option, and then place the cursor at the end of the text you want underlined before typing the UE option. Because this requires displaying the Printer Options menu two different times (once each when the cursor is at the locations where you want to begin and end underlining), it isn't a very efficient procedure for such a common print enhancement.

The **CONTROL-L** option lets you specify underlining in the word processor directly from the Review/Add/Change screen, without having to display the Printer Options menu. To use **CONTROL-L**, you simply move the cursor to the beginning of the section of text that you want underlined, then press **CONTROL-L**, and then move the cursor to the end of the section you want underlined and press **CONTROL-L** again. Just as with using UB and UE from the Printer Options menu, **CONTROL-L** places a caret at the underline begin and end locations to signify that this option will take effect there.

Underlining can only be accomplished if your printer is capable of underlining, and if AppleWorks has been configured so it can instruct your printer to underline (see: Printer Configuration[200]).

The underlining option affects only one paragraph at a time. If you want to underline two consecutive paragraphs, you must specify the Underline Begin option at the beginnings of both of those paragraphs.

Printing the display (⌂-H)

You can print the contents of the screen at any time in AppleWorks by using the Hard Copy[122] command (⌂-H). When you press ⌂-H, the current contents of the screen are printed on the printer you have configured as the ⌂-H printer. (See: Printer Configuration.[200])

In order for the Hard Copy command to work, you must have at least one printer configured in AppleWorks, and the printer must be properly connected to your computer and turned on.

It's useful to print the display when you want to make a paper record of information you can't otherwise print. You can print word-processor documents, spreadsheets, and database reports in a variety of ways, for example, but you can't use any of the three applications to print AppleWorks menus, disk catalogs, or printer-options screens. The Hard Copy command lets you print the contents of these screens on paper.

■ **Example**

Suppose you want to print a catalog of the files on a disk. Here's what you would do:

1. Choose option 2, *List all files on the current disk drive* from the Other Activities menu.[178]

2. When the list of files is displayed, press ⌂-H, and the display will be printed on your printer.

■ **Comments**

Besides file listings, you may want to print displays that show the printer-configuration options for a certain printer, so that if you remove that configuration you can always find the settings if you want to install it again later. When you print the display, you only print what is displayed on the current screen. Thus, if you are printing part of a file, you will only print the part that is showing on the screen at the time you use the Hard Copy command. The only elements of the AppleWorks screen that aren't printed with the Hard Copy command are the cursor and the highlight bars on menus or in prompt lines. Also note that AppleWorks will not allow you to print the screen's contents to a printer configured as a disk printer.

ProDOS

■ **Definition**

ProDOS is the Apple computer company's disk-operating system under which AppleWorks runs.

■ **Usage**

ProDOS is operating system software that handles the interaction between programs such as AppleWorks and the Apple's hardware—its disk drives, display screen, and printers, for example. ProDOS is supplied on your Apple-Works Startup Disk, and is loaded automatically when you load AppleWorks.

When you use AppleWorks, the program usually translates your instructions about hardware (print commands, or commands to list files on a disk drive, for example) into a language that ProDOS can understand. Thus, you normally don't have to know anything about ProDOS or how it works to use AppleWorks. But while ProDOS is usually an invisible housekeeper in the background, there are a few situations when you should understand something about ProDOS to use AppleWorks.

■ **DOS-ProDOS conversion**

ProDOS has been the standard operating system sold with Apple computers since early 1984. Before that, Apples had been sold for several years with an operating system called *DOS 3.3*. The ProDOS operating system isn't compatible with the DOS 3.3 operating system—programs written for one operating system won't run under the other, and files created on a program that runs under one particular operating system can't be used directly by a program that runs under the other operating system.

Since there are thousands of programs that run under DOS 3.3 (including VisiCalc, DB Master, and older versions of AppleWriter), Apple made it possible to convert data files made by DOS 3.3 programs to the ProDOS format, so they could be used by programs that run under ProDOS. The conversion also makes it possible to convert ProDOS data files to DOS 3.3 format. This conversion is performed with the DOS-ProDOS Conversion Program, which comes on the ProDOS User's Disk sold by Apple. (See: DOS-ProDOS Conversion Program.[104])

If you want to use ASCII,[13] DIF,[100] or VisiCalc[357] files created under DOS 3.3 in AppleWorks, you must first convert those files to a ProDOS format using the DOS-ProDOS Conversion Program. Even after some ASCII or DIF files are converted, however, AppleWorks may still not be able to use them. AppleWorks can only use standard DIF[100] and ASCII[13] files, so if your old DOS 3.3 files aren't in the standard DIF or ASCII formats, you may not get the results you expect. Likewise, the DOS 3.3 programs you want to share your AppleWorks files with must be able to use the DIF or ASCII file formats created by AppleWorks. Check the user's manual for the source or target DOS 3.3 programs for compatibility.

ProDOS and other operating systems: While ProDOS is not compatible with DOS 3.3, it is compatible with *SOS*, the operating system sold with the Apple III computer. DIF or ASCII files created on an Apple III under SOS can be loaded directly into AppleWorks without conversion.

There is also an integrated program especially for the Apple III called *III EZ Pieces*, which is the Apple III version of AppleWorks. You can use these files directly with AppleWorks, just as if AppleWorks itself had created them.

Because ProDOS is compatible with SOS, you can also share your ProDOS files with people who are using Apple III computers. You will probably have to put your files in standard formats (DIF or ASCII) first, though, depending on the Apple III program. (See: ASCII file;[13] DIF file.[100])

ProDOS volumes, subdirectories, and pathnames: ProDOS keeps track of the locations of data files through the use of volumes,[359] subdirectories,[336] and pathnames.[188] Every floppy disk you use under ProDOS must be given a name when it is formatted—this is the disk's volume name. If you use a hard disk, the hard disk will consist of one or more volumes, which have names as well.

A *volume* can be divided up into portions called *subdirectories*, which can be thought of as volumes within a volume. Each subdirectory is given its own name, and up to 130 files can be stored in a subdirectory, just as they could be stored on a volume. A *directory* is a list of files stored in a volume or subdirectory. When a directory of a volume is displayed, the subdirectory names will be displayed in the list just like a file name would, but the files stored in the subdirectories would not be seen. To get a directory of the files in a subdirectory, you must first specify that you want to work with that subdirectory. You do this by using a pathname,[188] which is explained a little later. You can think of the structure like this: If a volume is a drawer of information in a filing cabinet and a file is one piece of paper, a subdirectory can be thought of as a folder that holds several papers.

Files are, of course, individual units of data created by one of Apple-Works' applications. Files can be directly stored in a volume directory, or placed in a subdirectory for organizational purposes. This illustration shows the relationship between volumes, subdirectories, and files:

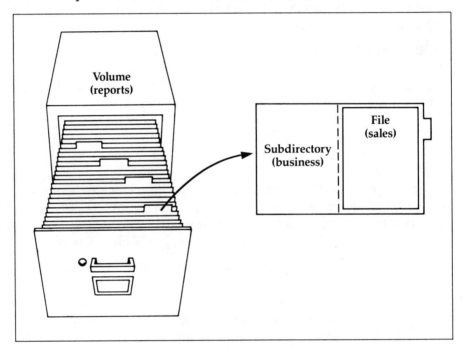

ProDOS keeps track of information in files, subdirectories, and volumes.

In order for ProDOS to remember the location of every file, subdirectory, and volume, it uses a system of *pathnames*. A pathname always contains the name of a volume and the name of the file stored on that volume. If the file has been placed in a subdirectory, the subdirectory name is also included. Pathnames always have the same format: */volume name/subdirectory name [if any]/file name*. A slash mark always begins a pathname, and slash marks always separate the volume name from the subdirectory name (if the file is stored in a subdirectory) and the file name.

When you are using AppleWorks with a floppy disk system, you usually don't have to specify a pathname. AppleWorks lets you name files when you create them, and then store them on a volume (or floppy disk) by indicating the number of the current disk drive where the volume is located (as indicated in the upper-left corner of the AppleWorks screen). Thus, if your current disk location is Drive 2, AppleWorks will automatically store your files on the disk in Drive 2.

If you are using a hard disk, you must store files by the volume name. Even in this case, however, AppleWorks lets you store the current volume name as the current disk location and then save files to it without having to specify the volume name each time. If you are using a hard-disk volume named /*Profile*, for example, you can specify this as the current disk location (by using options 1 or 6 on the Other Activities[178] menu) and then store all your files on it by simply saving them to the current disk. If you are storing files on a volume named /*Profile* in a subdirectory called /*Reports*, you would specify the current disk location to be: /*Profile*/*Reports*.

The only times when you must specify the entire pathname for a file are when you are loading a DIF, ASCII, or VisiCalc file into an AppleWorks application, when you are creating a DIF or ASCII file directly from an existing AppleWorks application, or when you are creating a subdirectory. In these cases, AppleWorks prompts you to enter the complete ProDOS pathname, and you must enter the pathname as /*volume name*/*subdirectory name [if any]*/ *file name [if any]*. If you don't enter the complete pathname, AppleWorks won't be able to locate or store your DIF or ASCII file, or create a subdirectory.

Even if you've been using floppy disks for storage, you must still specify the disk's volume name when you want to perform these operations. If you can't remember the volume's name, simply use the *Add Files* option from the Main Menu[158] or the *List all files* option from the Other Activities menu[178] to list the files on the disk—the volume name will appear at the top of the list. When you use the *List all files* option, the listing shows not only the AppleWorks files on a disk, but also subdirectories and DIF or ASCII files. Subdirectories are identified as such, and DIF or ASCII files (or files created by other programs) are classified as *Other* types of files. A *List All Files* menu with a volume directory that shows files, subdirectories, and "Other" file types is shown on the following page.

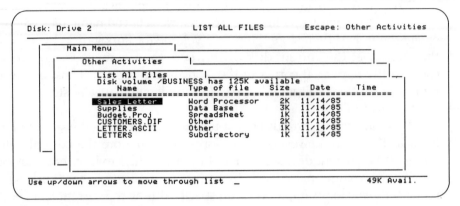

The List all files *option from the Other Activities menu displays the volume directory showing AppleWorks files, subdirectories, and "Other" types of files.*

Prompt and prompt line

■ **Definition**

A *prompt* is a phrase or sentence in the *prompt line* located at the bottom-left corner of the screen that helps you remember what action to take next, or what your current options are, as you work with AppleWorks.

■ **Usage**

The contents of the prompt line change according to the current activity you are performing in the program. When you don't remember what your options are at a given point, or you aren't sure what to do while working with AppleWorks, the prompt line is the first place to look. Here's an example:

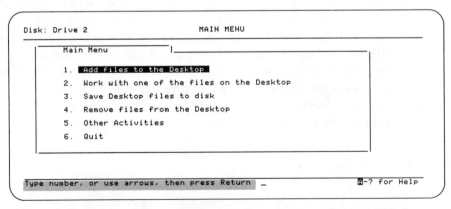

The prompt line always contains some helpful information about using AppleWorks.

Protection

■ **Definition**

Protection is a spreadsheet formatting option that lets you enter only a certain type of information into a cell or group of cells, or prevent the entry or alteration of data in a cell or group of cells.

■ **Usage**

You protect cells in the spreadsheet by using the Layout[146] command (⌂-**L**). Here are the basic steps:

1. With the Review/Add/Change screen of a spreadsheet displayed, move the cursor to the cell, or the first of a group of cells, that you wish to protect.

2. Press the Layout command (⌂-**L**).

3. The prompt line will present a list of cell-selection options. Choose *Entry, Rows, Column,* or *Block,* depending on the portion of the spreadsheet you want to protect, by pressing the first letter of the desired option, or by highlighting the option and pressing **RETURN**.

4. The list of Layout options will then appear. Choose the *Protection* option, and the list of specific protection options will appear in the prompt line, like this:

```
File: Investment                    LAYOUT          Escape: Review/Add/Change
========A=========B=========C=========D=========E=========F=========G=========H====
   1             Investment Analysis
   2
   3 Investment Amount: $10,000
   4 Discount Rate:        ▓▓▓▓▓▓.11
   5 Net Present Value: $10,130
   6
   7
   8   Year 1    Year 2    Year 3    Year 4    Year 5
   9
  10   $2,500    $2,500    $2,500    $2,500    $4,000
  11
  12
  13
  14
  15
  16
  17
  18
---------------------------------------------------------------------------------
C4: (Value) .11

Protection:   Allow? ▓Labels only▓ Values only  Nothing  Anything
```

There are four spreadsheet cell-protection options available through the Layout command.

5. Choose the protection option you want.

The different protection options have the following effects:

Labels only—only labels can be typed into the protected cells.

Values only—only values can be typed into the protected cells.

Nothing—nothing can be typed into the protected cells.

Anything—anything can be typed into the protected cells.

When the cursor is on a protected cell, the cell indicator in the lower-left corner of the screen will show the word *Protect*, followed by the first letter of one of the four options shown in the example above, to indicate how the cell is protected. You can override the current protection option, however, by using the Standard Values command (⌘-**V**), and specifying *No* under its Protection option. Setting this option to *No* will disable protection for the entire spreadsheet, even though the cell indicator will still show that protection had been applied to the cell using the Layout command. The default Standard Values setting for the Protection option is *Yes*.

For further information about cell protection, see Layout[146] and Standard Values.[330]

Quick Change (⌘-Q)

- **Definition**

The *Quick Change* command (⌘-**Q**) displays the Desktop Index,[98] which lets you view the files available on the Desktop,[97] and then lets you change to another file, if you like.

- **Usage**

Use the Quick Change command when you are working with one of several files on the Desktop, and you want to change to another Desktop file without returning to the Main Menu.[158] The command is called *Quick Change* because it lets you move quickly from one file to another.

■ **Example**

Suppose you have three files on the Desktop: a *Sales Letter* word-processor document, a *Customers* database file, and a *Cost of Sales* spreadsheet. You are currently working with *Sales Letter,* and you want to switch files so you can work on the *Cost of Sales* spreadsheet. Here's what you do:

1. Press the Quick Change command (♙-Q).

2. The Desktop Index will appear in the middle of the Review/Add/ Change screen of the *Sales Letter* file, and *Sales Letter* itself will be highlighted on the list, like this:

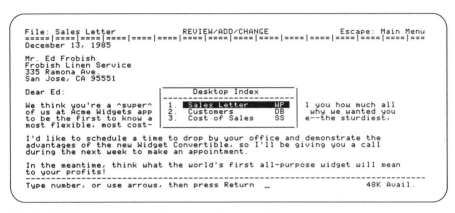

The Quick Change command displays the Desktop Index.

3. Type the number of the *Cost of Sales* file (3)—or use ↓ to move the highlight bar until *Cost of Sales* is covered—and then press **RETURN**.

4. The *Cost of Sales* spreadsheet will be displayed, and the Desktop Index will disappear.

■ **Comments**

You can use the Quick Change command from any application or menu in AppleWorks. Thus, you can always get to a Desktop file—or a different Desktop file—quickly.

If you change your mind after typing the Quick Change command and want to continue working with the current file, simply press **RETURN**. Since the current file is always highlighted when the Desktop Index is displayed, pressing **RETURN** will simply reselect the file you've been working with, and the Desktop Index will disappear.

The Desktop Index can also be displayed by choosing option 2, *Work with one of the files on the Desktop,* from the Main Menu.

Quick File file

■ **Definition**

A *Quick File file* is a file created by the program, *Quick File.*

■ **Usage**

Quick File is a database program that was written by AppleWorks developer Rupert Lissner. Quick File files may be used as sources for new AppleWorks database files. These files don't need to be converted from a different operating system, and they don't have to be placed in a standard format such as DIF[100] or ASCII[13]—they can be used directly to create new AppleWorks files.

To use a Quick File file in AppleWorks:

1. Make sure your disk of Quick File files is in the current disk location.

2. Choose option 1, *Add files to the Desktop,* from the Main Menu.[158]

3. Choose option 4, *Make a new file for the Data Base,* from the Add Files menu.[2]

4. Choose option 3, *From a Quick File (TM) file,* from the Data Base menu.[55]

5. Press **SPACE**. A list of Quick File files on the current disk will appear, and you can select a file from the current disk drive or subdirectory to be loaded into an AppleWorks database file.

6. After the file is loaded, type a name for the new AppleWorks database file, and then press **RETURN**. The new database file will be displayed.

Unlike DIF or ASCII files, Quick File files transfer to the AppleWorks database complete with category names. For further information about using Quick File files, see Database Overview[58] and Add Files menu.[2]

Quit screen

■ **Definition**

The *Quit* screen appears when you choose to exit the AppleWorks program.

■ **Usage**

Choosing option 6, *Quit*, from the AppleWorks Main Menu[158] produces the Quit screen. You should only use this option when you want to stop working with AppleWorks and either turn off your computer or begin using another program.

To use the Quit screen:

1. Choose option 6, *Quit*, from the Main Menu. AppleWorks will present the Quit screen. The prompt line at the bottom of the screen asks you if you really want to quit.

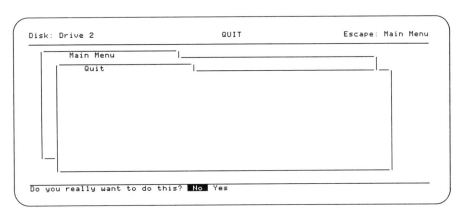

The Quit screen gives you a chance to change your mind about leaving AppleWorks.

2. If you answer *No* to the prompt, you will be returned to the Main Menu. What happens if you answer *Yes* to the prompt depends on the status of the Desktop at the time.

If there are no files on the Desktop when you answer *Yes* to the prompt, AppleWorks will quit, and you will be returned to ProDOS,[246] where you can select another application to run.

If there are files on the Desktop when you answer *Yes* to the prompt, but all files have already been saved to the current disk or you made no changes after loading the files from disk, AppleWorks quits and returns you to ProDOS.

If there are files on the Desktop that are new, or that have been changed from the way they were when loaded from disk, AppleWorks will present each new or changed file name, and give you a chance to save the file on the current disk or on a different disk, or to throw out the new file or changes made to a file loaded from disk. AppleWorks will then ask you to confirm that you really want to throw out the new file, or the changes made to a file loaded from disk. Once you have made a decision about each file, Apple-Works will quit to ProDOS.

■ **Comments**

If you change your mind about quitting at any time while there are still new or changed files on the Desktop, you can press **ESC**.

RAM

■ **Definition**

The *RAM* (or *Random Access Memory*) is the memory in your computer that stores programs and data.

■ **Usage**

When you load the AppleWorks program, it is loaded into your computer's RAM. When you add files from disk to the Desktop,[97] or create new files on the Desktop, those files are stored in RAM as well. RAM is measured in thousands of bytes, or *K*[144] (Kilobytes). You can always tell how much RAM you have available for Desktop files by looking at the Space Available indicator in the lower-right corner of the screen.

The Space Available indicator isn't displayed all the time—sometimes the prompt that tells you how to get help is in that position. If the Space Available indicator isn't showing and you want to display it, press the Help[123] command (⌂-?). The Space Available indicator will then appear in the lower-right corner of the screen.

The amount of RAM available for the Desktop is normally limited to 10K on a 64K Apple IIe and 55K on a 128K Apple IIe or IIc. You can greatly increase the amount of Desktop space available with one of several RAM expansion boards on the market. RAM expansion boards range in size from 64K to over two megabytes, so that the amount of space available on the AppleWorks Desktop can be increased from 55K to more than 2000K. Consult an Apple-specific magazine for companies that offer RAM expansion boards, or ask your Apple dealer.

Along with the AppleWorks program and your Desktop files, part of your computer's RAM is also used for the Clipboard.[35] The Clipboard, however, must share the amount of available RAM with the Desktop files. This means that if you are using most or all of the space on the Desktop for file storage, there will be less Clipboard space than there would be if the Desktop were nearly empty.

■ **Comment**
For further information about RAM, see Clipboard,[35] Desktop,[97] and K.[144]

Recalculation

■ **Definition**
Recalculation refers to the order and frequency with which an AppleWorks spreadsheet calculates itself.

■ **Usage**
When you enter spreadsheet formulas, they define a calculation that the spreadsheet is to perform. As soon as you type a formula and then press **RETURN**, the spreadsheet calculates the result of the formula. If a formula contains cell references, and you change a value in a cell referenced in that formula, the formula must be recalculated to show the current, correct result.

Normally, the AppleWorks spreadsheet is set to automatic recalculation: whenever a spreadsheet value or formula is changed, AppleWorks automatically recalculates the entire spreadsheet. You can, however, set the spreadsheet to manual recalculation, so the spreadsheet only recalculates when you tell it to.

The advantage to using manual recalculation is speed: If you have a large spreadsheet, it takes a second or two for it to recalculate each time you enter a value or formula. If the spreadsheet is set for automatic recalculation and you are entering a whole column or row of values, the spreadsheet will recalculate after each value is entered—you will have to wait a couple of seconds between entering each value. But if the spreadsheet is set to manual recalculation, it won't recalculate after each entry—you'll be able to enter a series of values more quickly.

When the spreadsheet is set to manual recalculation, you can tell it to recalculate at any time by pressing the Calculate[18] command (Ó-**K**).

The other recalculation option in the AppleWorks spreadsheet is the *order of recalculation*. In the default mode, the spreadsheet calculates in *column* order—from top to bottom down column A, then from top to bottom down column B, and so on to the right across the spreadsheet. You can change the order so the spreadsheet calculates in *row* order—from left to right across row 1, then from left to right across row 2, and so on down the spreadsheet.

Recalculation order is important when you have an equation in a column that must be solved before the equation in a column to the left can be solved. If a formula in cell C1 must be solved before the result of a formula in cell A3 is correct, for example, you would have to set the spreadsheet to calculate in row order (across rows) in order to solve these two equations in the proper order. Otherwise, the equation in A3 would be calculated before the equation in C1, and the result of A3 would be wrong.

You can change the settings for the order and frequency of recalculation by using the Standard Values[330] command (⌘-V).

■ **Comment**

For further information about recalculation, see Calculate.[18]

Record

■ **Definition**

A *record* is a single collection of information in a database file.

■ **Usage**

Database files have two basic levels of organization: categories and records. When you create a database file, you must create individual categories for the data to be placed in, such as *Name, Address, City, Phone*, and so on. Each category is a place to put a certain kind of information. Records contain one entry for each category, and all of the category entries in a record pertain to the same person, place, thing, or activity you are storing.

In a file of names and addresses, for example, *Name, Address*, and *City* would be categories in each *record*. In that file, one record would contain the name, address, and city for one person, and the next record would contain another person's name, address, and city, and so on.

When you look at the Multiple Record layout[168] of the database Review/ Add/Change screen, each *column* is a *category* of data, and each *row* is a data *record*. On the Single Record layout[243] of the database Review/Add/Change screen, each *screen* displays one record.

When you create records, it's important to place unified collections of data in each record. You wouldn't want to store Bob's name with Bill's phone number, for example, because that would make it very difficult for you to sort through the file and find either Bob's phone number or Bill's name. Once you decide what information will be placed in each category in a record, you must be consistent—if you place a phone number in the *Phone* category of one record and an address in the *Phone* category of another record, you won't be able to locate information very easily. The whole concept of organizing information into database files depends on your being consistent when entering and organizing information into categories and records.

■ **Comment**
For further information about creating records, see Database Overview.[58]

Record Selection Rules (⌘-R)

■ **Definition**
Record-selection rules (⌘-R) are logical conditions you apply to a database file so only records that match certain criteria are included in a report or layout.

■ **Usage**
When you normally display records on a database record layout or in a database report format, all the records in the file are included in the layout or report—if you scroll through the layout, you can view every record in the file, and if you print the report, every record in the file will be included. In many cases, however, you only want to view a certain group of records or print out a report containing only a certain group of records. From a database of customers, for example, you might only want to print a report containing records of all customers whose year-to-date purchases are greater than $2000. When you want to view or print out only certain groups of records in this way, you can use the AppleWorks record-selection rules. You can think of record-selection rules as a special kind of "filter" you apply to a database file—a filter that screens out unwanted records based on their contents.

Record-selection rules let you apply logical conditions and matching criteria to the records in a database file, so that only the records meeting those conditions or matching those criteria will be included in a layout or database report. You apply record-selection rules to a database file by pressing the Record Selection Rules command (⌂-R) from either the Multiple Record or Single Record layout screen, or from a database report format[79] screen. When you use record-selection rules on a layout screen, you restrict the records that are shown on the display to those matching the selection rules you set; and when you use record-selection rules on a report format screen, you restrict the records that will be included in the report to only those matching the rules you set.

Setting record-selection rules is a three-step process:

1. Select the category in your database file upon which you want to base your restriction.

2. Choose a logical operator to apply to the selected category.

3. Enter a matching criterion that, in conjunction with the logical operator, screens out unwanted records.

If we wanted to select only those records in which the year-to-date sales were greater than $2000, for example, we would (1) choose the *YTD Sales* category from the file; (2) choose the *is greater than* logical operator; and (3) enter the matching criterion of $2000.

AppleWorks makes it easy to set record-selection rules, because it presents the record-selection options in menus. The first menu presented is a list of the categories our file contains, so we can select the category upon which to base the restriction. The second menu contains a list of logical operators we can apply to that category. The third screen is simply a prompt at which we enter our matching criterion. Let's look at an example.

Suppose we have a file of customer names, and we want to select only the records in which the *Salesperson* is *Brohammer* and *YTD Sales* are greater than *$2000*.

1. With the Multiple Record or Single Record layout displayed, press the Record Selection Rules command (Ó-**R**). The menu of categories is displayed, showing all the data categories in our *Customers* file, like this:

```
File: Customers              SELECT RECORDS      Escape: Review/Add/Change
Selection:


============================================================================
  1.  Name
  2.  Company
  3.  Phone
  4.  Street
  5.  City
  6.  ST/Zip
  7.  Salesperson
  8.  YTD Sales




----------------------------------------------------------------------------
Type number, or use arrows, then press Return  _             48K Avail.
```

The first step in setting record-selection rules is to choose a data category upon which to base our selection.

2. We want our first rule to be based on the contents of the *Salesperson* category, so we type the number of that category (7), or move the highlight to the *Salesperson* category and press **RETURN**.

3. Once our category is selected, the second menu appears, giving us a list of logical operators from which to choose, as shown below:

```
File: Customers              SELECT RECORDS      Escape: Review/Add/Change
Selection: Salesperson


============================================================================
  1.  equals
  2.  is greater than
  3.  is less than
  4.  is not equal to
  5.  is blank
  6.  is not blank
  7.  contains
  8.  begins with
  9.  ends with
 10.  does not contain
 11.  does not begin with
 12.  does not end with

----------------------------------------------------------------------------
Type number, or use arrows, then press Return  _             48K Avail.
```

After choosing a data category, we choose a logical condition to apply to that category.

4. We want the contents of the *Salesperson* category to equal *Brohammer* (because we want to display only records for which Brohammer is the salesperson), so we choose *equals* as the logical condition and then press **RETURN**.

5. Once we choose the logical condition, the prompt line asks us to enter the comparison information, like this:

```
File: Customers                    SELECT RECORDS        Escape: Review/Add/Change
Selection: Salesperson equals

===============================================================================




                                                                          
                                                                          



----------------------------------------------------------------------------------
Type comparison information:  Brohammer_                              48K Avail.
```

After selecting a logical condition, we enter the comparison information by which to select our records.

Notice that as we build our selection rule, the rule itself appears below the file name at the top of the screen, so we can remember which selection criteria we have applied.

So far, we have defined a simple record-selection rule: *Salesperson equals Brohammer,* by which to restrict the contents of our layout screen. Apple-Works lets you define up to three selection criteria in a record-selection rule, however, and once you have defined one criterion, you are allowed to continue setting additional criteria.

6. After entering the comparison information and pressing **RETURN**, a "connector" menu appears, which allows us to extend our selection criteria by adding a second rule, as shown on the next page.

```
File: Customers                  SELECT RECORDS       Escape: Review/Add/Change
Selection: Salesperson equals BROHAMMER


================================================================================
  1.  and
  2.  or
  3.  through




----------------------------------------------------------------------
Type number, or use arrows, then press Return _              48K Avail.
```

You can refine selection rules by entering logical conditions and matching criteria for more than one category.

7. We want to add a second criteria (*YTD Sales* is greater than *$2000*) to our rule, so we choose option 1, *and*, from this screen to extend the selection rule. This addition to our rule now appears at the top of the screen.

8. After we choose *and* and press **RETURN**, the menu of category names appears again, and we select *YTD Sales* as the category this time, and press **RETURN**.

9. The menu of logical operators appears again, and we choose option 2, *is greater than*, as the option (because we want to select records in which *YTD Sales* is greater than *$2000*). Once we choose the logical operator, we're prompted to enter the comparison information, so we enter *$2000* and press **RETURN**.

10. The complete rule is now displayed at the top of the screen, and the "extender" menu appears again, giving us a chance to further refine our selection criteria. We don't want to extend our rule any further this time, so we press **ESC**. The selection rule is automatically applied to our file, and only those records in which the *Salesperson* category contains *Brohammer* and the *YTD Sales* category contains amounts greater than *$2000* will be displayed.

■ **About the logical conditions**

As you can see from the list of logical conditions in the second display above, you have a lot of flexibility in setting selection criteria for a category. We've seen how you would use the *equals* and *is greater than* operators. Here's how you might use the other operators:

Is less than: Use this condition to select records to include in the layout or report based on a category containing amounts. With it, you can specify only records in which the amount in that category is less than the comparison information you type. We might select records in which *YTD Sales is less than $2000*, for example.

Is not equal to: Use this operator when you want to select all records from our customers file except those for which *Brohammer* is the salesperson. For example, we might set a rule that specifies that the *Salesperson* category *is not equal to Brohammer.*

Is blank: Use this operator to locate those records in which a certain category doesn't contain data. Our customers file may contain some records for which *YTD Sales* haven't been calculated yet, for example. To find them, we might use the rule *YTD Sales is blank.*

Is not blank: We might use this condition as a way of finding records where a data flag has been entered. In our *Customers* file, for example, we might be using a category to track whether or not each customer responded to a recent direct-mail campaign. As the customer responses came in, our data-entry operator would simply put an *X* in a category called *Response.* To find all the records of customers who responded to the ad, we could use the rule *Response is not blank.*

Contains: Use this operator when you want to select by the contents of a category, but not on the exact contents of the category. Suppose we wanted to find all the customers whose zip codes began with *947.* We could use the rule *ST/Zip contains 947.*

Begins with: Use this operator when you want to select a range of numbers or alphabetic entries beginning with a certain letter, phrase, or number. If you wanted all records whose zip codes began with the numbers *947,* for example, you could specify *ST/Zip begins with 947.*

Ends with: Use this operator when you want to select a range of numbers or alphabetic entries ending with a certain letter, phrase, or number. If you wanted all the customers who were incorporated, for example, you could specify the rule *Company ends with Inc.*

Does not contain: If you knew you didn't want to target a certain mailing to customers on Elm Street, you could eliminate those records from a layout or Labels report with the rule *Street does not contain Elm Street.*

Does not begin with: Use this operator when you know which records you don't want, based on the beginning of data in a category. If, for example, you know you don't want records of customers in the 408 dialing area, you could select records with the rule *Phone does not begin with 408.*

Does not end with: Use this operator when you know which records you don't want, based on the ending of data in a category. If you knew that all the customers in zip codes ending in *0* were cheapskates, you could eliminate them from your Christmas-card list with the rule *ST/Zip does not end with 0.*

All these logical operators you can use are displayed at the bottom of page 281, but there are two more—those operating with times and dates. If your file contains one or more categories with the word *Time* or *Date* in their names, then the menu of logical operators also displays the conditions *is after* and *is before.* If your file contains such *Time* or *Date* category names, you can use *is after* and *is before* to select records based on times or dates in those categories. For example, you might have a category that recorded the date of a customer's first purchase, and then select records with the rule *Date first purchase is after May 1, 1984 and Date first purchase is before May 1, 1985.*

■ **Comments**

You can define a rule based on only one category, if you like—you simply select the category and logical operator, type in the comparison information, and then press **ESC** to signal that you are finished defining your rule. Or, using the extensions, you can define up to three sets of criteria for one rule. You could, for example, set the rule *Salesperson equals Brohammer and YTD Sales is greater than $2000 through YTD Sales is less than $4000* to select all of Brohammer's customers whose annual purchases are between $2000 and $4000.

If you aren't sure about whether you can select rules a certain way, try it. The logical operators and extensions provided in AppleWorks let you select records nearly any way you can imagine. Experiment!

Remove Files screen

■ **Definition**

The *Remove Files screen* is a display that lists the files currently on the Apple-Works Desktop,[97] from which you remove files from the Desktop and, optionally, save them on disk.

■ **Usage**

You produce the Remove Files screen by choosing option 4, *Remove files from the Desktop*, from the AppleWorks Main Menu.[158] Choose this option when you want to save Desktop files to disk and remove them from the Desktop at the same time. The Remove Files screen lets you save files to the current disk, or to a different disk.

To use the Remove Files screen:

1. Choose option 4, *Remove files from the Desktop*, from the AppleWorks Main Menu and press **RETURN**; the Remove Files screen will appear, as in this example.

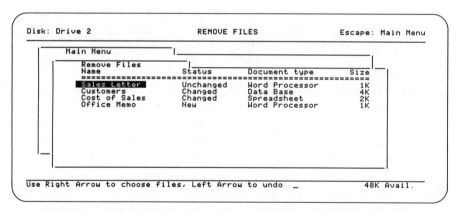

The Remove Files screen lets you remove files from the Desktop, and gives you a choice about whether to save them or not.

2. Select the file or files you want to remove from the list presented by highlighting a single file, or by selecting multiple files with the → key, and press **RETURN**.

3. AppleWorks automatically removes all selected files that have not been changed since they were added to the Desktop, and all files that have not been changed since they were last saved to disk.

The remaining files will be new or changed. AppleWorks presents a menu for each of these files that tells you whether the file is new or changed, and gives you a choice of either saving it on the current disk, saving it on a different disk, or throwing out the new file or the changes, like this:

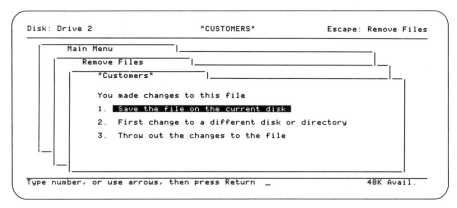

AppleWorks tells you about the file you are about to remove, and lets you choose whether to save it, and where.

4. If you choose to save a file to the current disk, AppleWorks will check the disk where you want the file saved to see if a file with the same name already exists on that disk. If a file with the same name doesn't exist on the disk in the current disk location, the file will be saved. If a file with the same name does exist, AppleWorks gives you a choice between replacing the existing information or saving the file under a new name, as shown here:

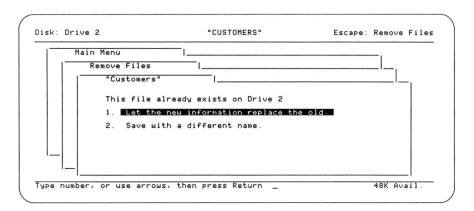

AppleWorks won't let you overwrite an existing file with the same name during a Remove Files operation without giving you a chance to save a new or changed file under a different name.

Remove a Printer menu

■ **Definition**

The *Remove a Printer menu* is a list of printer configurations currently stored in AppleWorks, from which you select a configuration to be deleted.

■ **Usage**

Use the Remove a Printer menu when you no longer need to store a particular printer configuration that was previously installed with the Add a Printer menu.[6] To use the Remove a Printer menu:

1. Choose *Other Activities* (option 5) from the AppleWorks Main Menu.[158]

2. Choose option 7, *Specify information about your printer(s)*, from the Other Activities menu.[178]

3. Choose *Remove a printer* (option 3) from the Printer Information menu.[212] The Remove a Printer menu will appear, as in this example:

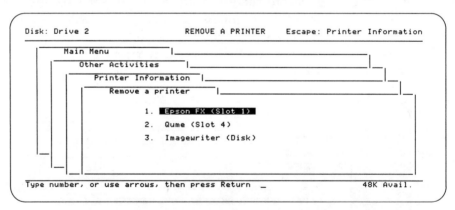

The Remove a Printer menu is used to delete previously stored printer configurations from AppleWorks.

4. Use the Arrow keys to move the highlight to the printer configuration you wish to remove, or type its number, and press **RETURN**.

5. The printer configuration will be deleted.

268

■ **Comments**

When you remove a printer from the Remove a Printer menu, you remove the printer configuration from the list of currently available printers that appears whenever you print a file.

Repeated label

■ **Definition**

A *repeated* is a character that has been duplicated across multiple cells.

■ **Usage**

When you design a spreadsheet, you can install repeated labels as dividing lines between sections, or beneath titles. A repeated label consists of a character, such as the equal sign (=) or the minus sign (−), typed repeatedly across a cell or group of adjacent cells.

Repeated labels are created on the Review/Add/Change screen of the spreadsheet. What you do is:

1. Move the cursor to the cell where you want labeling to begin.

2. Type a quote mark (") to tell AppleWorks you are entering a label.

3. Hold down the key of the character you want to enter as a label; the character will fill across the cursor cell and continue across the row to the right, until you release the key.

4. Press **RETURN** to enter the characters.

When you place the cursor on a cell containing a repeated label, the formula window will indicate this, as in this example:

```
File: Cost of Sales          REVIEW/ADD/CHANGE            Escape: Main Menu
========A========B========C========D========E========F========G========H====
   1│Acme Widget Company - Widget Sales Costs, Q4, 1985
   2│=============================================================
   3│
   4│Materials                     Oct      Nov      Dec      Qtr
   5│----------------              ===      ===      ===      ===
   6│
   7│Widget Oil                   1200     1410      960     2370
   8│Steel                        2500     3250     3000     8750
   9│Copper                       1000     1175      800     2975
  10│Magnesium                    1250     1100     1250     3600
  11│Grease                        120      150      135      405
  12│Rags                           50       50       50      150
  13│
  14│Labor
  15│----------------
  16│Salaries                     3000     3000     3000     9000
  17│Commissions                  2250     2250     2250     6750
  18│Hourly Wages                 2850     2850     2850     8550
 A2: <Label> Repeated--

Type entry or use ⌂ commands  _                           ⌂-? for Help
```

Cell A2 contains a repeated label, as shown in the entry line.

■ **Comments**

Unlike normal labels, AppleWorks considers a repeated label to be a label containing all the same characters and at least as wide as one cell. Note that even though the repeated label you enter into a cell could be 50 characters wide, when you later move the cursor onto that cell, the cell indicator in the lower-left corner of the screen will display the word *Repeated*, followed by only one of the characters that occupy that one cell—not all the characters that you originally typed in. When a long repeated label is entered and **RETURN** is pressed, AppleWorks will actually break the entry down into separate cells, which you can later change or edit individually. Also, if there is a value or formula in one of the cells to the right of where you began the repeated label, AppleWorks won't let the repeated label overwrite the contents of that cell.

Replace Text (⌘-R)

■ **Definition**

The *Replace Text* command (⌘-**R**) lets you automatically substitute new text for existing text in word-processor documents.

■ **Usage**

Use the Replace Text command in the word processor when you want to replace one or more occurrences of an existing string of text with other text.

■ **Example: Replacing text in the word processor**

Suppose you have created and stored a group of sales letters in preparation for the announcement of your new product, the Widget Convertible. You are just about to print the letters for mailing, when you learn that the product name has been changed from Widget Convertible to Widget Flexy. You want to change the letters as quickly as possible. Here's how to use the Replace Text command:

1. Make sure the document you want to work with is displayed on the Review/Add/Change screen.

2. Move the cursor to the beginning of the file.

3. Choose the Replace Text command (⌘-**R**). The prompt line will change to read:

   Replace? Text Case sensitive text

4. Choose *Case sensitive text*,[23] and press **RETURN**.

5. The prompt line will now read:

   Replace what?

Enter the word you want replaced (*Convertible*), and press **RETURN**.

6. The prompt line will now read:

   Replace with what?

Enter the word *Flexy*, and press **RETURN**.

7. The prompt line will now read:

   Replace? One at a time All

If you choose the default, *One at a time*, AppleWorks will stop at each occurrence of *Convertible*, highlight it, and display this prompt line:

   Replace this one? No Yes

If you press **RETURN** or **N**, AppleWorks will ask if you want to find the next occurrence. If you choose **Y**, AppleWorks will move on to the next occurrence of *Convertible* without changing this one and redisplay the prompt line; if you press **Y**, *Convertible* will be replaced with *Flexy* and AppleWorks will ask if you want to find the next occurrence. If you choose **Y**, AppleWorks will move on to highlight the next occurrence and redisplay the prompt line.

If you choose to replace *All*, AppleWorks will simply go through the entire document starting at the cursor position and replace every occurrence of *Convertible* with *Flexy*.

■ **Comments**

If you choose the option to replace *Text* when you first choose ⌂-**R**, the function will replace occurrences of the text whether they are capitalized or not, and whether they make up complete words or not. The *Case sensitive text* option will also replace parts of words as well, but if the word to be replaced is capitalized, only words with the same capitalization you specified will be replaced. If you want to change the word *ace* to *ice*, for example, the Replace Text command will not only change *ace* to *ice*, but *replace* to *replice*. It's always best to use the *Case sensitive text* option whenever you can. If the text you are replacing might occur in parts of words where you don't want it replaced, use the *One at a time* option to control which words will be replaced.

Report header

■ **Definition**

A *report header* is a section at the top of each page of a database report that specifies the name of the file, the name of the report, the page number, the record-selection rules[259] in effect (if any), the category names[23] (on a Tables report), and an optional report date.

■ **Usage**

Although most of the report-header information is always displayed on the screen, including it on a printed copy is optional. You can choose whether or not to print a report header by typing *PH* when the Printer Options menu[217] is displayed. Each time you type the letters and press **RETURN**, the *Print report Header at the top of each page* line under the *Formatting options* section will switch from *Yes* to *No* or vice versa.

■ **Example**

The report header in this database report includes category names, file name, report name, page number, report date, and record-selection rules in effect.

```
File:   Customers                                           Page   1
Report: Phone List                                          12/14/85
Selection: Company begins with A
   through  Company begins with F
Name                  Company                Phone         Salesperson YTD Sales
--------------------- ---------------------- ------------- ----------- ----------
Olive Ogilvy          Ace Jackhammer Service 555-6666      Brohammer   10,635.25
Wilson Peck           Apex Canning           555-3232      Smith        5,350.00
Wilson K. Jeeves      Butlerware, Inc.       555-3334      Smith          575.30
Mort Drucker          Drucker Drayage        555-2345      Smith        1,025.00
Arnold Ormsby         Flecko Paints          555-4567      Jones          787.35
Walter Canary         Flippo Dog Food        555-8606      Jones          125.60
Fred Fong             Fong Machine Tools     555-8765      Jones        4,675.20
Edwina Gumm           Fritzi Fashions        555-7890      Smith           87.50
Ed Frobish            Frobish Linen Service  555-1234      Smith       15,325.00
Fortuna Maldonado     Furniture City         555-2222      Brohammer    2,500.85
```

Report headers identify the name of a report, the file it came from, the category names, the record-selection rules in effect, the page number, and an optional report date.

Report Menu

■ **Definition**

The *Report Menu* is a list of report-producing options available in the Apple-Works database.

■ **Usage**

The Report Menu appears automatically when you use the Print command[193] (⌘-P) while a database file is displayed on the Review/Add/Change screen, either in Single Record or Multiple Record layout. All database files must be printed from a report format you create (see: Database Report Formats[79]). The Report Menu lets you use an existing report format you have already defined, create new Tables or Labels report formats, duplicate an existing format, erase an existing format, or continue working with the same format. To use the Report Menu:

1. Choose the Print command (⌘-P) while the Review/Add/Change screen of a database file is displayed. The Report Menu then appears:

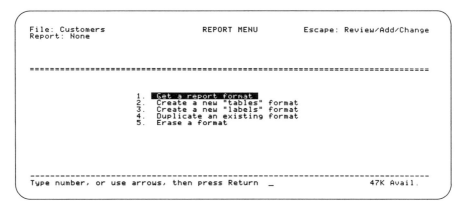

The Report Menu in the database lets you choose from a variety of report-making options.

2. Choose the report-making option you want. If you choose option 1, *Get a report format*, the Report Catalog will appear:

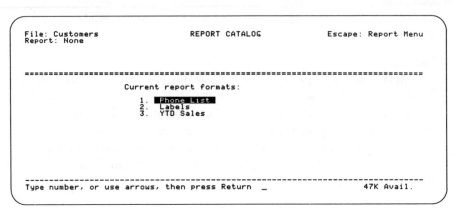

```
File: Customers              REPORT CATALOG           Escape: Report Menu
Report: None


===========================================================================
                    Current report formats:
                        1.  Phone List
                        2.  Labels
                        3.  YTD Sales




---------------------------------------------------------------------------
Type number, or use arrows, then press Return  _              47K Avail.
```

The Report Catalog lists report formats you have previously created for a database file.

This catalog also appears if you choose option 4, *Duplicate an existing format*, or option 5, *Erase a format*. In either case, you choose the format you want to get, duplicate, or delete from the catalog's list. If you choose to create either a new Tables or Labels format, the Report Format screen appears after you type in the name for the new report.

■ **Comments**
If no reports have been created for a file, option 2, *Create a new "tables" format*, will be highlighted on the Report Menu screen as the default selection. If you duplicate an existing format, you will be prompted to type a name for it. You can store up to 8 reports with a datafile. Complete instructions about how to create database reports will be found under the entry Database Report Formats.[19]

Reset (Ć-CONTROL-RESET)

■ **Definition**
The *Reset* command (Ć-**CONTROL-RESET**) clears the memory in the computer and restarts it.

■ **Usage**

Use the Reset command only when you are finished working with Apple-Works and want to start another program. The Reset command clears everything out of the Apple's memory and restarts the computer, just as if you had turned the computer off and then back on again.

You should always choose the Quit option from the Main Menu[158] when you want to stop working with AppleWorks, because you may have forgotten to save some of the files on the Desktop. Quit will check the Desktop for you and remind you to save any files you have forgotten to save.

Once you have quit AppleWorks, however, you may want to start another program by using the Reset command. Here's how.

1. Make sure you have quit AppleWorks. The screen should display the message:

```
        ENTER PREFIX (PRESS "RETURN" TO ACCEPT)

        /APPLEWORKS/
```

2. At this point, you could type the disk (volume) name and application name for the new program you want to run. You might not remember what those names are, however, so it's easier to use the Reset command. Remove the AppleWorks program disk from your disk drive (disk drive 1, if you have two drives), and replace it with the program disk for the new program you want to run.

3. Press the Reset command (♙-**CONTROL-RESET**). You must hold down all three of these keys at once, then release them to reset the computer.

4. The computer will restart, and the program in the disk drive will load.

■ **Comments**

If you have a hard disk drive,[353] you probably won't be able to restart another program in your floppy drive this way. Check your hard disk's manual to find out what happens when you press the Reset command.

If you're certain there are no files on the Desktop you want to save, you can use the Reset command at any time in AppleWorks. It's a faster way to quit the program and load another one than going through the Main Menu with the Quit option. Simply remove your AppleWorks program disk, insert the disk for the program you want to load, and press the Reset command.

CAUTION: The Reset command clears the Apple's memory. Be careful not to use it if you want to continue working with AppleWorks, or if you have any files on the Desktop that haven't been saved.

Reusing data

When you add an AppleWorks file to the Desktop[97] from a disk, you are only loading a copy of that file into memory—the original copy always remains safely on the disk unless you deliberately delete it using the Other Activities menu.[178] And, because you are working only with a copy of a file on disk, you can change the name or the contents of a file on the Desktop and thereby use some of your existing data for another purpose.

■ **Renaming files**

Suppose you have a sales letter you have sent to a customer named *Frobish*. You have created that letter and saved it under the name *Frobish.Ltr* on disk. Now you decide to send a slightly different letter to your customer *Ogilvy*. You could type the new letter over from scratch, but since the Ogilvy letter is similar to the Frobish letter, it's faster to reuse some of the data in the Frobish letter. To do this:

1. Load the file *Frobish.Ltr* to the Desktop (see: Add Files menu[2]).

2. Use the Name Change[171] command (⌘-N) to rename the file *Ogilvy.Ltr*.

3. Change the text of the letter so it's appropriate for your customer Ogilvy.

4. Save the new letter to disk with the Save[281] command (⌘-S). Since you renamed the file *Ogilvy.Ltr*, it will be saved under the new name, and the old file (*Frobish.Ltr*) will remain in its original state on the disk.

You can reuse data in any AppleWorks application this way. Along with the Name Change feature, there are other features of AppleWorks that make it easy to reuse data.

When you try to save a file using option 3 from the Main Menu, Apple-Works checks to see if there's another file by that name already stored on the current disk. If you forget to rename your file when you are working on it and then try to save it on disk, for example, AppleWorks will warn you and give you another chance. If there's another file by that name, you can choose to either replace the existing file with the new one, or to save the new file under a different name. By saving the new file under a different name, you will keep your original file intact and store the new one as well.

Restructuring a database file

In the word processor and the spreadsheet, the procedures for reusing data are fairly straightforward—you edit the word-processor document or change some of the labels or values in a spreadsheet, and then save the file under a new name. In the database, however, you have more options for restructuring a file on the Desktop.

Just as in the word processor and spreadsheet, you can change the name of a database file and edit the data stored in it. But with the database, you can also change the *structure* of the file. When you press the Name Change command from the database Review/Add/Change screen, you can change the file name, of course, but you can also change the names of categories, insert new categories, or delete existing categories. This feature lets you create a significantly different database file from an existing one.

Example: Suppose you have an existing file called *Customers*, and you want to use some of that file's data in a new file you want to call *Sales*. The *Customers* file contains a lot of data, but for the *Sales* file you only want to reuse the data in the categories for *Company*, *Salesperson*, and *YTD Sales*. Here's how:

1. Display the *Customers* file on the Review/Add/Change screen, and press the Name Change command (⌂-N). Next, the Change Name/Category screen[27] will appear, as in the example on the following page:

```
File: Customers          CHANGE NAME/CATEGORY     Escape: Review/Add/Change


Category names
================================================================================
Name
Company                                 Options:
Phone
Street                                  Change filename
City                                    Return    Go to first category
ST/Zip
Salesperson
YTD Sales




-------------------------------------------------------------------------------
Type filename: Customers                                        48K Avail.
```

The Change Name/Category screen lets you completely restructure a database file.

2. The blinking cursor will be located on the first character of the file name at the bottom of the screen (*Customers,* in the example). Delete the current name with the Clear[34] command (⌂-**Y**) and type the new name, *Sales.* Press **RETURN** when you're finished.

3. The cursor will move to the first category name at the top of the screen. Since this is a category you don't want in the new file, simply press the Delete[92] command (⌂-**D**). AppleWorks will display the following message, warning you that by deleting the category you will erase all custom screen layouts and report formats:

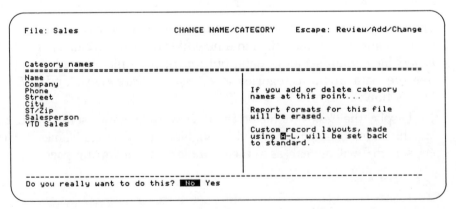

```
File: Sales              CHANGE NAME/CATEGORY     Escape: Review/Add/Change


Category names
================================================================================
Name
Company
Phone                                   If you add or delete category
Street                                  names at this point...
City
ST/Zip                                  Report formats for this file
Salesperson                             will be erased.
YTD Sales
                                        Custom record layouts, made
                                        using ⌂-L, will be set back
                                        to standard.


-------------------------------------------------------------------------------
Do you really want to do this? No  Yes
```

When you delete a category from a database file, AppleWorks warns you that you'll be erasing all report formats and custom layouts for this file.

278

You don't care if the existing layouts and report formats are erased, because the new file will have different layouts and report formats anyway. Press **Y** to answer *yes* to the question in the prompt line that appears at the bottom of the screen.

4. AppleWorks will display a second message warning you that you are about to erase all the data in the category *Name*—press **Y** to answer *yes* to the prompt to tell the program you really want to do this. The category *Name* and its data will be deleted from the file, and the cursor will move down to the next category, *Company*.

Use ↓ to move the cursor to the rest of the categories you want to delete (*Phone, Street, City,* and *ST/Zip*). Your file will now contain only the three categories you want, and its new name will be *Sales*.

```
File: Sales                CHANGE NAME/CATEGORY      Escape: Review/Add/Change

 Category names
 =================================================================================
 Company
 Salesperson                          Options:
 YTD Sales
                                      Change category name
                                      Up arrow    Go to previous category
                                      Down arrow  Go to next category
                                      -I             Insert new category
                                      -D             Delete this category



 ----------------------------------------------------------------------
 Type entry or use   commands                               50K Avail.
```

Once you delete unwanted categories, you have a new file with a new name that contains only the data you want.

Now you can save the new *Sales* file to disk, and the original *Customers* file will still be stored on disk in its original form.

Since you can restructure files this way with AppleWorks, you can reuse a lot of your existing data and save yourself hours of repetitive typing when you want to use the data in one file in different ways.

Row

■ **Definition**

A *row* is a continuous horizontal group of spreadsheet cells.

■ **Usage**

A row is one of the two ways in which data is grouped in a spreadsheet. Spreadsheets are matrices of *rows* and *columns,* and each intersection of a row and column[37] is a *cell.* Each row and column is labeled: Columns are labeled with letters and run from left to right, and rows are labeled with numbers from 1 to 999, running from the top of the spreadsheet to the bottom. An AppleWorks spreadsheet can contain a maximum of 127 columns and 999 rows of data.

```
File: FiveYear.Budget           REVIEW/ADD/CHANGE              Escape: Main Menu
=======A========B========C========D========E========F========G========H====
 1|
 2|               Acme Widgets - Budget Projection
 3|
 4|                    Q185      Q285      Q385      Q485      Q186      Q286
 5|
 6|Rent                2000      2000      2000      2000      2500      2500
 7|Utilities            502       489       480       500       510       530
 8|Material            2500      2495      2350      2500      2500      2650
 9|Salaries            2000      2000      2000      2250      2250      2250
10|Promotion            500       475       300       500       400       450
11|
12|Total Expenses      7502      7459      7130      7750      8160      8380
13|
14|
15|
16|
17|
18|
--------------------------------------------------------------------------
A6: <Label> Rent

Type entry or use ⌂ commands  _                              ⌂-? for Help
```

A row is one of the two major levels of organization in spreadsheets.

Because a row is one of the two major units of organization in a spreadsheet, AppleWorks provides options when you use certain commands that allow you to format or move data in increments of one or more entire rows. You can copy data from one row to another within a spreadsheet or between spreadsheets via the Clipboard, and you can change the format of data in one or more rows.

Ruler (⌘-1 through 9)

■ **Definition**

The *Ruler* is a method of moving the cursor quickly to different parts of an AppleWorks file.

■ **Usage**

The Ruler divides a file's length into eighths, and then moves you to the part of the file that corresponds to the number key (1 through 9) you press along with the ⌘ key.

    For example, when you press ⌘-**1**, the cursor moves to the beginning of a file. When you press ⌘-**9**, the cursor moves to the end of the file. Pressing ⌘ and a number from *2* through *8* moves the cursor directly to the part of the file proportionate to the number you type, whether it has to move up or down; the actual distance depends on how long the file is. If the file is one page long and you press the number *5*, the cursor will move to the middle of the page. If the file is 10 pages long, the cursor will move to page 5.

■ **Comments**

The Ruler is active in every AppleWorks application, and in every part of those applications that requires or allows cursor movement.

    If you are highlighting text to move, copy, or delete in a file, for example, you can use the Ruler to highlight large parts of a file when you are prompted to select the portion of the file that you want to perform the command on.

    Using the Ruler in cases like this is faster than scrolling with the cursor keys in a large file—you can highlight a large portion of the file quickly with the ruler, and then move the cursor to the exact place you want it with the regular Arrow keys.

Save (⌘-s)

■ **Definition**

The *Save* command (⌘-**s**) saves the file you are currently working with directly to the current disk.

■ **Usage**

When you use the Save command, the file is saved immediately on the current disk using the current file name. You have no options to change which disk it is saved to or which name it is saved under. The Save option works from any screen in any application file.

When you press ⌘-S, a screen message tells you that the file is being saved, and that you can cancel the save operation by pressing **ESC**. When the file has been saved, the message disappears, and your file is displayed again.

If you cancel a save operation by pressing **ESC**, and the file already exists on the current disk, the file on disk won't be changed. If the file doesn't yet exist on the disk, it simply won't be saved. Whether or not you cancel a save operation, however, the file remains as it was on the Desktop.[97]

▪ Comments

The Save command is useful for periodically saving your changes to a file as you work. It's always a good idea to save your work every 20 minutes or half hour at the most. That way, you will only lose the amount of work you did since the last save operation if the power should go out, or if your computer should malfunction.

Remember, when you use the Save command to save the current file, it will be saved on the current disk under the name the Desktop version of the file currently has. If a different file is stored on the current disk under that same name, then that file will be overwritten. In most cases, this isn't a problem, because you are simply updating an older version of the same file. If you inadvertently give your Desktop file the same name as a completely different file on the current disk and then use the Save command, however, your Desktop file will replace the other file on the disk. If you aren't sure if there is another file on the current disk with the same name, it is safer to use the Save Files screen.

Save Files screen

▪ Definition

The *Save Files screen* displays the files that are currently on the AppleWorks Desktop[97] and lets you select files to be saved to disk.

▪ Usage

Use the Save Files screen when you want to save one or more Desktop files to disk. The Save Files screen lets you save files to the current disk, or to a different disk.

To use the Save Files screen:

1. Choose option 3, *Save Desktop files to disk*, from the AppleWorks Main Menu.[158] When you select this option and press **RETURN**, the Save Files screen will appear, as in this example:

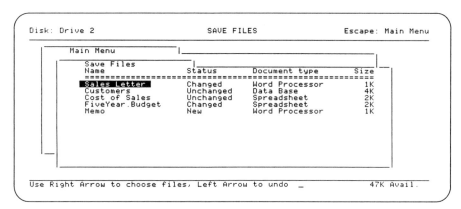

The Save Files screen lets you save to disk one or more of the files currently on the Desktop.

2. Use the → key to select the file or files you want to save from the list of files presented on the Save Files screen, and press **RETURN** when you are finished.

3. Before AppleWorks saves each file to disk, it offers you one or two sets of options, depending on the status of file you are saving. The first set lets you choose the location where you are saving the file:

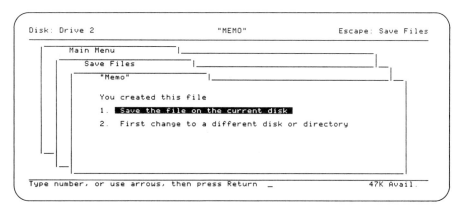

AppleWorks tells you about the file you are about to save, and lets you choose where to save it.

283

The title line of the menu tells you whether the file is new, or already exists. If the file already exists, it also tells you whether it has been changed or not.

4. If you are saving a new file, you can choose either the current disk or a different disk or directory as the place where the file will be saved. Once you make this choice and press **RETURN**, the file is saved.

If you are saving an existing file, AppleWorks will let you choose the save location, and after you choose option 1 to save the file, it then checks the location you have chosen as the current disk to see if a file with the same name exists there. If it does, it will report what it finds on a screen like this one:

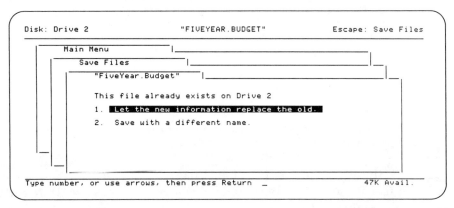

When you are saving a file to a disk that already contains a file with the same name, AppleWorks gives you the option of overwriting the old file, or saving the file under a different name.

If the location you select doesn't contain an existing file with the same name, the file will be automatically saved. If, however, the location does contain a file with the same name, AppleWorks will warn you about the situation and give you a choice between overwriting the existing file or saving the Desktop file under a different name.

■ **Comments**

Saving Desktop files to disk does not remove them from the Desktop. You must use the Remove Files[266] option from the Main Menu to actually take files off the Desktop.

When you use the Save Files screen, AppleWorks will never overwrite an existing disk file without giving you the opportunity to either save the file to a different directory or disk, or save it under a different name.

If you attempt to save a file with the same name as a file of a different type (such as ASCII or DIF), or from another AppleWorks application, you will be warned that you cannot replace the first file on disk. To save the file, you will first have to give it another name.

If you know you want to save a Desktop file to the current disk, and you don't care that a file with the same name will be overwritten, you can do this by issuing the Save[281] command (⌂-**S**) while you are working with the file on the screen.

Set Tabs (⌂-**T**)

■ **Definition**

The *Set Tabs* command (⌂-**T**) is used to set and clear tab stops in the word processor.

■ **Example: Setting tabs in the word processor**

The word-processor Review/Add/Change screen normally appears with tab stops set every five characters, so that the cursor will advance five spaces each time you press the **TAB** key. The stops are indicated as vertical lines in the bar at the top of the screen. You may want to set tab stops in different places than this, however.

Suppose you are preparing this price list for your customers:

```
File: Price List            MODIFY TAB STOPS      Escape: Review/Add/Change
▣====|====|====|====|====|====|====|====|====|====|====|====|===
                 Widget Prices - January, 1986

Dear Customer:

This is our new price list, effective January 1, 1986.
Please replace the old price list you have on file.

        Item                          Price




-------------------------------------------------------------
Tab stops:    S: Set   C: Clear   R: Remove all          (Column  1)
```

You can set new tab stops in the word processor with the Set Tabs command.

You could enter the data faster if you could tab to the beginning of each column, but the columns of items and prices begin where there are no current tab stops set. To set these new tab stops:

1. Press the Set Tabs command (⌘-T). A rectangular cursor will appear in the bar at the top of the screen, as shown in the example document. Note that the cursor will appear directly above the column the cursor was in when you pressed ⌘-T.

2. Press **R** to remove all the existing tab stops.

3. Use → or ← to move the cursor to the column where you want to set the first new tab, and press **S** to set a tab there. A new vertical line will appear to indicate the new tab stop.

4. Move the cursor to the next column where you want to set a tab, and press **S** again to set it.

5. Press **ESC** to exit the tab-setting mode so you can begin entering your data.

- **Clearing Tabs**

  To clear a tab stop (including a preset stop), press ⌘-T, move the cursor to the tab you want to clear, and press **C**.

Set Totals (⌘-T)

- **Definition**

  The *Set Totals* command (⌘-T) is used to total categories containing numeric information in a database Tables[79] report.

- **Usage**

  You use the Set Totals command on the Report Format menu[79] of a Tables report to calculate the total of the values in a category containing numbers. A total will then be placed at the bottom of each totaled category at the end of a *printed* report.

■ **Example: Setting Category Totals in the database**

Suppose you have the following sales report, which shows year-to-date sales to each customer:

```
File: Customers              REPORT FORMAT              Escape: Report Menu
Report: YTD Sales
Selection: All records


===============================================================================
--> or <--   Move cursor                    Ô-J  Right justify this category
  >  Ô   <   Switch category positions       Ô-K  Define a calculated category
--> Ô   <-- Change column width              Ô-N  Change report name and/or title
Ô-A  Arrange (sort) on this category         Ô-O  Printer options
Ô-D  Delete this category                    Ô-P  Print the report
Ô-G  Add/remove group totals                 Ô-R  Change record selection rules
Ô-I  Insert a prev. deleted category         Ô-T  Add/remove category totals
-------------------------------------------------------------------------------
Company                 Salesperson YTD Sales    L
-A--------------------- -B--------- -C--------   e
Ace Jackhammer Service  Brohammer   10,635.25    n
Apex Canning            Smith        5,350.00    5
Butlerware, Inc.        Smith          575.30    i
-------------------------------------------------------------------------------
Use options shown above to change report format          46K Avail.
```

You can total the values in a database Tables report category with the Set Totals command.

You want to set a Category Total for the *YTD Sales* category, so you know what your overall sales have been. To do this:

1. Move the cursor to the *YTD Sales* category.

2. Press the Set Totals command (Ô-**T**).

3. The prompt line will ask how many decimal places you want each value in the category, including the total, to be displayed with. Type *2*, since the values represent dollars and cents, then press **RETURN**.

4. The prompt line will ask how many spaces you want following the category. Since this is the rightmost category in the report, and since the report isn't very wide, it doesn't really matter, so press **RETURN** to choose *3* (the default).

5. The values in the category will now be displayed on the Report Format screen as rows of *9s* with the number of decimal places you chose, and a double line will appear at the bottom of the category to indicate that the category will be totaled when the file is printed.

Category Totals do not appear on the Report Format screen—they are only calculated and shown when you print the report with the Print[193] command (Ô-**P**). If you want to see the totals without printing the report on paper, print the report to the screen. If the report is long, you may have to press the spacebar several times in order to print the successive portions of the file on the screen until you reach the end of the report, where the total will be shown.

■ **Removing Category Totals**
To remove a Category Total, simply place the cursor on the totaled category and press the Set Totals command (⌘-T). The category will no longer be totaled; the rows of *9s* and the double line at the bottom will disappear, and the values in the category will be displayed and printed with the number of decimal places they had before the category was totaled.

Sharing data with other programs

The three AppleWorks applications create three different types of Pro-DOS[104] files that are incompatible with each other and with other programs. But you can store AppleWorks files in the standard ASCII[13] and DIF[100] formats, and you can also use ASCII and DIF files created by other programs as sources for new AppleWorks files. These standard file types make it easy to share data among the AppleWorks applications or with other programs.

There are two basic ways to share data between applications in Apple-Works: You can use the Clipboard[35] to transfer data from either the spreadsheet or the database into a word-processor document, and you can use the ASCII and DIF file types to transfer data among the spreadsheet, database, and word processor. These options are covered in the following sections.

■ **Sharing data via the Clipboard**
You can print all or part of a spreadsheet or database report to the Clipboard, and then copy or move the data from the Clipboard into a word-processor document. You must print (rather than move[163] or copy[40]) the spreadsheet or database data to the Clipboard, because printing it converts the data into a format that can be used by the word processor. Once the data is on the Clipboard, you can paste it into an existing word-processor document by placing the cursor where you want the data to be inserted and using the Copy or Move command to get it from the Clipboard.

Suppose you have some spreadsheet figures and you want to copy them into a word-processor document. Here's what to do:

1. Display the spreadsheet's Review/Add/Change screen, and move the cursor to the first cell of the area you want to copy to the spreadsheet.

2. Press the Print[193] command (⌂-P), which prompts you to select the data you want to move to the Clipboard (*All*, *Rows*, *Columns*, or *Block*). Make the appropriate choice, use the Arrow keys to select the data, and press **RETURN** to display the Print screen.[197]

3. Look at the Print screen, and make sure that the current printer options are wide enough to accommodate the data you have selected. (If the selected data is wider than the Printer Options allow for, some of your data will be cut off—see Spreadsheet Printing.[319]) If your data is wider than the Printer Options allow, either select a narrower set of data, or change the printer options to allow for the data you have selected.

4. Choose the option *The clipboard (for the Word Processor)* as the destination for your data, and press **RETURN**.

5. You'll be prompted either to type a report date to be printed at the top of the spreadsheet data when it is printed to the Clipboard, or just to press **RETURN**. After you press **RETURN**, the data will be printed to the Clipboard, and a message will appear on the screen telling you this.

6. Use the Desktop Index[98] to select the word-processor file where you want to paste the spreadsheet data. If the file isn't on the Desktop, add it to the Desktop via the Add Files menu.[2]

7. When the word-processor file is displayed, move the cursor to the place where you want the spreadsheet data inserted.

8. Press the Copy command (⌂-C), and choose *From clipboard (paste)* as the copy option. The data on the Clipboard will be inserted in the word-processor document starting at the current cursor position.

This process is much the same when you are moving database data into a word-processor document, except that the printing procedure from the database is slightly different (see Database Printing[67]). There are two considerations common to both applications: (1) The data you select for printing must be narrower than the current printer options in the source database or the spreadsheet file, or else some of the data won't transfer to the Clipboard, and (2) the printer options in the word processor must be set to accommodate the incoming data properly.

This second consideration arises because of the way the word processor treats data. Database or spreadsheet data is usually formatted in rows, and each row of data must remain intact. The default printer options in the database and spreadsheet allow 80-character lines.

In the word processor, however, the default printer options allow for only 60-character lines. When data moved from the Clipboard is too wide for the current printer options in the word processor, the data "wraps around" because of the word-processor's word-wraparound[375] feature. In the following word-processor document, you'll see that some database data has wrapped around because the word processor's printer options are too narrow to accommodate the lines as they were transferred.

```
 File: Customer Report          REVIEW/ADD/CHANGE              Escape: Main Menu
 ====|====|====|====|====|====|====|====|====|====|====|====|====|====|===
 list has been sorted to include only customers whose
 year-to-date purchases are greater than $500.

 Name                Company                Phone
 Salesperson YTD Sales
 ----------------    --------------------   -----------
 ----------- -----------
 Olive Ogilvy        Ace Jackhammer Service 555-6666
 Brohammer   10,635.25
 Wilson Peck         Apex Canning           555-3232       Smith
     5,350.00
 Wilson K. Jeeves    Butlerware, Inc.       555-3334       Smith
       575.30
 Mort Drucker        Drucker Drayage        555-2345       Smith
     1,025.00
 Arnold Ormsby       Flecko Paints          555-4567       Jones
       787.35
 Fred Fong           Fong Machine Tools     555-8765       Jones
     4,675.20
 ----------------------------------------------------------------------------
 Type entry or use ▣ commands               Line 12  Column  1     ▣-? for Help
```

When lines copied into the word processor from the Clipboard are wider than the current printer options allow, they wrap around on the screen.

As you can see in the example, the word processor's line length is too narrow to accommodate the data, and it has wrapped around on the screen. Fortunately, we can change the word processor's margin and Characters-per-Inch (CI) printer options to make room for these lines. Once we change the printer options, the lines will "unwrap" and the *YTD Sales* category will become the last column in the word-processor document, following *Salesperson.*

When you move data from the spreadsheet or the database to the word processor, you can change the word-processor's printer options to accommodate longer lines either before or after the data is moved. (See: Printer Options;[217] Word Processor Printing.[371])

Because you can change these printer options as often as every paragraph in the word processor, you can format your document so the margins and characters per inch are different only for the part of the document that contains the pasted-in data—simply move the cursor to the first line of the pasted-in data before changing the printer options to make lines containing the pasted data wider, then put the cursor on the first text line following the pasted data and change the printer options back to what they normally were.

In some cases, you may paste data into the word processor that is wider than 80 characters. Since the screen can only display 77 characters across, data wider than this will wrap around. It's possible to set the word-processor printer options to print lines up to 80 columns wide, however. If you have lines wider than the screen can display and your printer options are set to accommodate them, the lines will "unwrap" when they are printed on paper, even though they appear wrapped around on the screen. The maximum width of a printed line in AppleWorks is 225 characters.

▪ Sharing data via DIF and ASCII files

When you want to share data between the spreadsheet and the database, move word-processor data to the database, or share AppleWorks data with other programs, you can use the DIF and ASCII file formats. The following diagram shows the ways in which you can use DIF and ASCII files within AppleWorks and between it and other programs.

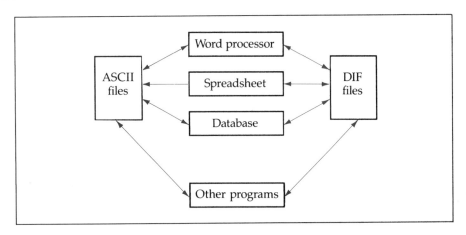

This diagram illustrates how the AppleWorks applications can create and share DIF and ASCII files.

As you can see from the diagram, each AppleWorks application can read and write at least one of the two standard file formats. This means you can always move data from one type of file to another. Specifically, the word processor can read and write ASCII files; the spreadsheet can read DIF files and write ASCII or DIF files; and the database can read or write ASCII or DIF files. Thus, if you wanted to move data from the spreadsheet to the database, you could save the spreadsheet as a DIF file, and then use the DIF file as the source for a new database file. You could save a word-processor document as an ASCII file and use it as the source for a new database file. You could store a database file as a DIF file and use it as the source for a new spreadsheet.

Here's the general procedure for moving data as DIF or ASCII files:

1. Display the spreadsheet, database, or word-processor file whose data you want to use, and then print it to disk as a DIF or ASCII file.

2. Use the Add Files menu to create a new file for the application where you want to use the data, and choose *From a DIF (TM) file* or *From a text (ASCII) file*, depending on the format your data was saved in on the disk.

3. Type the pathname[188] of the DIF or ASCII file you want to use, and then type a name for the new file.

4. The new file will be loaded into the current application. When you use DIF and ASCII files to move data like this, you must always create a *new* file with the DIF or ASCII file—you can't move DIF or ASCII data into an existing AppleWorks file.

There are some restrictions on the type of data that can be transferred via these formats. When you're transferring spreadsheet data, formulas do not transfer via DIF or ASCII formats. Thus, if you save a spreadsheet as a DIF file and then try to use that data in another spreadsheet program, only the labels, numbers, and values generated by the formulas will transfer, not the formulas themselves. When you're transferring database data as a DIF or ASCII file, Calculated Categories and Category Totals don't transfer, and category names don't transfer.

Finally, make sure that you specify the proper format for your data and use the file type that best suits the data. Both database and spreadsheet files can be saved to disk as either ASCII or DIF files, but only DIF files will preserve the row and column orientation of the original data. Therefore, you should use the DIF format for spreadsheet and database data. Use the ASCII format for spreadsheet and database files only when you are transferring the data to a program that won't accept DIF files, such as a word processor.

When you save files in the DIF format from the spreadsheet, you will be asked whether you want them saved in row or column order—you'll have to check the program you will be loading the file in to determine which order it expects the data to be in. The AppleWorks spreadsheet and database both expect DIF files they use to be in column order.

Single Record layout

▪ **Definition**

A *Single Record layout* is a view of the Review/Add/Change screen in a database file that shows only one record on the screen at a time.

▪ **Usage**

Use the Single Record layout when you want to see all the categories of data in individual database records.

When a database file that already contains information is loaded from disk to the Desktop, the Review/Add/Change screen always appears first in Multiple Record layout.[168] Multiple Record layout may not show all the categories of data in the file, though. You can change to Single Record layout to view all the data categories in one record at once. To change the view to Single Record layout:

1. Make sure the Multiple Record layout of the database file is displayed on the screen.

2. Press the Zoom[376] command ⌂-**z**. The screen will change to a Single Record layout, like this:

```
 File: Customers              REVIEW/ADD/CHANGE           Escape: Main Menu

 Selection: All records

 Record 11 of 15
=================================================================================
Name: Barney Flint
Company: Howard's U-Rent 'Em
Phone: 555-7608
Street: 878 14th St.
City: San Jose
ST/Zip: CA 95550
Salesperson: Brohammer
YTD Sales: 3,257.60




- - - - - - - - - - - - - - - - - - - - - - - - - - - - - - - - - - - - - - -
 Type entry or use ⌂ commands                            ⌂-? for Help
```

■ **Comments**

The single record that will be displayed when you change from the Multiple Record layout will be the one on which the cursor was located before you used the Zoom command.

To scroll forward or backward from one record to the next or previous record, use ⌘ and ↑ or ↓ in combination. When you use the Arrow keys alone, ↑ and ↓ move the cursor from one category to the next, and → and ← move the cursor horizontally within each data category.

If the cursor is on the last category in a record, pressing ↓ scrolls to the first category of the next record. If the cursor is on the first category of a record, pressing ↑ scrolls to the last category of the previous record.

If you press ↓ when the cursor is on the last category of the last record in a file, the screen will show a message telling you that you are past the last record, and you can then choose to enter new records at that point.

You can also use the Ruler[280] (⌘-**1** through **9**) to move proportionally through the records in a file.

If you use the Insert[127] command (⌘-**I**) to insert a blank record between two records on the Single Record layout, the inserted record will be placed before the record that is showing when you use the Insert command. For example, if record number 2 of a file is on the screen when you use the Insert command, a blank record number 2 will appear, and the old record number 2 will become record number 3, and the rest of the records in the file will be renumbered accordingly.

Spacing line

■ **Definition**

A *spacing line* is a blank line in a Labels database report.[79]

■ **Usage**

Use spacing lines to properly format the data in Labels database reports. When you first create a Labels database report, there are no spacing lines above or below the data in each category, as shown in the example on the following page.

```
File: Customers               REPORT FORMAT            Escape: Report Menu
Report: Labels
Selection: All records


==============================================================================
Name
Company
Street
City
ST/Zip
-----------------------Each record will print  5 lines---------------------




----------------------------------------------------------------------------
Use options shown on Help Screen                          -? for Help
```

Database reports with Labels format start out with no spacing lines in them.

If you print a report this way, records will be printed one after the other with no spaces between them. This will make the records hard to separate from one another in a printout, and it may make them difficult to print onto mailing labels. You can insert spacing lines into a report like this by using the Insert[127] command (-I):

1. Place the cursor on the line of the report below (or above) which you want the spacing line to appear.

2. Press the Insert command (-I). A complete list of categories you have deleted from the report format (if any) will appear, along with options to insert a spacing line above or below the cursor position, like this:

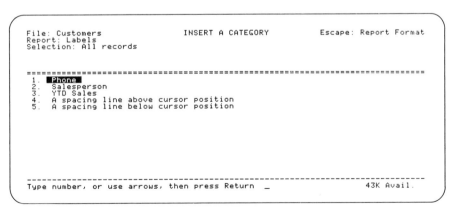

```
File: Customers             INSERT A CATEGORY          Escape: Report Format
Report: Labels
Selection: All records


==============================================================================
   1.  Phone
   2.  Salesperson
   3.  YTD Sales
   4.  A spacing line above cursor position
   5.  A spacing line below cursor position




----------------------------------------------------------------------------
Type number, or use arrows, then press Return  _          43K Avail.
```

Spacing lines are inserted in a database report by choosing an option from the menu displayed when you press the Insert command (-I).

295

3. Choose the option you want (to insert a line above or below the cursor position) and press **RETURN**. The spacing line will now appear in the report format.

To delete a spacing line from a report format, place the cursor on the spacing line and press the Delete[92] command (⌂-**D**). For more information about spacing lines, see Database Report Formats.[79]

Spreadsheet menu

- **Definition**

The *Spreadsheet menu* is a list of options that let you create new spreadsheet files in various ways.

- **Usage**

The Spreadsheet menu is displayed when you choose *Make a new file for the Spreadsheet* (option 5) from the Add Files menu:[2]

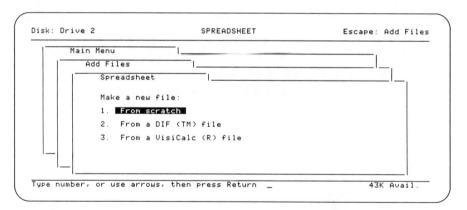

```
Disk: Drive 2                    SPREADSHEET              Escape: Add Files

       Main Menu          |_____
          Add Files          |_____ |
             Spreadsheet         |_____ |  |

             Make a new file:
             1.  From scratch
             2.  From a DIF (TM) file
             3.  From a VisiCalc (R) file




Type number, or use arrows, then press Return _            43K Avail.
```

1. *From scratch.* When you choose this option, the prompt line asks you to type a name for the new file. After you type a file name of up to 15 characters and then press **RETURN**, a new spreadsheet is displayed, and you can begin entering spreadsheet labels, values, and formulas.

2. *From a DIF (TM) file.* When you choose this option, the prompt line tells you to type the complete ProDOS pathname[188] of the DIF file[100] you wish to use. After you type the pathname and press **RETURN**, AppleWorks gets the file from disk (if AppleWorks is unable to locate

the DIF file under the pathname you specify, it will display the message, *Cannot find the file*). The prompt line then asks you to type a name for the new file. After you type the name and press **RETURN**, a new AppleWorks spreadsheet containing the data from the DIF file will be displayed.

DIF files have a specific format when stored on a disk. They normally contain data arranged in rows and columns, just as in a spreadsheet. When storing data in DIF format on disk, most programs that can generate DIF files give you the option of saving the data in either row or column order. The AppleWorks spreadsheet expects DIF files to have been stored in column order. If the data you load from a DIF file into a new AppleWorks spreadsheet file is misordered (that is, data that should be arranged across rows is arranged down columns), then the DIF file you loaded was stored in row order. (See: DIF file.[100])

3. *From a VisiCalc (R) file.* Use this option when you want to convert an existing VisiCalc[357] file into an AppleWorks spreadsheet file. VisiCalc was sold for years in a version that ran under the old Apple operating system, DOS 3.3. Files created with this version of VisiCalc must be converted to ProDOS files with the DOS-ProDOS Conversion Program before they can be used in AppleWorks. (See: DOS-ProDOS Conversion Program.[104]) VisiCalc was also sold in a ProDOS version, and files created with this version need not be converted.

When you choose this option, the prompt line asks you to type the ProDOS pathname of the VisiCalc file you want to use. A message on the screen will remind you that VisiCalc files may have to be converted from DOS 3.3 to ProDOS first.

After you enter the pathname of the file, AppleWorks gets the file from the disk. If AppleWorks can't find the file under the pathname you specify, it will display the message *Cannot find the file.*

Next, the prompt line will ask you to type a name for the new spreadsheet file. Once you enter the new file name, a new AppleWorks spreadsheet containing the transferred VisiCalc data and formulas will appear. (See: VisiCalc file.[357])

■ **Comments**

Some format elements from DIF files or VisiCalc files are incompatible with the AppleWorks spreadsheet, and these elements won't be transferred when you use a DIF or VisiCalc file as the source for a new spreadsheet file. Visi-Calc, for example, offers trigonometric functions such as sine and cosine that aren't available in AppleWorks. VisiCalc formulas containing these functions won't be transferred to a new AppleWorks spreadsheet. Whenever some of the data in a transferred DIF or VisiCalc file is rejected by the spreadsheet, AppleWorks displays the error message *Some Cells Were Lost From Row XX*, where *XX* is the number of the row from which the cells were lost.

Spreadsheet overview

The AppleWorks spreadsheet is a matrix of 999 rows and 127 columns whose intersections are *cells*[25] where you can enter, store, and manipulate text and numbers. Rows are numbered from 1 to 999, and columns are labeled A through Z; AA through AZ; BA through BZ; CA through CZ; and DA through DW.

Using standard arithmetic operators and special functions, you can calculate values in a variety of ways for budgeting, forecasting, inventory tracking, or other tasks. You can also adjust the format of text or numbers, and print them out on paper. Also, the spreadsheet can be split into two windows, which can be set to move in sync with each other during scrolling, or can be scrolled independently.

■ **Working with the spreadsheet**

You create a new spreadsheet file from scratch, from an existing DIF file,[100] or from an existing VisiCalc file[357] using the Spreadsheet menu. Because the spreadsheet can use DIF files, it is possible to use files created by the Apple-Works database (see: Reusing Data[276]).

Once you've named the new file (after loading the data from an existing DIF or VisiCalc file, if necessary), you can enter and work with spreadsheet data and formulas on the spreadsheet's Review/Add/Change screen.

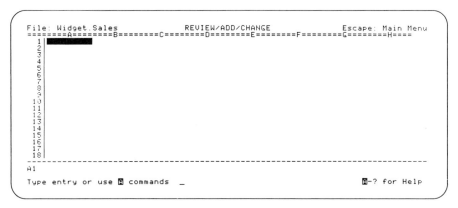

```
 File: Widget.Sales          REVIEW/ADD/CHANGE           Escape: Main Menu
========A=========B=========C=========D=========E=========F=========G=======H====
    1 |
    2
    3
    4
    5
    6
    7
    8
    9
   10
   11
   12
   13
   14
   15
   16
   17
   18
 ----------------------------------------------------------------------------
 A1
 Type entry or use [] commands  _                          []-? for Help
```

The Review/Add/Change screen is the place where you work with data in the spreadsheet.

The spreadsheet cursor occupies one cell at a time, and moves from cell to cell when you press the Arrow keys. You can enter numbers or letters in any spreadsheet cell by typing them and then pressing **RETURN** when you are finished. The entries will appear in the cell where the cursor is located at the time. (Detailed instructions for entering spreadsheet formulas, values, and labels are explained later in this entry.)

Entries on the spreadsheet can be moved[163] or copied[40] within the same spreadsheet; they can be moved or copied from one spreadsheet to another using the AppleWorks Clipboard;[35] and they can be transferred to an Apple-Works word-processor document by printing them to the Clipboard. And, besides printing all or part of a spreadsheet on paper or to the Clipboard, you can print to a disk, so a file will be stored with its formatting intact (see: Spreadsheet Printing[319]).

■ **Spreadsheet size limits**
Spreadsheet files can only be as large as the amount of available Desktop[97] memory will allow. The amount of memory occupied by a given spreadsheet depends not only on its size, but also on the complexity of entries in its cells—a spreadsheet filled with text labels won't occupy as much space as an

identically sized spreadsheet filled with numbers and formulas. The following table shows the maximum size of an AppleWorks spreadsheet, and the typical sizes of spreadsheets on systems with different Desktop sizes and RAM[256] configurations.

Maximum Size	127 Columns × 999 Rows, or 126,873 cells
Typical size with a 10K Desktop (64K system)	1000 cells
Typical size with a 55K Desktop (128K system)	6000 cells

- **Spreadsheet format defaults**

Typically, the AppleWorks spreadsheet is presented with a series of default format and operational settings:

Column widths	9 characters
Label format	Left justified
Value format	Appropriate, and right justified
Recalculation	Automatic
Calculation order	Down columns, left to right
Cell protection	On

These settings can be modified for the entire spreadsheet with the Standard Values[330] command, or they can be adjusted for one or more entries, columns, rows, or blocks (except Recalculation and Calculation order, which affect the entire spreadsheet). Column widths can be up to 75 characters.

- **Spreadsheet calculation specifications**

The spreadsheet will accept negative, positive, decimal, or exponential numbers. It cannot display every number it can store, however. Numbers larger than 10^{20}, or having more than seven decimal places, won't be displayed. Here's what happens when such numbers are entered:

If the number you enter is larger than 10^{20}, AppleWorks won't display the number, but will store it and calculate with it.

If the number has more than seven decimal places, AppleWorks rounds to the seventh decimal place, and stores and calculates the rounded number.

When AppleWorks can't display a number because it is larger than the width of the cell, it presents a row of number signs (#) in the cell to indicate this, and you must widen the column that cell is in to see the number.

Arithmetic operators and functions: The arithmetic operators and functions available in the AppleWorks spreadsheet are listed below:

Operator or Function:	Description:
+, −, *, /	Arithmetic operators (add, subtract, multiply, and divide).[9]
^	Exponent indicator.[22]
@ABS	Absolute value of a range, list, or expression.[1]
@AVG	Average of a range, list, or expression.[15]
@CHOOSE	Finds a value according to its position on a list.[32]
@COUNT	Counts the values in a list or range.[47]
@ERROR	Produces the message *ERROR* in a cell.[105]
@IF	Applies a logical condition to a cell, and presents different results depending on whether the condition is true or false.[125]
@INT	Converts a decimal number to an integer.[130]
@LOOKUP	Finds a value in a table according to the corresponding position of the comparison value named.[155]
@MAX	Returns the largest value in a list or range.[160]
@MIN	Returns the smallest value in a list or range.[161]
@NA	Produces the message *NA* in a cell.[170]
@NPV	Finds the current value of a predicted future cash flow at a specified discount rate.[175]
@SQRT	Finds the square root of a value.[327]
@SUM	Sums values in a range or list.[341]

Each of these functions is described in detail in its individual entry. In some cases, functions may be combined in formulas to perform more complex calculations.

■ **Spreadsheet command summary**

The following list describes the various keyboard commands that are used in the AppleWorks spreadsheet.

Command:	Description:
⌘-A	Arrange rows alphabetically or numerically.[10]
⌘-B	Blank cells, rows, columns, or block.[16]
⌘-C	Copy entries within worksheet, or to or from the Clipboard.[40]
⌘-D	Delete rows or columns.[92]
⌘-E	Toggle between overstrike and insert cursor.[105]
⌘-F	Find entries by cell coordinates or specified text.[109]
⌘-H	Print current display on a printer.[122]
⌘-I	Insert blank rows or columns.[127]
⌘-J	Move the cursor from one window to another.[144]
⌘-K	Recalculate formulas.[18]
⌘-L	Modify cell layout.[146]
⌘-M	Move rows or columns within worksheet, or to or from the Clipboard.[163]
⌘-N	Change file name.[171]
⌘-O	Show printer options.[217]
⌘-P	Print all or part of spreadsheet.[193]
⌘-Q	Show Desktop Index.[252]
⌘-S	Save current file to disk.[281]
⌘-T	Create a fixed-titles area.[114]
⌘-U	Edit an existing entry.[351]
⌘-V	Modify standard spreadsheet values.[330]
⌘-W	Split spreadsheet into two windows, or synchronize or remove windows.[360]
⌘-Y	Delete from cursor to end of entry.[34]
⌘-Z	Display spreadsheet formulas, or hide formulas.[376]
⌘-1 to ⌘-9	Move through a file proportionally.[280]
⌘-?	Display list of commands.[123]
⌘-Arrow keys	Scroll one screen in direction of arrow.

■ **Entering spreadsheet formulas**

Spreadsheet formulas can be thought of as "recipes," or sets of instructions that tell the spreadsheet to calculate certain values, or the contents of certain cells, in certain ways. Formulas usually contain arithmetic operators (+, −, *, /, and ^), and they may include a function, such as @SUM. All the spreadsheet's arithmetic operators and functions are described in individual entries in this book, but there are a few rules common to all formulas.

When you type a formula into a spreadsheet cell, the formula calculates the formula's result and displays the result in that cell. If you want to see the formula itself in the cell instead of the value that results from it, you must use the Zoom[376] command (⌂-**z**) to display it. Even when the formula is not displayed in the cell, however, you can see it in the spreadsheet's *entry line*, which is above the prompt line in the lower-left corner of the screen, when the cursor is on that cell. In the following example, the calculated result of the formula in cell A5 is displayed in the cell, and the formula itself is displayed in the entry line:

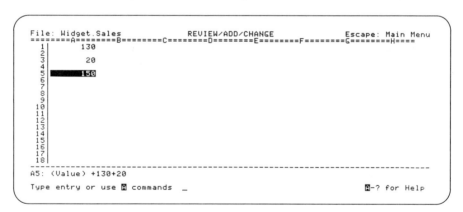

In this spreadsheet, a simple formula that adds 130 to 20 has been entered in cell A5. The cursor is located in cell A5, so the entry line displays the formula in the lower-left corner of the screen.

Using cell references: Although the formula in the example spreadsheet adds two specific numbers, we can also build formulas with cell references. In this case, the formula will use the contents of the cells as the values it calculates. If we referred to cells instead of numbers in the last example, the formula in cell A5 would be: *+A1+A3*.

You should refer to cells rather than actual numbers whenever possible in formulas, because this lets you alter the contents of a cell without having to change the formula. Suppose, for example, that you wanted to change the number in cell A1 to *150*. If you did this on the example spreadsheet, the formula result in cell A5 wouldn't change because the formula is calculating the specific numbers, *130+20*. If the formula told AppleWorks to add the contents of cells A1 and A3, however, you could change the number in cell A1 and the formula would then automatically recalculate with the new value and show the new result as *170*.

Entering formulas: When you enter a formula in AppleWorks, you have to follow certain format conventions. Formulas without functions must begin with either a plus sign (+), a minus sign (−), or an open parenthesis ((). These elements signal AppleWorks that you are beginning a formula. Otherwise, the spreadsheet thinks you are entering a number or a label (both of which are discussed later in this entry).

If you use an open parenthesis to begin a formula, you must end the formula with a closed parenthesis. AppleWorks will beep at you if you don't, and you won't be able to enter the formula.

Let's look at the example spreadsheet again. The formula in A5 could be modified in the following ways to produce the same result:

+A1+A3

+A3+A1

(A1+A3)

(A3+A1)

Because these formulas specify cell references, they will recalculate automatically when the value in A1 or A3 is changed.

To summarize, these are the steps you take to enter a formula:

1. Move the cursor to the cell where you want the result to appear.

2. Type either an open parenthesis ((), a plus sign (+), or a minus sign (−). This tells AppleWorks you are beginning a formula.

3. Type the formula.

4. When you finish typing the numbers or cell coordinates in the formula, press **RETURN**. (If you began the formula with an open parenthesis, you must type a close parenthesis ()) to end it before pressing **RETURN**.) AppleWorks will calculate the values you have specified in the formula with the arithmetic operators you have used.

Using parentheses: If your formula contains only two numbers or references, you don't need to use parentheses to identify it as a formula. When the mathematical expression contains more than two values, though, it's best to use parentheses so AppleWorks knows the proper order of calculation. Here's an example:

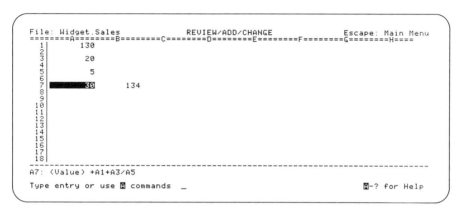

```
File: Widget.Sales              REVIEW/ADD/CHANGE              Escape: Main Menu
========A=========B=========C=========D=========E=========F=========G========H====
    1|       130
    2|
    3|        20
    4|
    5|         5
    6|
    7|██████████30     134
    8|
    9|
   10|
   11|
   12|
   13|
   14|
   15|
   16|
   17|
   18|
   ------------------------------------------------------------------------------
A7: (Value) +A1+A3/A5

Type entry or use ⌂ commands  _                              ⌂-? for Help
```

Without parentheses to specify the order of calculation, AppleWorks always calculates formulas from left to right.

In this case, AppleWorks, in the absence of specific instructions, simply made the calculations in order from left to right. Therefore, it first calculated *A1+A3* to arrive at *150*, and then divided by A5 to produce a result of *30*.

But suppose we want to add the value in cell A1 (*130*) to the result of cell A3 divided by cell A5 (*4*). To do this, we must use parentheses to build this formula: *(A1+(A3/A5))*. This tells AppleWorks to calculate the items in the inner parentheses first, and then add the result to A1. This formula is entered in cell B7 of the last example spreadsheet, and the final result is then displayed in the cell.

If you don't specify which calculations to make first with parentheses, AppleWorks always calculates from left to right. If you use parentheses, however, the program solves equations inside the most deeply embedded set of parentheses first, and then works its way outward.

The best rule of thumb when creating complex expressions is to always use parentheses to specify the groups of numbers you want calculated in a certain order. This way, you can be sure that AppleWorks will do things the way you want.

Entering cell coordinates by pointing: Another advantage to specifying formulas inside parentheses is that you can specify cell locations by *pointing*, rather than by typing. The idea behind cell pointers is that you are linking one cell's contents with the contents of another cell. Cell pointers let you set up spreadsheets so you can change just a few numbers by hand, and have the changes reflected in other cells. Let's look at another example:

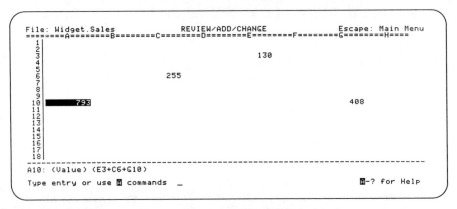

You can specify cell locations by pointing to them with the cursor.

Suppose we want to add the values in the preceding spreadsheet. To type in the cell locations, we first have to figure out the coordinates of each cell. Since these values aren't close to the labels at the edges of the spreadsheet, this isn't so easy. It would be even harder to quickly identify each cell if the values we wanted were surrounded by other numbers. But AppleWorks lets us use the cursor to point to the cells we want to include, and enter their locations that way. Here's how we would build this addition formula in cell A10 by pointing with the cursor keys:

1. Place the cursor in cell A10, and type an open parenthesis ((.

2. Move the cursor to the first value to be added, in our example cell E3.

3. Type a plus sign. The cursor will return to the formula cell, and the formula now looks like this: *(E3+.*

4. Move the cursor to the second value to be added, in our example cell C6.

5. Type another plus sign. It will be automatically placed after the reference to C6, and the cursor will return to the formula cell. The formula now says: *(E3+C6+.*

6. Move the cursor to the last cell to be specified, in our example cell G10.

7. Type a closing parenthesis, and the cursor returns to the formula cell. Press **RETURN** to end the formula. The formula calculates automatically, and the result appears in cell A10.

This is a very simple example, but pointing to cell references can really speed up building a complex formula that contains references located all over a large worksheet. In addition, it eliminates the possibility that you will type a reference or value improperly, because the value you point to is automatically entered.

If you want to edit a formula or change a cell pointer, you can either type something else from scratch in the same cell, or (if the formula is a long one) you can use the Undo[351] command (⌕-**U**) to display it in the entry line, and then edit it there.

Using functions with formulas: So far, we've been talking about formulas that consist only of mathematical expressions. However, the AppleWorks spreadsheet also offers a number of mathematical functions that can make your spreadsheets more accurate and easier to build.

Many of the functions available in the AppleWorks spreadsheet are simply shortcuts to certain kinds of arithmetic. The @AVG function, for example, simply averages the values expressed in the argument that follows it: The formula *@AVG(4+3+5)* produces a result of *4*, and we could calculate this without using the @AVG function by entering the formula *((4+3+5)/3)*. But if we are averaging a large number of values, or if the values are scattered in many places in the spreadsheet, it's simply faster and easier to use the function.

A formula with a function is divided into two parts: the function itself, and the value or group of values on which the function is to be performed. This value or group of values is always enclosed in parentheses, and is called the *argument*.[7]

All functions begin with the *at* sign (@), followed by a function name. The @ sign tells AppleWorks that you are entering a function name. Without the @ sign, AppleWorks would treat the function name simply as text.

After the function name has been entered, you can then type the *argument*—a value, a list of values, a range of values, or a combination of these—inside parentheses. Some functions will accept groups of values or cell coordinates separated by arithmetic operators; others will accept ranges of values or cell coordinates (where you need only specify the beginning and ending points of a continuous range); still others will accept lists of values or cell coordinates (which are separated by commas instead of arithmetic operators).

In some cases, an argument can itself contain a function and an argument. Typically, formulas contain one function, as in *@AVG(B3.B18)*, but a formula could contain other, nested formulas within its argument, as in this example: *@SQRT(@SUM(C29.C35))*.

The specific requirements for each function are discussed in detail in the separate entry for each function. For now, though, let's look at some examples on this spreadsheet:

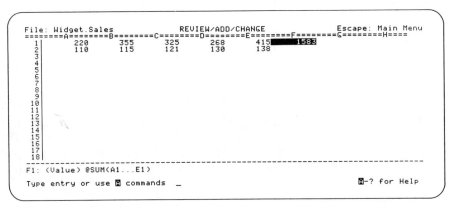

When you are specifying large groups of numbers in formulas, some AppleWorks functions can make the job much easier.

Suppose we want to add all the numbers in a row of cells: A1, B1, C1, D1, and E1. We could, of course, type in an expression that adds all five values *(A1+B1+C1+D1+E1)*. This takes time, however. We can use the *@SUM* function to make things easier because it automatically adds a range or list[155] of numbers. In this case, typing a list would be as much trouble as specifying all the cells in an expression, but since these cells are contiguous, we can specify them as a *range*, so that only the beginning and ending cell in the range (two references) need to be entered, instead of specifying every cell in the group (five references).

When you specify a list of numbers or references, each number or reference must be separated by a comma. Lists may contain either or both numbers or cell references, or they may also contain functions or ranges. When you specify a range, the beginning reference must be separated from the ending reference by a period (AppleWorks automatically converts the period to ellipses when you enter the formula). All lists, values, and ranges used with functions must be enclosed in parentheses.

In the last example, the @SUM formula used to sum the values in cells A1 through E1 is entered in cell F1 and displayed in the entry line. The calculated result is displayed in the cell. The steps for entering the formula are:

1. Place the cursor on the cell where you want the result to appear (F1, in this case).

2. Type the @ sign, which tells AppleWorks you will be entering a function.

3. Type *SUM*, the name of the function you want to use.

4. Type an open parenthesis, to specify the beginning of the argument.

5. Type the first cell in the range (*A1*).

6. To separate the beginning of the range from the end of the range, type a period (.).

7. Type the ending cell in the range (E1, followed by a closing parenthesis, and then press **RETURN**. All cells from A1 through E1 are added together and the result is placed in cell F1.

In this example we typed the cell references to specify the range. We could also point to the first cell in the range, type a period, move the pointer to the last cell in the range, press **RETURN**, type a closing parenthesis, and press **RETURN** to enter them automatically.

This is the basic procedure for entering a formula with a function. Specific instruction in the use and entry of each type of function can be found under the individual function entries.

■ Entering spreadsheet labels and values

You can enter and store two types of data in an AppleWorks spreadsheet: *labels* and *values*. Labels are usually words, such as *Sales, Cost, Rent*, and so forth, that identify columns and rows of numbers. Values are always either numbers, cell references, or formulas. Values may contain text elements, such as function names, but they are still stored, calculated, and formatted as values by the spreadsheet.

Usually, you know whether a spreadsheet entry is a label or a value, or you can tell by the context of the spreadsheet. If you can't, however, Apple-Works spreadsheets have a *cell indicator* to remind you. The cell indicator is located in the lower-left corner of the screen, just below the bottom line of the spreadsheet, as shown in this example:

```
File: Cost of Sales          REVIEW/ADD/CHANGE              Escape: Main Menu
========A========B========C========D========E========F========G========H====
   1│Acme Widget Company - Widget Sales Costs, Q4, 1985
   2│
   3│
   4│Materials                      Oct      Nov      Dec      Qtr
   5│------------------             ===      ===      ===      ===
   6│
   7│Widget Oil                    1200     1410      960     2370
   8│Steel                         2500     3250     3000     8750
   9│Copper                        1000     1175      800     2975
  10│Magnesium                     1250     1100     1250     3600
  11│Grease                         120      150      135      405
  12│Rags                            50       50       50      150
  13│
  14│Labor
  15│------------------
  16│Salaries                      3000     3000     3000     9000
  17│Commissions                   2250     2250     2250     6750
  18│Hourly Wages                  2850     2850     2850     8550
-------------------------------------------------------------------------------
F1: (Label, Layout-L)  1985

Type entry or use ⌂ commands  _                          ⌂-? for Help
```

The cell indicator shows the type of entry contained in a cell.

In this case, the cursor is in cell F1, which contains a number. But the number was entered as part of a label (the spreadsheet title in the top row), so it is identified by the spreadsheet as a label. When used in labels, numbers have no mathematical value in the spreadsheet. (The different cell-indicator designations for labels and values are explained in the next section.)

Although the cell indicator shows the formatting of an entry and identifies it as a label or value after it has been entered, you can see the contents of the entry as you type by looking in the entry line, as we've seen in the examples. Labels or values can be up to 75 characters long. Once you enter the label or value by pressing **RETURN**, the entry line disappears. If you wish to edit an entry later, you can place the cursor on the entry you want to edit, and then either retype it or use the Undo[351] command (⌂-**U**). The Undo command will make the original entry reappear in the entry line, and you can then edit the entry there.

Typing labels in the spreadsheet: To enter a label into a spreadsheet cell, you must type it and then press **RETURN**. Labels are typically made up of letters, and when you type a letter in a spreadsheet cell, AppleWorks automatically assumes you are beginning a label. Sometimes, though, you will want to type a number, a dash, or a space at the beginning of a label. In this case, you have to specifically tell AppleWorks to treat what you type as a label. You do this by first typing a quotation mark ("). This sets up the spreadsheet to treat what follows as a label, whether it's a number, punctuation mark, arithmetic operator, or whatever. A good rule of thumb is that if you want to enter a label beginning with a non-alphabetic character, type a quotation mark first.

If the label you type is longer than a column width, AppleWorks automatically extends your typing area into the *empty* and unprotected cell or cells to the right. In the last example spreadsheet, the top row of the spreadsheet contains a continuous label that runs from columns A through F. The label began with a letter, so AppleWorks knew it was a label and automatically allowed us to extend the label across several columns. An extended label can't move into a cell that already contains a value, or that has been protected against label entry with the spreadsheet's cell-protection feature.

One type of label that you will use to make a spreadsheet easier to read is a *repeated label*.[269] Repeated labels are made by pressing a key and holding it down, so that the same character completely fills one or more cells. Repeated labels generally extend to the right of the original cell across one or more columns. As you can see in the following spreadsheet, repeated labels are identified as such by the cell indicator:

```
File: Cost of Sales              REVIEW/ADD/CHANGE              Escape: Main Menu
========A========B=========C=========D========E========F========G========H====
   1│Acme Widget Company - Widge  t Sales Costs, Q4, 1985
   2│========----------------------------------------------------
   3│
   4│Materials                        Oct      Nov      Dec      Qtr
   5│-----------------                ===      ===      ===      ===
   6│
   7│Widget Oil                      1200     1410      960     2370
   8│Steel                           2500     3250     3000     8750
   9│Copper                          1000     1175      800     2975
  10│Magnesium                       1250     1100     1250     3600
  11│Grease                           120      150      135      405
  12│Rags                              50       50       50      150
  13│
  14│Labor
  15│-----------------
  16│Salaries                        3000     3000     3000     9000
  17│Commissions                     2250     2250     2250     6750
  18│Hourly Wages                    2850     2850     2850     8550
------------------------------------------------------------------------------
A2: (Label) Repeated--

Type entry or use Ⓐ commands  _                          Ⓐ-? for Help
```

The cursor is positioned on a repeated label, and the cell indicator displays this. (Column C has been widened in this spreadsheet, and it has affected the appearance of the extended label in row 1.)

Although repeated or extended labels look like they're all one entry, they are actually individual entries spread across several columns. You have to keep this in mind when you change the column widths or delete columns from a spreadsheet, because doing either of these may affect the appearance of extended labels, as shown in the last example.

How the spreadsheet formats labels: When you first begin a spreadsheet, the default format for labels is *left justified:* All labels will align on the left boundary of their cell. Other formats are *centered* (the label is centered in the cell), and *right justified* (labels are aligned on the right cell boundary). The cell indicator shows these label-formatting differences. For example, if the label *Materials* were entered into three cells each with a different format, the result would be:

Label:	Format:	Cell Indicator:
Materials	left justified	(Label, Layout-L) Materials
Materials	right justified	(Label, Layout-R) Materials
Materials	centered	(Label, Layout-C) Materials

To change the format of an individual label, use the Layout[146] command (⌂-L), which is described in its own entry.

To change the default format of a spreadsheet so *all* labels will be centered or right justified, you use the Standard Values command, which is described in the Standard Values[330] entry.

Typing values in the spreadsheet: You can enter values into the spreadsheet in three ways:

☐ by typing a number;

☐ by typing a cell pointer that refers to a number in another cell;

☐ by typing a formula or function.

As explained in the "Entering spreadsheet formulas" section earlier in this entry, values can contain numbers, arithmetic operators (+, −, *, /, or ^), decimal points, or functions, and they can be typed in or entered as cell coordinates by pointing. AppleWorks can store negative, positive, and exponential numbers. Whenever you enter a value that contains arithmetic operators and press **RETURN**, AppleWorks automatically does the calculation and presents the result in the cell where it's entered (unless you've chosen *manual* recalculation on the Standard Values menu).

Decimal values: If you type a decimal number, AppleWorks will only display up to seven decimal places. If you type a number that has more than seven decimal places, AppleWorks will round the number off to seven decimal places. Thus, if you type *23.7777888*, the number will be stored and displayed (if you have made the column wide enough). But if you type *23.77778888*, AppleWorks will round the number to *23.7777889*.

How the spreadsheet formats values: Columns in an AppleWorks spreadsheet are usually nine characters wide, but you can widen or narrow individual columns, groups of columns, or all the columns with either the Layout[146] (⌘-L) or Standard Values command (⌘-V). If you type a number larger than a column can display (a number with many numbers to the right of the decimal point, for example), AppleWorks will display only as many numbers as will fit in the column, but it will store the entire number and also calculate with it.

If AppleWorks cannot display a number completely in a cell, meaning there are more numbers to the left of the decimal point than the column width will display, it fills the cell completely with a row of number (#) signs to indicate this. Whether you can see the whole number or not, though, AppleWorks will store and calculate it. You can widen the column to display the whole number. Regardless of column width, AppleWorks can't display values with more than seven values to the right of a decimal point (it will always round off those numbers), and it can't display numbers larger than 10^{20}.

When AppleWorks cannot display a number because it is too large (exponents larger than 10^{20}, for example), the cell where the number was entered will contain four number signs (#).

These are the different value formats available in the spreadsheet:

Appropriate format usually displays numbers as you type them, except that numbers can't contain dollar signs ($) or commas. Dollar sign and comma formatting elements for numbers must be specified with a Layout (⌘-L) or Standard Values (⌘-V) command.

Fixed format displays numbers with a specific number of decimal places (from 0 to 7). If you have the format set to Fixed, with 0 decimal places, the number 23.777 will be shown as *24* (but the spreadsheet will store the entire number for calculations).

313

Dollars format displays numbers with the number of decimal places you specify (0 to 7), and a dollar sign in front of them. For example, 23.777 will be shown as *$23.78*, if you specified 2 decimal places. Also, numbers in the thousands and up will be displayed with commas, and negative numbers will be shown in parentheses.

Commas format displays numbers with a number of decimal places (from 0 to 7) that you specify. It automatically places commas between thousands, and it shows negative numbers inside parentheses.

Percent format multiplies an entry by 100, and puts a number of decimal places (from 0 to 7) that you specify after it, along with a percent sign. For example, 23.777 will be shown as *2377.70%*, if you specified 2 decimal places.

The following table shows the ways the same value can be shown in the spreadsheet's cell indicator and displayed in a cell:

Value:	Format:	Cell Indicator:	Cell:
23.77	Appropriate	(Value, Layout-AO) 23.77	23.77
23.77	Fixed, 0 decimal places	(Value, Layout-FO) 23.77	24
23.77	Dollars, 2 decimal places	(Value, Layout-D2) 23.77	$23.77
23.77	Percent, 2 decimal places	(Value, Layout-P2) 23.77	2377.00%

The default format for values typed into the spreadsheet is *Appropriate*. You can change the format of a specific value with the Layout command (⌘-L), and you can change the default format of the entire spreadsheet with the Standard Values command (⌘-V).

Spreadsheet planning

The key to building efficient and successful spreadsheets is *planning*. Once you're an old hand at making spreadsheets, you'll have some experience to draw upon and you won't have to be as careful about your initial planning; but as a beginner, you should have a good idea of what your spreadsheet should look like and what it should accomplish before you begin. The techniques described in this section will help you build more efficient spreadsheets in AppleWorks.

■ **Choosing the right tool**

Before you begin your spreadsheet, think about what you want to do and whether or not the spreadsheet is the right tool for the job. If you want to store, arrange, and sort facts, such as names and addresses, you'd be much better off using the AppleWorks database because of its superior sorting and selecting capabilities. The database can also perform simple calculations, such as multiplying or dividing the data in one category by the data in another category, or summing the values in one or more categories. If you're creating a weekly list of invoices that includes the product type, the amount paid, and the total by product for the week, for example, you can perform these calculations with the Group Totals[118] and Set Totals[286] commands in the database.

Generally, spreadsheets are best for showing the relationships between a lot of different values, such as budget projections and sales forecasts. In many cases, we use spreadsheets to show how values change over periods of time such as weeks, months, or years. Spreadsheets are also the only tool to use when you are performing a variety of different calculations on some values, or you are performing the same calculations on different values and want to see the results of your changes quickly.

With these initial strengths of the spreadsheet in mind, let's look at some techniques for building better spreadsheets.

■ **Making a plan**

When you're new to spreadsheeting, it's hard to decide which information should go where. It's always best to begin by entering labels to identify the data you'll be entering. In most cases, a spreadsheet shows inflows of money or distributions of money or some other commodity (such as manpower, parts, electricity, or whatever) over a period of time. Normally, the labels that indicate different periods of time are entered at the tops of columns across the spreadsheet, and the labels that identify different types of expenses or income are entered in rows down the left-hand side of the spreadsheet (in column A). This type of spreadsheet arrangement is shown in the example on the following page.

```
File: FiveYear.Budget        REVIEW/ADD/CHANGE          Escape: Main Menu
========A========B========C========D========E========F========G========H====
 1
 2                Acme Widgets - Budget Projection
 3
 4                    Q185     Q285     Q385     Q485     Q186     Q286
 5
 6 Rent             2000     2000     2000     2000     2500     2500
 7 Utilities         502      489      480      500      510      530
 8 Material         2500     2495     2350     2500     2500     2650
 9 Salaries         2000     2000     2000     2250     2250     2250
10 Promotion         500      475      300      500      400      450
11
12 Total Expenses   7502     7459     7130     7750     8160      8380
13
14
15
16
17
18
----------------------------------------------------------------------------
H12: (Value, Layout-F0) @SUM(H6...H10)

Type entry or use ▣ commands  _                            ▣-? for Help
```

In a spreadsheet, time periods usually occupy columns, while different types of expenses or income occupy rows.

If you are new to spreadsheeting, try making a rough sketch of your spreadsheet on paper before building it with AppleWorks. This will give you an overall view of the spreadsheet, and you can make major design changes before you ever have anything in the computer. If your spreadsheet is very wide and not very long, such as the last example, you may decide to reverse the layout and place the time labels in rows and the item labels at the tops of columns. This way, you'll have a much easier time printing the spreadsheet on standard-width paper.

Your paper sketch of the spreadsheet doesn't have to be exact, though. You will probably have some touching-up to do as you enter the data into AppleWorks. Fortunately, AppleWorks makes it easy to insert blank rows or columns or change the format of labels and values in the spreadsheet, as discussed in the Spreadsheet Overview[298] entry.

■ **Building a spreadsheet quickly**

You will often have a lot of individual labels and numbers to enter in your spreadsheet, but you can save time and work more effectively if you *copy* data as much as possible. Since most spreadsheets show changes in values over time, you must enter essentially the same formulas to calculate those values in each time period.

Looking back at the last example, we can see that the formula required for the *Total Expenses* row is basically the same for each quarter—we're adding the values in rows 6 through 10 for each column. Because the calculation is the same, we can enter just one @SUM[341] formula in cell C12, and then copy it as a *relative* formula into columns D12 through H12 (or wherever the last column of numbers is). Making this copy is much faster than entering formulas individually into every column. (See the Copy[40] entry for an explanation of this command.)

As you build your spreadsheets, look for situations like this where the formulas are basically the same, and then copy formulas whenever possible. Of course, you can also copy labels if the labels are very similar and require only minor changes (otherwise, it will be as time-consuming to edit each label as it would have been to enter each label individually).

■ Using a reference area

Some spreadsheets, particularly investment analyses, make repeated use of certain interest-rate, payment, or other fixed values in many different formulas. When you will be using the same value repeatedly, it helps to put that value in a *reference area*, and then refer to it in each formula that uses it instead of entering the value manually in each formula. This allows you to change the value in the reference area, and have all the formulas that refer to it change as well.

In the following sample spreadsheet, the Net Present Value (NPV) formula entered in cell C5 relies on the interest-rate figure in cell C4. As you can see, the @NPV[175] formula in cell C5 refers to cell C4 for the interest rate.

```
 File: Investment               REVIEW/ADD/CHANGE         Escape: Main Menu
 =======A========B========C========D========E========F========G========H====
  1|              Investment Analysis
  2|
  3|Investment Amount: $10,000
  4|Discount Rate:           .11
  5|Net Present Value: $10,130
  6|
  7|
  8|    Year 1    Year 2    Year 3    Year 4    Year 5
  9|
 10|    $2,500    $2,500    $2,500    $2,500    $4,000
 11|
 12|
 13|
 14|
 15|
 16|
 17|
 18|
 ------------------------------------------------------------------------
 C5: (Value, Layout-D0) @NPV(C4,A10...E10)

 Type entry or use ▣ commands  _                      ▣-? for Help
```

Use a reference area in a spreadsheet so you can change a value and have the change reflected in all formulas that use that value.

We could have entered the actual interest rate (.11) in the formula in cell C5, but because we have used the contents of cell C4 instead, we can change the rate in C4 and have the formula in C5 automatically change to reflect the new rate. Other good candidates for reference areas are amortization tables, commission analyses, and depreciation schedules.

■ **Using space efficiently**

If you will be printing your spreadsheet on paper, try to anticipate printing problems as you build your spreadsheet. The problem with most spreadsheets is that they are wider than the paper on which they're being printed, so anything you can do to make the best use of horizontal space in your spreadsheet will pay off.

One technique is to use efficient column labels. The spreadsheet's default column width is nine characters, but frequently columns may contain numbers that are only four or five characters across. If you're trying to squeeze as many columns on a sheet of paper as possible, it makes sense to use column labels that are no wider than the numbers in those columns. In the first example above, the column labels are the same width as the numbers in those columns, so we could reduce the column widths on this spreadsheet to five characters instead of nine and squeeze more data on one page without making the column labels unreadable.

Another tip is to use special formatting only when it's absolutely necessary. Using the *Dollar* format in the second example adds two characters to the width of each of the numbers in the cash-flow sequence (the dollar sign and comma). If we used decimal places after these numbers, they would be even wider. In most cases, it isn't necessary to use dollar signs in a spreadsheet, because the assumption is that you're working with dollars anyway. If your numbers are particularly large (a million or more), you can represent them as four-digit numbers, and then insert a note at the top of the spreadsheet that all numbers are thousands. Instead of entering *1023000*, for example, you could enter *1023*. (Spreadsheet formatting is covered in the Layout[146] and Standard Values[330] entries.)

■ **Finishing touches**

While you may be tempted to enter a title for your spreadsheet before you begin entering data, try to hold off until the end. During the spreadsheet-building process, you may find yourself making columns wider or narrower, or inserting or deleting columns. If you have a spreadsheet title at the top of the screen, this title will become scrambled as you reformat the columns. Once you've entered all your data and set the column widths the way you want, you can safely enter a spreadsheet title at the top of the screen. If you forgot to leave room for a title, just insert a few rows above your data.

As you work with the spreadsheet and begin solving problems with it, you will discover other techniques that will help you get the job done faster and better.

Spreadsheet printing

This entry explains the five different ways you can print a spreadsheet file. The five print options are:

☐ To a printer for a paper copy;

☐ To a disk printer as a formatted ASCII file;

☐ To a disk as an ASCII[13] file;

☐ To a disk as a DIF[100] file;

☐ To the Clipboard[35] for moving to a word-processor document.

■ General printing procedures

When you print a spreadsheet file, you must always follow the same basic sequence:

1. Make sure the document you want to print is displayed on the Review/Add/Change screen.

2. Select the printer options or print enhancements you want to make on the file (if any). Printer options are available from the Printer Options[217] menu, which is displayed when you press ⌂-O.

3. Press the Print[193] command (⌂-P). The Print screen[198] will appear, as shown in the following example, and the prompt line will ask you whether you want to print all of the file, or if you only want to print certain columns, rows, or a block of data, as shown in the following example. Choose the option you want and press **RETURN**.

```
 File: FiveYear.Budget              PRINT            Escape: Review/Add/Change
 ========A========B========C========D========E========F========G========H====
  1
  2                     Acme Widgets - Budget Projection
  3
  4                        Q185     Q285     Q385     Q485     Q186     Q286
  5
  6 Rent                  2000     2000     2000     2000     2500     2500
  7 Utilities              502      489      480      500      510      530
  8 Material              2500     2495     2350     2500     2500     2650
  9 Salaries              2000     2000     2000     2250     2250     2250
 10 Promotion              500      475      300      500      400      450
 11
 12 Total Expenses        7502     7459     7130     7750     8160     8380
 13
 14
 15
 16
 17
 18
 ------------------------------------------------------------------------------
 H12: (Value, Layout-F0) @SUM(H6...H10)

 Print? █All█  Rows  Columns  Block
```

When you first press the Print command (⌂-P), you must choose the part of the file you want to print.

4. Next, choose the printer or other destination where you want the file printed: either a printer, an ASCII or DIF file, or the Clipboard. These options are shown on the Print screen, as you can see in this example:

```
File: FiveYear.Budget                    PRINT            Escape: Review/Add/Change
================================================================================

                      The information that you identified
                      is 198 characters wide.

                      The Printer Options values allow
                      80 characters per line.

                      Where do you want to print the report?

                      1. █Epson FX█
                      2.  Imagewriter (disk)
                      3.  The clipboard (for the Word Processor)
                      4.  A text (ASCII) file on disk
                      5.  A DIF (TM) file on disk


         --------------------------------------------------------------------

         Type number, or use arrows, then press Return  _           42K Avail.
```

Before printing a spreadsheet file, you must choose the destination where it's to be printed.

Notice also in the preceding example that the width of the data you have selected for printing is displayed at the top of the screen, together with the printing width allowed by the current printer-options settings. If you are going to print to a printer, a disk printer, an ASCII file, or the Clipboard, your data selection must be narrower than the width allowed by the printer options. If the data selection is wider, you must make it narrower, which is explained in the following sections. If you are printing to a DIF file on disk, you don't have to worry about the width of your data selection—the entire selection will print to the DIF file no matter how the printer options are set.

With these general print procedures in mind, let's look at the specific procedures for printing to the various spreadsheet print destinations.

■ Printing on printers

When you print to a printer, you must be sure that AppleWorks has been configured for that printer, that the printer is turned on, and that it can handle any printer options you may have specified for the file (see: Printer Configuration;[200] Printer Options[217]).

The choice of printers offered on the Print screen displayed after step 4 in the last example will depend on which printers you have previously configured. You can store up to three printer configurations at a time (including a disk printer).

After you choose the printer on which you want the file printed, the prompt line will ask if you want to enter a report date to be printed at the top of the spreadsheet. If you don't want a date printed, press **RETURN**. (You won't be prompted to enter a report date if you have the PH (*Print report header at top of page*) printer option set to *No* (see: Printer Options[217]). You will then be asked how many copies you want printed. Type a number and press **RETURN**, or just press **RETURN** to accept the default of one copy, and the file will be printed.

If your printer doesn't begin printing the file, check to make sure it is turned on, and that the printer cable isn't loose. Most printers also have an "on line," "ready," or "selected" indicator that shows whether the printer is ready to print. Make sure this indicator shows the printer is ready (there may be a "select" button you push to light the indicator), and that there is paper in the printer. If your problem persists after this, call your Apple dealer and ask for further advice.

Adjusting the width of the data: If the data you have selected is narrower than the width allowed by the printer options, then the data will print properly. If the data is wider than the printer options allow, however, only the amount of data that falls within the printer options will print. For example, in the last screen display the data selected is 198 characters wide, but the printer options only allow for lines 80 characters wide. If this file were to be printed this way, only the first 80 characters from the left margin of the document on each line would print—the other 118 characters would not be printed.

If your data selection is too wide for the printer options, there are a few remedies: You can either make the data selection narrower (by narrowing columns, for example), or you can change the printer options to accept a wider selection, by changing such printer options as CI (Characters-per-Inch) or the platen width on the Printer Options menu, to allow for more data on one line. Also, instead of selecting *All* of the document to print, for example, you might select only certain columns. Here's how:

1. Press **ESC** to leave the Print screen and return to the Review/Add/Change screen of the spreadsheet. Doing this cancels your previous data selection.

2. If you want to change the data selection, press the Print command again (⌂-**P**) and reselect the data to print. If you want to alter the printer options, press the Printer Options command (⌂-**O**) before

321

pressing the Print command and change the options for platen width and characters per inch (CI). As you change the options, the number of characters allowed on a line will change, and this will be shown on the Printer Options menu, like this:

```
File: FiveYear.Budget          PRINTER OPTIONS      Escape: Review/Add/Change
==============================================================================

-------Left and right margins--------        ------Top and bottom margins-------
PW: Platen Width           8.2 inches     PL: Paper Length        11.0 inches
LM: Left Margin            0.0 inches     TM: Top Margin           0.0 inches
RM: Right Margin           0.0 inches     BM: Bottom Margin        0.0 inches
CI: Chars per Inch        16              LI: Lines per Inch       6

    Line width            8.2 inches          Printing length     11.0 inches
    Char per line (est)  131                  Lines per page      66

            --------------------Formatting options--------------------
    SC:  Send Special Codes to printer                        No
    PH:  Print report Header at top of each page              Yes
         Single, Double or Triple Spacing (SS/DS/TS)          SS


--------------------------------------------------------------------------------
Type a two letter option code  _                               43K Avail.
```

When you change the printer options to allow for more data on a line, the amount of data permitted on a line is shown on the Printer Options menu as Char per line (est).

You can use the estimated Characters-per-Line reading on the Printer Options menu to compare with the width of a data selection you have made. If you want to select data that is 100 characters wide, for example, you know that the printer options must be set so the estimated Characters-per-Line reading is at least 100. (See: Characters-per-Line Indicator.[31])

Troubleshooting printer problems: Printing from the spreadsheet is a very straightforward process, but it's possible to get results you don't expect. If your printer is printing your file but isn't printing it the way you want, there are two likely causes for this: the printer options and the printer-configuration settings.

The first thing to do is check the printer options. If a file is printing with single spacing and you want double spacing, for example, make sure the double-space option is set on the Printer Options menu.

If you are sure you have set all the printer options correctly, then you should check your printer-configuration settings. These settings are covered in detail in the Printer Configuration entry, but it's important to remember that many of the printer options you specify won't take effect if your printer configurations aren't properly set.

If you change the size of a file's printed characters from 10 CI to 12 CI with the Printer Options menu, for example, this change won't be made if you haven't configured AppleWorks to print at 12 CI. So if you aren't getting the right printing effects on paper and you're sure that your printer options are set correctly, check the printer configuration for that printer to see whether you have configured AppleWorks to make your printer perform those options properly.

Another configuration-related problem is your interface. You may not have configured AppleWorks properly for your printer interface. Check the interface code you have entered (or check to see whether you entered one at all). See the entry, Printer Interface Configuration,[214] for more about configuring interface cards.

One final thing to check when sorting out printer problems is the printer itself. You can specify certain printer options, and AppleWorks can be configured properly to handle them, but they still won't take effect if your printer can't handle them. If you specify a platen width of 10 inches and your printer has an 8-inch platen, you can't print lines that are 10 inches wide. Check your printer manual before configuring Apple-Works to work with the printer, and make sure the configurations you enter are supported by your printer.

■ **Printing to a disk printer**

When you want to store a file on disk with all the formatting it would have if printed on paper, you must print it to a disk printer. It's useful to print to a disk printer when you want to send a file via modem, or plan to give the disk the file is on to someone else who will print it out later. When the file is printed to the disk, it is printed as an ASCII[13] file, so you can send it via modem. Also, the file is printed with the specific format and print enhancements you specified (such as margins or text alignment), so somebody else using a different word-processing program can load it and print it out exactly the way you intended.

A disk printer is set up just like an ordinary printer—by configuring it from the Printer Information menu.[212] The only difference is the way this "printer" is connected to your Apple. The detailed steps for configuring disk printers are covered in Printer Configuration, but the overview is:

1. Choose option 2, *Add a printer,* from the Printer Information menu.

2. Choose a printer configuration that matches the printer on which the file will ultimately be printed.

3. After you choose the printer configuration, you will be asked to name the printer. You will be given a menu of slot locations and the option *Print onto disk or another Apple.* When you choose this option, any file printed to this printer will be "printed" onto disk under the pathname you specify.

Once you have set up the printer this way, it appears on the Print screen along with any two other printers you may have configured, as well as the other listed print destinations—the Clipboard, or an ASCII or DIF file. (The Print screen is the list of available print destinations that appears when you press the Print command.) To help you remember that this is a disk printer, AppleWorks puts the word *disk* in parentheses after the disk-printer option.

To print your file to the disk, choose the disk-printer destination, enter a report date if you like, specify a pathname, and the file is printed to disk. All margins, line spacing, and other options you specified will be retained in the format of the file on disk.

■ **Printing to the Clipboard**

Another print destination to which you can send spreadsheet files is the Clipboard. Printing files to the Clipboard is different from copying or moving data to the Clipboard: When you copy or move spreadsheet data to the Clipboard, you can only use that data in spreadsheet files, but when you print data to the Clipboard, the data is converted into a format that can be used in word-processor files. Thus, you must print spreadsheet data to the Clipboard when you want to transfer that data into a word-processor document. And, once you have printed spreadsheet data to the Clipboard, you can't copy it back into a spreadsheet file—you can only move it to a word-processor document.

Printing to the Clipboard is much like printing to a printer. You select the data you want to print, and then choose the option *The clipboard (for the Word Processor)* as the destination. Just as with printing to a printer, you must be sure that the data you select is narrow enough to fit within the width limits set by the printer options. If your data is wider than the limits, only the part of the data that fits within the printer options limits will be printed to the Clipboard.

As with printing to a printer, you also have the option to print a report date in the header at the top of the file when you print to the Clipboard. Once you print your data to the Clipboard, AppleWorks displays this notice telling you that the data is on the Clipboard:

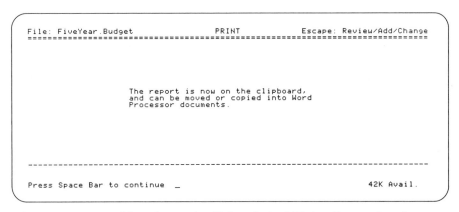

```
File: FiveYear.Budget                PRINT              Escape: Review/Add/Change
================================================================================




                          The report is now on the clipboard,
                          and can be moved or copied into Word
                          Processor documents.




         ----------------------------------------------------------------------

 Press Space Bar to continue  _                                  42K Avail.
```

When you print spreadsheet data to the Clipboard, AppleWorks tells you when the operation is complete.

Once your data is printed to the Clipboard, you must press **SPACE** or **ESC** to return to the spreadsheet's Review/Add/Change screen.

■ **Printing to an ASCII file**

Another possible print destination for a spreadsheet file is to disk as a plain ASCII file.[13] An ASCII file contains ordinary characters without any formatting. It's useful to print ASCII files when you want to send your file via modem, or when you want to use it in another program that can read ASCII files. Standard AppleWorks files have a unique format other programs can't read, so the ability to produce files in ASCII format makes it easy to share files with many other programs. (See: Sharing Data with Other Programs.[288])

When you store spreadsheet files in the ASCII format, however, you eliminate all the row-and-column formatting for the labels and values in the spreadsheet. Instead of appearing as data in rows and columns, spreadsheet data in ASCII format appears as a continuous series of values or labels. Since this format makes it difficult or impossible for someone to determine how the labels and values were arranged in the original spreadsheet, ASCII is a poor format for spreadsheet data when you want to move the data into another spreadsheet program.

Nevertheless, you may be forced to print a file to disk in ASCII format, because the program you want to use the data in may not be able to use DIF files. To do this, display the document you want to print and press the Print command (⌂-P), just as you do when printing to a printer. You must choose the portion of the document you want to print to the ASCII file (even though in most cases you will be printing the entire file). After that:

1. Choose the option *A text (ASCII) file on disk* as the print destination.

2. Type the complete ProDOS[246] pathname[188] under which you want the file stored on the disk, and then press **RETURN**. The file will be stored on disk.

Remember, when you print to an ASCII file, you must make sure your data's width falls within the limits set by the printer-options settings. If your current printer options permit you to print data 80 characters wide, for example, and the data you want to print to an ASCII file is 102 characters wide, only the first 80 characters of that data will be printed. The Print screen (where you choose an ASCII file as the print destination) shows you how wide your data selection is, and how much of your data can be printed with the current printer-options settings.

■ **Printing to a DIF file**

A DIF file[100] is a much more suitable place for storing spreadsheet data you want to share with another program because it maintains the original row-and-column orientation of the data. To print to a DIF file, you follow most of the same steps you do when printing to an ASCII file. Because DIF files store data in row-and-column order, though, you must tell AppleWorks how to store the data.

When printing to a DIF file, you press the Print command (⌂-P) and select the portion of the file you want to print, just as with the other print options in the spreadsheet. After this:

1. Choose the option *A DIF (TM) file on disk* as the print destination.

2. The prompt line will then ask whether you want the file stored in row or column order. The order you choose depends on the order expected by the program that will be using the DIF file. If you will be using the file to create an AppleWorks database or spreadsheet file, choose column order.

3. Type the complete ProDOS[246] pathname[188] under which you want the file stored, and then press **RETURN**. The file will be stored on disk under the pathname you specified.

   Complete information about making and using DIF files is contained in the DIF file entry.

@SQRT

■ **Structure**

@SQRT(argument)

■ **Definition**

@SQRT is a spreadsheet function that computes the square root of a value and places it in the cell where the function is entered.

The argument can be:	Such as:
A numeric value	@SQRT(967)
Mathematical expressions	@SQRT(7 ∗ 63)
Other functions	@SQRT(@SUM(@AVG(B3.B5)+30))

■ **Example**

In the following spreadsheet, the @SQRT formula in cell B7 and displayed in the entry line first subtracts the side stress factor from the perimeter stress factor, multiplies the result by the axis stress factor, and enters the square root of the result in the cell:

```
File: Stress Factors          REVIEW/ADD/CHANGE          Escape: Main Menu
========A=========B=========C=========D=========E=========F=========G========H====
 1           Widget Stress Factors, (ft/lbs. per sq. inch)
 2    -------------------------------------------------------------------
 3 |Axis            350
 4 |Perimeter        85
 5 |Sides            15
 6 |
 7 |Square Rt 156.5247
 8 |
 9 |
10 |
11 |
12 |
13 |
14 |
15 |
16 |
17 |
18 |
   -------------------------------------------------------------------
B7: (Value) @SQRT((B4-B5)*B3)

Type entry or use Ⓐ commands  _                        Ⓐ-? for Help
```

AppleWorks can calculate square roots of individual values or of mathematical expressions.

You could also calculate the square root of just one value. If you wanted to calculate only the square root of the axis stress factor, for example, you could type *@SQRT(350)*, or *@SQRT(B3)*.

Formatting decimal numbers: When calculating square roots, the result will not often be a whole number. The AppleWorks spreadsheet will only calculate square roots or any other numbers to an accuracy of seven decimal places. However, the spreadsheet's default-value format, *Appropriate*, will not display all seven decimal places if there is more than one number to the left of the decimal point. When that happens, use the Layout[146] command (⌂-**L**) to widen the column until the complete value is displayed. The problem is, you won't always know that the number is longer than the one displayed. If you're working with scientific calculations, it can be critical for you to know exactly what the complete value is in a cell. In those situations, you want a *flag* in the cell that will warn you that the number is longer than the one displayed. You can set this "flag" with the Layout command's *Fixed* option. With it, you can specify the number of decimal places to be displayed (up to seven places). Then, if the cell is not wide enough to display the entire number, a series of number signs (#) will appear in the cell. You can then either put the cursor on the cell and consult the entry line for the complete number, or else you can widen the column containing the formula.

As an example, cell B7 in the example spreadsheet now displays the number *156.5247*. However, AppleWorks actually calculated the square root to seven decimal places, or *156.5247584*. Let's change the value format of cell B7 in the example spreadsheet to display all seven decimal places. In the process we'll also have to widen column B.

1. Press the Layout command (⌂-**L**). The prompt line changes to read:

    Layout? Entry Rows Columns Block

2. Press **RETURN** to choose the default *Entry* Layout option. The prompt line now reads:

    Layout? Value format Label format Protection

3. Press **RETURN** to choose the default *Value format* option. The prompt line now reads:

   Value format? Fixed Dollars Commas Percent Appropriate Standard

4. Press **RETURN** to choose the default *Fixed* option. The prompt line now reads:

   How many decimal places?(0–7)

5. We want the number displayed to the maximum seven decimal places, so type *7* and press **RETURN**.

A row of number signs now appears in the cell because it's not wide enough to display the complete number. To widen it:

1. Press the Layout command (⌥-L) to display the first *Layout?* prompt line.

2. Press **C** to choose the *Columns* option.

3. The column the cursor is in becomes highlighted, and since that's the only one we want, press **RETURN** again to select it.

4. The second *Layout?* prompt line appears; press **C** to choose the *Column width* option. The prompt line now reads:

   Press ⌥ and arrows to change column widths

5. Hold down the ⌥ key and press the → key until the number appears in the cell, replacing the number signs.

6. Press **RETURN** to end the operation and return to the spreadsheet.

■ **Comments**

If a cell location specified in an @SQRT formula contains text, the function treats it as if it were the number *0*.

If a value that is specified in the argument of the @SQRT function contains a negative number, the cell where the function has been placed will display the message *ERROR*. It is not possible to calculate the square root of a negative number.

Arguments that are specified in @SQRT formulas may themselves contain functions. If we wanted to obtain the square root of the sum of a group of numbers, for example, we could use a formula such as the following: @SQRT(@SUM(C17…C25)).

Standard Values (⌂-V)

- **Definition**

  Standard values are format and data-entry values that can be set in the Apple-Works spreadsheet and database. In the spreadsheet, you can use standard values to control the format of data. And in the database, you can use standard values to specify that certain categories in all new records you insert or append already contain the same information, saving you the trouble of typing the information in each record.

 Standard values in the spreadsheet

The AppleWorks spreadsheet has certain standard formatting and data-entry options that are preset whenever you create a new file, as shown in the following table.

Standard values:	*Default setting:*
Label Format	Left justified
Column Width	Nine characters
Cell Protection	On
Recalculation Order	Columns
Recalculation Frequency	Automatic

These values affect the entire spreadsheet, so that all columns in the spreadsheet are nine characters wide, all labels appear left justified when entered in cells, and so forth. You can change these values for individual cells, rows, columns, or blocks of cells with the Layout[146] command (⌂-L), but if you want to change the values for the entire spreadsheet, you should use the Standard Values command.

To use the Standard Values command, display the Review/Add/Change screen for the spreadsheet whose standard values you want to change, and then press the Standard Values command (⌂-V). A menu of options will appear in the prompt line, as shown in the example.

```
File: Cost of Sales          STANDARD VALUES       Escape: Review/Add/Change
========A========B========C========D========E========F========G========H====
 3
 4 Materials                    Oct      Nov      Dec      Qtr
 5 ------------------           ===      ===      ===      ===
 6
 7 Widget Oil                  1200     1410      960     2370
 8 Steel                       2500     3250     3000     8750
 9 Copper                      1000     1175      800     2975
10 Magnesium                   1250     1100     1250     3600
11 Grease                       120      150      135      405
12 Rags                          50       50       50      150
13
14 Labor
15 ------------------
16 Salaries                    3000     3000     3000     9000
17 Commissions                 2250     2250     2250     6750
18 Hourly Wages                2850     2850     2850     8550
19
20
-------------------------------------------------------------------------------
G18: (Value) @SUM(D18...F18)

Standards? Value format  Label format  Column width  Protection  Recalculate
```

The Standard Values command in the spreadsheet lets you set a range of format and data-entry options.

Let's look at the options on this menu one at a time.

Value format: Choose the *Value format* option whenever you want to change the way values are displayed when they are entered into the spreadsheet. When you choose the *Value format* option, the following submenu appears in the prompt line:

Value format? Fixed Dollars Commas Percent Appropriate

Fixed format displays numbers with a set number of decimal places. When you choose the *Fixed* format option, the prompt line asks you how many decimal places you want after each number you enter. Enter a number between 0 and 7, and then press **RETURN** to set that value. After that, all numbers already in the spreadsheet will be reformatted to reflect the new value, and new numbers you enter or numbers generated by formulas will have the number of decimal places you chose. If you specified 2 decimal places, for example, a number entered as *22* would be displayed as *22.00*.

Dollars format displays numbers with a set number of decimal places and with a dollar sign in front of them, and commas setting off thousands, hundred thousands, etc. When you choose the *dollars* format option, you are prompted to enter the number of decimal places you want values to have. You enter a number between 0 and 7, and then press **RETURN** to set that value. If you specified 0 decimal places, for example, a number entered as *22* would be displayed as *$22*. Also note that any negative value will be displayed in parentheses.

Commas format displays numbers with a set number of decimal places, and with commas setting off each increment of a thousand. When you choose the *commas* format option, you are asked to enter the number of decimal places you want values to have. You enter a number between 0 and 7, and then press the Return key to set that value. If you specified 2 decimal places, for example, a number entered as *1000* would be displayed as *1,000.00*. As with the *Dollars* option, negative values will be displayed in parentheses.

Percent format displays numbers with a set number of decimal places, multiplies the number by 100, and then puts a percent sign after it. When you choose the percent format option, you're asked to enter the number of decimal places you want values to have. You enter a number between 0 and 7, and then press **RETURN** to set that value. If you specify 2 decimal places, for example, a number entered as *2* would be displayed as *200.00%*, and a number entered as *.5* would be displayed as *50.00%*.

Appropriate format is the default standard-value format in the spreadsheet. In this format, numbers are represented as closely as possible to the way you enter them. The spreadsheet will not accept certain format enhancements when you enter a number, however. If, for example, you enter a number as *22.00*, it will be displayed as *22.00*. If you enter a number as *22%*, though, the spreadsheet won't accept the percent sign as part of the value and you won't be allowed to enter it. In appropriate format, the spreadsheet accepts numbers and a decimal point, but not dollar signs, commas, or percent signs.

Label format: Choose the *Label format* option when you want to change the way labels are displayed in the spreadsheet. When you choose the *Label format* option from the Standard Values menu, this submenu appears in the prompt line:

> **Label format? Left justify Right justify Center**

The *Left justify* option, which is the default value, formats labels so they are aligned with the left side of the cell in which they are entered.

The *Right justify* option formats labels so they are aligned with the right side of the cell in which they are entered.

The *Center* option formats labels so they are centered in the cell in which they are entered.

Column width: The *Column width* format option lets you set the width of all the columns in a spreadsheet. When you choose the *Column width* option from the Standard Values menu, you are prompted to press ⌂ and ← to narrow or → to widen the spreadsheet's columns. As you press these keys, all the columns become wider or narrower. When the columns are the width you want them, press **RETURN** or **ESC** to return to the Review/Add/ Change screen.

Protection: The *Protection* option on the Standard Values menu allows you to either activate or deactivate the cell-protection facilities that are available under the Layout[146] command.

When you choose the *Protection* option, you are given two options: *No* and *Yes*. In new spreadsheet files, the default protection option is set to *Yes*, which means protection is active, and you can set cell protection with the Layout command. If you want to deactivate the protection facilities (and thereby disable the protection options available under the Layout command), set the protection under the standard values to *No*.

Recalculate: When you choose the *Recalculate* option, the following submenu appears in the prompt line:

Recalculate? Order Frequency

The *Order* option lets you specify the order that the spreadsheet recalculates. The two options are *Rows* and *Columns*. The *Columns* option, which is the default order, means the spreadsheet will calculate each column top to bottom and working to the right. The *Rows* option means the spreadsheet will calculate each row left to right starting with row 1 and work its way down.

The *Frequency* option lets you specify whether spreadsheet formulas recalculate *automatically* (each time you change or enter a spreadsheet value), or *manually* (only when you use the Calculate[18] command (⌂-K)).

The default standard value for recalculation is *Automatic*. When you are entering a lot of numbers at a time, however, you may not want to wait as the spreadsheet recalculates between each value entered. In this case, you should choose the *Recalculate* option from the Standard Values menu and set recalculation to *Manual*. With recalculation set to *Manual*, you can enter a series of numbers in various cells, and then recalculate the spreadsheet by pressing the Calculate command (⌂-K) when you're done.

Comments: The standard-values options change all the standard values settings in a spreadsheet, but they do not override custom format options you have set in certain cells, rows, columns, or blocks with the Layout command. Thus, if you have entered values with the default *Appropriate* format and you change the standard value to *Dollars* format, the existing values will be reformatted as dollars; but if you have used the Layout option to set the format for existing numbers to *Percent,* changing the standard values option to *Dollars* won't change values represented as percent into values represented as dollars. The only values that change throughout the spreadsheet (affecting all cells, regardless of whether they contain a custom format) are the *Recalculate, Column width,* and *Protection* options.

To change the format of cells already using a custom format, you will have to move the cursor to those individual cells, rows, columns, or blocks and use the Layout command to change the custom format you entered in them. Changing standard values does, however, affect the format of all future entries.

Standard values in the database

In the database, the Standard Values command is used to enter the same data automatically in one or more categories of new records. In a new database file, there are no standard values set for categories.

To set standard category contents for new records in the database, press the Standard Values command (⌂-**v**) when the file's Review/Add/Change screen is displayed. When you do this, you're presented with a Single Record layout screen showing all the file's category names, like this:

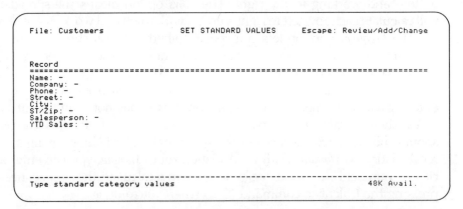

```
File: Customers          SET STANDARD VALUES     Escape: Review/Add/Change


Record
================================================================================
Name: -
Company: -
Phone: -
Street: -
City: -
ST/Zip: -
Salesperson: -
YTD Sales: -




--------------------------------------------------------------------------------
Type standard category values                               48K Avail.
```

The Standard Values command in the database lets you set standard data that will automatically be entered into each new record.

To set the standard values on this screen, simply type the information you want to be automatically entered in the categories you select. If you were entering a lot of records for salesperson *Smith*, for example, you could enter the standard value *Smith* in the category *Salesperson*. After that, all new records you inserted or appended in the file would automatically contain the entry *Smith* in the *Salesperson* category.

Comments: You can delete or change a standard value by pressing the Standard Values command again, moving the cursor to the category whose value you want to delete or change, pressing the Clear[34] command (⌂-Y), and then either typing the new data or pressing **RETURN**.

You can enter standard values in as many database categories as you like. The Standard Values command is so easy to use in the database that it makes sense to use it even if you have just a few records that will contain the same data in one or more categories. You can also edit or change the standard value in a category as you append or insert new records.

Entering or changing standard values in the database does not affect the contents of existing records.

Sticky Space (⌂-SPACE)

- **Definition**

   The *Sticky Space* command (⌂-SPACE) places a nonbreaking blank space in a word-processor document.

- **Usage**

   Use the Sticky Space command when you are typing a long phrase or proper name in a word-processor document, and you don't want the words placed on separate lines by the application's word-wraparound[375] feature. Normally, the word processor moves the last word on a line down to a new line when there isn't room for it on the current line. A sticky space holds two words together, so that the wraparound feature moves them both when it moves that portion of your text down to the next line.

■ **Example**

Suppose you compose this promotional letter announcing a new product:

```
File: New Year.Ltr              REVIEW/ADD/CHANGE              Escape: Main Menu
=====|====|====|====|====|====|====|====|====|====|====|====|====|====|====|===
January 6, 1986

Mr. Ed Frobish
Frobish Linen Service
335 Ramona Ave.
San Jose, CA 95551

Dear Ed:

All of us at Acme Widget Manufacturing want to wish you and yours a happy
and prosperous new year.  Now that the holidays are over, it's time to
begin thinking about the competitive forces at work in this robust business
quarter.  Personally, Ed, I think the Frobish Linen Service can meet the
challenge and continue its growth with the all-new, revolutionary Wonder
Widget--the Widget Whose Time Has Come.

I'll be calling you next week to arrange a time to present this exciting
new product.

Sincerely Yours,
-----------------------------------------------------------------------------
Type entry or use ⬛ commands           Line 17   Column  1       ⬛-? for Help
```

Notice that the two words or the product's name appear on different lines at the end of the first paragraph. You want to fix the letter so the product's name appears on one line. Here's how to use the Sticky Space command to do it:

1. Place the cursor on the *W* in *Widget*, and press the **DELETE** key twice. This will delete the spaces between *Wonder* and *Widget*. The format will change, so the two words appear together on the last line without a space between them.

2. Press the Sticky Space command (⌂-**SPACE**). A caret[22] symbol (^) will appear between *Wonder* and *Widget*. This is the Sticky Space symbol. When you print the document, the caret symbol won't be printed, but the two words will be printed together on the same line with a space between them.

Subdirectory

■ **Definition**

A *subdirectory* is a gathering place where you can store a group of files under a common name on a floppy- or hard-disk volume.[122]

■ **Usage**

A subdirectory is a named location you create on a floppy- or hard-disk volume. You can use subdirectories to organize related files under a descriptive name, and to keep the main catalog of a floppy- or hard-disk volume relatively short and uncluttered.

To create a subdirectory, choose option 3, *Create a subdirectory,* from the Other Activities menu.[178] Once you have chosen the option, you must type the complete ProDOS pathname[188] (the volume name and the subdirectory name) for the new subdirectory. After you create a subdirectory, you can store files in it, and those files won't show up when you list files on the whole disk—only when you change the current disk location to that subdirectory and then list the files stored there.

■ **Example**

Suppose you are using a floppy disk called *Business* to store two different kinds of files: files pertaining to a sales report you are doing, and files relating to general business activities, such as a calendar, a list of business contacts, and a time sheet. The disk is in Drive 2. When you list the files on this disk, you are listing the files in the volume directory, and the disk shows more files than you can see on the screen at once without scrolling with the Arrow keys, as you can see in this example:

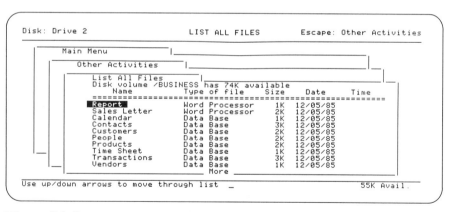

When a disk directory gets too crowded, you can use subdirectories to make it smaller.

To make the files a little easier to get to, you want to create a subdirectory called *Sales*, where you can store all your sales-report files:

1. If you aren't at the Main Menu,[158] press **ESC** until the Main Menu is displayed. Make sure your disk, *Business*, is currently in one of your disk drives.

2. Choose option 5, *Other Activities*, from the Main Menu.

3. Choose option 3, *Create a subdirectory*, from the Other Activities menu. You will be prompted to enter the complete pathname of the new subdirectory, as shown below:

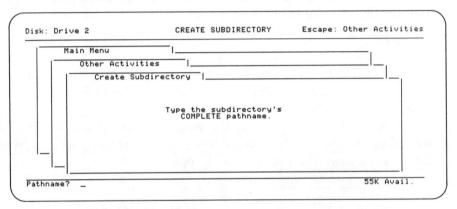

```
Disk: Drive 2              CREATE SUBDIRECTORY      Escape: Other Activities

        Main Menu              |_____
          Other Activities         |_____|__
            Create Subdirectory      |_____|__



                         Type the subdirectory's
                           COMPLETE pathname.




     __
        |_____|

   Pathname?  _                                              55K Avail.
```

When you make a subdirectory, you must type the complete pathname of the subdirectory so AppleWorks knows which name to give it.

4. Type the complete pathname of the subdirectory. The complete pathname includes the name of the volume (*Business*) and the name you want the subdirectory to be (*Sales*), preceded by slash marks, like this: */Business/Sales*.

5. Once you type the pathname, press **RETURN**. Appleworks will attempt to create the subdirectory */Sales* on the volume */Business*. If it is successful, you will see a message that reports the successful creation of the subdirectory. If AppleWorks isn't successful (either because the volume you specified isn't in a disk drive or doesn't exist on your hard disk, or because there is already a subdirectory with the name you have chosen on the volume you have specified), then it will report its failure.

With your subdirectory called *Sales* successfully created on the volume *Business*, you can now move all your sales-related files there. To do this, add the sales files to the Desktop[97] (you may have to add them in more than one group, if there are more than 12), save them into the subdirectory *Sales*, and then remove the original copies of the sales files from the main-volume directory. Here are the steps:

1. Press **ESC** to return to the Main Menu if you're not already there.

2. Make sure your current disk location is either */Business* or the disk-drive number where the */Business* disk is located.

3. Choose option 1, *Add Files to the Desktop*, from the Main Menu.

4. Select the files you want to add with →, and then add all these files to the desktop by pressing **RETURN**.

5. Press **ESC** until the Main Menu is displayed.

6. Choose option 3, *Save Desktop files to disk*, from the Main Menu.

7. Use → to select all the files you have just added to the Desktop, and then press **RETURN**.

8. You will be asked whether you want to save the files on the current disk, or if you want to first change to a different disk or directory. You want to change to the subdirectory */Business/Sales*, so choose option 2, *First change to a different disk or directory*.

9. The Change Current Disk menu[25] will appear, letting you choose the new location to which you want to save the files. Choose option 3, *ProFile or other ProDOS directory*, and then type the complete pathname of the new subdirectory where you want to save the files: */Business/Sales*.

10. After you type the new pathname and press **RETURN**, you can save all the files to the subdirectory.

At this point, you have two copies of these files on your *Business* disk: one copy of each file is in the */Business* volume directory, and one copy is in the */Business/Sales* subdirectory. You don't want to waste disk space with two copies of identical files, so you want to delete the original copies of the files from the *Business* volume directory. To do this:

1. Press **ESC** to return to the Main Menu if you're not already there.

2. Choose option 5, *Other Activities*.

3. From the Other Activities menu, choose option 1, *Change current disk drive or ProDOS prefix*.

4. The Change Current Disk screen will appear. Choose option 3, *ProFile or other ProDOS directory*, and type the pathname */Business.* (If */Business* is a hard-disk volume, you should also choose option 3, and type the pathname */Business.*) Alternatively, you can choose either option 1 (Drive 1) or option 2 (Drive 2), depending on which one contains your volume disk. AppleWorks will then use the volume name in the specified disk drive.

5. With the current disk changed back to */Business*, the Other Activities menu will appear again. Now, choose option 4, *Delete files from disk.* All the files on the volume */Business* will be listed. Use → to select the duplicate files which you have saved to */Business/Sales*, and then press **RETURN**. AppleWorks will display each file name individually and warn you that you are about to permanently remove that file from the disk. Press **Y** to confirm, since another copy of each file is stored under the */Business/Sales* subdirectory.

6. Now, you have deleted the files from the *Business* volume directory, but there is still a copy of each file on the Desktop. You can continue working with these files, or you can remove them from the desktop by choosing option 4, *Remove files from the Desktop*, from the Main Menu.

Now, you can list the files on the */Business* disk using the *Add files to the Desktop* option from the Main Menu, and the listing is much shorter. The sales files that were cluttering the listing are now located in the subdirectory *Sales*, and you can't see their names when you list the files on the whole disk. The shorter file listing looks like this:

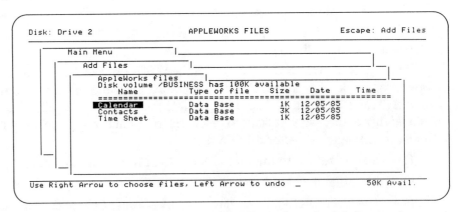

With some files in a subdirectory, the listing of files in the main disk directory is much shorter.

Notice that the *Sales* subdirectory isn't displayed. It is not displayed because the list of files presented when you add files only contains AppleWorks application files—not DIF, ASCII, or other types of files or subdirectories. To see the subdirectory listed, you must use the *List all files on the current disk drive* option (option 2) from the Other Activities menu—this listing will show every file and subdirectory on the disk, whether or not it is an AppleWorks application file.

When you want to add files from your new subdirectory to the Desktop, you must change the current file location to the ProDOS prefix, */Business/Sales* by choosing option 1 from the Other Activities menu. After you do this, the *Add files to the Desktop* option will produce a listing of only the files in the *Sales* subdirectory.

■ **Comments**

Subdirectories are especially helpful when you are using a hard-disk drive: Since a hard disk could contain hundreds of files, you'll want to place those files in logical groups instead of scrolling through page after page of file listings each time you want to locate a file.

You can't delete a subdirectory from a disk unless there are no files stored in it. Therefore, you must delete all files from a subdirectory before you can delete the subdirectory itself.

For more information about subdirectories, see Other Activities menu;[178] Pathname;[188] and ProDOS.[246]

@SUM

■ **Structure**

@SUM(range or list)

■ **Definition**

@SUM is a spreadsheet function that totals a group of values and presents the result in the cell where the function appears.

The argument can be:	Such as:
Numeric values	@SUM(−402,30,40)
Cell ranges	@SUM(B4.B23)
Lists	@SUM(B4,E7,A9)
Other functions	@SUM(@AVG(B3.B5)+30)

■ **Example: Summing a range of cells**

In the following spreadsheet, the @SUM formula entered in cell E9 and displayed in the entry line sums the range of cells E5 through E7:

```
 File: Oil Orders              REVIEW/ADD/CHANGE            Escape: Main Menu
 =======A=======B=======C=======D=======E=======F=======G=======H====
   1                    The Widget Company - Widget Oil Orders
   2  --------------------------------------------------------------
   3
   4                    Jan      Feb      Mar      Apr      May      Jun
   5  Wonder Widget     200      300      400      500      450      400
   6  Widget Light       85       88       92      110       98       90
   7  Widget Crude      500      450      550      600      550      475
   8
   9  Orders Delivered  785             ████1042
  10
  11  Partial Orders             750
  12
  13
  14
  15
  16
  17
  18  --------------------------------------------------------------
 E9: (Value) @SUM(E5...E7)

 Type entry or use ◘ commands  _                         ◘-? for Help
```

The @SUM formula can sum the figures in a continuous range of cells.

■ **Example: Summing a list of cells**

Suppose in the example that the order for Widget Light Oil wasn't received for the month of April. Consequently, we only want to add the amounts for Wonder Widget Oil (cell F5) and Widget Crude Oil (cell F7), skipping the amount in cell F6. So, we'd move the cursor to cell F9 and enter this formula:

@SUM(F5,F7)

The total of Wonder Widget and Widget Crude orders (1100) would then be displayed in cell F9.

■ **Editing an @SUM formula**

If you want to edit an @SUM formula after it's been entered, place the cursor on the cell where the formula is entered and then press the Undo[351] command (⌂-U). The formula will appear in the entry line, where you can edit it.

■ **Comment**

If you specify a mathematical expression by itself in the argument of an @SUM formula, the function treats the expression as a single item, and individual numbers in the expression will not be calculated. If you were to enter *@SUM(2∗3)*, for example, the result would be *6*. If you added another item, like *@SUM(2∗3,5)*, the function would return the value *11*. Note that the @SUM function only sums items in its argument that are separated by commas, and that any mathematical expression between commas is calculated before the @SUM function uses its value.

Time

■ Definition
Time is a special type of data category in a database file.

■ Usage
The word *Time* (or *time*) in a database category automatically formats all your time entries in that category in the same way, and enables you to sort records chronologically according to those entries.

A database file will store any type of numeric or text information. Normally, the data you enter is formatted just the way you enter it, and you can sort records in any category in either alphabetic or numeric order depending on the type of information in the category. If you use the word *Time* as part of a category name, however, AppleWorks automatically formats time entries as HH:MM (AM or PM), and lets you sort records chronologically according to time entries, as well as alphabetically and numerically.

In the following file, for example, we have used the word *Time* in the category *Start Time*.

```
 File: Employees            REVIEW/ADD/CHANGE          Escape: Main Menu
 Selection: All records


 Name          Phone        Title          Hire Date     Start Time
 ================================================================================
 Susan Best     555-0707    Salesperson    Oct  9 85       9:00 AM
 Audie Brohammer 555-6543   Salesperson    Jul 16 84       9:00 AM
 Fred Smith     555-2342    Salesperson    Nov  3 84      10:00 AM
 Martin Grunion 555-8099    Clerk          Apr 13 85       8:30 AM





 ------------------------------------------------------------------------------
 Type entry or use ⬚ commands                          ⬚-? for Help
```

If you use the word time *in a category name, times you enter are automatically formatted consistently, no matter how you enter the data.*

Now, all the times we enter in *Start Time* are formatted HH:MM (AM or PM), no matter how we type the data in. We could well have entered Best's start time as *9* or *9:00*, and AppleWorks would automatically translate it to the *9:00 AM* format shown above.

If you don't enter an *A* (or *AM*) or *P* (or *PM*) after a time entry, AppleWorks assumes you mean that the time falls during normal business hours: 7:00 AM through 6:59 PM. Thus, if you enter a time as *6*, AppleWorks will assume you mean *6:00 PM*, not *6:00 AM*. If you want to enter a non-business time, such as 1:00 AM, you must specify *AM*, or at least *A*, after the time entry. AppleWorks will then convert the time to the standard format. You can also enter the time in military format, and it will automatically be converted to the HH:MM format in AppleWorks. If you enter 1300, for example, AppleWorks will convert this to *1:00 PM*.

Another advantage to using the word *Time* in a category name is that it makes it possible to arrange that category chronologically. If we type the Arrange[10] command (⌂-**A**) with our cursor located on the *Start Time* category in the last example, the chronological options will then appear on the Arrange screen, like this:

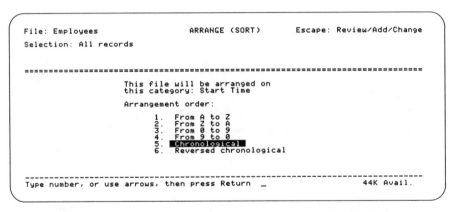

```
File: Employees              ARRANGE (SORT)        Escape: Review/Add/Change
Selection: All records

================================================================================
                    This file will be arranged on
                    this category: Start Time

                    Arrangement order:

                       1.  From A to Z
                       2.  From Z to A
                       3.  From 0 to 9
                       4.  From 9 to 0
                       5.  Chronological
                       6.  Reversed chronological


--------------------------------------------------------------------------------
Type number, or use arrows, then press Return  _              44K Avail.
```

When a category name contains the word time, you can arrange the data in it chronologically.

■ **Comments**

You must use the word *time* in a category name to inform AppleWorks that you are working with time information. If you enter times in a category whose name doesn't contain the word *Time*, the database will treat the data as ordinary text—it won't be formatted consistently, and you won't be able to sort it chronologically.

Tricks and Tips

This section contains a few suggestions for getting more out of the Apple-Works program. Some of the items are actual applications for AppleWorks, and others are general tips to help you use the program more efficiently.

- **Using the Desktop**

One of the major advantages of AppleWorks is that it lets you keep up to 12 files on the Desktop[97] at a time. If you're used to working with stand-alone programs you haven't had this luxury, so you may not be taking advantage of it in AppleWorks.

The obvious use for this multiple-file capability is when you're working on a project, such as a paper or report, that requires you to use several files. You can load all the relevant files onto the Desktop at once, and then move between them quickly. But you can also use the Desktop to store "desk accessory" files that help you do your daily work. Here are some examples:

Calendar: Use the database to set up a simple appointments calendar with categories for date, time, and activity. If you add this file to the Desktop each day, you're only a keystroke away from your calendar when you need to consult it. You can also use the record-selection rules[259] to print out a schedule for each day or week.

Calculator: Keep a new spreadsheet file on the Desktop as you work, and you're always a keystroke away from an intelligent calculator.

Notepad: Keep a new word-processor file on the Desktop and use it to make notes to yourself throughout the day. You can print the file at the end of the day, or delete the notes if you don't need them anymore.

Rolodex: Make a simple database file with names, addresses, and telephone numbers, and then add it to the Desktop each day so you have quick access to your business and personal contacts.

"Do List": Use a word-processor file to make a daily "Do List" for yourself. You could even make a template with dates for the whole week, and then enter things to do as they arise.

You can probably think of other handy files to put on your Desktop to help you through your business day.

Numbering pages in separate word-processor documents

Most word processors for the Apple limit the size of a document to the available RAM[256] space. This is true with AppleWorks. If you are writing a long document, such as a novel or thesis, you will probably run out of file space in the word processor before you run out of things to write. This means you'll have to create two or more separate documents for the whole project.

Most long pieces of writing have natural breaks (chapters, sections, or whatever), so it's easy to begin a new section in a new file. Because the files are separate, however, you have to take an extra step to make the page numbering continuous from one file to the next. To maintain continuous page numbering, make a note of the last page number in the first file, and then use the Page Number (PN) printer option[237] in the second file to specify that the page numbering begins with the next number in the sequence. If, for example, the last page in the first file is 25, specify that the first page in the next file be numbered 26 by using the PN printer option.

Using efficient category names in the database

As with the spreadsheet, Tables database reports are often wider than the paper you will ultimately print them on. You can make individual report categories narrower to squeeze more data on each line, however. To make it as easy as possible to shrink each database category, try to use category names that are no wider than the data the category will contain. If a category will contain zip codes, for example, name the category *Zip* (which is shorter than the five-digit entries in the category itself), rather than *Zip Code.* This way, you can shrink the category to its narrowest width (in this case, five characters), and the entire category name will still show.

Another way to conserve horizontal space in a file is to combine categories. In an address file, for example, you'll use much less horizontal space by combining the state and zip data in one category called *ST/Zip* than you would if you used separate categories.

Two special category names that can save you some formatting work are *Date* and *Time.* When you use these words in a category name, the date and time information that you enter is automatically formatted a certain way by AppleWorks (see Date[90] and Time[343]).

Database data-entry shortcuts

There are two ways to speed up data entry into a database file when some of the information in each record is the same. If you want to insert the same information into many existing records in a file, you can enter it on the Multiple Record layout.[168] Make sure that the cursor moves down after you press **RETURN** (if it doesn't, press the Layout[146] command (⌘-L), press **ESC**, and choose *Down* as the cursor movement direction). Then, move the cursor to the record containing the first blank category where you want to copy the data from the same category in the record above it. The category containing the entry you want to copy must be directly above the category the cursor is in. Press the Ditto[103] command (⌘-'). The entry above will then be copied into the category where your cursor is located, and the cursor will move down one record to the next category.

The Ditto command always copies the entry in the record directly above, so you have to be sure that this entry is the one you want to duplicate. If you are sure, however, you can simply continue pressing the Ditto command—each time you do, the entry above will be copied into the same category in the record where the cursor is located. You can quickly move down a Multiple Record layout duplicating an entry this way.

The other way to enter data quickly works only with new or inserted records. If you use the Standard Values[330] command (⌘-V), you can enter data you want to automatically appear in each new or inserted record into one or several categories on a special screen that displays the categories using the Single Record layout. After you do this, the data you entered as standard values will automatically appear on all new records you insert or append. Thus, if the entry for the category *State* is usually or always *CA*, you can use the Standard Values command to automatically enter *CA* in all new records. You can always change the Standard Values settings so the database will insert different data, or so it won't automatically insert any data, which is its default state. Also, when entering new records that contain data already in place via the Standard Values command, you can edit or change that data.

Duplicating a database file

Suppose you fill up a database file and need to create a new file to handle more records. What you want is a file whose categories and report formats are identical to the existing file, but which doesn't contain any entries yet. The easiest way to do this is to duplicate the current file and delete the existing records.

After you make sure there is a copy of the file on your disk, add the file to the Desktop (see: Add Files menu[2]). Next, use the Name Change[171] command (⌃-N) to change the file name to something slightly different. (If the first file is *Customers*, you might name the second one *Customers.1*. Now, you have a new file that has the same categories and report formats—all that remains is to delete the records.

You can't delete all the records in a database file—AppleWorks always keeps one record in the file. To delete the rest of the records, move the cursor to the first record in the Multiple Record layout and press the Delete[92] command (⌃-D). Use the Ruler[280] to highlight the entire file (press ⌃-9), and then press **RETURN**. All records will be deleted except the first one. Then edit the first record so it contains the data for the first record in the new file.

You can use a similar technique when you want to split a file. If a *Customers* file is filling up, for example, you might want to split the file into two, with the names from *A* through *M* in the first file and the names from *N* through *Z* in the second file. To do this, make sure the *Customers* file is safely stored on disk, then add it to the Desktop. Rename the file *Customers.1*. Arrange the file on the *Name* category from *A* through *Z* (see: Arrange[10]). Move the cursor to the first name in the file that begins with *N*, and delete that record and all the other records below it. Now, this file contains only the names from A through M. Add the original *Customers* file to the Desktop again, and rename it *Customers.2*. This time, delete all the records for names *A* through *M*, and you will have a second file that contains only the *N* through *Z* names. Save both new files on disk, then delete the original *Customers* file from the disk.

Calculating in the spreadsheet

Sometimes when you're entering spreadsheet data, you need to perform a quick calculation to determine a number you must enter. The simplest thing to do is move the cursor to an unused portion of the spreadsheet and make the calculation in a blank cell. Once you arrive at the answer, you can copy the value to the cell where it belongs.

In large spreadsheets, it can be useful to set up a special calculator area that's always located in the same place. To do this, move to an unused area of the spreadsheet and type the word *CALC* in a cell. Now, whenever you want to move to that area quickly, you can use the Find[109] command (⌃-F)—just enter the word *CALC* as the text to find, and the cursor will jump there.

The Find command in the spreadsheet remembers the last text string or cell coordinate you found. Once you enter *CALC* as the string to find the first time, you can move quickly to the *CALC* area after that by simply pressing the Find command and then **RETURN**.

Getting around a large spreadsheet

Another tip for large spreadsheets is to name different areas so you can move the cursor to them quickly with the Find command, because it's a lot easier to remember a name than a particular cell location. Suppose, for example, that you are doing a cost-of-sales analysis, and you have created separate areas of a spreadsheet for analyzing sales commissions, figuring the month's sales, and figuring your cost of products. Identify each separate area by typing a label above it—*Commissions, Sales,* and *Products,* for example. When you want to jump quickly to the different areas, you can use the Find command and enter the name of the area where you want to move.

Backing up and copying files

Unfortunately, it sometimes happens that a data disk or hard-disk subdirectory becomes unreadable by the computer. Consequently, it's a good idea to back up your files on a separate storage disk for safekeeping. Also, in the normal course of working with your files you will sometimes want the same file on different disks. Although there's a utility on the ProDOS User's Disk for copying files from one disk to another, it's usually easier to simply save the files when you're working with AppleWorks. There are two ways to do this. The simplest is to display the file on the screen and then use the Save command. Make sure your data disk is in the current disk drive, then display the file and press ⌂-S. The file will be saved to that disk. Remove that disk and insert a second disk where you want the file saved, and then press the Save command again. Now there are copies of the file on two disks. The second way to save files on different disks is to use the Save Files[282] option from the Main Menu. Save the file to the first disk, replace that disk with the second disk, and save the file again.

Avoiding disk clutter

If you create and use a lot of DIF[100] or ASCII[13] files, you can clutter up your data disk with them without realizing it. The Add Files feature doesn't show non-AppleWorks files in the file listing, so it's easy to forget that the disk contains DIF or ASCII files. So, every now and then, use the *Delete files* option from the Other Activities menu[123] to list all the "other" files on the disk and delete files you no longer need.

■ **Naming DIF and ASCII files**

You can't save an AppleWorks file on the same disk with a *DIF* or *ASCII* file that has the same name. Thus, you should be careful about how you name DIF or ASCII files when transferring data from one application to another. Remember that the DIF or ASCII files are probably temporary—the data is in transition from one program or application to another program or application. With this in mind, you don't want to use the best file names for these temporary files.

Suppose you have a database file called *Sales*, for example, and you want to transfer the data to a spreadsheet file. When you save the database file as a DIF file, you must give it a name. The name that occurs to you is *Sales.SS*. If you name the DIF file *Sales.SS*, however, you won't be able to use that name with the spreadsheet because you won't be able to save the new file to disk with that name while the DIF file is on the same disk. It would be better to name the file *Sales.DIF*. That way, you can use the *Sales.SS* name on the new spreadsheet file when you create it and eventually save it.

The restriction on using the same name only takes effect when you save a file to disk, not when you name it. AppleWorks won't stop you from naming a spreadsheet *Sales.SS* while there's a DIF file stored on disk under the same name, but when you try to *save* the spreadsheet file, AppleWorks will tell you another file by that name already exists, and it will then terminate the save process.

Another tip about naming DIF and ASCII files is to use the suffix *DIF* or *ASCII* as part of the file name (such as *Sales.DIF* or *Sales.ASCII*). Since Apple-Works simply identifies both of these types of files as "other" when you list files, it helps to use a suffix so you know which type of file is which.

As you use AppleWorks you will discover your own tips and tricks to make the program more efficient.

Underlining (CONTROL-L)

■ **Definition**

The **CONTROL-L** command is an alternate way to specify underlining in word-processor documents.

■ **Usage**

There are two ways to underline text in the word processor: via the Printer Options menu,[217] or with **CONTROL-L**. The **CONTROL-L** command is the fastest way for you to underline text, because you can issue it directly from the keyboard while the Review/Add/Change screen is displayed—you don't have to choose it as an option from the Printer Options menu.

You can only underline up to one paragraph at a time—that is, underlining will begin at the point you specified, but will terminate at the end of that paragraph, even if no "end underlining" command was used to terminate underlining.

To use **CONTROL-L** in a document:

1. Place the cursor where you want underlining to begin.

2. Press **CONTROL-L**. A caret symbol (^) will appear, signifying that text will be underlined from that point.

3. Move the cursor to the place where you want underlining to end.

4. Press **CONTROL-L** again. Another caret symbol will appear to signify the end of underlining.

■ **Comments**

In order for this underlining command to work, the printer you are printing on must be capable of underlining, and AppleWorks must have been configured to instruct that printer to underline (see: Printer Configuration[200]).

This option is not available in the spreadsheet or the database, because these applications don't support underlining.

The caret symbol is used to represent many printer options. You can tell which option is being represented by a particular caret symbol by placing the cursor on the caret. When you do this, the option that caret represents is shown in the line-indicator area at the bottom of the screen. (See: Caret.[22])

Undo (⌂-U)

■ **Definition**

The *Undo* command (⌂-U) is used to edit the contents of a spreadsheet cell.

■ **Usage**

When a label, value, or formula in a cell is just a few characters long and you want to change it, you can simply place the cursor in the cell, type the new information, and press **RETURN**. The new information will replace the old information. When a cell's contents are long and complex, however, and the change you want to make is minor, it's simpler to use the Undo command to edit the existing entry.

■ **Example**

Suppose you are working with this *Cost of Sales* worksheet:

```
File: Cost of Sales          REVIEW/ADD/CHANGE              Escape: Main Menu
=======A========B========C========D========E========F========G========H====
  3
  4 Materials                   Oct      Nov      Dec      Qtr
  5 ------------------          ===      ===      ===      ===
  6
  7 Widget Oil                 1200     1410      960▮▮▮▮2370
  8 Steel                      2500     3250     3000     8750
  9 Copper                     1000     1175      800     2975
 10 Magnesium                  1250     1100     1250     3600
 11 Grease                      120      150      135      405
 12 Rags                         50       50       50      150
 13
 14 Labor
 15 ------------------
 16 Salaries                   3000     3000     3000     9000
 17 Commissions                2250     2250     2250     6750
 18 Hourly Wages               2850     2850     2850     8550
 19
 20
--------------------------------------------------------------------------
G7: (Value) @SUM(E7...F7)

Type entry or use ▯ commands  _                        ▯-? for Help
```

You want to add the Widget Oil expenses in row 7 for the quarter, and you enter the formula in cell G7 as it is shown in the entry line.

In going over the spreadsheet, you realize that you made a mistake in the formula: Instead of summing all three months (columns D through F), you have summed only columns E and F. You could re-enter the entire formula, but it's easier to edit it instead. Here's how:

1. Place the cursor in cell G7. The formula contained in the cell appears in the entry line at the bottom of the screen.

2. Press the Undo command (⌘-U). A copy of the formula appears below the cell indicator, with a blinking cursor on the formula's first character. You can now edit the formula.

3. Use → to move the cursor to the 7 in the reference E7, and press **DELETE** to delete the letter *E*.

4. Type the letter *D*, and press **RETURN**.

5. The edited formula now appears in the formula window and the new amount in cell G7.

■ **Comments**

The Undo command works in any part of the spreadsheet's Review/Add/Change screen. The command is not active in the word processor or the database.

Using a hard disk

You can use AppleWorks on computer systems with one or two floppy-disk drives, but for faster performance you may want to use a hard disk to store your data files or the AppleWorks program itself.

Hard disks typically operate at speeds that are five to ten times faster than floppy-disk drives, so files can be loaded from or saved to them five to ten times more quickly. To store data files on a hard disk, you must create a ProDOS[246] volume on the hard disk (according to the instructions supplied by the hard-disk manufacturer), and then make that volume the standard data-disk location in AppleWorks by using option 6 of the Other Activities[178] menu. When a ProDOS volume is the standard data-disk location, it must be specified with a ProDOS *pathname*.[188]

Once you make your hard disk's volume the standard file location in AppleWorks, you can save files to it or add files from it much more quickly than you can from floppy disks. But if you really want to improve the performance of AppleWorks, you should run the program itself from the hard disk.

■ Copying AppleWorks to a hard disk

AppleWorks is a fairly large program—it occupies nearly all of the space on its Program Disk. Since there are far more program instructions stored on that disk than can be loaded into a standard Apple's memory at once, AppleWorks must periodically read further instructions from the floppy disk as you work. (You will notice your program disk drive running during certain AppleWorks operations, such as printing, asking for help, or moving from one application to another.)

When AppleWorks pauses to read further program instructions from disk, you must wait until it reads them. If those program instructions are on a hard disk instead of a floppy disk, your waiting time is cut dramatically because of the hard disk's greater speed. Fortunately, AppleWorks isn't a copy-protected program, so it's easy to copy the entire program onto a hard disk. Here are the steps:

1. Turn on your hard disk, follow the manufacturer's instructions and create a ProDOS volume on your hard disk (if there isn't one already).

2. Boot the ProDOS User's Disk in your floppy-disk drive. (You may have to purchase the User's Disk separately from your Apple dealer.)

3. When the User's Disk menu appears, choose the *PRODOS FILER (UTILITIES)* option.

4. Choose *FILE COMMANDS* from the Filer menu.

5. Choose *COPY FILES* from the File Commands menu.

6. Remove the User's Disk from your disk drive, and place the AppleWorks Startup Disk in the drive instead.

7. The cursor on the screen should be located between parentheses in the blank area where you enter the pathname of the disk from which you want the copy to be made, as shown in this example:

```
*****************************************
*                                       *
*               COPY FILES              *
*                                       *
**PREFIX: /USERS.DISK/*******************
--COPY--
    PATHNAME: (*
                                       )

    TO PATHNAME:




    --ENTER PATHNAME AND PRESS <RET>--
```

To copy files from the AppleWorks disk to your hard disk, use the Copy Files command to display this screen and enter the source and destination pathnames.

Type the pathname */appleworks/* = and press **RETURN**. The cursor will move down to the blank where you enter the pathname for the disk to which you want the copy made.

8. Type the pathname of your actual ProDOS hard-disk volume with this format: */volumename/* = and press **RETURN**.

Note: The equal sign (=) after the volume name tells ProDOS to copy all the files on the volume. If you wanted to copy only one file, you would type the name of that specific file instead.

9. You will be prompted to insert the correct disks and press the Return key. Since the correct disks are already inserted, you can simply press **RETURN**, and all the files on the Startup Disk will be copied to the hard-disk volume you specified.

Note: Your ProDOS hard-disk volume may already contain a copy of the ProDOS operating system file. Since the AppleWorks Startup Disk also contains a copy of ProDOS, you will be asked if you want to delete the existing ProDOS file and replace it with the copy of ProDOS that's on the Startup Disk. You will be asked to type a *Y* or *N* (*Yes* or *No*); type *N* for *No*. The copying process will then continue until all the files have been copied.

10. When the copy is complete, turn your Startup Disk over so the AppleWorks Program Disk is facing up, and reinsert it in your disk drive. Press **RETURN** to move the cursor back to the blank for the source-disk pathname, and type the pathname */appleworks/* = and press **RETURN**.

11. The cursor will move down to the blank for the destination-disk pathname. Type the pathname and format entered in step 8 and press **RETURN**. Press **RETURN** again when you are prompted to insert the disks in the disk drive, and the copy will be made.

Once all the files from the AppleWorks Startup and Program disks are on your hard disk, you can run the program from there. The steps you take to boot the program from your hard disk will vary, depending on how your hard disk is set up.

■ **Booting AppleWorks from a hard disk**

Hard disks vary among manufacturers, but most of them let you make space for more than one operating system—you might have a volume for the CP/M operating system, some volumes for the DOS 3.3 operating system, and one or more volumes for ProDOS. When you turn on your hard disk and computer with such a system, you select which operating system's volume you want to work with. Once you choose the ProDOS volume, you "boot" that volume, just as you would boot a floppy disk in a disk drive. When you set up your ProDOS volume on a hard disk, you usually copy both the ProDOS operating system and the ProDOS Utilities from the ProDOS User's Disk onto that volume.

Usually, ProDOS volumes on hard disks contain a copy of the files on the ProDOS User's Disk. One of these files, *BASIC.SYSTEM*, produces the User's Disk Main Menu. Whenever you boot a disk or hard-disk volume under Pro-DOS, ProDOS looks for a file with the suffix *SYSTEM* and loads that file. If there is more than one file with this suffix on the disk, ProDOS will load *BASIC.SYSTEM* instead of any other.

If your hard disk's ProDOS volume contains the User's Disk files as well as AppleWorks, the User's Disk Main Menu will always appear when you boot that volume. To load AppleWorks from the User's Disk Main Menu, follow these steps:

1. Boot the ProDOS volume so the User's Disk Main Menu appears.

2. Choose the *PRODOS FILER (UTILITIES)* option to produce the Filer menu.

3. Choose the *FILE COMMANDS* option to produce the File Commands menu.

4. Choose the *SET PREFIX* option from the File Commands menu. You will be shown the current prefix. If this prefix matches the name of your ProDOS volume, press **ESC** to return to the File Commands menu. If the prefix doesn't match the name of your ProDOS volume, type the new prefix (your volume name) and press **RETURN**.

5. Press **ESC** to return to the Filer menu.

6. Choose *Quit* from the Filer menu. The prefix will then be shown at the top of the screen, and the prompt will say *Quit and Load—Pathname: BASIC.SYSTEM*. You don't want to load *BASIC.SYSTEM*, however, so type *APLWORKS.SYSTEM* and press **RETURN**. ProDOS will then look on your hard-disk volume for the file *APLWORKS.SYSTEM* and load it. The Getting Started screen will then appear.

Booting AppleWorks automatically: If AppleWorks is the program you would normally use from your hard-disk volume, you can set your volume up so AppleWorks loads automatically whenever you boot into that volume.

All ProDOS programs contain a startup file with the suffix *.SYSTEM*, because ProDOS has no way of knowing which file to load first unless one of them has this suffix. We've seen that the ProDOS User's Disk contains a file called *BASIC.SYSTEM*. AppleWorks uses a file called *APLWORKS.SYSTEM* for this purpose—it produces the Getting Started screen you see upon first booting the Startup Disk.

If you want ProDOS to load the *APLWORKS.SYSTEM* file when you boot your hard-disk volume, you will have to rename *BASIC.SYSTEM* (and any other *.SYSTEM* files) on that volume and eliminate the *.SYSTEM* suffix.

Using the *RENAME FILES* option from the User's Disk File Commands menu, you can rename *BASIC.SYSTEM* so it is simply called *BASIC*, for example. Without its *.SYSTEM* suffix, this file will no longer be the one ProDOS loads automatically. Rename any other files with *.SYSTEM* after them until *APLWORKS.SYSTEM* is the only *.SYSTEM* file on the volume. Once you have done this, *APLWORKS.SYSTEM* will be the file that is loaded when you boot the volume.

You can still access the User's Disk Main Menu, even if you have set up AppleWorks to be the program that loads automatically when you boot your hard-disk volume. To get to the User's Disk Main Menu, you simply quit AppleWorks and type the name of the renamed *BASIC.SYSTEM* file as the next application to load. Just remember to enter whatever name you gave to *BASIC.SYSTEM* when you renamed it—this new name is now the name of the file that produces the User's Disk Main Menu when it is loaded. If you renamed *BASIC.SYSTEM* as *BASIC*, for example, you would type *BASIC* as the name of the next application to load, and then the User's Disk Main Menu would be displayed.

Once AppleWorks is on your hard disk, you can load and save files to either floppy disks or the hard disk just as you normally would. The standard data disk location is still whatever it was when you last set it (see: Other Activities menu[178]). If you want to save data files on the hard disk, you must enter a hard-disk volume or subdirectory as the current-disk location. You do this by choosing option 3, *ProFile or other ProDOS directory*, from the Change Current Disk screen. (See the entries: Pathname;[188] Subdirectory[336]; Other Activities menu.[178])

VisiCalc file

■ **Definition**

A *VisiCalc file* is a spreadsheet file that is created by the VisiCalc program.

■ **Usage**

VisiCalc was the first spreadsheet program written for microcomputers, and the first version of VisiCalc ran on the Apple II. VisiCalc was an extremely popular program, but it is no longer being sold. There are tens of thousands of Apple owners who used the program at one point, and who would now like to use their VisiCalc files in the AppleWorks spreadsheet.

You can use VisiCalc files as sources for new AppleWorks spreadsheets by choosing option 3 *From a VisiCalc (R) file* from the Spreadsheet menu[296] to add a new spreadsheet file to the Desktop. After you choose this option, you must type the pathname[188] of the VisiCalc file, and then the file is loaded into a new AppleWorks spreadsheet.

The VisiCalc program is in some ways different from the AppleWorks spreadsheet, and there are some types of data that won't transfer from a Visi-Calc file to AppleWorks. First of all, the VisiCalc file must be a ProDOS file.[246] VisiCalc was sold in both DOS 3.3 and ProDOS versions. If the file you want to use was created with the DOS 3.3 version of VisiCalc, you'll have to convert it to ProDOS (with the DOS-ProDOS Conversion Program[104] on the ProDOS User's Disk) before you can load it into AppleWorks.

Even if the VisiCalc file you load is a ProDOS file, however, some types of data may not transfer. VisiCalc spreadsheets can contain trigonometric functions such as sine, cosine, and tangent, for example, while the AppleWorks spreadsheet doesn't offer these functions. If the VisiCalc file you try to load contains formulas that use functions which are not supported by Apple-Works, those formulas will not transfer to the new AppleWorks spreadsheet.

Whenever data elements of a VisiCalc file won't transfer to a new Apple-Works spreadsheet, you are informed of this by an error message that is displayed on the screen. The message tells you which row(s) of the spreadsheet contain missing data.

Along with incompatible calculating functions, there are other features in VisiCalc that can't transfer to AppleWorks. VisiCalc allows you to *chain* formulas together—you can write one formula that refers to a formula in another cell. Chain formulas can't transfer to AppleWorks, because AppleWorks doesn't support this feature.

Another potential transfer problem can occur because of the respective data capacities of VisiCalc and AppleWorks. AppleWorks' data structure is such that you can't place a formula in every cell in a row (from column A to column DW). You could place plain numbers or text in every cell, but if you begin in column A of the spreadsheet and fill every cell to the right with formulas, you will run out of data storage space in that row somewhere around column BW, depending on the type of formula you are entering. (Formulas use more storage space than plain text or numbers.) VisiCalc can store more formulas in any given row, so it could contain rows with more formulas in them than can be stored in a row of an AppleWorks spreadsheet.

If you should load a VisiCalc file having rows that hold more data than AppleWorks can store, you will see a message telling you that some data did not transfer into the affected rows. In this case, you won't be able to enter any more data into those rows, however, because the data capacity of those rows will already have been reached.

Volume

■ **Definition**

A *volume* is a physical location for ProDOS[246] data files and subdirectories.[336]

■ **Usage**

A volume is storage media that can contain ProDOS files and subdirectories. Usually, volumes on a typical Apple system are floppy disks, but hard disks can be divided up into one or more volumes in which you store files. It's important to remember that when you store data on a volume, it remains there even after you turn off your computer. This is different from your computer's Random Access Memory (RAM[256]), which loses all the data it's holding when you turn off or reset[274] the computer. Floppy disks are often called volumes, because one floppy disk contains one volume of storage space, while a hard disk could contain several volumes, since it can store many times the amount of data a single floppy disk can. When you add or list files in AppleWorks, for example, the program refers to the current volume as the current disk.

Whether a volume is on a floppy disk or a hard disk, though, it must have a name. You are asked to name each floppy disk you format under ProDOS—that name becomes the volume name. When you format a hard disk, you can sometimes give names to its volumes (but sometimes the software that formats the hard disk automatically creates and names volumes).

A volume name always begins with a slash mark (/). When you format a floppy disk using the option from the AppleWorks Other Activities menu,[178] you are asked to type a disk name. You don't have to begin that name with a slash, because AppleWorks supplies the slash for you. If you format a disk or name a volume with ProDOS, however, you must use the slash at the beginning of the name you type.

A volume name is the first part of a ProDOS pathname. The pathname must contain at least a volume name and a file name in this type of format: */volume name/file name.* A pathname can also contain a subdirectory name. (See Pathname[188] and Subdirectory.[336])

When you list the files on a volume, the list produced is called the *volume directory*. You can produce two types of volume directories with AppleWorks. When you use the *Add files to the Desktop* option from the Main Menu,[158] the volume directory of the current disk that AppleWorks displays only shows the AppleWorks files on that volume and not other types of files. This is because AppleWorks assumes you want to add files to the Desktop, and you can't add non-AppleWorks files directly to the Desktop.

If you use the option on the Other Activities menu to list all the files on the current disk, however, AppleWorks will show you other types of files as well as AppleWorks files. Even when you list all the files on a disk, however, you might not be able to see the names of every file—some of the files may be stored in a subdirectory, and only the name of the subdirectory will be shown in the volume directory.

Window (⌂-w)

■ **Definition**

The *Window* command (⌂-w) creates two separate viewing windows in a spreadsheet file, letting you view two different parts of a spreadsheet at once.

■ **Usage**

Normally, the Review/Add/Change screen of a spreadsheet file only shows the spreadsheet in one window. If you want to see two different parts of the spreadsheet at once, you can split the display into two windows, either vertically or horizontally, and each can be scrolled separately or together.

■ **Window options**

When you press ⌂-w in the Review/Add/Change screen of the spreadsheet, you are presented with this prompt line:

Windows? Side by side Top and bottom

Side by side: This option splits the window vertically along the left side of the column the cursor is in when you press the command, allowing you to look at two different groups of columns. An example is shown at the top of the next page.

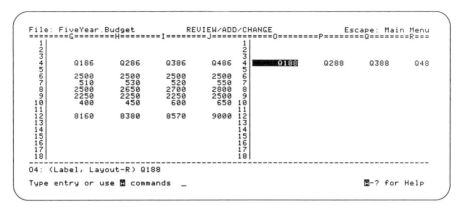

The Side by side *window option splits a spreadsheet vertically into two windows.*

Now, you could scroll whichever window the cursor is in without affecting the other window.

To move the cursor between windows, you use the Jump Windows[144] command (⌂-J).

Top and bottom: This window option splits the screen horizontally along the top of the row the cursor is in when you press the command, allowing you to look at two different groups of rows. You can use the Jump command (⌂-J) to move the cursor from one window to the other.

Synchronizing two-window scrolling: When you first use the Window command to split the display into two windows, only the window the cursor is currently in will scroll. If you want both windows to scroll at the same time, press ⌂-W a second time to display this prompt line:

> Windows? One Synchronized

If you press **s** to choose the *Synchronized* option, the prompt line will disappear and thereafter when you scroll one window, the other will scroll in the same direction. However, both windows will scroll only in the direction of the window split: If the windows are split horizontally, for example, both windows will scroll horizontally but only the window the cursor is in will scroll vertically.

If you choose to synchronize scrolling in both windows and later want to turn it off, press ⌂-W again: The prompt line will contain the option *Unsynchronized.* Choosing this option will return you to the default of scrolling in only the window the cursor is in.

Returning to one window: When you want to eliminate the two windows and return to just a single-window display, press ⌂-**W** to display the *Windows?* prompt line and press **O** to choose the *One* option.

Word Processor menu

■ **Definition**

The *Word Processor menu* is a list of options that let you create new files for the word processor from one of two sources.

■ **Usage**

The Word Processor menu is displayed when you choose option 3, *Make a new file for the Word Processor,* from the Add Files menu:[2]

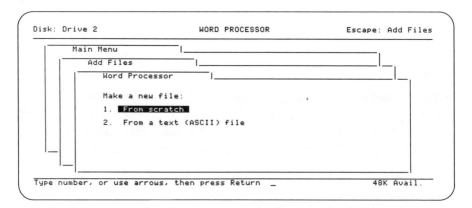

```
Disk: Drive 2              WORD PROCESSOR           Escape: Add Files

        Main Menu          |_____
          Add Files        |_____|__
            Word Processor  |_____|_

            Make a new file:
            1.  From scratch
            2.  From a text (ASCII) file



Type number, or use arrows, then press Return  _        48K Avail.
```

Option 1—From scratch: When you choose this option, the prompt line asks you to type a name for the new file. When you type a file name of up to 15 characters and press **RETURN**, a new word-processor file is displayed, and you can begin entering text or formatting commands.

Option 2—From a text (ASCII) file: This option lets you use data in an existing ASCII file[13] as the source for a new AppleWorks word-processor file. The common sources of ASCII files are other word-processing programs that can save their files in the ASCII format and files created by capturing data via modem.

When you choose this option, the prompt line asks you to type the complete ProDOS pathname[188] of the ASCII file. When you type this pathname and press **RETURN**, the ASCII file on disk is loaded into RAM,[256] and is converted to a new AppleWorks word-processor file.

If AppleWorks is unable to locate the ASCII file at the pathname you entered, it will display the message *Cannot find the file.*

If the file is successfully located, it will be converted to a new Apple-Works word-processor file. The prompt line will ask you to enter a name for the new AppleWorks word-processor file. Once you have entered the file name and pressed **RETURN**, the new file will be displayed.

■ **Comment**
When you use an existing ASCII file as the source for a new word-processor file, a copy of the original file remains on the disk.

Word Processor overview

The AppleWorks word processor lets you create, store, modify, and print text documents. You can format the text with enhancements such as boldfacing, underlining, super- and subscripting, and you can control the position of the text when it is printed on paper. You can transfer data to the word processor from the AppleWorks spreadsheet and database via the Clipboard[35] (see: Spreadsheet Printing;[319] Database Printing[67]), or you can create files by typing them from scratch or using the data from an existing ASCII file.[13] You can print word-processor files on paper, or you can print them to a disk as standard ASCII files.

■ **Working with the word processor**
You create a new AppleWorks word-processor file either from scratch or from an existing ASCII file, using the Word Processor menu.[362] Or, if you want to work with an existing word-processor file, you can simply add the file to the Desktop[97] and begin working with it. With a new file, you must type a name for the new file before you can enter text in it or view the transferred ASCII

text. Once you type a file name and press **RETURN**, AppleWorks displays the word processor's Review/Add/Change screen, and you can work with your new file:

```
  File: Sales Letter            REVIEW/ADD/CHANGE          Escape: Main Menu
  =====|====|====|====|====|====|====|====|====|====|====|====|====|====|===
  _




















  ---------------------------------------------------------------------
  Type entry or use ⌂ commands         Line 1   Column  1      ⌂-? for Help
```

The Review/Add/Change screen is used to view, enter, delete, or modify text in the word processor.

■ **File-size limits**

Like other AppleWorks files, the amount of available Desktop space determines how large a word-processor file can be. The following table shows the maximum size of an AppleWorks word-processor file, and the maximum sizes of word-processor files on systems with different Desktop sizes and RAM[256] configurations:

Maximum size	2250 lines
Typical size with a 10K Desktop (64K system)	166 lines
Typical size with a 55K Desktop (128K system)	933 lines

(The "typical" measurements assume 60-character lines of text with no blank lines anywhere in the document. The actual number of lines you will be able to get into a word-processor file depends on the content and format of each document.)

- **Word Processor command summary**

The following list contains all the keyboard commands used with the Apple-Works word processor; complete information for each is contained in its respective entry at the denoted page numbers.

Command:	Description:
Ċ-C	Copy text within a file, or to or from the Clipboard[40]
Ċ-D	Delete text[92]
Ċ-E	Toggle between insert and overstrike cursor[105]
Ċ-F	Find text by page number, search string, or marker[109]
Ċ-H	Print current display on a printer[122]
Ċ-K	Calculate page breaks for printing[18]
Ċ-M	Move text within file, or to or from the Clipboard[163]
Ċ-N	Change file name[171]
Ċ-O	Show printer options[217]
Ċ-P	Print all or part of file[193]
Ċ-Q	Show Desktop Index;[252] switch to another file on the Desktop
Ċ-R	Replace text with new text, either one occurrence at a time or throughout document at once[270]
Ċ-S	Save current document to the current disk[281]
Ċ-T	Set or remove tabs[285]
Ċ-Y	Delete from cursor to end of line[34]
Ċ-Z	Display format settings and carriage returns[376]
Ċ-1 to Ċ-9	Move through a file proportionally[280]
Ċ-?	Display list of commands[123]
Ċ-↑ and ↓	Scroll one screen vertically in direction of arrow
Ċ-→ and ←	Move cursor one word in direction of arrow
CONTROL-Y	Delete from cursor to end of line[34]
CONTROL-L	Begin or end underlining[350]
CONTROL-B	Begin or end boldfacing[220]

■ **Format defaults and options**

When you begin working with a word-processor file, it is set for certain default formats:

Platen Width (PW)	8.0 inches
Left Margin (LM)	1.0 inch
Right Margin (RM)	1.0 inch
Characters per Inch (CI), or Pitch	10
Unjustified Text (UJ)	
Page Length (PL)	11 inches
Top Margin (TM)	0.0 inches
Bottom Margin (BM)	2.0 inches
Lines printed per Inch (LI)	6
Single Spacing (SS)	

These settings can be changed for an entire word-processor document, or they can be changed for individual paragraphs or groups of paragraphs (see: Printer Options[217]). Every *new* word-processor document has listed default settings, however.

■ **Entering word-processor text**

To enter text in a word-processor file, you simply type. The keys on the Apple keyboard[145] work much like they do on a typewriter: The **SHIFT** and **CAPS LOCK** keys make capital letters; the **TAB** key moves the cursor to the next tab stop; the **RETURN** key moves the cursor down to the beginning of the next line; the **DELETE** key backspaces and erases characters; and the **SPACE** key moves the cursor ahead one character and leaves a blank space. As you type down to the bottom of the screen, the text automatically *scrolls* upward to give you additional lines to type on. You can scroll vertically back to the beginning of the file, or elsewhere within the file, by using the Arrow keys or the Ruler.[280] The Arrow keys also move the cursor horizontally.

In a new file, the AppleWorks word processor has default format settings for margins, line spacing, and other elements, as described above. You can change these settings as you like, but the individual commands specifying where the settings take place don't appear on the screen unless you use the Zoom[376] command (⌂-Z) to display them.

When you reach the right-hand margin of a document while typing a line, a feature called *word wraparound*[375] automatically moves the cursor down to the next line and allows you to continue typing without having to press **RETURN**, as you would on a normal typewriter. The word-wraparound feature keeps complete words together—if a word begins near the right-hand margin and is too long to fit on the current line, the entire word is moved down to the next line so it isn't split in the middle.

The horizontal bar at the top of the Review/Add/Change screen contains vertical lines every five characters. These indicate the AppleWorks preset tab stops. When you clear tab stops or set additional tab stops, these lines may disappear (or new lines may be added) to show the new tab positions. (See: Set Tabs.[285])

Another default in new word-processor files is the cursor[50] itself, which is an *insert* cursor: If you place the cursor in the middle of a line of text and begin typing, the text in front of it will be pushed ahead, and your new text will be inserted. The insert cursor is shown as a blinking underline. You can change the cursor to an *overstrike* cursor by pressing ⌂-E: This cursor replaces text as you type, instead of pushing it ahead. The overstrike cursor is shown as a blinking rectangle. (See: Edit Cursor.[105])

You can delete text from a word-processor file in several ways. If you want to delete a character or characters you have just typed (and which are directly to the left of the cursor), you can use the **DELETE** key. This acts like the Backspace key on a typewriter, except that it erases text it passes over as it moves backward. You can also use the Clear[34] command (⌂-Y) to erase everything on the current line from the cursor's position to the right margin. Finally, you can press the Delete[92] command (⌂-D), use the Arrow keys to highlight a portion of text, and then press the **RETURN** key to delete it.

Text can be moved about within a word-processor file or to the Clipboard with the Move[163] command (⌂-M). When you use this command, you first choose the destination of the data you want to move, then highlight the portion of text you want to move using the Arrow keys and press **RETURN** to end the selection. Then either move your cursor to the new location, or the selected data is automatically moved to the Clipboard as the move destination, if you chose that option. The Copy[40] command (⌘-C) works the same way, except that it leaves a copy of the text you select in its original position.

You can print text from the word processor onto paper, or onto a disk as an ASCII file, by using the Print[193] command (⌘-P). You can control the appearance of the text on paper by selecting format options from the Printer Options[217] menu (⌘-O).

▪ Formatting text with the word processor

The AppleWorks word processor uses a "what you see is what you get" approach to formatting. Generally, you enter words on the Review/Add/Change screen in the places where you want them to appear on a printed page, as shown in this example:

```
 File: Sales Letter            REVIEW/ADD/CHANGE              Escape: Main Menu
 =====|====|====|====|====|====|====|====|====|====|====|====|====|====|====|===
 December 13, 1985

 Mr. Ed Frobish
 Frobish Linen Service_
 335 Ramona Ave.
 San Jose, CA 95551

 Dear Ed:




 ----------------------------------------------------------------------
 Type entry or use ⌘ commands          Line 6   Column 22      ⌘-? for Help
```

The Review/Add/Change display helps you determine how your document will look on paper.

There are several features in this display that help you determine where your text will be on a page. One feature is the *line indicator,* which is located in the bottom-center of the screen, below the dashed line. The line indicator always shows the current position of the cursor: which line of the document it is on, and which column it is in. In the example, the cursor (located at the end of the word *Service*) is 22 characters from the left-hand margin. Notice, however, that the cursor appears to be on line 4 of the document, and the line indicator tells us it is on line 6.

This discrepancy occurs because of the second feature of the Review/ Add/Change screen: visible printer options. Because there are two printer-option settings entered at the top of this document, each of which occupies a line, the line indicator tells us the cursor is on line 6. These lines won't be printed when you print the document, but they occupy space when the document is stored on disk or displayed on the Review/Add/Change screen. To see these options, you must use the Zoom command (⌃-**z**). The options will then appear, as in this example:

```
File: Sales Letter              REVIEW/ADD/CHANGE              Escape: Main Menu
=====|====|====|====|====|====|====|====|====|====|====|====|====|====|====|===
--------Chars per Inch: 12 chars
--------Left Margin:  0.7 inches
December 13, 1985*
*
Mr. Ed Frobish*
Frobish Linen Service_
335 Ramona Ave.*
San Jose, CA 95551*
*
Dear Ed: *




-------------------------------------------------------------------------------
Type entry or use ⌂ commands           Line 6  Column 22      ⌂-? for Help
```

*Some printer options in the word processor occupy lines in a document. The Zoom command (⌃-**z**) displays or hides them.*

Since AppleWorks can't show you the effect of some printer options that affect at least a paragraph on the screen, it shows the printer option in a separate line between paragraphs on the screen to indicate where the option will occur. Use the Zoom command to help you remember the current margin, pitch, line spacing, justification, and other format settings. Some format settings, such as headers and footers, always appear on the screen, whether you use the Zoom command or not.

Another way in which the word processor shows format settings is by placing a caret[22] symbol (^) where the format option is used. The caret is used to represent the underlining, boldfacing, super- and subscripting, enter keyboard, and page numbering Printer Options,[217] and also any sticky spaces[335] you may have used. All the other options are represented on individual lines, as shown in the last example. When a caret is used to represent a format option, the line indicator displays the type of option when the cursor is placed on the caret, as shown here:

```
File: Sales Letter              REVIEW/ADD/CHANGE              Escape: Main Menu
=====|=====|=====|=====|=====|=====|=====|=====|=====|=====|=====|=====|===
December 13, 1985

Mr. Ed Frobish
Frobish Linen Service
335 Ramona Ave.
San Jose, CA 95551

Dear Ed:

I just wanted to tell you how much all of us at Acme Widgets appreciate
your business.  We think you're a ▉super^ customer!




--------------------------------------------------------------------------
Type entry or use ▉ commands          Boldface Begin          ▉-? for Help
```

The line indicator shows the specific type of format enhancement represented by a caret when the cursor is placed on the caret symbol.

To alter the format of a document with printer-option settings, you must use the Printer Options menu. This menu is displayed when you type the Printer Options command (⌘-O). If you are using a printer option that affects individual words or characters (such as boldfacing or underlining), the option you type on the Printer Options menu will take effect beginning with the current position of the cursor in the document. If you are using an option that takes effect only between paragraphs of text (such as margin settings or line spacing), the option will take effect from the first carriage return above the cursor's current position.

Once you display the Printer Options menu, you can't move the cursor around in a document. Because of this, you have to position it where you want the option to begin *before* displaying the Printer Options menu.

Descriptions of the printer options and how to use them are found in the Printer Options[217] entry.

■ **Comment**

In addition to the entries cited in this overview, additional information about the word processor can be found in the Reusing Data[276] and Word Processor Printing[371] entries.

Word Processor printing

There are three different ways you can print a word-processor file: You can print onto paper; you can print a formatted ASCII file to a disk printer; and you can print unformatted data to an ASCII file[13] on disk. This tutorial explains these options.

When you print a word-processor file, you must always follow the same basic sequence:

1. Make sure the document you want to print is displayed on the Review/Add/Change screen.

2. Select the printer options or print enhancements you want to make on the file (if any). Printer options are available from the Printer Options[217] menu, which is displayed when you press Ú-O.

3. Press the Print[193] command (Ú-P). AppleWorks will ask you whether you want to print the file from the beginning of the file, from the current page, or from the line that the cursor is on, as shown in the following example. Choose the option you want and press **RETURN**.

```
File: Sales Letter             PRINT MENU        Escape: Review/Add/Change
====|====|====|====|====|====|====|====|====|====|====|====|====|====|===
December 13, 1985

Mr. Ed Frobish
Frobish Linen Service
335 Ramona Ave.
San Jose, CA 95551

Dear Ed:

We think you're a ^super^ customer, and I wanted to tell you how much all
of us at Acme Widgets appreciate your business.  That's why we wanted you
to be the first to know about our new Widget Convertible--the sturdiest,
most flexible, most cost-effective widget around.

I'd like to schedule a time to drop by your office and demonstrate the
advantages of the new Widget Convertible, so I'll be giving you a call
during the next week to make an appointment.

In the meantime, think what the world's first all-purpose widget will mean
to your profits!
---------------------------------------------------------------------------
Print from? Beginning  This page  Cursor
```

When you first press the Print command (Ú-P), you must choose the part of the document you want to print.

4. Next, choose the destination where the document will be printed: either a printer or a text (ASCII) file on disk.

You always follow these same steps when printing, no matter how you are printing the file. From here on, however, the procedure varies depending on the print destination for the file.

- **Printing on printers**

When you print to a printer, you must be sure that AppleWorks has been configured for that printer, that the printer is properly connected and turned on, and that the printer can handle any printer options you may have specified for the file (see: Printer Configuration[200]). Once you complete steps 1 through 4 on the previous page, the basic procedure goes like this:

1. Choose one of the printers listed on the Print Menu as the destination for your file. The selection of printers available will depend on which printers you have previously configured AppleWorks to use. You can store up to three printer configurations at a time, as explained in the Printer Configuration entry.

2. After you choose the printer on which you want the file printed, enter the number of copies you want to make. AppleWorks can print up to nine copies of a document in one printing operation.

3. Once you type the number of copies you want and press **RETURN**, the file will be printed.

If your printer doesn't begin printing the file, check to make sure it is turned on, and that the printer cable isn't loose. Most printers also have an "on line," "ready," or "selected" indicator that shows whether the printer is ready to print. Make sure this indicator shows the printer is ready (there may be a "select" or "on line" button you push to light the indicator), and that there is paper in the printer. If your problem persists after this, call your Apple dealer and ask for further advice.

Troubleshooting printer problems: Printing from the word processor is very straightforward, but it's possible to get results you don't expect. If your printer is printing your file but it isn't printing it the way you expected, there are two likely causes: the printer options and the printer configuration settings.

The first thing to do is check the printer options. If a file is printing with single spacing and you want double spacing, for example, use the Zoom[376] command (⌂-**Z**) to make sure the double-space option appears in the file. (The default is single spacing, so if you haven't specified the double-space option, you won't get double-spaced printing.)

It's very easy to forget a printer option at a crucial point: You may specify single spacing for a part of a document, and then forget to return to double spacing afterward, for example. If your document isn't the way you want it to look, make sure all the correct printer options have been specified (see: Printer Options[217]).

If you are sure you have put all the printer options in the right places, then you should check your printer-configuration settings. These settings are covered in detail in Printer Configuration,[200] but it's important to remember that many of the printer options you specify won't take effect if your printer configuration isn't properly set.

If you change the size of a document's characters from 10 CI (characters per inch) to 12 CI with the Printer Options menu, for example, this change won't be made if you haven't configured AppleWorks to print at 12 CI on your printer. So if you aren't getting the right printing effects on paper, and you're sure your printer options are set correctly, check the printer configuration for that printer to see if you have configured AppleWorks to make your printer perform those options properly.

Another configuration-related problem could be your interface. You may not have configured AppleWorks properly for your printer interface. Check the interface code you have entered (or check to see whether you entered one at all). See the entry Printer Interface Configuration[214] for more about configuring interface cards. One final thing to check when sorting out printer problems is the printer itself. You can specify certain printer options, and AppleWorks can be configured properly to handle them, but they still won't take effect if your printer can't handle them. If, for example, you specify triple spacing from the Printer Options menu but your printer can't do triple spacing, then you won't get it. Check your printer manual before configuring AppleWorks to work with the printer, and make sure the configurations you enter are supported by your printer. It won't do you any good to enter a configuration for 24 CI printing, for example, if your printer won't print smaller than 16 CI.

■ **Printing to a disk printer**
When you want to store a file on disk with all the formatting it would have if printed on paper, you must print it to a disk printer. It's useful to print to a disk printer when you want to send a file via modem, or you are giving the file on disk to someone else who will print it out later. When the file is printed to the disk, it is printed as a text-only (ASCII) file, so you can send it via modem. Also, the file is printed with the specific format and print enhancements you specified (such as margins, justification, and line spacing), so somebody else using a different word-processing program can load it and print it out exactly the way you intended.

A disk printer is set up just like an ordinary printer—by configuring it from the Printer Information menu.[212] The only difference is the way this "printer" is connected to your Apple. To configure a disk printer:

1. Choose option 2, *Add a printer*, from the Printer Information menu.

2. Choose a printer that matches the printer on which the file will ultimately be printed.

3. Give the printer a descriptive name.

4. After you name the printer, you are prompted to choose how the printer is accessed. Instead of choosing a slot number, choose *Print onto disk or another Apple*. Thereafter, any file printed to this printer will be printed onto disk.

Once you have set up the printer this way, it appears on the Print Menu along with any two other printers you may have configured (you can have a total of three printers). To help you remember that this is a disk printer, AppleWorks puts the word *disk* in parentheses after the disk-printer name when you are choosing which printer to print a file on.

To print your file to disk, first choose the disk-printer destination. Then type the complete ProDOS pathname under which you want the file stored on the disk, and then press **RETURN**. The file will be stored on disk as a for-matted ASCII file. All margins, line spacing, and other options you specified will be retained in the format of the file on disk.

■ **Printing to an ASCII file**

The third possible print destination for a word-processor file is to disk as an ASCII file. An ASCII file contains only the actual text of the file without any formatting (see: ASCII file[13]). It's useful to print ASCII files when you want to send your file via modem, or you want to use it in another program that can read ASCII files. Standard AppleWorks files have a unique format other pro-grams can't read, so the ability to produce files in ASCII format makes it easy to share files with many other programs.

To print a file to disk in ASCII format, you display the document you want to print on the Review/Add/Change screen, press the Print command (⌥-P), and select the portion of the document you want to print, just as you do when printing to a printer. After that:

1. Choose *A text (ASCII) file on disk* as the print destination.

2. Type the complete ProDOS pathname under which you want the file stored on the disk, and press **RETURN**. The file will be stored on disk.

Remember that ASCII files (including those created by a disk printer) don't appear in the directory of a volume when you use the Add Files to the Desktop option—to see an ASCII file listed, you must use the option to list all files on the current disk drive, which you can access from the Other Activities menu.[178]

Word wraparound

■ **Definition**

Word wraparound is a feature in the word processor that automatically senses when the last word in a line is too long to fit within the margins of that line, and moves the word down to the beginning of the next line in the document.

■ **Usage**

In the AppleWorks word processor, word wraparound is like an automatic carriage-return feature. When you type on a typewriter and approach the right margin of the page, you must press the carriage-return key or return the carriage by hand to begin typing on the next line. In AppleWorks, the word wraparound feature does this for you.

As you type on a line, AppleWorks always keeps track of the horizontal position of the cursor. When the cursor reaches the right margin of a document, word wraparound automatically moves the cursor to the beginning of the next line. If you are in the middle of typing a word when the cursor reaches the margin, the word you are typing will be moved down to the next line along with the cursor.

Word wraparound helps you type faster, because you don't have to worry about how many words will fit on a given line—AppleWorks makes sure each line contains only enough text to fit within the margin, and moves your cursor down to the next line automatically. Word wraparound is always active in the word processor—you can't turn it off.

If you type a phrase that you want to remain all on one line, but the word-wraparound feature puts some of the words on the next line, you can use sticky spaces[335] to keep the words together on one line.

Zoom (⌂-z)

- **Definition**

  The *Zoom* command (⌂-z) displays printer-option settings[217] in the word processor, formulas (instead of values) in spreadsheet cells, and switches between the database's Single Record[293] and Multiple Record[168] layout screens.

- **Usage**

  In the word processor, the Review/Add/Change screen normally does not show most printer options you have specified for the file, and it doesn't show the locations of carriage returns in the file. Use the Zoom command to display these format settings, then use the Zoom command again to hide them.

  When you enter a formula in the spreadsheet and press **RETURN**, the value calculated from that formula is displayed in the cell—not the formula itself. Use the Zoom command to show the formulas in the cells where they have been entered, then use the Zoom command again to show the values.

  In the database, use the Zoom command to switch from the Mutiple Record layout to the Single Record layout, or vice versa.

 Example: Zooming in the word processor

Suppose you are preparing a price list for your customers, but you can't remember whether the section that lists prices was formatted for double or single spacing. To check, you use the Zoom command:

1. Press ⌂-z.
2. The format settings in the file will be displayed, as in this example:

```
File: Price List              REVIEW/ADD/CHANGE              Escape: Main Menu
============|==========================|=====================================
--------Top Margin:  1.0 inches
--------Centered
               Widget Prices - January, 1986*
--------Unjustified
*
Dear Customer:*
*
This is our new price list, effective January 1, 1986.*
Please replace the old price list you have on file.*
*
         Item                    Price*
--------Double Space
          Economy Widget          $19.95*
          Standard Widget         $26.80*
          Deluxe Widget           $34.50*
          Widg-O-Matic            $28.90*
          Widget Carrying Case    $10.00*
          Widget Overhaul Kit     $16.25*
          Widget Cleaning Kit     $12.60*
          Widget Supercharger     $45.95*
-------------------------------------------------------------------------
Type entry or use ⌂ commands          Line 1  Column  1       ⌂-? for Help
```

The Zoom command displays format settings in a word-processor document.

376

3. You can continue adding or changing text with the settings displayed, or you can press ⌂-**z** again to make them disappear.

Comments: Zoom is also necessary if you want to delete a printer-option setting from a document because normally you can't see the setting to select it for deletion. To delete a hidden printer option, use Zoom to display the printer options, move the cursor to the option you want to delete and press the Delete[92] command (⌂-**D**), then press **RETURN**.

 Example: Zooming in the spreadsheet
When you build a complicated spreadsheet that you want to share with others, it helps to have a printout of the formulas you used. You can display the formulas in a spreadsheet's cells with the Zoom command:

1. Make sure the Review/Add/Change screen is displayed.

2. Press the Zoom command (⌂-**z**).

3. The formulas you have entered will be displayed in their cells, as shown in the following example. You can then print them out with either the Print[193] or the Hard Copy[122] command.

```
File: Budget.Proj            REVIEW/ADD/CHANGE            Escape: Main Menu
========A=======B=========C=============D=============E==============F=======
  1
  2              Acme Widgets - Budget Projection
  3
  4                        Jan          Feb          Mar            Qtr
  5
  6 Rent          2000         2000         2000         @SUM(C6...E6)
  7 Utilities      502          489          480         @SUM(C7...E7)
  8 Material      2500         2495         2350         @SUM(C8...E8)
  9 Salaries      2000         2000         2000         @SUM(C9...E9)
 10 Promotion      500          475          300         @SUM(C10...E10)
 11                 0            0            0
 12 Total Expenses @SUM(C6...C10)@SUM(D6...D10)@SUM(E6...E10)@SUM(C12...E12)
 13
 14
 15
 16
 17
 18
--------------------------------------------------------------------------
F12: (Value) @SUM(C12...E12)

Type entry or use ⌂ commands  _                          ⌂-? for Help
```

The Zoom command displays formulas in spreadsheet cells.

Comments: You will probably have to widen the columns in your spreadsheet in order to display the formulas in them completely. In the example spreadsheet, columns C through F have been widened to display all of the entered formulas.

Example: Zooming in the database

Suppose you are working with the Mulitple Record layout of a customer's file, and you want to take a quick look at all the data in a particular record. Use the Zoom command:

1. Move the cursor to the record you want to view completely.

2. Press the Zoom command (⌂-z).

3. The Single Record layout will be displayed, and you can view all the data categories in the record your cursor was located on.

Comments: Once you Zoom to the Single Record layout, you can then scroll through the file with the ⌂ and ↑ or ↓ keys. To change back to the Multiple Record layout, press ⌂-z again.

Appendix: Alphabetic List of Entries

@ABS
Add Files menu
Add a Printer menu
Argument
Arithmetic functions
Arithmetic operators
Arrange (⌂-A)
ASCII file
@AVG
Blank (⌂-B)
Calculate (⌂-K)
Caret
Case sensitive text
Category
Cell
Change Current Disk menu
Change Name/Category
     screen (⌂-N)
Change A Printer menu
Characters-per-Line indicator
@CHOOSE
Clear (⌂-Y)
Clipboard
Column
Column width
Copy (⌂-C)
@COUNT
Current disk location
Cursor
Custom printer
Data Base menu

Database overview
Database printing
Database report formats
Date
Default
Delete (⌂-D)
Desktop
Desktop Index (⌂-Q)
DIF file
Displaying a database report
Ditto (⌂-')
DOS-ProDOS Conversion Program
Edit Cursor (⌂-E)
@ERROR
ERROR
File
Find (⌂-F)
Fixed Titles (⌂-T)
Formula
Functions
Group Totals (⌂-G)
Hard Copy (⌂-H)
Help (⌂-?)
@IF
Insert (⌂-I)
@INT
Interacting with AppleWorks
Internal Rate of Return (IRR)
Iterative calculations
Jump Windows (⌂-J)
Justify (⌂-J)

K
Keyboard
Layout (⌂-L)
Len indicator
List
@LOOKUP
Main Menu
Margin indicator
@MAX
@MIN
Move (⌂-M)
Multiple Record layout
@NA
Name Change (⌂-N)
@NPV
Other Activities menu
Page break
Paste
Path
Pathname
Pointer
Print (⌂-P)
Print Menu
Print the Report menu
Print screen
Printer configuration
Printer Information menu
Printer interface configuration
Printer Options (⌂-O)
Printing the display (⌂-H)
ProDOS
Prompt and Prompt Line
Protection
Quick Change (⌂-Q)
Quick File file
Quit screen
RAM
Recalculation
Record
Record Selection Rules (⌂-R)

Remove Files screen
Remove a Printer menu
Repeated label
Replace Text (⌂-R)
Report header
Report Menu
Reset (CONTROL-⌂-RESET)
Reusing data
Row
Ruler (⌂-1 through 9)
Save (⌂-S)
Save Files screen
Set Tabs (⌂-T)
Set Totals (⌂-T)
Sharing data with other programs
Single Record layout
Spacing line
Spreadsheet menu
Spreadsheet overview
Spreadsheet planning
Spreadsheet printing
@SQRT
Standard Values (⌂-V)
Sticky Space (⌂-SPACE)
Subdirectory
@SUM
Time
Tricks and Tips
Underlining (CONTROL-L)
Undo (⌂-U)
Using a hard disk
VisiCalc file
Volume
Window (⌂-W)
Word Processor menu
Word Processor overview
Word Processor printing
Word wraparound
Zoom (⌂-Z)

Index

A

@ABS function, 1–2, 8, 117
Absolute values, 1–2, 43
ACCESS communications software, 14
Add Files menu, 2–6
Add a Printer menu, 6–7, 54, 201
Apple Parallel Interface card, 205,
       214–15
AppleWorks
  booting from hard disks, 355–57
  copying to hard disks, 353–55
  error messages, 134–36
  quitting, 159, 255–56
AppleWorks Interface Configuration
      Utility, 214
Arguments
  absolute value of, 8
  square root of, 9
  types of, 7–8
Arithmetic functions, 8–9
Arithmetic operators, 9–10
Arrange command, 10–13, 65
ASCII files, 13–15
  formatted, 73
  identifying, 189
  naming, 350
  printing to, 76–77
  printing spreadsheet files to, 325–26
  sharing data via, 291–93
@AVG function, 8, 15–16, 117

B

Blank command, 16–17

C

Calculate command, 18–21
Caps lock key, 146
Caret symbol, 22
Case sensitive text, 23
Cell, 37. *See also* Spreadsheet
  coordinates, 25
  editing, 351–52
  erasing data in, 16–17
  labels, alignment of, 148–49
  number of non-blank, 8
  pointer, 191–92
  protecting, 148–50, 251–52, 333
  searching for, 112, 114
  specifying location of, 306–7
Change Current Disk menu, 3, 25–26
Change Name/Category screen,
      27–29, 60
Change A Printer menu, 29–30, 72
Characters
  boldface, 210
  per inch, 206–8
  per line indicator, 31–32
  subscript, 210
  superscript, 210
  underlining, 211
@CHOOSE function, 8, 32–33, 117
Clear command, 34–35, 63
Clipboard, 35–37
  copying data with, 35–36, 40–41,
      45–47
  copying database records with, 64
  memory available on, 36, 40
  moving data to, 35–36, 163

Clipboard *(continued)*
  and Paste command, 187
  printing data with, 35–36
  printing spreadsheet files to, 324–25
  sharing data with, 288–91
  transferring files with, 107–8
Column, 37–39
  erasing data in, 16–17
  indicator, 38–39
  width, changing, 39
Commands
  Arrange, 65
  Blank, 16–17
  Calculate, 18–21
  Clear, 34–35, 63
  Copy, 35
  Delete, 34, 63, 81–82, 92–97
  Ditto, 103–4
  Edit Cursor, 51
  Find, 109–14
  Group Totals, 118–22
  Hard Copy, 122–23
  Help, 123–24
  Insert, 82, 127–30
  Jump Windows, 142
  Justify, 142–44
  Layout, 39, 63, 146–54
  Move, 35–36, 163–68
  Name Change, 171–75
  Paste, 187
  Print, 64, 193–95
  Quick Change, 252–54
  Record Selection Rules, 65, 84
  Reset, 274–76
  Save, 281–82
  Set Tabs, 285–86
  Set Totals, 286–88
  Standard Values, 39, 64
  Undo, 34, 351–52
  Window, 360–62
  Zoom, 62, 169, 376–78
Control key, 145
Copy command, 35, 40–47
Copying
  database records, 46–48
  spreadsheet

Copying *(continued)*
  entries, 41–43
  formulas, 43–45, 46
  text in word processor, 41
@COUNT function, 8, 47–48, 117
Current disk location, 49
Cursor, 50–54
  Edit, 105
  insert, 50
  overstrike, 105
  overtype, 50
  with Ruler, 280–81

D

Data Base menu, 27, 55–58
Database
  arithmetic operators in, 10
  Calculated Category in, 19–21
  calculations, 65–66
  categories, 23–25
    adding, 27–28
    deleting, 27–29, 35, 95–96
    justifying, 142–44
    moving between, 169
    naming, 29, 60, 173–75, 356
    rearranging, 63
    subtotals, 118–22
    totaling, 286–88
    widths, 71–72
  character spacing, 238–40
  characters-per-line estimate, 31–32
  commands, 66–67
  creating new files
    from ASCII files, 14, 55–56
    from DIF files, 4, 57–58
    from Quick File files, 4, 56–57
    from scratch, 4, 55
  cursor movements in, 52–54, 62,
    152–54
  data-entry shortcuts, 347
  date entries, formatting, 90–91
  files
    deleting categories from, 96–97
    duplicating, 347–48
    limit of size, 64–65

Database *(continued)*
    naming, 26–29, 59, 173–75
    restructuring, 277–79
    saving as ASCII files, 77
format defaults, 64
Labels report, 35, 79, 87–90, 142–44
    blank lines in, 294–96
    blank lines, removing, 234–35
    deleting categories in, 88
    inserting blank lines in, 89
    inserting deleted categories in,
        88–89
    justifying categories in, 89–90
    printing, 70–72, 74–75
layout
    multiple, 62–63, 168–69
    single, 169
lines-per-inch, 230–31
margins, 231–32
memory available, 64–65
moving data in, 166–68
Multiple Record layout, 62–63
paper length, 236–37
platen width, 241
printing, 67–79, 195, 197–98
    to ASCII files, 76–77
    Characters-per-Inch (CI)
        setting, 70
    Characters-per-Line indicator, 70
    to Clipboard, 78–79
    with control characters, 242–43
    dashes, 236
    dates, 69
    to DIF files, 78
    mailing labels, 228–29
    to printers, 69–70
    to screen, 74–76
    troubleshooting, 72–73
Quick File file, 254
quitting, 255–56
records, 24, 258–59
    copying, 46–47, 64
    deleting, 63–64, 95
    displaying data in, 378
    inserting, 62–63
    inserting blank, 129–30

Database *(continued)*
    layout, 150–54
    logical conditions applied to,
        259–65
    moving via Clipboard, 64
    moving into word processor, 78
    repeating, 103–4
    searching for, 113
    sorting, 12–13, 65
    transferring to word processor, 64
report formats, 159–60
reports
    creating, 273–74
    displaying, 102
    headers, 272
    line length, 70–71
    naming, 173–75
    previewing, 74–76, 102
    printing to screen, 64
saving, 281–82
sharing data with word processor,
    288–91
Single Record layout, 61, 293–94
standard values, 334–35
Tables report format, 35, 79–87
    line spacing in, 229–30
    calculating data in, 85–87
    categories, arranging data in,
        82–83
    categories, changing order
        of, 82
    creating new reports in, 80
    deleting categories, 81–82
    inserting categories, 81–82
    Len indicator, 31–32, 71, 81, 154
    printing, 71–72, 75–76
    selecting records from, 84
    totaling categories, 286–88
    widths, category, 81
time formats, 343–44
Database overview, 58–67
Dates, formatting in database files,
    90–91
Default option settings, 92
Delete command, 34, 63, 81, 92–97
Delete key, 34, 146

Deleting
  data
    from spreadsheet, 94–95
    from word processor, 93
  database
    categories, 95–96
    records, 95
Desktop, 97–98
  adding files to, 2–6
  calculator, 345
  calendar, 345
  files
    adding, 158
    list of, 98–99
    loading, 158
    removing, 158, 266–68
    saving, 158
    saving to disk, 282–85
    storage limit, 108
    viewing available, 252–54
  memory available on, 5
  notepad, 345
  Rolodex, 345
  Space Available indicator, 256
Desktop Index, 3, 98–99, 252–54
DIF files, 100–101
  creating new database files from, 4
  creating new spreadsheet files
      from, 5
  identifying, 189
  naming, 350
  printing database data to, 78
  printing spreadsheet files to, 326–27
  sharing data via, 291–93
Directories
  creating, 180–81
  listing non-AppleWorks files, 5
  subdirectories, 190, 336–41
Disks
  data-disk location, selecting, 183
  directory, files available on, 3
  drives, changing, 25–26, 178–79
  files
    deleting, 181–82
    list of, 180
  formatting blank, 182–83

Disks (continued)
  hard, directories on, 188–90
Ditto command, 103–4
DOS-ProDOS Conversion
      Program, 104
Drives, changing, 3

E

Edit Cursor command, 51
@ERROR function, 9, 105–6, 117
ERROR message, 106–7
Escape destination, 132
Escape key, 145

F

Files, 107–8
  adding new, 2–6
  ASCII, 13–15
  backing up, 349
  creating new database, 4–5, 14
  creating new spreadsheet, 5
  creating new word-processor,
      3–4, 14
  deleting from disks, 181–82
  DOS, converting to ProDOS
      files, 104
  erasing, 35
  lists of, 133–34, 180
  naming, 108
  ProDOS
    converting to DOS, 104
  removing from Desktop, 266–68
  renaming, 276–77
  restructuring, 277–79
  saving, 281–82
    in ASCII format, 14
    to different disk, 26
    to disk, 267
    disk location for, 132
  sending via modem, 73
  switching between, 99
Find command, 109–14
  repeating, 111–12
Fixed Titles, 114–16

Fixed Titles *(continued)*
  removing, 115
Formulas, 116–17
  copying, 43–45
  spreadsheet, 33
Functions, 117–18
  and arguments, 7–8
  arithmetic, 8–9
    @ABS, 1–2, 8
    @AVG, 8, 15–16
    @CHOOSE, 8
    @COUNT, 8, 47–48
    @ERROR, 9, 105–6
    @LOOKUP, 9, 155–57
    @MAX, 9, 160–61
    @MIN, 9, 161–62
    @NA, 9, 170–71
    @SQRT, 9, 327–29
    @SUM, 9, 341–42
    @CHOOSE, 32–33
    @IF, 125–27, 130–31
    @NPV, 136–38, 175–77

G

Group Totals command, 118–22

H

Hard Copy command, 122–23, 201
Hard disks
  booting AppleWorks from, 355–57
  copying AppleWorks to, 353–55
  directories, 188–90
Help command, 123–24

I

@IF function, 117, 125–27
Insert command, 82, 127–30
Insert mode, 105
Insert New Records screen, 60
@INT function, 9, 117, 130–31
Interactive calculations, 138–41
Internal Rate of Return (IRR), 136–38

J

Jump Windows command, 142
Justify command, 142–44

K

K symbol, 144–45
Keyboard
  Caps Lock key, 146
  Control key, 145
  Delete key, 146
  Escape key, 145
  Reset key, 146
  Return key, 146
  Shift key, 145
  symbol keys, 145
  Tab key, 145

L

Labels reports, 32. *See also* Database,
          Labels reports
Layout command, 39, 63, 146–54
Len indicator, 154
Lines per inch, 209
Logical operators, 127, 259–65
@LOOKUP function, 9, 118, 155–57
Lookup table, 155–57

M

Main menu, 26, 59, 131–32, 158–59
Margin indicator, 159–60
@MAX function, 9, 118, 160–61
Memory, clearing, 274–76. *See also*
          Random Access Memory
          (RAM)
Menus
  Add Files, 2–6
  Add a Printer menu, 6–7, 54, 201–2
  Change A Printer, 29–30
  Change Current Disk, 25–26
  Main, 26, 131–32, 158–59
  names, 132

Menus *(continued)*
  options
    canceling, 132
    choosing, 132
    default, 132
  Other Activities, 26
  Print, 196–97
  Printer Information, 30, 74, 201,
      212–13
  Print the Report, 197–98
  Remove Files, 34
  Report, 79, 273–74
  Spreadsheet, 296–98
  Word Processor, 362–63
@MIN function, 9, 118, 161–62
Move command, 35, 163–68
Multiple Record layout, 168–69

N

@NA function, 9, 118, 170–71
Name Change command, 171–75
Net Present Value, 136–38
@NPV function, 118, 136–38, 175–77

O

Operating systems
  DOS 3.3, 246–47
  ProDOS, 246–50
  SOS, 247
Other Activities menu, 26, 178–85

P

Page breaks, 185–87
Paste command, 187
Pointers, 191–92
Print command, 64, 193–95
Print menu, 7, 196–97
Print the Report menu, 197–98
Print screen, 198–200
Printer Codes screen, exiting, 22
Printer-control codes, entering, 22
Printer Information menu, 30, 74, 201,
      212–13

Printer interface configuration, 214–17
Printer Options command, 217–45
  settings, 22
Printer Options menu, 22, 217
Printers
  codes, 205–6
  configurations, 54, 184–85, 203–5
    changing, 29–30, 211, 213
    custom, 7
    installing, 6–7
    removing, 213, 268–69
    stored list of, 213
    storing, 211
  custom, 54, 201–2
  disk, 73–74
  interface cards, 30, 205, 217
  interfaces, 214–17
    parallel, 214
    serial, 211, 214
  pausing, to enter keyboard text,
      223–24
  standard, 201–2
Printing
  catalog of disk files, 245
  to Clipboard, 64
  screendumps, 122–23, 245
  spreadsheets, 198–200
Printing the display, 245
ProDOS, 246–50
  converting DOS files to, 246–47, 297
  pathnames, 49, 187–90, 247–50
  volumes, 188–90, 247–50, 359–60
  subdirectories, 247–50
Prompt lines, 132, 250

Q

Quick Change command, 252–54
Quick File file, 254
  creating new database files from, 4
Quit screen, 255–56

R

Random Access Memory (RAM), 35,
    256–57

Random Access Memory (*continued*)
  expansion cards, 97
Ranges
  average value in, 15–16
  largest value in, 9
  number of non-blank cells in, 8
  smallest value in, 9
Recalculation, 257–58
Record Selection Rules command, 65,
    84, 259–65
Records, 24. *See also* Database
Relative values, 43–45
Remove Files menu, 34
Remove Files screen, 266–68
Remove a Printer menu, 268–69
Repeated labels, 269–70
Report Format screen, 10, 19–21,
    64, 102
Report header, 272
Report menu, 79, 273–74
Reports. *See* Database, reports
Reset command, 274–76
Reset key, 146
Return key, 146
Review/Add/Change screen, 19, 61,
    68, 102
Rows, 37–38, 149, 280
  erasing data in, 16–17
Ruler, 51, 280–81

S

Save command, 281–82
Save Files screen, 282–85
Saving
  files, 281–82
    in ASCII format, 14
    to different disks, 26
    disk location for, 132
Screen names, 132
Set Tabs command, 285–86
Set Totals command, 286–88
Sharing data with other programs,
    288–93
Shift key, 145
Single Record layout, 293–94

Sorting
  records, 12–13
  rows, 10–12
Space Available indicator, 256
Spacing line, 294–96
Special Codes screen, exiting, 22
Spreadsheet
  arithmetic functions, 8–9
  arithmetic operators, 10, 301
  building quickly, 316–17
  calculating, 19, 257–58, 300–301,
    348–49
  caret symbols, 22
  cells, 37–38
    coordinates, 25
    editing, 351–52
    erasing data in, 16–17
    labels, alignment of, 148–49
    number of non-blank, 8
    pointer, 191–92
    protecting, 148–50, 251–52, 333
    searching for, 112, 114
    specifying location of, 306–7
  character spacing, 238–40
  characters-per-line estimate, 31–32
  columns
    inserting blank, 127–28
    layout, 149–50
    widths, 39, 332–33
  command summary, 302
  copying to Clipboard, 45
  creating new files
    from DIF files, 5, 296–97
    from scratch, 5, 296
    from VisiCalc files, 5, 297–98
  cursor movements in, 50–51, 52
  deleting data from, 94–95
  entries, 41–43
  error messages, 135–36
  exponents, 22
  files, naming, 171–73
  Fixed Titles, 114–16
    removing, 115
  format defaults, 300
  formulas, 33, 116–17
    circular, 138–41

Spreadsheet *(continued)*
   copying, 43–45, 46
   dependent, 138–40
   displaying, 377
   entering, 303–5
   order of precedence, 10
   pointers in, 191–92
   using functions with, 307–9
  functions
   @CHOOSE, 32–33
   @COUNT, 47–48
   @ERROR, 105–6
   @IF, 125–27, 130–31
   list of, 155, 301
   @LOOKUP, 155–57
   @MAX, 160–61
   @MIN, 161–62
   @NA, 170–71
   @NPV, 175–77
   @SQRT, 327–29
   @SUM, 341–42
  labels
   entering, 309–12
   formatting, 332
   repeating, 269–70
  layout, 146–47
   Appropriate format, 148
   Commas format, 147
   Dollars format, 147
   Fixed format, 147
   Labels format, 148
   Percent format, 147–48
   Standard format, 148
   Value format, 147
  line spacing, 229–30
  lines-per-inch, 230–31
  margins, 231–32
  moving data in, 165–66
  moving through quickly, 349
  paper length, 236–37
  platen width, 241
  printing, 194, 198–200, 309–27
   to ASCII files, 325–26
   to Clipboard, 324–25
   with control characters, 242–43
   to DIF files, 326–27

Spreadsheet *(continued)*
   to disk printer, 323–24
   on printers, 320–21
   quitting, 255–56
   troubleshooting, 322–23
   width, 321–22
  ranges, 155
  recalculating, 19, 333
  reference area, 317
  rows, 37–38, 149, 280
  saving, 281–82
  sharing data with word processor,
   288–91
  size limits, 299–300
  sorting rows in, 10–12
  split-screen viewing, 360–62
  standard values, 330–34
  values
   entering, 309, 312–14
   formatting, 331–32
   square root of, 327–29
  windows, moving between, 142
  working with, 298–99
Spreadsheet menu, 296–98
Spreadsheet overview, 298–314
Spreadsheet planning, 314–18
@SQRT function, 9, 118, 327–29
Standard Values command, 39, 64,
   330–35
Sticky Space command, 335–36
Subdirectories, 190, 336–41
  creating, 180–81
@SUM function, 9, 118, 341–42

T

Tab key, 145
Tables Report Format screen, 31
Text
  boldfacing, 220–21
  case sensitive, 23
  centering, 221
  copying, 41
  deleting, 34
  entering, 366–68
  formatting, 368–70

Text *(continued)*
  indenting, 227–28
  justifying, 221–22
  markers, 241–42
  replacing, 270–71
  underlining, 244–45, 350–51
  unjustifying, 222–23
Time, 343–44

U

Underlining, 350–51
Undo command, 34, 351–52
Using a hard disk, 353–57

V

VisiCalc files, 100, 357–59
  creating new spreadsheet files
      from, 5
  identifying, 189
Volume, 359–60
  names, 188–90

W

Window command, 360–62
Windows
  moving between, in spread-
      sheets, 142
Word processor
  blank lines, inserting, 242
  blank space, nonbreaking, 335–36
  caret symbols, 22
  character spacing, 238–40
  columns in, 38–39
  command summary, 365–66
  creating new files
    from ASCII files, 4, 14, 362–63
    from scratch, 3, 362
  cursor movements in, 51
  default formats, 365
  deleting data from, 93
  files
    naming, 171–73
    printing, 193, 196–97

Word processor *(continued)*
  saving, to disk, 281–82
  size limits, 364
  form letters, 223–24
  line spacing, 229–30
  lines-per-inch, 230–31
  margins, 231–33
  moving data in, 164–65
  page breaks, 185–87
    displaying, 186
    forcing, 233–34
    overriding, 224–25
  page footers, 225–26
  page headers, 225–26
  page numbering, 237–38
    in separate documents, 346
  paper length, 236–37
  platen width, 241
  printer options, 219–23, 376–77
  printing, 371–75
    to ASCII files, 374–75
    to disk printer, 373–74
    from keyboard, 223–24
    pausing, 235–36
    to printers, 372
    subscript, 243–44
    superscript, 243–44
    troubleshooting, 372–73
  proportional spacing, 240
  quitting, 255–56
  searching for text in, 109–11
  setting tabs, 285–86
  text
    boldfacing, 220–21
    case sensitive, 110, 271
    centering, 221
    copying, 41
    deleting, 34
    entering, 366–68
    formatting, 368–70
    indenting, 227–28
    justifying, 221–22
    markers, 241–42
    replacing, 270–71
    underlining, 244–45, 350–51
    unjustifying, 222–23

Word processing *(continued)*
  using Database data in, 78
  word wraparound, 375
  working with, 363–64
Word Processor menu, 362–63
Word processor overview, 363–70
Word wraparound, 375

Z

Zoom command, 62, 169, 376–78

Charles Rubin

Charles Rubin has been writing about microcomputers since 1981. He is a contributing editor for *Personal Computing,* and a consulting editor for *A+* magazine. His work has also appeared in *PC Week, LOTUS, InfoWorld,* and *Macworld* magazines. His books include the best-selling *APPLEWORKS,* and *THE ENDLESS APPLE,* both published by Microsoft Press, and *Thinking Small: The Buyer's Guide to Portable Computers.* Charles lives in Oakland, California, and has been using an Apple IIe since 1983.

The manuscript for this book was prepared and submitted to Microsoft Press in electronic form. Text files were processed and formatted using Microsoft Word.

Cover design by Steve Renick.
Cover airbrushed by Charles Solway.
Interior text design by Craig A. Bergquist & Associates.
The high-resolution screen displays were created on the Apple II, formatted on the Apple Macintosh, and printed through the Microsoft MacEnhancer on the Hewlett-Packard LaserJet.

Text composition by Microsoft Press in Palatino with Times Roman Italic and Helvetica Bold, using the CCI composition system and the Mergenthaler Linotron 202 digital phototypesetter.

OTHER TITLES FROM MICROSOFT PRESS

AppleWorks
Boosting Your Business with Integrated Software
Charles Rubin $16.95

The Apple Macintosh Book, Second Edition
Cary Lu $19.95

Excel in Business
Number-Crunching Power on the Apple Macintosh
Douglas Cobb and the Cobb Group $22.95

The Printed Word
Professional Word Processing with Microsoft Word on the Apple Macintosh
David A. Kater and Richard L. Kater $17.95

MacWork MacPlay
Creative Ideas for Fun and Profit on Your Apple Macintosh
Lon Poole $18.95

Presentation Graphics on the Apple Macintosh
How to Use Microsoft Chart to Create Dazzling Graphics for Corporate and Professional Applications
Steve Lambert $18.95

Microsoft Macinations
An Introduction to Microsoft BASIC for the Apple Macintosh
The Waite Group, Mitchell Waite, Robert Lafore, and Ira Lansing $19.95

Macintosh Midnight Madness
Utilities, Games, and Other Grand Diversions in Microsoft BASIC for the Apple Macintosh
The Waite Group, Mitchell Waite, Dan Putterman, Don Urquhart, and Chuck Blanchard $18.95

Creative Programming in Microsoft BASIC for Optimal Macintosh Performance
Steve Lambert $18.95

Microsoft Multiplan: Of Mice and Menus
Models for Managing Your Business with the Apple Macintosh
The Waite Group, Bill Bono, and Ken Kalkis $16.95

Inside MacPaint
Sailing Through the Sea of FatBits on a Single-Pixel Raft
Jeffrey S. Young $18.95

Online
A Guide to America's Leading Information Services
Steve Lambert $19.95

Silicon Valley Guide to Financial Success in Software
Daniel Remer, Paul Remer, and Robert Dunaway $19.95

Out of the Inner Circle
A Hacker's Guide to Computer Security
"The Cracker" (Bill Landreth) $9.95 softcover $19.95 hardcover

Available wherever fine books are sold.